The Far Western Frontier

The Far Western Frontier

Advisory Editor
RAY A. BILLINGTON
Senior Research Associate
at the Henry E. Huntington Library
and Art Gallery

"OREGON:

ITS

HISTORY, CONDITION AND PROSPECTS

BY REV. GUSTAVUS HINES

ARNO PRESS
A NEW YORK TIMES COMPANY
New York • 1973

O/NW 917.95 HINES   20 00
Hines, Gustavus
Oregon its history,
 condition and prospects

O/NW
917.95
cp 1

Reprint Edition 1973 by Arno Press Inc.

Reprinted from a copy in The State
Historical Society of Wisconsin Library

The Far Western Frontier
ISBN for complete set: 0-405-04955-2
See last pages of this volume for titles.

Manufactured in the United States of America

Library of Congress Cataloging in Publication Data

Hines, Gustavus, 1809-1873.
   Life on the plains of the Pacific.

   (The Far Western frontier)
   First ed. published in 1850 under title: A
voyage round the world.
   Reprint of the 1851 ed.
   1. Northwest, Pacific. 2. Oregon. 3. Missions
--Oregon. 4. Voyages and travels. I. Title.
II. Title: Oregon: its history, condition, and
prospects. III. Series.
F880.H66 1973   917.95   72-9450
ISBN 0-405-04978-1

OREGON:
ITS
HISTORY, CONDITION AND PROSPECTS

REV GUSTAVUS HINES.

LIFE ON THE PLAINS OF THE PACIFIC.

OREGON:

ITS

HISTORY, CONDITION AND PROSPECTS:

CONTAINING A DESCRIPTION OF THE

GEOGRAPHY, CLIMATE AND PRODUCTIONS

WITH

PERSONAL ADVENTURES AMONG THE INDIANS

DURING A RESIDENCE OF THE AUTHOR ON THE

PLAINS BORDERING THE PACIFIC

WHILE CONNECTED WITH

THE OREGON MISSION:

EMBRACING EXTENDED NOTES OF

A VOYAGE AROUND THE WORLD.

BY REV. GUSTAVUS HINES.

BUFFALO:
GEO. H. DERBY AND CO.
1851.

Entered according to Act of Congress, in the year 1850, by
GEO. H. DERBY & CO,
In the Clerk's Office for the Northern District of New York.

PREFACE.

If this volume does not commend itself to the favorable considerations of the reading public, it will not be owing to any deficiency of material in the possession of the author, to enable him to furnish a most interesting and instructive work. Though his opportunities for the acquirement of that kind of knowledge resulting from observation, and necessary to qualify one to instruct and entertain mankind, during seven years of constant journeyings in various parts of the world, both by sea and land, have been perhaps greater than usually falls to the lot of even authors of books of travel, yet, conscious of his want of the requisite qualifications to array his work in that fascinating drapery necessary to charm the reader at once into an unqualified approval, the author casts himself upon the public with all due deference.

The principal apology necessary to offer for the publication of this work, is a desire to connect with entertainment the promotion of a more extensive and particular knowledge of those interesting portions of the world where it has been the privilege of the author to travel, and make his observations.

While the world is literally teeming with fictitious publications, here is presented a volume of facts, for the most of which the author is alone responsible; and in the absence of the tinsel adorning of a glowing and high-sounding style, the truthfulness of what is narrated is the principal merit to which the work is entitled.

The "History of the Oregon Mission," to which the first chapter of the work is devoted, has been drawn from the most reliable sources, and, principally from the short notes of the late Rev. Jason Lee, and the Journal of the late Cyrus Shepherd, the first missionary teacher in Oregon.

This part, the author flatters himself, will supply the Christian public with a needful desideratum, with respect to the true character of that important Mission, and of the courageous and self-denying men who were the first to carry the Gospel across the Rocky Mountains, and to proclaim it along the shores of the Pacific Ocean.

The Journal, commencing with the departure of the Missionaries in the Ship Lausanne in the fall of 1839, will introduce the reader to all that is interesting relating to the largest expedition of the kind that ever sailed from an American port. It will acquaint him with "Life on the Ocean Wave," and the different interesting phenomena of the great deep. It will introduce to him the people of other countries, and give him information with respect to many of their customs. It will present him with a glimpse of oriental scenery, and occasionally unfold the beauties and sublimities of the mountain landscape. It will conduct him through perils by sea and perils by land, and perils among the most savage, degraded and treacherous of the human race.

The Atlantic, the Pacific, and the Indian Oceans; Brazil, Chili, the Sandwich Islands, Oregon, China, the Spanish Islands, and even Africa herself, have all been laid under contribution to enrich the Journal; and from these different fields of observation have been collected facts, circumstances, and incidents of history, which cannot fail to enlist the attention and excite the interest of the reader, and to induce him to pursue the narrative, until, with the author, he shall have circumnavigated the globe.

The last few Chapters of the book are devoted exclusively to the Geography and History of the Oregon Territory. From a residence of several years in Oregon, connected with the fact that he made it a leading object to become informed from personal observation, not only with the geography of the country, with its productions; the soil, climate, seasons, mountains, valleys, prairies, forests, rivers, &c.; but also with every circumstance of importance which has ever transpired in connection with either the civil, political or religious interests of the country, the author believes himself to be qualified to present the inquiring public with more correct information regarding that portion of the world, than has hitherto been furnished from any source. For some of the facts connected with the History of Oregon, the author would acknowledge his indebtedness to the able and interesting Memoirs of Mr. Greenhow, the recent translator and librarian of the department of State, at Washington.

With these remarks, conscious of the uprightness of his intentions, the author would now place his offering upon the public altar; counting no other favor in its behalf than that to which the merit of his performance is justly entitled.

TABLE OF CONTENTS.

CHAP. I.—History of the Oregon mission, from its commencement to the departure of the great reinforcement, in the fall of 1839, in the ship Lausanne.   9

CHAP. II.— Journal of a voyage from New York to Oregon — Time and circumstances of departure—First evening—Last look at the Highlands—Initiatory rites —Great distress — Sea sickness indescribable — Fourth day— Captain Spaulding —First and second officers — Passengers in the cabin — Character of the expedition—First Sabbath at sea—Police regulations—A rich treat—Centenary meeting —Results—Vessel ships a sea—Wind increases — Tremendous gale—North-east trade — Description of the trades —Whale — Allowance of water — Porpoise — Vessel — Amusing surprise—Astronomy— Northern constellations — Magellanic clouds—Interesting Sabbath—Land ho !—Cape Frio—Lighthouse—Splendid scenery—Arrival at Rio de Janeiro — Historical sketch—Don John—Brazil independent—Don Pedro the first—Compelled to abdicate—State of the country—Foreign residents—Religion—City—Buildings—Missionaries—Slavery—Reflections.   .   38

CHAP. III.—Journal continued — Departure from Rio — Rev. Mr. Spaulding — French fleet—Violent storm –Flying jib boom carried away—Dinner lost—Storm abates—Christmas—Heat—Doubling Cape Horn — Gale nineteen days — Under bare poles — Prosperity— Sight of land—Brig Andes—Arrival at Valparaiso— Small pox—Danger—Description of the city—Its civil and political condition— Religion—Superstition, illustrated by amusing incidents—Protestantism—Importance of Valparaiso—Adventures round about the city — Great discrepancy— Appropriate name.   62

CHAP. IV.—Journal continued—Raising anchor—View of the Andes—Brig—Pacific ocean rightly named—Capture of a sea monster—Difficulty among the sailors' —Spoken by a whaler—Captain Sawyer—Island of Mauî—Hawaii—Oahu—Honolulu—Remarks on the island—Oahu and its city—Sabbath—Introduction to the royal family—Interview—Anniversary of the landing of missionaries—Visit to the Para — Battle ground — Kamehameha I.—Waiakiki — Valley of Manoah — Source of prosperity—Difficulty with the French—Arrogance of Captain La Place—Impression upon the Hawaiians.   73

CHAP. V.—Journal continued—Departure from Honolulu—Slow progress—Fresh breeze—Coast of Oregon—Old pilot—Captain delivers up the vessel—Crossing the fearful bar—Deep anxiety—Cast anchor in Baker's Bay—Rev. Daniel Lee—Chenook Indians—Clatsops ascend the river—Fort George—Run aground—Difficulty of ascending—Arrival at Vancouver—Meeting called—Missionaries receive their appointments—Sent off to their stations—First encampment in Oregon—Ascending the Wallamette in canoes — Tum Water — Portage — Champoeg — Horseback ride—Arrival at the Mission Station.   85

CONTENTS.

CHAP. VI.—Exploring tour to the Umpqua—Preliminaries—Departure—Delightful country — Encampment—Amusing incident — Fording river — Mountain La Beache—Elk river—Umpqua fort—Indian fight—Frenchman in charge—Meeting with the Indians — Old chief's confession — Hostile Indians — Danger of going among them — Resolved to go—Voyage to the coast — Indians accompany us — Interesting encampment—Indians on the coast—Meeting with them—Speeches of the chiefs—Results of the meeting—Talk to God—Solicitude of our Protectress—Watching—Presents—Departure—Description of the country—Return to the fort —Story of the Frenchman's wife—Dangers we had escaped—Perilous adventures of the mountaineers—Tour continued—mountainous country—Fording Elk river —Giant tree—Aromatic tree—Umpqua Indians—Head chiefs—Shocking story—Burst of heathen passions—Difficulty with guide—Settled—Fear of treachery—Confirmed—Request of We-We—Refused—Warning—An Indian can be honest—Unhappy results of not trusting him—Night—Lost in a forest—Sabbath—Indians again—Homeward route—Fine country—Delightful scenery—Home. . . 93

CHAP. VII.—Tour to Vancouver—Reception at the fort—Preaching in the hall—Business completed — Expedient to keep warm—Cold weather—difficult navigation—The rapids—Forest encampment—Strange visitor—Affecting intelligence—Death of Rev. James Olley—My Mohican guest—Return home—Meeting—Fruitless attempt to recover a dead body. 120

CHAP. VIII.—Another Tour — Rock Island rapids—The Jesuit— Stormy encampment — Return — Hospitality—Story of our host — Mr. Cornelius Rogers — Party increase—La Butte — Lonely Sabbath—Arrival home — Mr. Rogers and party—Meeting at the hospital — Indian messenger—Sad tidings—Great bereavement—Esq. Crocker—Call to civil duties—Thomas McKay—Great rain—Estate of Mr. Rogers—Return—Great freshet—Damages—Safe arrival home. 130

CHAP. IX.—Panic—Indian troubles—Tour to the interior—Causes—Precautions—Excitement increases—Mr Brewer's letter—The sub-agent—Expedition resolved upon — Opposed by Dr. McLaughlin — Departure — A squall — Ascent of the Columbia—Mount Hood—Romantic scenery—Sabbath encampment—Reflections —Remarkable rocks—Cascades—How formed — Indian tradition confirmed—La Dallas—Canasissa—Negotiation—De Shutes—John Day—Sabbath Reflections—Arrival at Dr. Whitman's — Interview with the Kayuse chiefs — Excursion —Adventure of Mr. Perkins—Party proceeds—Snake river — Red wolf—Laperai—Accident — Grotesque exhibition — Temperance training—Rev. Mr. and Mrs. Spaulding—Return to Dr. Whitman's—Interesting negotiation — Closing feast—Homeward—Story of the Walla-Walla chief—Peter Ogden—Arrival home. . 142

CHAP. X.—Homeward bound—Departure from Oregon — Lost in a fog—Vancouver—Unexpected meeting—Night running—Labor lost—Dreary encampment—Sabbath—Pillar Rock—Fort George—Clatsop plains—A whale — Entertainment —Embarkation — Detention—Great cave—Weigh anchor — Remarkable escape from shipwwreck—Driven back — Second trial successful—Voyage — Mani —Night danger — Arrival at Oahu—Shipping — English fleet—News from home — Rev. Jason Lee — " Hoa Tita "—Affecting separation — Admiral Thomas —Great alarm—Detention—How improved. 192

CHAP. XI.—View of the Sandwich Islands—How formed—Volcano—Coral reefs — Names of Islands — When discovered — Singular tradition—Cook's death—Population — Previous condition—Long and bloody war — Results — Missionary statistics—Effects of Missionary labor— Seamen's chaplaincy—Romanism—Kamehameha III.—Reformation—Singular custom—School for young chiefs—Influence of missionaries the king's cabinet—Important history of two hundred and seventy-six days — Increase of cabinet — Paper king — Protection—Commerce—Whale fishery—Productions—Society—Temperance—Destination of the Islands. 207

CHAP. XII.—Return to Oregon — Embarkation — Passengers — Horace Holden—Thrilling story—The whaleman—Voyage—Arrival in the Columbia river—Disagreeable navigation — Yearly meeting of the missionaries — Appointments —Arrival of Rev. George Gang — Reasons for his appointment — Great changes—Mr. Lee—George Abernethy—Powers of the new superintendent—Special meeting — Voyage — Laymen dismissed — Miscellaneous — Transporting supplies —

CONTENTS. vii

Another meeting—Oregon Institute—Finances of the mission brought to a close—Number of missionaries returned—Number remaining in the field. . . 233

CHAP. XIII.—Final departure and voyage home—Notice of Captain Sylvester—Arrangements to leave—Mode of departure—Vancouver again—Clatsop Plains—On board the brig Chenamos—Difficult navigation—Danger—Get into the bay—Fair breeze—Exit—Fellow Passengers—T. J. Hubbard—Wave and Devenport—Mode of taking a porpoise—Scarcity of men—Scarcity of incident—Pilot fish—Make land—Spoken by the English brig Frolic—Shipping—Arrival at Oahu—Reception—Review of the mission. 244

CHAP. XIV.—Voyage to China—Change of calculations—Embark on board the Leland—Accident—Departure—Cabin associates—The captain—Rules to judge of character—The island of Grigan—The Ladrones—Dangerous reefs—Gale—Bashu islands—Spanish possessions in the Pacific—Formosa—Chinese Sea—Ship Montreal—Ty phongs—The contending pilots—Appearance of the coast of China—Arrival at Hong Kong—Reception of Keying—Review of the British troops—Sabbath disregarded—The Rev. Charles Gutzlaff—Island of Hong Kong—City of Victoria—Population—Schools—Morrison Education Society—Morrison Hill—Success of the school—Rev. S. R. Brown—Churches—Missions—Where established—Missionaries—Climate of Hong Kong—Soldiers' Burying Ground—Wesleyan Methodists—Short voyage—City of Macao—Grand prior—Bazaar—Temple—Camoen's cave—Voyage to Canton—Description of the "Provincial City"—Adventures in the city—Temple of Honan—Dr. Parker—Dr. Devan—Proclamation of Keying—Counter proclamation—Flower Garden—Dr. Bridgeman—Great excitement—Danger of an outbreak—Thrust out of the city—Night excursion—On board the Leland—Things that strike the foreigner—Boat population—Pirates. 255

CHAP. XV.—Voyage from Hong Kong to New York—Chinese Sea—Islands—Strait of Gasper—Java Sea—Strait of Sunda—Perilous condition of the Leland—Loss of cable and anchor—Ship saved—Sumatra and Java—Pulo Bassa—Malays—Indian Ocean—Cape of Good Hope—Cast anchor in Table Bay—Cape Town—Colony—Vineyards—Produce—Missionary labor—The responsibility of churches—Difficulty on board—Captain fined—His character—The supercargo—Mrs. Hooper—Adieu to Africa—Cleansing the ship—Man overboard—Splendid eclipse of the sun—Reflections—The gulf stream—Coast of New Jersey—New York. 300

CHAP. XVI.—Oregon Territory—Its geography—Boundary and extent—Harbors—Capes—Face of the country—Snow mountains—Rivers—Mouth of the Columbia—Columbia Bar—Channel—Kinds of fish—Timber—Climate—Summer and winter—Fertility of the soil—Clatsop plains—Bottom lands—Puget's sound—The garden of Oregon—Middle region—Upper region—Capabilities of the country. 317

CHAP. XVII.—Oregon territory—Its history—Spanish discoveries—Measures of the English—Sir Francis Drake—Heceta—Isle of Grief—Bodega discovers Killemook head—Discoveries of Captain James Cook—Captain John Mearls—Cape Disappointment—Robert Gray, of Boston—First visit to the coast—Second visit, discovers the Columbia river—Captain Vancouver—Braughton. . . . 348

CHAP. XVIII.—Oregon territory—History continued—European nations involved in war—Pacific trade carried by the Great Republic—Ship Boston seized by the Indians—Land expeditions—Captain Jonathan Carver—Sir Alexander McKenzie—Lewis and Clark—Project of John Jacob Astor—Captain Thorn and the Tonquin—McDougal and Concomley—Fate of the Tonquin—Wilson Price Hunt—Depression at the fort—Encouragement—Ship Beaver arrives—Declaration of war—Thompson and the North-West Company—Ross Cox—Astoria in danger—Visit of McTavish and Stuart—Alarming news—Effect on the American company—Sloop of war—Racoon and Captain Black—Astoria falls into the hands of the British—Astor's magnificent enterprise terminated. 364

CONTENTS.

CHAP. XIX.— Oregon territory — History continued — Astoria restored to the Americans—Description of the fort—North West Company remain in the country—Rival companies—Hudson's Bay Company—How formed—Extent of its operations—War between the two companies—Both merged in one—The Honorable Hudson's Bay Company—Policy of the company—Number and situation of trading forts — Immense power of the company — Colonizing the country—Sir George Simpson's Colony — Settlements — Fort Vancouver — Gentlemen of the fort—Perils of the fur trade—A thrilling tragedy. 376

CHAP. XX.—Oregon territory — History continued — Mr. Ashley's expedition — Smith, Jackson, and Sublette—Rocky Mountain Fur Company—Interesting journey—Country explored—Independent parties—Bonneville—Red wolf— Captain Wyeth—Opposed by H. B. C.—Results—Immigration for settlement—Character of population — Sources whence it proceeds — Enterprise — Portions of country occupied. 407

CHAP. XXI.—Oregon territory—Political history—Necessity of organizing a body politic — First meeting of the people — Second meeting—Exigencies met—Organization dies — Exploring squadron — Great excitement—Commander Wilkes— Opposed to organizing—Subject slumbers—Sub-agent—Mass meeting—Old subject revived—Indians troublesome—Talk of war—Dr. McLaughlin—Third meeting—Government organized—Fourth meeting—Officers qualified—Laws enacted —Effect produced — New legislative committee — Laws revised—Alterations— Election of a Governor and House of Representatives—Peaceable state of community—Joel Turnham—Thrilling incident. 417

OREGON:

ITS

HISTORY, CONDITION AND PROSPECTS.

CHAPTER I.

History of the Oregon mission, from its commencement to the departure of the great reinforcement, in the fall of 1839, in the ship Lausanne.

In the year 1832, four Indians, belonging to the Flat Head tribe, living west of the Rocky Mountains, performed a wearisome journey on foot to St. Louis, in Missouri, for the purpose of inquiring for the Christian's Book and the white man's God. Early in 1833, notice of this wonderful event was given in the Christian Advocate and Journal, published in New York, and a general feeling of christian sympathy was produced in all the churches of the land for these interesting heathen, and a proposition was made that the Missionary Board of the Methodist Episcopal Church proceed forthwith to establish a mission among the Flat Head Indians. This measure was strongly advocated by Dr. Fisk, Dr. Bangs, and many others, while none were opposed to the accomplishment of so worthy an object. While the subject was being agitated, Dr. Fisk corresponded with the Rev. Jason Lee, of Stanstead, C. E., having formerly been his tutor in the Wilbraham Academy, to ascertain whether he would undertake the superintendence of an Indian mission beyond the Rocky Mountains. Mr. Lee was then employed on an Indian mission, under the direction of the Church in Canada ; but yielding to the solicitations of Dr. Fisk, and from a conviction of duty, he left Canada, and repairing to Boston in June,

1833, where the New England Conference was then in session, he was received into that body as a member on probation, ordained by Bishop Hedding, and, on the recommendation of the Board of Managers of the Missionary Society of the M. E. Church, was appointed to the superintendence of the Oregon mission.

In the following August, Rev. Daniel Lee, a nephew of Rev. Jason Lee, was appointed to labor in the same field. When they received their appointment, they knew of no way of getting to the field assigned them, unless they ventured alone across the continent, through hostile tribes, or could find some vessel bound to the North-West coast, around Cape Horn, that would take them on board; and they continued in suspense in regard to their mode of proceeding, until November, when notice appeared in the public journals that Captain N. J. Wyeth, of Cambridge, Mass., had recently returned from a tour west of the Rocky Mountains, and that he contemplated returning to Oregon in the following spring. On receiving this intelligence, J. Lee immediately repaired to Boston, had an interview with Capt. Wyeth, and readily obtained permission to accompany him back to Oregon. Capt. W. had also made arrangements to send a vessel, called the "May Dacre," round to the Columbia river, loaded with goods; and while in Boston Mr. Lee procured the necessary outfit for his mission, and shipped it on board of Capt. Wyeth's vessel. Here, also, by the consent of the Board, Mr. Lee engaged Cyrus Shepard, a lay member of the church, to accompany him. During the interval between the time that they received their appointment, and the period fixed upon for their departure, the Lees held a number of missionary meetings in various parts of the country, with very encouraging results. Early in March, 1834, they left New England for the west, and on arriving in Missouri, P. L. Edwards, also a lay member, was connected with the mission party, which now numbered four.

This company, after holding a most interesting missionary meeting at St Louis, proceeded to Fort

Independence, on the frontiers of Missouri, which is a place of general rendezvous before starting for the mountains, where they met Capt. Wyeth and his party, on the 24th of April, 1834.

On the 25th, the expedition left Independence, and commenced their wearisome and perilous journey across the Rocky Mountains, and on the 20th of June they arrived at the general rendezvous of the American Fur Traders on Kane's Fork, which is a branch of the Colorado of the West.

Here they continued till the 2nd of July, to recruit their jaded animals, and then proceeded on, and on the 15th, arrived at a place on the Snake river, west of the mountains, where Wyeth and his men built a trading station, which he called Fort Hall. Here the missionaries tarried until the 30th of July; and as Capt. Wyeth was detained longer for the purpose of finishing his fort, the mission party resolved to proceed, in company with Mr. Thomas McKay and Capt. Stewart, and on the first day of September they arrived in safety at Fort Walla Walla, on the Columbia river. They ascertained, on their journey down from Fort Hall, that the Flat Head tribe of Indians was not only very small, but very disadvantageously situated for the establishment and support of missionary operations among them; and this brought them to the determination to proceed down to the lower country, to find a more eligible site for the location of their mission.

Leaving their horses at Walla-Walla, they proceeded down the Columbia in one of the Hudson's Bay Company's boats, and after a tedious voyage of eleven days, against strong head winds, they arrived in safety at Vancouver on the 15th of September, and the following night slept under a roof, for the first time for one hundred and fifty-two nights. Worn out with the excessive labor and fatigue of their long journey, they could well appreciate the kind hospitality with which they were entertained by the gentlemen of the Fort; but they gave themselves but two days to rest, and to consult with their hosts, who were well acquainted with all the Indian tribes, concerning the object they had in view; and on the 18th, J. and D. Lee were off on an exploring tour through the country, to "make observations relative to the best location for the mission."

Examining the Wallamette valley and other portions of the country, they returned to Vancouver on the 27th, still undecided as to the proper place to make the location.

The merits of the different portions of the country were considered, the Flat Heads, the Nez Perces, the Kayuses, and other tribes, were faithfully reviewed, but to the exclusion of all others, the Wallamette valley was *strongly* recommended by Dr. John McLaughlin and the rest of the gentlemen of Vancouver, as the most eligible place for the establishment of the centre of their operations.

On Sunday, the 28th, Jason Lee preached twice at Vancouver, to a congregation of English, Irish, French, half-caste, &c., which were the first sermons ever preached in the place, and doubtless the first that many of the people had ever heard.

It was finally decided, "after much prayer for direction as to the place," to locate the mission in the Wallamette valley, and as the brig May Dacre had safely arrived in the Columbia with the goods belonging to the mission, measures were immediately taken to receive them from Capt. Lambert, and convey them to the place selected for the station. The brig lay at the mouth of the Multnomah, or lower mouth of the Wallamette, and the site for the mission was seventy-five miles up the river; but, after "much toil and hard labor," Mr. Lee succeeded in getting up all the goods, and they were landed on the mission premises on the 6th day of October.

The rainy season was commencing, and as they had no house to shelter either themselves or their goods from the inclemency of the weather, they went immediately to work to prepare logs, &c., to build a house. The rain fell in torrents long before their house was erected, yet they labored constantly during the day, and at night were obliged to lie down together in a small tent, scarcely large enough to contain them, and, wrapped in their wet clothes, seek a few hours' repose to prepare them for the toils and storms of the ensuing day. Their house was 32 feet by 18, and on the 3d of November they moved their goods into it, though they had put on but ten feet of the roof. So soon as they got their house thus partly covered, they began to receive Indian children into their family, with the design of establishing a mission school, and also to labor for the spiritual benefit of all the Indians, and the few French people who had settled in the country. Meetings were established at the house of Mr. Joseph Gervais, and held every Sabbath, the principal attendants being French and half-caste.

On the 14th of December, Mr. Jason Lee visited Vancouver, where he preached, and baptized four adults and seventeen children. In consideration of these services he received, in donations, from the gentlemen of the company, the sum of twenty dollars, for the benefit of the mission. During the winter of 1835, the missionaries were alternately employed in improving their house, procuring supplies, preaching the gospel, and teaching the Indian and half-caste children to read and write.

Thrown entirely upon their own resources, in the spring, to guard against future want, they commenced cultivating the ground. There was no alternative; they must do so, or starve. While they saw some fruits of their labors in other respects, this department of their work, during the summer, was greatly prospered, for in the fall, after they gathered in their crops, they found themselves with a good supply of wheat, peas, oats, and barley, and two hundred and fifty bushels of potatoes in their cellar. This, with six barrels of salmon which J. Lee purchased fresh of the Indians at the Wallamette Falls, and salted with his own hands, and took up the river to the mission, furnished them with the means of subsistence for the following year.

Soon after the missionaries first arrived, Mr. Cyrus Shepard was employed at Vancouver, to teach the children belonging to the Fort, but losing his health, he was obliged to leave his school. On the 1st of March he ascended the river in company with Mr. Lee, and from that time remained on the Wallamette station.

Late in August a circumstance happened which shows to what dangers the missionaries were exposed. A boy whose Indian name was Ken-o-teesh, belonging to the Si-le-lah tribe, was received into the mission in April, and died on the 19th of the following August. A few days after his death, his brother came to the mission, determined to seek revenge for the death of Ken-o-teesh, by taking the life of Daniel Lee and Cyrus Shepard. He remained over night, and was prevented from accomplishing his design only by the interposition of an Indian who accompanied him. Bent upon glutting his vengeance on somebody, he crossed the river, and fell upon a band of unarmed Indians, and savagely murdered several of them.

In the month of September, nearly the whole mission family were attacked with the intermittent fever, and the mission house was converted into an hospital, without an attending physician. A scene of distress now presented itself, and our missionaries not only suffered personally, but were obliged to descend to the most menial services, in waiting upon the Indian children, for whose comfort they manifested the utmost care.

Mr. Daniel Lee and Mr. P. L. Edwards left the mission premises the last of September, the former for Vancouver to obtain medical aid, and the latter to embark on board the Brig May Dacre for the United States. Remaining awhile at Vancouver without benefit to his health, Mr. Lee, by the advice of Dr. McLaughlin, embarked on board one of the Hudson's Bay Company's ships, bound for the Sandwich Islands, and in consequence of this, Mr. Edwards relinquished the idea of leaving the country at that time, and returned to the mission, and late in October established a school for the winter, at Campment du Sable, or Champoeg.

To provide for future contingencies, the missionaries sowed that fall twenty-seven bushels of wheat.

On the 26th of November, the Rev. Mr. Parker a Presbyterian Clergyman from the State of New York, arrived at the mission, where he was most cordially received. He had been sent out by the A. B. C. F. M. to explore the country, and ascertain the most eligible site for a mission. He remained at the station two days only, when he returned to Vancouver. Dr. Marcus Whitman accompanied him over the Rocky Mountains, but on arriving at the Snake river, the doctor returned to the States for the purpose of inducing the Board to appoint missionaries forthwith to Oregon.

The enlargement of the mission family by receiving Indian children from time to time, rendered it necessary, at the close of this year, for the missionaries to build an addition to their house, 32 by 16 feet. This they did principally with their own hands. In reviewing the year, the missionaries found cause for thankfulness in the success which had attended their labors, though they had been called to pass through some trying scenes, and to meet with many discouragements. They had received fifteen children into the family, of whom four had died, and one had been dismissed, leaving ten under their instruction. These were making rapid progress in manners, science, and useful labor; and by the blessing of God the missionaries had a sufficiency of wholesome food for themselves and the children.

In February, 1836, hearing it rumored abroad that certain Americans, who had arrived in the country, were about to commence the manufacture of rum, and fearing, from a knowledge of the material of which the Oregon community was composed, that intemperance would sweep over their field of labor, the missionaries invited the settlers to the mission house, and formed the Oregon Temperance Society, the first organized west of the Rocky Mountains. Three only, besides the members of the mission, signed the pledge at first, but subsequently the number increased to eighteen.

About the first of March a vessel arrived in the Columbia from the Sandwich Islands, bringing intelligence that the health of Daniel Lee had much improved, but for the general good of the cause he had concluded to remain till another opportunity should present itself for returning to Oregon. The natives of Oahu had made a contribution to Mr. Lee for the benefit of the Oregon mission, amounting to two hundred and fifty dollars. At the same time that this intelligence reached the mission, a letter was received by Jason Lee from Dr. McLaughlin, inclosing a subscription for the benefit of the mission, to the amount of one hundred and thirty dollars, all from the gentlemen at Vancouver. As the letter shows in what light these intelligent persons viewed the mission at that time, I insert a copy. It is as follows:

"FORT VANCOUVER, 1st March, 1836.
THE REV. JASON LEE:

Dear Sir,—I do myself the pleasure to hand you the inclosed subscription, which the gentlemen who have signed it request you will do them the favor to accept for the use of the mission, and they pray our Heavenly Father, without whose assistance we can do nothing, that of his infinite mercy he may vouchsafe to bless and prosper your pious endeavors—and believe me to be, with esteem and regard, your sincere well wisher and humble servant,

JOHN MCLAUGHLIN."

The business of the mission continued as usual, without any thing especial taking place, until the 30th of April, when we find Mr. J. Lee at the death bed of G. Sergent, a native of New England, whom he found in extreme agony both of body and mind. As Mr. Lee entered, the dying man told him that as he had lived a life of wickedness, he was about to die an awful death. The missionary pointed him to the Redeemer of the world, and commended him to God in prayer. He appeared deeply affected, and responding a hearty *amen*, in a short time ceased to breathe.

Teaching the children, preaching to both the settlers and natives, visiting the sick, attending funerals, and harvesting their crops, employed the time of the missionaries during the summer; and in the fall, to make their "bread sure," they sowed thirty-four bushels of wheat.

In the latter part of August there arrived a vessel in the Columbia river from England, by the way of the Sandwich Islands, having on board the Rev. Daniel Lee, who had recovered his health, and Rev. Mr. Beaver and lady. Mr. Beaver had been sent out as chaplain to the Hudson's Bay Company at Vancouver. He was a clergyman of the Church of England. Mr. Lee arrived at the mission at a very seasonable time to render himself useful, not only in his appropriate missionary work, but also in assisting to take care of the sick members of the mission family. At this time Mr. J. Lee was suffering under a severe attack of the intermittent fever. Partially recovering from this attack, he started for Vancouver on the 6th of September, taking with him a favorite Indian girl whom he called Lucy Hedding, to obtain medical aid in her behalf.

On the 12th, he returned, bringing information of the arrival at Walla-Walla of the Rev. Mr. Spaulding and wife, Dr. Whitman and wife, and Mr. Grey, who had been sent out as missionaries by the A. B. C. F. M. As Mr. Lee had taken the lower country, they decided upon locating their mission in the interior, among the Kayuse and Nez Perce Indians. These were the first American ladies that ever crossed the Rocky Mountains, and their arrival in the country formed an epoch in the history of Oregon.

During the month of September, nearly all the mission family were sick at once, with the intermittent fever, and another was taken to Vancouver, by Mr. Edwards, for medical aid. Mr. Edwards returned on the 30th, bringing with him Lucy Hedding, who had received no benefit from medicine. She died on the 5th of October.

On the 22nd, J. Lee had a third attack of the fever, so severe as to deprive him of reason for a short time. He continued to suffer, without medical advice, until the 21st of November, when, in a very reduced state, he set out for Vancouver, where he arrived two days afterwards.

During his absence, died Joseph Pournaffe, a member of the mission school, aged 17 years. This lad was very attentive to religious instruction, and left off play and work on the Sabbath, immediately on being told it was wrong. He often expressed much thankfulness that the missionaries had come to the country, to learn him to read, and tell him about God. He was a promising youth, and, if he had lived, would probably have been a blessing to the country. As it was, the missionaries had much consolation in his death, for he gave them satisfaction that their labors had not been in vain.

On the 28th of December, after an absence of five weeks, J. Lee returned from Vancouver with his health somewhat improved, though still quite feeble.

Eighteen children and adults had been admitted into the mission family during this year; two had died and one had run away. The missionaries found on their hands, the last day of December, twenty-five persons; but having enlarged their farming operations, by the blessing of God they found themselves in the possession of supplies amply sufficient to sustain them until another harvest.

On the 2nd day of January, 1837, the members of the mission found cause to rally their forces, to support the cause of temperance. A meeting of the Temperance Society was called at the mission house; one member who had violated the pledge, was excluded, and three more were added to the Society. As the reports concerning the distillation of ardent spirits were about to be verified by a couple of men, named Young and Carmichael, it was unanimously resolved by the meeting to send them a written request, signed by all the members of the Oregon Temperance Society, to desist from their unholy enterprise. The following is a copy of the correspondence which took place between the Society and Messrs. Young & Carmichael, and is inserted to show what stand the missionaries took in guarding the morals of the community, and the extent of the influence they exerted. But for these measures, intemperance would have devastated the country.

"Messrs. Young & Carmichael:

"*Gentlemen,* — Whereas we, the members of the Oregon Temperance Society, have learned with no common interest, and with feelings of *deep regret,* that you are now preparing a distillery for the purpose of manufacturing ardent spirits, to be sold in this vicinity; and, whereas, we are most fully convinced that the vending of spiritous liquors will more effectually paralyze our efforts for the promotion of temperance, than any other, or all other obstacles that can be thrown in our way; and, as we do feel a lively and intense interest in the success of the temperance cause, believing as we do, that the prosperity and interests of this infant and rising settlement will be materially affected by it, both as it respects its temporal and spiritual welfare, and that the poor Indians, whose case is even now *indescribably* wretched, will be made far more so by the use of ardent spirits; and whereas, gentlemen, you are not ignorant that the laws of the United States prohibit American citizens from selling ardent spirits to Indians under the penalty of a heavy fine; and as you do not pretend to justify yourselves, but urge pecuniary interest as the reason of your procedure; and as we do not, *cannot* think it will be of pecuniary interest to you to prosecute this business; and as we are not enemies, but friends, and do not wish, under existing circumstances, that you should sacrifice one penny of the money you have already expended; we, therefore, for the above, and various other reasons which we could urge,

"1st. *Resolved,* That we do most *earnestly* and *feelingly* request you, gentlemen, forever to abandon your enterprise.

"2nd. *Resolved,* That we will and do hereby agree to pay you the sum you have expended, if you will give us the avails of your expenditures, or deduct from them the bill of expenses.

"3d. *Resolved*, That a committee of one be appointed to make known the views of this society, and present our request to Messrs. Young & Carmichael.

"4th. *Resolved*, That the undersigned will pay the sums severally affixed to our names, to Messrs. Young & Carmichael, on or before the thirty-first day of March next, the better to enable them to give up their project."

Then followed the names of nine Americans, and fifteen Frenchmen, which then embraced a majority of the white men of the country, excluding the Hudson's Bay Company, with a subscription of sixty-three dollars, and a note appended as follows:

"We, the undersigned, jointly promise to pay the balance, be the same more or less.

"Jason Lee,
Daniel Lee,
Cyrus Shepard,
P. L. Edwards."

To the above request Messrs. Young & Carmichael returned the following answer:

"Wallamette, 13th Jan., 1837.

"To the Oregon Temperance Society:

"*Gentlemen,*—Having taken into consideration your request to relinquish our enterprise in manufacturing ardent spirits, we therefore do agree to stop our proceeding for the present. But, gentlemen, the reasons for first beginning such an undertaking were the innumerable difficulties placed in our way by, and the tyranising oppression of the Hudson's Bay Company, here under the absolute authority of Dr. McLaughlin, who has treated us with more disdain than any American citizen's feelings could support. But as there have now some favorable circumstances occurred to enable us to get along without making spiritous liquors, we resolve to stop the manufacture of it for the present; but, gentlemen, it is not consistent with our feelings to receive any recompense whatever for our expenditures, but we are thankful to the Society for their offer.

"We remain, yours, &c.,
"Young & Carmichael."

The missionaries from the first had proved a great blessing to the country, not only in a spiritual and moral point of view, but in furnishing employment to many individuals otherwise without the means of livelihood; and setting an example of industry and perseverance in the temporal departments of their work, they gave a spur to all business operations, and the community seemed at once to spring from that state of inactivity into which it had been thrown by the domineering policy of the Hudson's Bay Company, into one of great enterprise and prosperity. In the early part of January a circumstance transpired which enabled the members of the mission and others, to carry out a design which they had previously formed, and in the execution of which the temporal interests of the country would be greatly promoted. This design was to send an expedition to California to purchase and drive to Oregon a band of neat cattle for the supply of the settlers. The circumstance referred to was the arrival in the country of Wm. A. Slocum, Esq., of the United States Navy. Up to this period there were no cattle in the country, except what belonged to the Hudson's Bay Company, and they would not sell, but compelled the settlers, if they had cattle at all, to take cows merely for their milk, and return them with their increase. This looked too much like oppression to Mr. Jason Lee, and he resolved, if possible, to break up the cattle monopoly, believing that he would thereby confer a lasting benefit to the country. On the arrival of Mr. Slocum, he proposed to take to California, any number of persons that might be needed, free of expense except board; and a meeting was immediately called at the mission house, for the purpose of forming a California Cattle Company, and making the necessary arrangements for the expedition. Each person belonging to the Company was to share in proportion to the amount of money he invested, and the persons who went with the expedition were to be paid a stipulated sum per month in cattle. P. L. Edwards and Ewing Young, were appointed to take charge of the Company, and Thursday the 19th of January was fixed upon as the day for the vessel to sail.

Mr. Slocum, while in Oregon, manifested a deep interest in the welfare of the rising settlement, and especially in the prosperity of the Oregon mission. He highly approved of the method the missionaries had pursued to benefit the Indians, and said he was perfectly astonished at the improvement those had made who were under the care of the mission. In company with Mr. Jason Lee, he visited the several farms in the settlement, and on the 14th, took his leave of the Wallamette, Mr. Lee accompanying him to Vancouver. A letter signed by the missionaries, commendatory of the course Mr. Slocum had pursued in the country, had been put into his hands before leaving, and he returned them the following answer, which contained a donation of fifty dollars for the benefit of the mission. This letter was put into the hands of Mr. Lee during his last interview with Mr. Slocum.

"AMERICAN BRIG LORIOT, OFF THE WALLAMETTE,
Oregon river, 18*th January,* 1837.

"MY DEAR SIRS :—I have much pleasure in acknowledging the receipt of your kind favor of the 16th, and I beg leave to thank you for the expressions of regard contained therein. It was indeed a source of regret that I could continue no longer at your mission on the banks of the Wallamette, for the visit was to me one of exceeding interest. On my return to the civilized parts of our country, I shall not hesitate to express my humble opinion that you have already effected a great public good, by practically showing that the Indians west of the Rocky Mountains are capable of the union of mental and physical discipline, as taught at your establishment. For I have seen with my own eyes, children, who, two years ago, were roaming their own native wilds in a state of savage barbarism, now being brought within the knowledge of moral and religious instruction, becoming useful members of society, by being taught the most useful of all arts, agriculture, and all this without the slightest compulsion.

"As an evidence of my good will towards the laudable efforts you are making in this remote quarter, debarred of almost every comfort, deprived of the associations of kindred, and of *home*, I beg you to accept herewith, the sum of fifty dollars; only regretting that my means at present will not allow me to add more, I pray you to accept, my dear sirs, the assurances of the unfeigned regard of,

"Your friend and ob'nt servant,
"Wm. A. Slocum, U. S. N."

Mr. Slocum's vessel left the Columbia river about the first of February, and arrived safely in the Bay of San Francisco, on the coast of California. The cattle company proceeded immediately to purchase a large band of cattle, and a number of horses, with which they started for Oregon. In crossing a range of mountains separating the two countries, they were attacked by the Rascal Indians, and a number of their cattle were killed, but they at length succeeded in driving back their foe, and saving the remainder. Contrary to the predictions and wishes of the members of the Hudson's Bay Company, who indirectly opposed them at the outset, they arrived in safety in the Wallamette valley with six hundred head of cattle, and distributed them among the settlers, according to the provisions of the compact. This successful enterprise, which laid the foundation for a rapid accumulation of wealth by the settlers, was mainly accomplished through the energy and perseverance of Rev. Jason Lee.

Sometime in July, 1836, We-lap-tu-lekt, an Indian of the Kayuse tribe, came to the mission on the Wallamette, and brought two of his sons, whom he desired to have remain to be educated. He had travelled with the missionaries, while on their way from Fort Hall to

Walla-Walla, and seemed very attentive to religious instruction, and desirous that missionaries should settle in the Kayuse country; but none having yet come, he resolved to visit the mission in the lower country. He was so well pleased that he determined to return to his country, and bring his family down to the mission, as soon as possible. This he accomplished by the 6th of September, when he settled his family near the mission station. Some of his children attended the school, and appeared to be making rapid improvement, but in February, 1837, his family began to suffer with disease. Two of his children died in quick succession, and a third was fast sinking with a burning fever. We-lap-tu-lekt was frightened, and supposed that all his family would die, if he did not leave the place. He accordingly fled in a canoe, but just at the moment of his landing at Vancouver, another of his family expired. These repeated deaths in one family, and the fact that most of the mission children were sick, and some had died but recently, began to create a prejudice in the minds of the Indians, against having their children remain with the mission, and after this it was not so easy to procure and retain them.

In February, 1835, Mr. Lee addressed letters to the Board in New York, earnestly soliciting them to send out a reinforcement. In compliance with this request, the Board appointed Dr. Elijah White and wife, Mr. Alanson Beers and wife, Miss Ann Maria Pitman, Miss Susan Downing, Miss Elvina Johnson, and Mr. W. H. Wilson, assistant missionaries. This company sailed from Boston in July, 1836, and, after several months detention at the Sandwich Islands, entered the mouth of the Columbia river in May, 1837. Intelligence of their arrival in the Columbia was received on the 18th of May, and the following day J. Lee went down the river in a canoe to meet them and conduct them to the station. On the 27th he returned with five of them, the others remaining awhile at Vancouver. Their arrival in the country was hailed by the four lonely brethren, who had hitherto composed the mission, with great gladness, and the more so because they were thenceforth to be cheered by the presence and sympathy of intelligent females, from their own native land, especially as they had found, long before this, that " it was not good for man to be alone."

The next day after the arrival of the reinforcement at the station, Sam-nik, a Calapooa chief, was brought to the mission house, dreadfully mangled, having been shot by another Indian, while sleeping in his lodge. He desired surgical aid. This was the second circumstance of the kind that had transpired within a short time.

The last of May, the mission was visited by Captain Hinckley and lady, of the vessel that brought out the reinforcement, and the first of June, J. Lee accompanied them back to Vancouver. On his return, the 13th of that month, he found Cyrus Shepard dangerously sick with inflammatory fever; but under the faithful care of Dr. White, he soon recovered.

On the 4th of July, the annual meeting of the Oregon Temperance Society was held at the mission house, when short and appropriate addresses were delivered by J. Lee, D. Lee, A. Beers, W. H. Wilson and Dr. White. Twelve new members were added, and a most satisfactory influence was gained for the cause of temperance.

On Sabbath, the 16th of July, a large assembly for Oregon convened in the pleasant grove of firs, in front of the mission house, for the purpose of religious worship. The services were conducted by Rev. Daniel Lee, and commenced by his uniting in lawful matrimony, according to the form laid down in the Methodist Discipline, the Rev. Jason Lee with Miss Ann Maria Pitman, Cyrus Shepard with Miss Susan Downing, and Charles Roe with Miss Nancy, an Indian girl of the Calapooa tribe. This was followed by an appropriate discourse, and the sacrament of the Lord's Supper. It was a season of thrilling interest to all present. Two persons who professed to have recently experienced the comforts of religion, united with the church, and one of them, though brought up a Quaker, was baptized, and both partook of the sacrament.

No particular change took place in the mission in consequence of the arrival of the reinforcement, with the exception of the enlargement of its financial operations. Two log houses, for the accommodation of the families, and a blacksmith shop, were immediately erected. A short time after, a frame house was built, located one mile from the station back from the river, and was occupied by the family of Dr. White. This was the only comfortable house as yet owned by the mission. During the same season Mr. Lee bought out a Frenchman who had built a small house, and opened a farm so near the mission premises as to be much in the way. By this purchase the mission enlarged its farming improvements, and having now a large band of cattle, resulting from the California expedition, Mr. Josiah Whitcomb was employed by the mission to take charge of the farming operations, as it was impossible for the Lees to attend to them and look after the spiritual wants of the people.

The number of children and adults in the mission continued to increase, notwithstanding the numerous deaths that had taken place, until the average number attending the day and sabbath school was from thirty to thirty-five. The school was under the judicious management of Cyrus Shepard, and at this period was in a very flourishing condition. The scholars were taught the English language, and made rapid proficiency in reading, writing, spelling, geography, and arithmetic.

As the sickly season came on, some of the missionaries performed two tours through the country, for the benefit of their health. On the 2d of August, Mr. and Mrs. Lee and Mr. Shepard, accompanied by Mr. Desportes as a guide, started up the Wallamette river on horseback, and journeying leisurely for several days, towards the south, took a circuit eastward, and striking the head waters of the Molala river, followed down that stream to the north, towards where it forms a junction with the Wallamette. Crossing the latter river at Champoeg, they returned in safety to the mission, after an absence of ten days. They saw and imparted instruction to a few bands of Indians on their route, and returned with reanimated health.

On the 14th of August, Mr. J. Lee and Mr. C. Shepard, with their wives, accompanied by Joseph Gervais as guide, left the mission to perform a land journey to the Pacific coast. They traveled one day and a half, through a very beautiful and fertile country, crossing the Wallamette and Yamhill rivers, and encamped the second night at the foot of the mountains which separate the Wallamette valley from the Pacific ocean. Next day they commenced crossing the mountains, but found the trail exceedingly difficult, on account of the abruptness of the ascending and descending, and the numerous large trees that had fallen across it. This rendered their progress very slow, and the third night they encamped in a deep, dark valley, among the mountains, twelve miles from the shore. During the night it was very rainy, and also the following day ; but they moved camp in the morning, and at 5 p. m. pitched their tent in a beautiful cypress grove, within a short distance of the shore, so that their encampment commanded a fine view of the broad expanse of the Pacific ocean.

Here they continued for one week, visiting the Killemook Indians, who inhabit that portion of the country, and preaching to them as they were able. They enjoyed the clams and other shell-fish, which they procured from the delightful sandy beach, and invigorated themselves by frequent bathing in the salt water. On the 26th, they left their pleasant encampment, and after four days' toil in crossing the mountains, jumping the logs, fording the streams, and traveling over the prairies, they arrived at the mission, after an absence of sixteen days. They were better qualified, from the improvement of their health, to pursue the business of their calling.

On the 4th of September following, Mr. Daniel Lee and Mr. Shepard started for Vancouver on business, and arrived there on the 6th. On the following day, a canoe arrived at Vancouver, direct from the mouth of the river, bringing the Rev. Daniel Leslie and Rev. H.

K. W. Perkins, who had recently entered the river, in the ship Sumatra. They, with Mrs. Leslie and three children, and Miss Margaret Smith, constituted a second reinforcement to the Oregon mission. They sailed from Boston on the 20th of January, 1837, and reached the place of their destination, on the Wallamette river, the 20th of September. Soon after the arrival of Mr. Perkins, a union betwixt himself and Miss Elvira Johnson, who came out in the former reinforcement, which had been long in contemplation, was consummated. They were married on the 21st of November, 1837, by Rev. David Leslie.

On the 25th of December, a general meeting was called at the mission house, and an Oregon Missionary Society was formed. A liberal subscription was raised, to be expended the ensuing year, for the benefit of the Calapooa Indians.

At the close of this year, the missionaries were all residing at or near the Wallamette station, and were laboring in their respective departments, not without effect, some in sustaining the interests of the mission school, some in preaching to the Calapooas, and the white settlements, some in different mechanical branches, and some in taking care of the farm and the rapidly increasing stock of cattle and horses. Several members of the mission school had died during the year, and mortal diseases unceasingly prevailed among the Indians throughout the country; yet, in view of all the circumstances of the case, the missionaries were encouraged, and began to take measures for the enlargement of their operations.

Attending to the interests of the temperance cause, Mr. J. Lee set out, soon after the 1st of January, on an exploring tour to the Umpqua country, in company with Mr. Birnie, one of the traders of the Hudson's Bay Company. This country lies some two hundred miles south of Vancouver, and it was reported to contain several thousand Indians, and as offering a fine field for missionary operations. The late rains had swollen the rivers and creeks to such a degree, that it was almost impossible for Mr. Lee to proceed; yet, after several days of toilsome and dangerous journeying, through the mud and rain, and fording the rapid streams that crossed his path, he succeeded in reaching the trading post of the Hudson's Bay Company, situated on the Umpqua river, forty miles above its mouth. The information he received here was of an encouraging nature, and such was the difficulty of traveling, that he resolved to extend his observations no farther. Accordingly he returned to the Wallamette, where he arrived on the 11th of March, 1838, under the impression that, so soon as a competency of missionaries could be provided, a station should be established somewhere in the Umpqua valley.

About this time, a meeting of all the missionaries, preachers, and laymen was called, to consult on the subject of establishing a new station; and, after the merits of several portions of the country were presented, it was unanimously resolved, that a mission be commenced at the Dalls, on the Columbia river, about ninety miles above Vancouver. Daniel Lee and H. K. W. Perkins were appointed by the superintendent to the new mission. They left the Wallamette station, to repair to their new field, on the 14th of March, Mr. Perkins leaving his wife behind, until they could make arrangements for the convenience of a family.

Before Daniel Lee and Mr. Perkins left the Wallamette, a general consultation was held on the subject of a still greater enlargement of the missionary work, in Oregon. In the estimation of the meeting, "the harvest was plenteous and the laborers were few." The Umpqua, Killamook, Klikitat, Clatsop, Chenook, Nezqualy, and many other tribes, were destitute of missionaries ; and in view of these different stations, and the general wants of the country, they passed a unanimous resolution, advising the Rev. Jason Lee to make a visit to the United States for the purpose of representing before the Board of Managers of the Missionary Society of the M. E. Church and the public generally, the true condition of the country, and of the Indians, and soliciting the men and means which, in their judgment, were necessary, for the successful prosecution of the missionary work.

Mr. Lee concurred in the opinions thus expressed by the members of the mission, and accordingly took leave of his wife and brethren on the Wallamette, on the 26th day of March, 1838, and commenced the long and hazardous journey back across the Rocky mountains. He was accompanied by P. L. Edwards, of the mission, a Mr. Ewing, of Missouri, and two Indian boys of the Chenook tribe, called Wm. Brooks and Thos. Adams. It was a trying scene when Mr. Lee took his departure from his companions in labor and suffering in Oregon, and the more so from the consideration that he was leaving his beloved wife, to whom he had been married less than a year; but in his opinion, it was his duty to return, and call for fellow-laborers; and, though worldly interests and enjoyments demanded his continuance in Oregon, yet he practised on the principle, that all such things should give place to considerations of duty.

It was the first of April before Mr. Lee found himself prepared to take his departure from Vancouver, towards the Rocky mountains; but before we follow him in his toilsome and perilous journey home, we will contemplate some of the circumstances which were transpiring among those whom he had left in the valley of Oregon.

On the 21st of April Rev. H. K. W. Perkins arrived at the mission from the Dalls, and brought a favorable report from the new station. The Indians are known by the name of the Wasco tribe, and they call the place where they live, Wascopam. They were found to number from twelve to fifteen hundred; were much pleased with the idea of the establishment of a mission among them, and were willing to assist in preparing a place for the accommodation of the missionaries.

On the 26th of April, Mr. and Mrs. Perkins left the Wallamette in a canoe manned by Indians, to take up their residence at Wascopam. The voyage from the Wallamette station to the Dalls, was first down the Wallamette river the distance of seventy miles to its mouth, and then up the Columbia river the distance of ninety-five miles. Both rivers are dangerous, in consequence of the numerous rapids, but after several days of exposure and fatigue, Mr. and Mrs. Perkins arrived in safety at the Dalls, and by the assistance of Mr. D. Lee and the Indians, soon established themselves in comfortable quarters. Mr. D. Lee had already acquired a knowledge of the Chenook language as spoken in the vicinity of Vancouver, which the Wascoes generally understood, and could preach immediately to the Indians without the aid of an interpreter. As the Walla-Walla tribe was contiguous, and their language understood by many of the Dalls Indians, Mr. Perkins, in addition to learning the Chenook, applied himself to the acquirement of the Walla-Walla, and it was not long before he could preach to the Indians in both languages. The plan adopted was to circulate among the Indians, and preach to them wherever they could be found; and from the reception which the missionaries met, and the apparent attention given to the gospel, seldom was there ever an Indian mission established under more favorable auspices.

Things moved on quite prosperously in all the departments, under the direction of Rev. David Leslie, whom Mr. Jason Lee had appointed his substitute during his absence, until the 26th day of June, when an event transpired among the little band on the Wallamette, which, from the circumstances attending it, threw a gloom over the hitherto cheering aspects of the mission. Ann Maria, wife of the Rev. Jason Lee, gave birth to a son on the 6th of June, which she was doomed to see expire a few days afterwards. At the time of its death unfavorable symptoms appeared in Mrs. Lee, and on Tuesday, the 26th, at six o'clock A. M., she calmly closed her eyes in death. The following day the afflicted band of missionaries committed to the grave the remains of this youthful mother, with her little son clasped in her arms. When this took place Mr. Lee had been absent three months, and was far on his way to the United States; but through the kindness of Dr. McLaughlin, an express was sent off immediately, to carry to Mr.

Lee the sad tidings of the death of his companion. It was about the first of September when Mr. Lee arrived at the Methodist mission among the Shawnees, on the frontiers of Missouri, then under the superintendence of Rev. Mr. Johnson, and having retired to his room, late in the evening, he was offering up a tribute of thanksgiving to Him who had been his preserver while on his toilsome journey through the hostile tribes of the mountains, when he heard a rap at his door. Rising, he admitted the stranger, who placed a package of letters in his hands, and immediately left the room. He broke the black seal of one, and the first line conveyed to him the heart-rending intelligence that his Ann Maria, and her little son, were numbered with the dead. Leaving the afflicted missionary to indulge his grief alone, we return to review other scenes in the valley of the Columbia.

On the 14th day of August, information was received in the Wallamette, that Mrs. Perkins, at the Dalls, was very sick, and stood in great need of medical aid, and other assistance. Accordingly Rev. D. Leslie, Dr. I. Bailey, and Mrs. White with her little daughter then eight months old, embarked for the Dalls in a canoe manned by Indians, and six days afterward arrived there in safety. In the mean time Dr. Whitman, from the mission in the interior, had visited Mrs. P., and when the company arrived from the Wallamette, her health was nearly restored; consequently, on the morning of the 22nd, Mr. Leslie and Mrs. White left the Dalls to return home. They descended the Columbia to the cascades the first day, and the next morning made a portage of some three miles, and again all were seated quietly in the canoe, and the Indians struck out into the strong current. Below them were rapids which, in consequence of the high water, were worse than they anticipated. The river at this place is about one mile and a half wide, and the canoe was about one-third of a mile from the nearest shore. They saw the dashing of the waters before them, but such was the strength of the current that already bore them down, that it was impossible to shun the dangerous point. Soon the canoe was carried among the rolling surges, filled, capsized, and instantly all were plunged into the frightful gulph. Mr. Leslie, on rising to the surface of the river, thought of Mrs. White, and seeing her beneath his feet, immediately plunged after her, if possible to bring her to the surface. He caught hold of her clothes, and came up to the surface, struggled for a moment to keep her above the water, but was obliged to relinquish his hold. He now thought that by giving her up he might possibly save his own life, but it then occurred to him that she was entrusted to his care, and at once resolving to do his best to save her if he died in the attempt, plunged after her again, and seizing her clothes, brought her to the surface. Discovering the canoe drifting but a short distance from him, bottom up, he soon regained it, and got hold of the hand of an Indian, who had risen on the other side of the canoe, and succeeded in keeping the head of Mrs. White above the water. By this time they had been carried by the current partly across the river towards the farther shore; and fortunately some Indians were on that side with a canoe, who, on discovering their situation, immediately put off to their relief. These friendly natives took them into their canoe, and then taking the capsized canoe in tow, succeeded in gaining the shore. All were safe but the babe; that was missing, but on righting the canoe, it was found to have drifted along with it to the shore, but the vital spark had fled. They were forty miles distant from a civilized habitation, but the Indians kindly proffered to take them into their canoe, and carry them down to Vancouver. Wrapped in their wet blankets, with the corpse of the little infant lying in one part of their canoe, they descended to that place, where they had all the assistance afforded them which sympathy could devise, or their distressed circumstances demand. On Friday, the 24th, they left Vancouver, and on Saturday evening they arrived at the Wallamette, and the following day deposited the body of the infant in the mission burying grounds, Mr. Leslie improving the occasion by an appropriate discourse founded on Deut. viii. 6: "O, how wonderful in working is our God, and his ways past finding out."

Thus the missionaries were constantly exposed. If they passed from one portion of the country to another, they were obliged to commit themselves in their frail craft, to the treacherous element, or travel by land through hostile tribes of savages.

Mr. Grey, of the mission in the interior, made about this time a hair breadth escape. While on his way from the Rocky mountains to Missouri, with one or two white men and a number of Indians, he was attacked by a band of Sioux warriors; his Indians were all killed, and himself was twice wounded by musket balls. While he and the white men with him were making their escape on horseback, across a river, the Indians fired at them from the shore, and a ball passed through the hat of Mr. Grey, cutting the hair from the top of his head. The white men escaped with one horse apiece, having been robbed of every thing besides.

About the first of September, Rev. Daniel Lee left the Dalls with a party of Indians, to go to the Wallamette station by land across the Cascade mountains, to ascertain whether it would be practicable to drive back a small band of cattle for the accommodation of the mission farm. Supposing that a week would be the longest time that it would require to perform the journey, he took provisions to last him only during that time; but in consequence of the extreme difficulty of the traveling through the dense thickets, over the high mountains, up and down the precipices, and fording the rapid streams, it required twice as long as he anticipated. Consequently they consumed all their provisions, and after going hungry for some length of time, they were driven to the necessity of killing a poor, jaded horse, on the flesh of which they supported themselves till they arrived at the Clakamas, where they procured salmon, having consumed the last morsel of their horse that very day. Not at all discouraged by these difficulties, Mr. Lee resolved to drive the cattle through, and engaging two men from the settlement to accompany him, he started with his band on the 26th of September. After ten days of excessive labor and fatigue, he arrived safely at Wascopam without loss. This measure for stocking the little farm they had opened at the Dalls, was adopted by the missionaries for the purpose of securing, at less expense, the means of subsistence.

In the month of December of this year the Rev. D. Leslie had the misfortune of losing his house, and most of his furniture, bedding, clothing, &c., by fire. This loss was the more severely felt, as it was difficult in that new country to replace the articles destroyed.

At the close of this year the mission school under the care of Cyrus Shepard, had increased to nearly forty scholars, notwithstanding the fearful mortality that reigned among the children. About one-third of all that had been received up to this period, had died, and most of the remainder were in a sickly condition. At this time Mr. Shepard was obliged to give up the care of the school, in consequence of personal affliction. A swelling appeared on one of his knees, which at first created but little concern, but at length assumed a very alarming aspect. All the medical and surgical skill of the country were expended upon him to no purpose; the limb was amputated, but it was too late to save life. Death ensued a short time after the operation. In Mr. Shepard the mission lost one of its most valuable members, a fond wife was bereft of a kind and faithful companion, and two little girls were rendered fatherless.

Soon after this event, by an arrangement of the mission, Dr. Elijah White connected with his professional duties, the care of the mission school; and the business of the various departments proceeded as usual through the winter.

At the Dalls a great religious excitement prevailed among the Indians through the labors of D. Lee and H. K. W. Perkins. This excitement extended fifty or seventy-five miles along the Columbia river, chiefly among the Wasco and Chenook Indians, of whom more than one thousand in the course of a few weeks apparently embraced the christian religion. Such were the evidences of a genuine change in these Indians, that the missionaries, after witnessing their praying habits for a few weeks, baptized them, and received them formally into the church. They were then formed into classes, and stated preaching was established in the different villages where they resided; and for the time being the hearts of the missionaries were encouraged, from beholding the apparently happy success with which their labors were crowned.

On the Wallamette also, under the labors of Rev. D. Leslie, a revival of religion took place among the white settlers, the Hawaiians, who were in the employment of the mission, and the Indians connected with the mission school. A number of each class were converted and received into the church.

While these things were transpiring in Oregon, Rev. J. Lee was zealously employed in accomplishing the objects of his visit to the United States. He arrived in the city of New York about the first of November, and on the 14th he was present at a meeting of the Missionary Board, and stated at length the object of his visit He urged with much earnestness the importance of extending the missionary work in Oregon; and in view of this he plead with great zeal the necessity of sending to that country a large reinforcement. In his opinion it was essential, for the prosperity of the mission, to supply it with the requisite means to furnish itself with food, buildings, etc.; and all the necessary implements for husbandry, and mechanical purposes, should be sent out by the Board. To meet all these demands would require a very heavy outlay, and for this and some other reasons, Mr. Lee met with warm opposition from some of the members of the Board, who sincerely doubted the expediency of the measure; but the superintendent, who had just come from the field of operation, perseveringly and powerfully urged the claims of the mission, and, sustained by Dr. Fisk, Dr. Bangs and others, finally succeeded in obtaining from the Board all, yea more than he demanded; for in his opinion but two ministers were required, but in the estimation of a majority of the Board, if there were to be as many laymen sent out as Mr. Lee called for, two ministers would not be sufficient. Accordingly, on the 6th of December, 1838, the Board passed a resolution to send to Oregon five additional missionaries, one physician, six mechanics, four farmers, one missionary steward, and four female teachers; making in all thirty-six adult persons. These were all selected and appointed within a few months, the laymen by Dr. Bangs and Mr. Lee, and the missionaries by the Bishop having charge of the Foreign missions. The appointments took place from various parts of the United States, the New England, NewYork, Troy, Genesee, Illinois, and North Carolina Conferences contributing more or less, to make the numbers of the reinforcement complete. During the summer of 1839, Mr. Lee, attended by Wm. Brooks and Thomas Adams, the two Indian boys whom he brought with him, traveled quite extensively through the New England and Middle States, holding missionary meetings in all the important places, and collecting funds for the Oregon mission. His success was unparalleled, and an interest was excited throughout the land amounting to enthusiasm. Crowds thronged to see and hear the pioneer missionary beyond the Rocky mountains, and the converted Indians who accompanied him. Liberal collections were taken up for the Oregon mission in almost every place, and these, with the appropriations of the Board for the purchase of goods, amounted to forty thousand dollars. Furnished with all kinds of tools for agricultural and mechanical purposes, and with the necessary articles for the construction of a saw-mill and grist-mill, the great reinforcement, with Mr. Lee at their head, at length found themselves ready for sea.

CHAPTER II.

Journal of a voyage from New York to Oregon — Time and circumstances of departure — First evening — Last look at the Highlands — Initiatory rites — Great distress — Sea-sickness indescribable — Fourth day — Captain Spaulding — First and second officers — Passengers in the cabin — Character of the expedition — First Sabbath at sea — Police regulations — A rich treat — Centenary meeting — Results — Vessel ships a sea — Wind increases — Tremendous gale — North-East trade — Description of the trades — Whale — Allowance of Water — Porpoise — Vessel — Amusing surprise — Astronomy — Northern constellations — Magellanic clouds — Interesting Sabbath — Land, ho! — Cape Frio — Lighthouse — Splendid scenery — Arrival at Rio de Janeiro — Historical sketch — Don John — Brazil independent — Don Pedro the first — Compelled to abdicate — State of the country — Foreign residents — Religion — City — Buildings — Missionaries — Slavery — Reflections.

It was in the evening of the 9th day of October, 1839, that a company of fifty-two persons, sixteen of whom were children, were collected together on the quarter deck of the ship Lausanne, which then lay quietly in the bight, betwixt the east coast of New Jersey and Sandy Hook. The preceding day had been one of most thrilling interest to every person composing that excited, though confiding, group. They had bidden, as they all then supposed, a last adieu to the land of their nativity; and all the endearing ties that bound them to home and friends, had been torn asunder. In their hearts burned an intense desire to become the instruments of introducing the blessings of religion and civilization, to the benighted heathen in a foreign land; and for this purpose they had resolved upon braving the dangers of the deep, and to endure the difficulties and deprivations incident to a residence in a heathen land.

It fell to the lot of the writer to be associated with this self-denying band, to mingle with them while they lingered on their native shore, as if loth to make the sacrifice, to witness them, as, at the given signal, they hastened to commit themselves to that frail bark, which was destined to become their prison home for so many tedious days and stormy nights, and, with them, to share the perils of a voyage of more than twenty-two thousand miles.

Before we take our departure from Sandy Hook, the reader will expect to be entertained with some of the principal events which took place the day preceding the evening on which these voluntary exiles were for the first time assembled on the deck of the Lausanne.

The morning rose beautiful and serene, with not a cloud to obscure the rising sun, and not a breath of wind to ruffle the surface of the waters. It was at nine o'clock of this day, when, by a previous arrangement, the mission family, attended by their beloved friends of New York and vicinity, assembled at White Hall Dock, at the foot of Broadway, where lay the steamboat Hercules, which had been engaged to take the passengers to the Lausanne, which then lay in East River, and then to tow the ship down through the Narrows, into the vicinity of Sandy Hook. Two hundred and fifty persons, who had endeared themselves to our hearts by their kindness and solicitude for our welfare, accompanied us on the steamboat, when we embarked, and among them were the Rev. N. Bangs, D. D., and the Rev. Dr. Anderson, the former being the secretary of the Missionary Society of the M. E. C., and the latter, the secretary of the A. B. C. F. M.

It was precisely fifteen minutes past ten o'clock, when the signal was given for the boat to leave the wharf, and, in a few moments, we were along side the Lausanne, while the multitude that lined the shore, were invoking many blessings on our enterprise, and by words and signs were bidding us a last farewell.

The ship was immediately fastened to the boat, and we were speedily gliding down the beautiful harbor of New York, first looking back upon the city, whose hundred gilded steeples were flashing in the sun light, and then upon immense shipping, crowded for miles up and down the East and North rivers; now looking for a moment upon Castle Garden, Governor's Island, the North Carolina seventy-four, Brooklyn, the Fort, and then upon the Jersey shore, Long Island coast, Staten Island, with all its delightful scenery; and every thing within the range of our vision was gazed upon with so much the more interest, as they belonged to our own native country, and, in all probability, we were to see them no more.

The time that elapsed from our leaving the wharf, till the steamboat left us to return, was full of deep and lively interest. The conversation was fraught with the most intense feeling and anxiety, which were manifested ever and anon, by floods of tears, and expressions of the most ardent wishes for our welfare and success. The hymns that were sung were remarkably appropriate, and tended to increase the flame already burning on the altar of every heart. The religious services, conducted by Dr. Bangs, Dr. Anderson, and the Rev. Mr. Davis, were peculiarly solemn and affecting, and closed by the baptism of the infant son of the Rev. J. P. Richmond, who was christened "Oregon," the name of the country to which we were bound. While yet the impressions which these services had made upon all present were the most lively and tender, it was announced that the two vessels must separate. At this time all the missionaries, with their attendants, were on the steamboat. We had passed the Narrows, and were rapidly approaching Sandy Hook, when the parting scene commenced. Now parents and children, brothers and sisters, and friends and acquaintances, embraced each other for the last time on earth, and amidst tears, prayers and farewells, the missionaries passed from the boat to the deck of the Lausanne. The grapplings were immediately cast off, and the Hercules sailed gracefully around us, while from each deck the emblems of purity and affection, snow white handkerchiefs, were fluttering in the air, until by a point of Long Island, at the Narrows, the vessels were hidden from each other's sight.

Though there was no wind to favor us, an ebb tide carried us slowly down to the usual anchorage, inside of

Sandy Hook, where we were glad to have a little time to arrange our cabin and state room affairs, before going to sea.

The evening of the day of embarkation was serene and peaceful, and after the stirring events of the day had been rehearsed by the passengers assembled on the deck of our noble vessel, all repaired quietly to their berths, and, after a good night's rest, arose on the morning of the 10th of October, in good health and spirits, for their voyage. At half past six o'clock in the morning, we weighed anchor, and spreading our canvass to a gentle western breeze, were carried majestically past the Hook, and were soon tossed upon the waves of the broad Atlantic.

The passengers were all immediately called upon to perform the initiatory rites to which all have to submit, who, for the first time, invade the dominions of Neptune. This, however, did not prevent many from taking a last look of the Highlands of Never Sink, which disappeared in the smoky distance at three o'clock in the afternoon of the first day. In passing through this terrible ordeal of initiation, there are occasional intervals of relaxation, and on Sunday, the 13th, the "North-Easter," which had been blowing from the first day out, lulled; a calm succeeded, and operated like a charm upon the sick inmates of the Lausanne; for all so far recovered as to be able to present themselves on the quarter deck.

As we are now on the fourth day out fairly under way, having lost sight of land, and experienced one severe storm, and, for the first time since leaving Sandy Hook, collected on the deck of the vessel, the reader will expect a more particular account of the company to which, collectively, he has already been introduced. Embracing the officers and crew, there were seventy-five souls on board, fifty-four of whom were passengers. The ship was commanded by Capt. Spaulding, who had been employed by the owners, Farnham & Fry, in view of his qualifications, to take charge of such an expedition, for so long a voyage. Twenty years' experience as master of a vessel, had established the captain's

2*

reputation as a skillful navigator, which, in connexion with his general kindness to the passengers, and his efforts to make them as comfortable as their crowded condition on the vessel would admit, proves that the selection, if not the best that could have been made, was as good as could have been reasonably expected. The first and second mates, though wanting in strict morality, were excellent seamen, and well understood the business of navigation. The second mate, Mr. Coffin, had performed eight voyages around Cape Horn.

The crew were composed of English, Americans, Irish, Germans, Danes, and Swedes. This variety was selected, as the captain said, because among such a crew it is less difficult to preserve order, than it is with a crew exclusively Americans.

Finding ourselves thus officered and manned, and witnessing the management of our vessel through one protracted storm, we concluded that, extraordinaries excepted, we should be conducted in safety to the land of our destination.

The passengers in the cabin, embracing children, numbered fifty-four. Of these eight were ministers of the gospel; seven of whom, namely, Jason Lee, J. H. Frost, A. F. Waller, W. W. Kone, G. Hines, L. H. Judson, J. L. Parrish and J. P. Richmond, were connected with the missionary expedition to Oregon; and one, the Rev. Shelden Dibble, was a Presbyterian missionary, on his way to his field of labor, in the Sandwich Islands. We had one physician, Dr. J. L. Babcock, who had been appointed to take care of the health of the members of the mission, and all the remainder had been connected with the enterprise, by the appointment of the Missionary Board of the M. E. Church, as farmers, mechanics, and teachers, to labor for the promotion of religion and civilization, in the territory of Oregon. With the secular department of the work, two of the above named preachers, L. H. Judson, and J. L. Parrish, were also connected.

The persons composing this, the largest expedition of the kind that had ever sailed from our shores, presented a great variety in consequence of the extensive range of country from which they had been collected. Coming together from Massachusetts, Connecticut, New York, Maryland, North Carolina, Illinois, and Missouri, and bringing with them many of the different peculiarities of these several portions of our Union, it would not be surprising, confined as they were for so long a time, under circumstances peculiarly calculated to "try men's souls" if, from time to time, they came so far in collision with each other's views and prejudices, as to produce a momentary rupture. One striking trait, however, as difficult to exhibit as it is excellent in its influence, appeared in the conduct of the company huddled together in the cabin of the Lausanne. It was this; a disposition to sacrifice self, for the promotion of the common weal. This excellency of character was fully manifested on the part of the ladies, of whom we had nineteen on board.

Dismissing this general description of the company, I proceed to give a few of the incidents of our voyage, first, assuring the reader that long and tedious descriptions of the management and evolutions of the vessel, the peculiar technicalities of navigation, the clewing, handling, or reefing of sails, and the various phenomena which belong exclusively to the avocation of those who "go down to the sea in ships and do business on the great waters," will be studiously avoided. The seaman's vocabulary constitutes an unintelligible jargon to all landsmen; and as this Journal is designed for the benefit of such as are not accustomed to the seas, this vocabulary will not be resorted to, except where it may be thought necessary to express the subject in a clearer light, or to render a description more full and explicit. Waiving all such explanations hereafter, and continuing directly on our voyage, in the regular course of events, I come now to give a description of our first Sabbath at sea.

Though a storm had been raging for days, yet the Sabbath brought with it almost a perfect calm. In consequence of the sickness of the passengers no arrangements had been made with regard to the services of the day; but the weather being so fine, it was thought practicable, notwithstanding all had not recovered from their sickness, to have public worship. The Rev. Mr. Dibble having performed a number of voyages, was sufficiently inured to the motion of the vessel, to be able to preach; and being requested to officiate, the passengers and some of the crew collected on the quarter deck, and listened to a most interesting, appropriate, and profitable discourse, from the words of the Apostle Paul: "For scarcely for a righteous man, will one die, yet peradventure for a good man, some would even dare to die."

To many, it was a season "of refreshing from the presence of the Lord;" and we found our vessel to be none other than the "house of God, and the gate of Heaven." In the evening, all that were able, came together on deck, for the purpose of holding a prayer meeting, and while the meeting was in progress, a fine breeze sprung up, and as the wind whistled through our rigging, the voice of prayer was ascending to the throne of God. The meeting closed, and all quietly retired to their berths, committing themselves to the care of Him who rides upon the wings of the wind, and who holds the mighty ocean in the hollow of his hand. Thus closed our first Sabbath at sea, leaving the delightful impression that we were not to be deprived of the privileges of the sanctuary, though far away amidst the solitude of the ocean.

For the purpose of promoting harmony on board, in the evening of the 16th, rules were adopted, by a vote of the passengers, to regulate the police of the cabin during the voyage. These rules fixed the time of rising, the time for morning and evening prayers, the order to be observed at the table, and the course of conduct to be pursued with reference to the children. We found it to be as necessary to have law in our little floating world, as it is on land; and the laws thus voluntarily adopted, proved salutary in their influence, throughout the whole voyage.

This arrangement was carried out, during the seven months of our confinement on the Lausanne, without deviation, except when the motion of the vessel was so violent as to render it altogether impracticable. Persons were also appointed to make arrangements for holding a centenary meeting, on board the vessel, and for preparing a journal of our voyage, to be sent back to New York, for publication in the C. A. Journal.

On the 18th, it was determined that our meeting preparatory to the centenary, should be held on Monday, the 21st instant, at 10 o'clock, A. M., at which addresses should be delivered, and subscriptions solicited. It was also resolved, that, in connection with our brethren throughout the world, we would meet together on the 25th inst., and celebrate the day in the following manner:

Prayer meeting in the morning, preaching at 2 o'clock, and love-feast in the evening.

On Monday, the 21st, a strong head wind prevailed, and the violence of the motion of the ship was so great, that the preparatory meeting was deferred until the 23d. Two addresses were delivered on the occasion, after which a subscription was taken, which, by a previous resolution, was to be appropriated for the moral elevation of the Indians, west of the Rocky mountains. And, although we were floating upon the bosom of the deep, nearly a thousand miles from land, being in latitude 35 degrees, 44 minutes, north, and longitude 55 degrees, 15 minutes, west, yet it was a season of peculiar interest; and the sense of obligation which all felt, in view of the benefits conferred upon them and the world, through the influence of Wesleyan Methodism, was exhibited by placing on the altar, by the missionaries, a thank offering, amounting to six hundred and fifty dollars, twenty of which were contributed by the Presbyterian missionary, the Rev. S. Dibble.

On the 25th, the centenary of Methodism was celebrated on the Lausanne, according to previous arrangement; and, having been selected for the purpose, the writer endeavored to improve the occasion by a discourse, from Zachariah, xiv. 6, 7, 8.

While the interesting services of this day and evening were in progress, our gallant ship, by a strong breeze, was wafted over the rolling deep at the rate of nine knots an hour.

Thursday, 31st. All the passengers begin to prefer the deck to the cabin or state-rooms, and whether sick or well, storm or calm, they will make their appearance on deck several times a day, if they can possibly get out themselves, or get any one to assist them out. This preference arises first, from the heat of the cabin, which as we proceed south, is getting quite unendurable; second, from the nauseous scent, which, at any time, would be disagreeable to the olfactories, and, to sea-sick stomachs, is truly repulsive; third, from the crowded condition of the cabin, there being a large number of chests, trunks, boxes, baskets and other things, scattered along the gangway and under the tables, so that it is almost impossible to find a place to set one's foot. This day an incident transpired, as disagreeable to some as it was a fruitful source of laughter to others. The wind had been blowing with increasing violence for a number of hours, and the sea had become unusually rough. By the mismanagement of the man at the wheel, the vessel shipped a tremendous sea, which came rushing over on the deck, and extended from the bow to the stern, and rose so high as to wet the lower part of the top sails. Mrs. Lee, Mrs. Hines and Mrs. Frost were on deck at the time, the two former too sick to hold up their heads, and the latter waiting upon them to some gruel. They were bolstered up in their chairs, which leaned back against the scuttle, with their faces to the windward, and received the whole weight of the huge sea, as it poured its overwhelming flood on the ship's deck. For a moment they scarcely knew whether they were in the ocean, or on the vessel, but when the flood passed over, they found cause for thankfulness in the fact, that, with their thorough drenching, they had received no serious injury.

November 1st. The wind has gradually increased in strength since yesterday, and consequently the sea runs very high. Though I find myself so sick, in consequence of the violent motion of the vessel, that I loathe almost every thing my eyes behold, yet occasionally I draw myself up to the windward by ropes, and, looking over the bulwarks, contemplate the grandeur and sublimity of the mighty ocean, as she proudly and majestically rolls onward her mountain waves. During the night, we were called to encounter a severe gale. For forty-eight hours the wind had been blowing with increasing strength, attended occasionally with rain. But early in the evening the sky became perfectly clear, and the stars glistened with unusual brightness, which gave indication that a still more violent blast awaited us. About midnight, at the loud and well understood call of the second officer, all hands were immediately on deck; for in the midst of a storm, every sailor is converted into a fearless hero. The listening sailors waited for a moment the word of command, when "Clew your main sheet; clew up your main top sail; handle your main top gallant sail; clew your fore tack; close reef your fore top sail;" were heard above the roar of the winds and waves, and met with a prompt obedience. This being done, the captain was called, for the time was considered somewhat perilous. When the captain appeared on deck, the officer said to him, "There is a gale coming, sir, still more heavy than any thing we have had. Shall I not handle the foretop gallant sail, and lay to the gale?" The captain hesitated a moment, when the mate cried out, "The fore top gallant sail must be taken in, sir, or lost in a minute." "Close reef your fore top gallant sail," was heard above the roar of the angry elements, and was obeyed with amazing promptness by the faithful sailors, who had been as quick as thought to every word of command. After the sails had all been taken in, except enough to keep the vessel steady, the man at the wheel was charged to "mind his weather helm." At this moment the whole fury of the blast was upon us. The sea was lashed to foam, and the wind, with fitful gusts, swept angrily across our deck, and howled dismally through our rigging. At every blast of the tempest, the ship creaked in every joint, and, careening to the water's edge, swung her towering masts majestically in the heavens. The huge waves came rolling over our weather bow, and occasionally washed the entire length of our vessel. But the time had now arrived to lay to the wind. "Hard up!" thundered the watchful captain; "Hard up, sir!" replied the faithful helmsman. The gallant ship turned her face to the wind, and defied the fury of the storm. She lay upon the waves, apparently as light as a feather, and increased the confidence of all in her capacity, by the triumphant manner in which she rode out the gale. At 3 o'clock in the morning the wind slackened, and changing suddenly into the west, brought us again on our course, and at four we were gliding over the billows, at the rate of nine knots an hour.

On the morning of the 8th, we began to be affected by the north-east trade wind. There are two of these winds, one north and the other south of the equator, extending quite around the globe, with the exception of those intermediate spaces where they are broken off by land breezes. The trade north of the equator, called the north-east trade, commences between the 28th and 30th degrees of north latitude, and continues to the 8th, the distance of twenty degrees. In sailing to the south, you begin to feel the south-east trade between the 3d and 4th degrees of north latitude. The intermediate space, consisting of a strip about five degrees, or three hundred miles wide, is the region celebrated on account of its variable winds, sudden squalls, and extended calms. Here vessels are sometimes detained, by dead calms, beneath the vertical rays of a burning sun, for forty or fifty days; and captains consider that a voyage across this region is unusually prosperous, if it is performed in one week.

The south-east trade continues from the 3d degree north, to the 30th degree south of the equator; its current varying from the east to south by east.

These winds are probably produced by two causes in connection. First, the constant tendency of the air to restore its equilibrium. The cold air of the poles rushes in towards the equator, and sets the heated and rarified air around the equator in motion, and the heat of the sun, upon the elastic air, has a tendency to increase the motion, by expanding the air; and thus a contention is produced betwixt the cold and heated air, the former exerting itself to supplant the latter, and *vice versa*. Second, the diurnal revolution of the earth on its axis. If it were not for these daily revolutions, these winds would blow direct from the poles to the equator, whereas their current now runs diagonally with that line. There is also a current in the ocean, which runs with the trade winds, and is evidently produced by the revolutions of the earth. These two causes combine to produce that regularity in these winds, without which it would be difficult, if not impossible, to navigate the Atlantic and Pacific oceans. These important currents are called trade winds, because they are more favorable to commerce, or trade, than all other winds that blow.

In the afternoon of this day, the passengers were thrown into an excitement by the announcement, by the captain, of "a whale along side." No one had ever seen one of these monsters of the deep, and of course there was a general rush to the bulwarks, to get a glimpse of him before he should disappear.

Even those who were still confined to their berths, by sea sickness, must be assisted on deck, to have a view of the whale. There were two of them, and they played around the vessel for an hour, and occasionally showed the entire length of their huge forms, above the surface of the water, thus giving all an opportunity to satisfy their curiosity concerning the largest of the inhabitants of the ocean. On the firing of a gun, they instantly disappeared.

On the 19th, we were in the latitude of Monrovia, on the western coast of Africa, and within three hundred and fifty miles of that place. This is our nearest approach to the continent of Africa. In these latitudes vessels usually experience heavy falls of rain, so as to be able to replenish all their empty water casks; however, we realized but little, and most of our exhausted casks remained dry. This subjected us to the inconvenience of being thrown upon an allowance of water, which was a precaution the captain said was necessary to enter into, in order to make our water hold out, till we should reach the port of Rio de Janeiro. We were here relieved from the monotony of our voyage, which began to be quite disagreeable, by a number of incidents always interesting at sea, and always described in the journals of voyagers. The first was the appearance of an immense school of porpoises. There must have been tens of thousands of them, as they appeared to cover hundreds of acres. They continued around the vessel for some time, leaping and bounding high out of the water in every direction. They are a warm blooded fish, and leap out of the water for the purpose of breathing. They are from three to five feet long, and weigh from one hundred and fifty to three hundred pounds. The second was, the being spoken by two French sloops of war. We had seen several vessels since leaving port, but none had approached near us, until the 21st of November, when, early in the morning, a French sloop of war, of twenty-four guns, came dashing on our stern, as if she intended to run us down. The stars and stripes were immediately flying from our spanker yard, to show Monsieur who we were. In response, the French colors were soon seen, streaming in the wind. After manœuvering a little on our stern, she finally passed us to the windward within a few rods, presenting a remarkably fine appearance. The other vessel referred to was a sloop of eighteen guns, and spoke us on the 23d. She first appeared far to the windward, but bore down towards us, and fell on our stern about three miles off. After chasing us for several hours she finally succeeded in coming along side to the leeward, and, after we examined each other for a half hour or more, and passed through with the usual salutations of showing the colors of our respective nations, she bade us good bye, but allowed us to keep in sight of her during the day.

On the morning of the 25th, before a strong south east trade, at the rate of seven knots, we passed from the northern to the southern hemisphere. The following evening was remarkably dark, though calm and serene, and we were gliding almost imperceptibly along at the rate of three knots, before a gentle breeze, when, all at once, there appeared within ten feet of the vessel, floating on the water, a large fire, which flamed up several feet high, and appeared about three feet in diameter. The Rev. W. W. Kone first discovered this remarkable phenomenon, and with his exclamations of wonder at what it might be, a great excitement was produced among the passengers, while the captain *appeared* to be more at a loss to know what this strange fire could mean, than any other. All were gazing at it with intense interest, and many began to philosophize concerning it. Some said it was a remarkable collection of phosphorus; some called it electricity, and some one thing and some another. At length it began to be whispered that there was some trick about it, and finally, all the theories that had been advanced concerning it, laughable from their absurdities, fell to the ground, on the discovery of the fact that it was nothing but a burning tar barrel, which the sailors had got permission from the captain to lower from the bow of the vessel, for the purpose of exciting the inquisitive curiosity of the passengers. The incident, though trifling in its nature, for the time being was a source of considerable merriment.

It was not a little interesting to us, as we proceeded southward, to witness new and magnificent constellations of stars rising to our view, and those near the north pole, with which we had been familiar from our childhood, sinking from our sight, below the northern horizon.

The north polar star, which to us had ever been elevated more than forty degrees in the heavens, was lost behind the mountains of ice which rise in majestic grandeur amid the Arctic ocean; while the Great and Little

Bear, the Great and Little Dog, Andromeda, Cassiopea, Taurus and Orion, were fast receding northward, to rise again to our view when we should approximate the latitudes over which we had sailed. But while we were leaving these old acquaintances of the hypoborean regions, new and no less interesting ones presented themselves in the southern sky, to cheer us on our lonely voyage around the stormy cape.

Among the celestial scenery of the south, there is nothing more interesting than those two remarkable spots in the heavens, which are known by the name of the Magellan clouds. These phenomena do not present the appearance of clouds, as their name would indicate, but they are quite luminous, resembling in their aspect the brightest spots in the Milky Way, and supposed, like the latter, to consist of innumerable stars, not discernible to the naked eye. They are situated near the south pole of the heavens, and are about fifteen degrees apart, the smaller being nearest the pole. In the diurnal revolutions of the earth, they each describe a circle round the pole, the diameter of the smaller circle being about fifteen, and that of the latter about twenty-five degrees. As there is no star at the south pole answering, to the southern hemisphere, the purpose that the north star serves to the northern, these clouds serve in navigating the South Pacific ocean. It is said by some that there is another cloud of a dark appearance not far distant from these, but of this we could see nothing. It is quite certain that no such dark cloud exists. These clouds derived their name from the distinguished navigator, who also gave his name to the straits leading from the Atlantic to the Pacific ocean, and separating Terra del Fuego from Patigonia.

December 1st was the last Sabbath we spent before making the coast of Brazil, and as it was a fair sample of the manner in which all our pleasant Sabbaths were employed, the reader will perhaps be gratified with a short description of it. The day was inexpressibly fine; a bland and reviving breeze tempered the rays of the vertical sun, and bore us almost imperceptibly over the gentle undulation of the deep. At the usual hour of worship in the temple of Jehovah on land, a bell was rung so as to be heard from the after cabin to the forecastle, to call the people together; and immediately sixty-five persons were comfortably seated on the quarter deck, beneath an awning, spread to intercept the too intense rays of the tropical sun. The minister for the occasion gave out the sublime hymn commencing

"Before Jehovah's awful throne,"

which was sung "with the spirit and with the understanding also," to the immortal tune of "Old Hundred." The voice of solemn prayer succeeded, and was followed by an appropriate sermon from the words, "They all with one consent began to make excuse." At the close of the exercises all appeared to feel that, from whatever else they would be excused, they would not be excused from receiving the forgiveness of sins, the consolations of religion, hope in death, and everlasting life. In the afternoon all assembled again, and listened to an interesting discourse from the text, "And they remembered his words." The excellency and wisdom of the words of Christ, were dilated upon in such a manner as to impress all with the truth of the remark, that "He spake as never man spake." The closing scene of this day's exercise was one of true sublimity. Surrounded with the darkness and stillness of evening, all again bowed down on the deck of the Lausanne, and offered up their fervent aspirations to the throne of God. The wind began to whistle through our canvass as we retired to our berths, feeling truly grateful for the privileges of the holy Sabbath, though enjoyed amidst the boundless wastes of the Atlantic.

On leaving New York our course was nearly southeast until we approached the continent of Africa; then making an angle, we sailed nearly south-west until we approached the coast of Brazil; and it may be a matter of surprise to many, that we should sail so much out of our way, to get to the city of Rio Janeiro. The object of making so much easting was, first, to secure the benefits of the north-east and south-east trade winds, and second, to avoid being driven by these winds and the currents of the ocean, to the northward of Cape St Rogue, the easternmost point of land on the coast of Brazil. All vessels bound to the south of Cape St. Roque pursue nearly the same track, and cross the equator between the twentieth and twenty-third degrees of west longitude.

Early in the morning of the 8th of December, the cry of "Land, ho!" brought most of the passengers immediately to the deck. The captain had remarked the evening previous, that we should see land in the morning to the north-east of us, if the wind continued in the same direction, which proved to be the case ; and the high bluffs of Cape Frio (cold cape) appeared in full view about twenty-five miles off. The sight of land was hailed with the utmost joy, it having been fifty-nine days since the high lands of Never Sink, the last land we saw, were hidden in the dim distance. As we proceeded down towards Rio, the coast presented a grand and picturesque appearance, not vastly dissimilar to that of the mountains, as seen from the deck of a steamboat on the Hudson river. The day was calm, and the sky overcast with clouds, and many of the mountains reared their lofty heads above the strata of the lower clouds, so that these were seen lowering around the mountains, and presenting the appearance of vast quantities of smoke, rolling down their apparently smooth and conical sides. Our eyes being once more privileged with beholding land, though at a distance, our attention was again called to the solemnities of the holy Sabbath.

Monday, the 9th, we were hovering around the entrance of the harbor of Rio de Janeiro. A slight breeze from land prevented us from proceeding directly into the harbor, and this gave us an opportunity to contemplate the scenery of the shore. The preceding night had been one of unusual darkness, occasioned by the dense fog by which we were enveloped; but this rendered the appearance of the revolving light, which came peering through the midnight gloom from the distant isle, still more delightful.

As the sun approached the meridian, and dissipated the mists of the morning, the land zephyr died away, and a gentle breeze from the ocean filled our already expanded sails, wafting us directly towards the harbor. As we approached the shore, the scenery presented to our view was beautifully grand, beyond description. On our left, the "Sugar Loaf" mountain reared its lofty summit, to the height of eight hundred feet, sloping on the side towards the water, but perpendicular on the opposite; also, the island of serpentine rock, elevated several hundred feet, with the light-house resting on its top, and "Redonda," perfectly conical in its formation, being about fifty rods in diameter at its base, and rising more than five hundred feet; while, about ten miles in the distance, appeared a majestic mountain, whose cloud-capped summit towered to the height of three thousand feet above the ocean, and seeming to look down contemptuously on every thing beneath. It is called the "Parrot's Beak." The main shore is very broken, some parts of it being elevated far above the rest, while the huge "crags" on their rugged summits, appear to frown down upon the agitated waters, which dash harmlessly against their base. On our right, the mountainous coast could be distinctly seen the distance of sixty miles, to Cape Frio; while on our left, to a distance, if possible, still greater, pile after pile of huge, massy rocks were thrown together in the wildest confusion, rising thousands of feet above the level of the ocean, and, as they receded from us, appearing less and less, until, in the dim distance, they were lost from our sight. These, together with a view of the imperial city of Rio de Janeiro, lying quietly in the bosom of the bay of St. Janarius, conspired to give variety to the splendid panorama, by which, on entering the harbor, we found ourselves encircled. The grandeur and sublimity of the scene were worthy of the pencil of the most skillful artist, and truly enchanting to the lover of nature; and it was with the most thrilling emotions of delight, that we gazed upon the romantic and picturesque scenery before us. As we drew near the shore, the mountains lining the entrance of the harbor, lost the sterile appearance which they had presented from a distance, being changed, by the beautiful verdure which covered their summits, into a delightful green. The valleys between the mountains were clothed with luxuriant evergreens, and here and there a round elevation presented, in beautiful variety, a few cocoa-nut trees, which were scattered sparsely over them. Soon our attention was invited to animate nature. At the mouth of the channel, leading into the bay and harbor of Rio, is a very strong fortification, and the heads of armed men could be seen above the ramparts as we passed. We were hailed from this fort, as also from an armed vessel lying at a distance. From another fort, still nearer the city, a man bawled out, through a speaking-trumpet, requiring us to proceed no farther, but to bear off to the right and come to anchor, which we immediately obeyed, although it subjected us to the inconvenience of rowing one mile and a half, to gain the shore.

It was two o'clock, P. M., of the 9th, when we came to anchor, and the rest of the day was spent in receiving those visits from government officers, which are required previous to their admitting any on shore. The gentlemen who visited us were intelligent and affable, and, coming from a Roman Catholic government, were quite astonished to see so many priests on board, especially when they were informed that they all had wives.

On the morning of the 10th, the captain, with six of the passengers, went ashore. We were, however, required by the government, to pass along side an armed schooner, which was stationed in the harbor, for the purpose of giving them an opportunity to examine our baggage, to see that we had no contraband goods in our possession, which very unceremonious process, we were informed, we must submit to, as well when we returned from the shore to the vessel, as in passing from the vessel to the shore. As we were to lie here a number of days, we looked upon this custom-house arrangement as imposing upon us a useless and disagreeable task. Immediately on landing, we proceeded to the mercantile establishment of Gardiner & Campbell, who are English residents. Gardiner had formerly resided some time in the city of New York. Here we were soon met by the Rev. Justin Spaulding, who had resided in the place for three years, as a missionary of the Methodist E. Church, and from whom, in connection with his family, and the family of his colleague, the Rev. D. P. Kidder, (who himself was absent on an exploring tour to the north,) we met with a most cordial reception. We found them commodiously situated, in a large building, well furnished for their accommodation, and located in a retired part of the city of Rio de Janeiro, about one mile from the place of landing. Mr. Spaulding assured us that, though he could not furnish the whole company with beds, yet his rooms were open, and he should expect us to occupy them freely, by night and by day, while we remained in the place. And, indeed, all that christian love and kindness could do, these missionaries cheerfully performed, to render our stay with them happy and interesting.

The splendid city of Rio de Janeiro, which is the capital of the Empire of Brazil, presents to voyagers to this portion of the world, an object of considerable interest. A better location for a commercial city can scarcely be imagined. It is surrounded by a country of vast extent, of inexhaustible fertility, and equal in resources to the most enlarged expectations. Its harbor is one of the best in the world. The entrance to it is narrow, though sufficiently deep to admit vessels of the largest size to pass with perfect safety, and then extending out into a bay thirty miles long, and fifteen broad, and being favored almost every day with both land and sea breezes, which enable vessels readily to pass in and out, being of suitable depth for all sizes of vessels, and surrounded by mighty mountain barriers, which break off the winds on every side. It is unquestionably one of the safest and most commodious anchorages on the whole face of the globe. With these natural advantages to favor her, we might expect that Rio would have experienced a rapid growth from the time when

3

Portugal planted her first colony on the borders of that lovely bay; but a mistaken policy, developed in many periods of her history, has tended greatly to retard her progress; and, consequently, she continued comparatively small until Don John, the Portuguese king, left the mother country, and removed to his Brazilian territories, and built his palace within the precincts of this city. This circumstance transpired in 1803.

At the present time the city is one of considerable extent. It contains one hundred and fifty thousand inhabitants, of various nations, and of every shade of complexion. Here are some native Portuguese, more native Brazilians, a few French, Africans, Jews, Americans, and about one thousand English.

The city lies in the form of a parallelogram, and some of the streets present a splendid appearance. The houses are principally built with stone, and are covered with tiles. Some of the buildings, and especially the royal palace, and some of the churches and convents, are splendid specimens of architecture; but a great share of the city, however, appears like a vast assemblage of state prisons. Rio de Janeiro suffers much in point of beauty and cleanliness, when compared with the cities of many of our Eastern and Middle States. It presents an antiquated and sombre aspect, without that appearance of life and animation, which characterize the cities of the Anglo-Americans.

The religious state of the city is truly deplorable. The Roman Catholic religion here exists in all its nameless mummeries and superstitions. "Strictly speaking," said a Protestant missionary who has resided three years in the city, "there is no religion here." This same missionary informed me that of all the people with whom he had become acquainted by three year's residence among them, there were but two that he had the least reason to suppose were christians, in the proper sense of the word.

But, if true religion consists in the erection of splendid cathedrals, and in decorating them with golden images, and the lambent flame of huge wax candles constantly burning, and with hangings of the finest embroidery; or, if it consists in convents, filled with priests and nuns, with all their attendant ceremonies and image worship, then Rio de Janeiro contains more than any other city I have ever visited. But, if it consists in a consecration of soul and body to God, and a life corresponding with the gospel of Christ, then, of the tens of thousands of Rio, who bear the christian name, how few are pious! how few will be saved!! But signs of a better state of things begin to show themselves in this bigoted city. The English residents have a minister among them, and have recently built a church, in which they statedly worship after the Protestant form. The Rev. J. Spaulding and the Rev. D. P. Kidder, of whom mention has been made, were laboring with energy and zeal, in the cause of their Divine Master, both in preaching the gospel and in the circulation of bibles and tracts. These missionaries were frequently encouraged in their labors of love, by those evidences which appeared from time to time, that their efforts were not altogether in vain. An individual, through the influence of a tract, became dissatisfied with Popery, and came to Mr. Spaulding and earnestly enquired what he must do to be saved. Subsequently he partook of the sacrament of the Lord's supper with Protestants; but the Romish priests, having ascertained this, determined, at all hazards, to put a stop to his attending Protestant meetings. Accordingly, one morning, when this gentleman arose, he discovered a paper which had been pushed into his room under the door, during the night. He took up the paper and read in substance as follows: "Unless you desist from attending these Protestant associations, you may expect to find yourself stabbed." This circumstance drove him almost to despair, but subsequently he indulged a hope in Christ, and discarded the Church of Rome; but, from fear of falling a victim to the madness of bigoted and persecuting priests, his intercourse with the Protestants was carried on with the utmost secrecy. Thus the true leaven was working in spite of all the efforts made by the Papists to suppress it, and it was hoped that it would continue to work until the whole lump was leavened.

The slavery of Rio is one of the most prominent characteristics which present themselves to the traveler, on arriving at this place. And, to those of us who had never seen slavery in its practical effects, it was "enough to make one's heart bleed," to witness these ill-fated sons of Ham driven about by their cruel task-masters, and compelled to perform their tasks in a state of almost perfect nudity, exposed to the burning rays of a vertical sun. As cruel, however, as Brazilian slavery appears to be at first sight, there are some mitigating circumstances connected with it, when compared with the slavery of some other countries. Unlike the laws in the Southern States of our Republic, which give the master the same control over his slaves that he has over any kind of property, those of Brazil guarantee to the slave a number of important privileges. First, the slave is required to labor for his master from morning until two o'clock, which is the business portion of the day; and the remainder of the day he has to himself. Second, the slave is entitled, by law, to two days in each week to employ as he sees fit. These two provisions give the slave nearly one half of the time, and the property he accumulates, when thus at liberty, belongs to himself. He is compelled, however, to procure his own food, without expense to his master. If, by industry or good fortune, he succeeds in obtaining his freedom, which is not an unfrequent occurrence, he is immediately entitled to all the privileges of a freeman, and his offspring are not liable to be enslaved. But, notwithstanding these extenuating circumstances connected with Brazilian slavery, it is a system of cruelty and oppression. The naked appearance of the slaves, the ponderous burdens they are compelled to bear, their frequent flagellations, and when worn out with fatigue, their lying around the streets and under the walls of buildings like cattle, and at other times like horses dragging around their drays, unmercifully loaded, all had a tendency deeply to excite our sympathies for suffering humanity, and to increase our abhorrence for this system of cruelty and blood. It was cheering, while beholding some of the worst evils of the system, to indulge the reflection that the time will come when slavery must be abolished throughout the world. Incompatible with civil and religious liberty, and opposed to the doctrine of Christ, it must feel the paralyzing influence of those benevolent principles which are destined to destroy the pride and tyranny of the human heart, and to induce man to acknowledge in his fellow man, an equal and a brother. Thus it appears, that, while there are a few things in and about Rio which are calculated to excite our admiration, there are many which are truly deplorable. Enveloped in a midnight gloom, forgetful of her God, and bound with chains of bigotry and superstition, Rio de Janeiro is indeed a valley of the shadow of death. But the beauty and grandeur of the natural scenery by which she is environed, the salubrity of the climate, the spontaneous growth of the most delicious fruits, with all the natural advantages by which she is distinguished, in connexion with the pure religion of the meek and lowly Jesus, would constitute her an earthly paradise.

CHAPTER III.

Journal continued — Departure from Rio — Rev. Mr. Spaulding — French Fleet — Violent storm — Flying jib boom carried away — Dinner lost — Storm abates — Christmas — Heat — Doubling Cape Horn — Gale nineteen days — Under bare poles — Prosperity — Sight of land — Brig Andes — Arrival at Valparaiso — Small pox — Danger — Description of the city — Its civil and political condition — Religion — Superstition, illustrated by amusing incidents — Protestantism — Importance of Valparaiso — Adventures round about the city — Great discrepancy — Appropriate name.

THE time fixed upon for leaving Rio, to proceed on our voyage, was Saturday morning, the 14th of December. Accordingly, at that time, we were all prepared for weighing anchor; but a strong south wind commenced blowing directly into the harbor, and detained us during the whole day. In the morning, the Rev. Mr. Spaulding came on board, and continued with us for several hours, during which he gave us a very interesting address. He also gave a short account of the mission in Rio, in which he related some striking anecdotes, illustrative of the success with which his labors had been crowned. Before leaving, he commended us to God and to the word of His grace, in fervent prayer, and then, bidding us an affectionate farewell, lowered himself by a rope into a small skiff, which lay under the lee of the Lausanne, and was conveyed back to the shore. The season was one of deep interest, and kindred feelings palpitated every heart. And, as this fellow missionary left us to immure himself again in what is worse than heathenism itself, we could but invoke the God of battles to prepare his way, and sustain him with omnipotent grace, that he might witness more abundant success attending his labors, and finally see the man of sin fall to rise no more.

The south wind had abated the next morning, and a land breeze was favorable for our leaving the harbor.

Consequently, after the customary visits by government officers, we raised the anchor, and spreading our sails again to the wind, bid adieu to the dominions of Don Pedro the second, and were soon tossed upon old ocean's billows, with our vessel's prow directed towards the cape of storms.

The same morning, a French fleet of war of eight sail, weighed anchor, and passed majestically out of the harbor before us. This fleet was destined to join the blockading squadron before Buenos Ayres, and to bombard the city, provided the United Provinces did not comply with the imperious demands of the French.

The first day out we had a violent storm; the sea was very rough, and nearly every one of the passengers was called again to suffer with sea sickness. In the course of the storm the vessel encountered a number of mountain waves. At one time, through the carelessness of the helmsman, she plunged her bows so far into the water that her jib and flying jib went completely under, and when she rose, her flying jib boom was carried away, and the sails were both rent into shreds from top to bottom. A table was set for dinner in the captain's cabin, and all the dishes were thrown clear from the table into the steward's locker, and dashed to pieces. The shock given to the vessel was exceedingly violent, and caused it to tremble in every joint. This was on Sunday. The following day the wind abated, and, changing a few points, became more favorable. For a number of subsequent days, a fine breeze wafted us rapidly onwards, and on Christmas day, at 12 o'clock, M., we were in latitude thirty-nine degrees, thirty minutes, south.

This was the warmest Christmas we had ever seen, the thermometer ranging at eighty in the shade. Rev. Jason Lee delivered, on the occasion of Christmas, an appropriate discourse, on the subject of the advent of Christ.

Wednesday, January 8th, 1840. For a number of days past we have been favored with a prosperous wind, and are now within four degrees of Cape Horn. Thus far, our way has been remarkably prospered. The weather is now very calm, with a gentle breeze from the north-west; but we are approaching the region of storms, and can scarcely hope to double the Cape with the delightful weather we are now experiencing.

Friday, 10th. According to our expectations, the slumbering winds were aroused, and we began to experience the difficulties of doubling Cape Horn. About 9 o'clock, A. M., a severe gale came down upon us with the most threatening violence. Every stitch of canvass was immediately taken in, and for more than forty-eight hours we lay under the bare poles, the very sport of both wind and water. The gale was said by the captain to be one of the most violent he had ever experienced. On the 15th, the wind had so far abated that we were able again to carry sail, but found by an observation at noon, that we had been driven several degrees out of our course.

Monday, 27th. For many days past we have been baffled with contrary winds, and indeed this is the nineteenth day since we have had any thing like a fair breeze. Our course has been west, but we have been compelled to run almost every point of compass, and the most of the time to contend with violent gales. In consequence of head winds we were carried nearly to the sixty-first degree of south latitude; and Cape Horn being in the fifty-sixth, we were nearly three hundred miles south of the Cape. By an observation this day we found our longitude to be sixty-eight degrees, twelve minutes, which is a few miles west of the Diegoes. We have therefore left the Atlantic ocean, and are now on the waters of the Pacific. It is not common for vessels to be driven so far to the south in doubling the Cape. Perhaps the greater part pass round within sight of the Cape or the Diegoes; but the only land discernible from our vessel, in the vicinity of the Cape, was Staten Land, which presented its lofty summit to our view the day before we experienced the commencement of the Cape Horn gales. Though it was midsummer, in the southern hemisphere, while we were doubling the Cape, yet at sixty-one degrees we found it excessively cold. Hail frequently fell on deck, and though no icebergs appeared in sight, it was judged, from the coldness of the atmosphere, that they were at no great distance. At this season of the year, in this latitude, the sun rises a few minutes after three and sets a few minutes before nine, and daylight scarcely disappears during the whole night. We have to proceed but seven degrees farther south, and the day will be one month long, at the sun's farthest declination south.

During our long detention here, by successive storms, we were frequently entertained by the appearance of the huge monsters of the deep, and a vast variety of the feathered tribes of the ocean. Whales, lashing the briny element, and spouting the huge spray high into the air; porpoises, gamboling over the waves like flocks of antelopes over the western plains; the auk or penguin, which is a link connecting the feathered with the finny tribe, with the albatros, stormy petrel, cape pigeon and many others, appeared from time to time around us, in large numbers, contributing much to amuse us, and diverting our attention even from the successive tempests, that howled around us for nineteen days.

On the 28th, Providence again favored us with a fair wind, and enabled us to direct our course to the north, and for several days we were carried forward at the rate of seven and nine knots an hour.

On the 3d of February, we found ourselves off the western entrance of the Straits of Magellan.

Our passage round the Cape was a stormy one for the season of the year, but the winds and waves were under the control of the Almighty, who seemed to smile on our enterprise, and interpose in our behalf while navigating the tempestuous waters of the southern ocean.

We now steered our course for Valparaiso, on the coast of Chili, where we intended to take in water and other supplies. Our passage up the coast was barren of incident worthy of special notice, until the morning of the 18th, when our eyes were once more delighted with the sight of land, the coast of Chili, about forty miles

3*

south of Valparaiso Head, presenting its dark outlines thirty miles distant over our starboard bow.

The wind died away as we approached the shore, and we were consequently unable to proceed directly into port. A number of vessels appeared near us, bound to the same place, with one of which we had a friendly interview. She proved to be the brig Andes, of Liverpool, forty-eight days from Sydney, New South Wales. We had a shower of rain, with lightning, at ten o'clock, and the rest of the day were becalmed within ten miles of land. A dead swell bore us slowly towards the shore, and in the evening we could distinctly hear the surf of the ocean, breaking against the rocks. The captain manifested great anxiety, lest we might be dashed to pieces on the iron bound coast. At twelve o'clock at night a light breeze sprung up, and enabled us to remove to a safer distance from the shore. The following morning, after the rising sun had dissipated the fog that enveloped the shore, the high bluffs, called Valparaiso Head, appeared directly before us. A fresh ocean breeze sprang up, and bore us directly towards the harbor, and on our right appeared a beautiful bay, which washed a broad and delightful sandy beach. Variety was given to the prospect, by the appearance of strange looking birds on the wing, passing from one side of the bay to the other. At noon we rounded Valparaiso Head, and the city, harbor, and shipping were spread out in full view before us. We dropped our anchor half a mile distant from the landing, and were immediately boarded by government officers, who examined us before permitting us to go on shore. A number of American gentlemen also came on board, and showed themselves remarkably polite and friendly. They informed us that the small pox had made terrible havoc among the inhabitants of the place, especially the natives, but that it had, in a measure, subsided. They said that all the foreigners who had been vaccinated, had entirely escaped, and that they did not apprehend there would be any danger in our going ashore, and purchasing whatever necessaries we desired; that there would be as much danger in taking the disease from those who came on board from the shore, as from going on shore ourselves. Accordingly we came to the conclusion to act as though no fatal epidemic prevailed in Valparaiso, except that, on going ashore, we would avoid those places where the disease continued to rage most, especially the hospital, presuming that, in our case also, vaccination would prove a safeguard against contracting the disease. Having attended to the preliminaries, a number of the passengers accompanied the captain on shore, and, upon landing, found the city of Valparaiso much as it appears to be on entering the harbor, very forbidding in its aspects. The streets are generally narrow, and badly paved, and the houses are generally low, being but one story. This is designed to preserve them from the destructive effects of the frequent earthquakes, which take place along the Chilian coast.

The city lies around a beautiful bay which constitutes its harbor, and is about one mile and a half long, and varying much in breadth in consequence of the mountains behind the city, which, in some places, extend down nearly to the shore of the bay. These mountains have been dug away at their base, so as to afford room for two or three tiers of buildings back from the shore.

This space being filled, the inhabitants retired back on the sides of the mountains, where there are a number of contracted plains, which form eligible sites for building. Here a number of gentlemen, mostly foreigners, have erected their fine cottages, and live in princely style. But in the hill part of the city, as well as near the shore, there is but little regularity or beauty. The number of inhabitants is variously estimated from eight to twelve thousand, among which are fifty Americans, and some English, Germans and French. The foreigners are by far the most interesting part of the population, and do nearly all the heavy business of the place.

The civil and political condition of the country was any thing but prosperous. The people were frequently breaking out in rebellion · the city was under martial law, and the whole country seemed to be verging towards a state of anarchy. It was the time of their election, and such was the excitement that prevailed, particularly among the peasantry, that it was extremely dangerous for foreigners to go far back from the city, as they were generally taken to be the enemies of the Republic, and were looked upon, by the Chilians, as their lawful prey. Robberies and murders were frequent and from the weakness and inefficiency of the government, were committed with impunity. However, the Chilians are quite partial to Americans, because they are citizens of a sister Republic.

The religion of the country is Romanism, which here exhibits itself in all its principles of intolerance and persecution, as well as in its superstitions and bigotry. A circumstance or two, illustrative of the ignorance and superstition of the Chilian Papists, I will relate. At the time of the great earthquake, in 1822, which nearly destroyed the city of Conception, and greatly injured Valparaiso, when the shock was first felt in the latter, a large number of the inhabitants fled for safety to the Catholic cathedral, under the impression that Heaven would interpose in behalf of the sacred edifice, and prevent its destruction. To render themselves still more secure against the danger which threatened them, they took down the venerable images of St. Peter and St. Paul, from the places they had occupied from time immemorial, and placed them as a guard at the door of the cathedral. The principal seat of the earthquake being in the sea, the water rushed from its bed into the city; the foundations of the city trembled; the earth heaved with convulsions, and the cathedral, with one tremendous crash, tumbled into a heap of ruins, and five hundred persons were either killed by the falling walls and timbers of the building, or drowned by the flood of waters that deluged the place. The shock subsided; the waters returned to their place; and the next day the images of Peter and Paul were found floating in the harbor. The indignant survivors took the image of Peter, he being the more guilty of the two, and perforated a hole through his body, and pinned him upon the beach, at low water mark, as a punishment for his cowardice, and for deserting them in the hour of danger. As he abandoned them to so awful a calamity, they abandoned him to the fury of the waves.

Although the laws of Chili do not tolerate any religion but Romanism, yet there is a minister of the English church in the city, who is permitted to preach to the foreign residents without molestation. They will not permit a Protestant to preach in the language of the country; if one should attempt it, he would immediately be driven from their coast, or forfeit his life. As a matter of course, there is but little chance for missionary operations among the people, except so far as the English, American and German residents are concerned. Among these an intelligent, prudent, and devoted missionary, might render himself abundantly useful. But the time will come, notwithstanding the fierce opposition that now rages against Protestantism, when the vain mummeries of Popery must pass away, and the darkness that now shrouds the people with a midnight gloom, shall be succeeded by the light of the glorious Sun of righteousness, which shall rise upon this benighted country with healing in his wings.

The importance of Valparaiso lies in its eligible situation for commerce, it being the entrepot for a great portion of the Republic of Chili. The high hills or mountains, which surround the city on three sides, and extend many miles back, are actually as barren as their appearance from the ocean indicates, affording but a scanty allowance of vegetation for a few sheep, goats, and donkeys. All the supplies of fruit, meat, vegetables, &c., for the city and shipping, are brought on the backs of mules and asses, from valleys which lie from forty to a hundred miles distant; and even the wood for fire, brickbats, tiles, and other materials for building, are brought in the same manner.

With this description of the place, I now proceed to relate a few adventures. Immediately on landing, we proceeded up through the city; took a view of the custom house, which, by the way, is a fine building, went into a number of stores, and finally came round to the market, where we found an abundance of fruit, similar to that of New York. We regaled ourselves on peaches, pears, plums, grapes, &c., but soon discovered a boy lying near us on a couch, and partly covered with a rug. We enquired what the matter was with him, and were informed that he was just recovering from the small pox. Looking around us, we saw a number in a similar condition, and concluded that we should give the virtue of vaccination a faithful trial. Tying up some fruit in our handkerchiefs for our families on board, we returned to the vessel for the night.

Not being able to weigh anchor the next morning as we expected, we entertained ourselves with another excursion on shore. Purchasing a few articles to take back to the ship when we returned, we bent our course up the beach, south of the city, and taking a narrow footpath, which wound up a steep declivity, soon found ourselves on an artificial steppe of some thirty or forty feet square, and which commanded a beautiful view of the bay and harbor of Valparaiso. From this we ascended another declivity one hundred feet high, nearly perpendicular, and from its top enjoyed a lovely prospect of the city and surrounding country. Continuing our course, we passed a number of deep ravines, climbed a number of high bluffs, and came to the lighthouse, which stands on the summit of Valparaiso Head. From this place, we discovered, near the shore, a cross erected on a rock, and approaching it, found that it was the sign of a burying ground, or rather a depository for dead bodies. In the language of scripture it might be called "Golgotha, the place of a skull;" for the ground was literally covered with human bones. Here had been dug a deep hole about twelve feet square, into which those who had died with the small pox in the city, had been indiscriminately thrown. They were conveyed here from the hospital, and other places, in carts and wheelbarrows, so soon as they were dead, and perhaps sometimes before; and, uncoffined and unshrouded, were cast into one common reservoir, where their bones will mingle, undistinguished, till the resurrection morn. Turning from this sickening sight, we proceeded over a high point of land, and came down to the shore of a beautiful bay, which constituted a resort for a variety of sea fowl; and having refreshed ourselves with bread, and bathed in the ocean, we collected a few shells and other curiosities, and turned our course backward towards the landing. Rising over a high and barren hill, in the rear of the city, we entered a deep ravine, very narrow at the botton, and forming a channel for a small rill of water. Each bank was covered with a spontaneous growth of the sage plant and other shrubbery, while, by the side of the brook, groups of females from the city were seen, who had resorted thither for the purpose of washing their clothes. As we passed down the narrow path which had been cut into the almost perpendicular sides of the mountains, we met a large number of donkeys driven by natives, with two casks slung across each one of their backs for the purpose of conveying into the city. For some distance up this ravine, there are dwellings erected where there is sufficient room, and in many places small mud-walled cottages have been stuck into the side of the mountain, where places have been excavated for that purpose. This ravine led us directly into the back part of the city; and, after taking a view of the cathedral, which had been rebuilt on the same site since its destruction by the earthquake, and collecting a few necessaries for the comfort of our families on our continued voyage, we bid adieu to the Chilian coast, very unfavorably impressed as regards the condition of the country.

One thing which particularly struck us on examining the city of Valparaiso and the country in its immediate vicinity, was the wonderful discrepancy betwixt the name and the place. Valparaiso signifies Vale of Paradise; and certainly no word has ever been more abused than this, in its application to this place. Considering its irregularity; the narrowness and filthiness of the streets; the squalid appearance of many of its inhabitants; the obscenity which presents itself in almost every direction; the loathsome diseases which prevail; the gloomy character of its religion, and the barrenness of the surrounding country, Valparaiso is well entitled to a re-baptism, and might appropriately be called, the "Valley of the Shadow of Death."

CHAPTER IV.

Journal continued — Raising anchor — View of the Andes — Brig — Pacific ocean rightly named — Capture of a sea monster — Difficulty among the sailors — Spoken by a whaler — Captain Sawyer — Island of Mowi — Hawaii — Oahu — Honolulu — Remarks on the Island — Oahu and its city — Sabbath — Introduction to the royal family — Interview — Anniversary of the landing of missionaries — Visit to the Para — Battle ground — Kamehameha I. — Waiakiki — Valley of Manoah — Source of prosperity — Difficulty with the French — Arrogance of Captain La Place — Impression upon the Hawaiians.

On the morning of the 22d of February, we were all ready to proceed on our voyage, and commenced raising our anchor, but the anchor of a French barque getting foul of ours, we were obliged to raise both at the same time, and were consequently detained until four o'clock in the afternoon. At this time a land breeze favored our departure, and again unfurling our canvass to the wind, we directed our course for the Sandwich Islands. After we had proceeded a few miles from the shore, we enjoyed, from the deck of our vessel, a clear and distinct view of the towering Cordilleras. This astonishing range of mountains, which extends from the Isthmus of Darien to the Straits of Magellan, is situated here, sixty or seventy miles from the shore, and there is something peculiarly grand in their appearance at this vast distance; and surely a near view must be sublime beyond description. Some of them present a white appearance, as if covered with snow, and others assume a sombre hue, representing the moral darkness which surrounds the whole country. Some of them lift their towering summits far above the clouds, and seem to look down with contempt upon the storms which howl around their base. While contemplating this most stupendous range of mountains on the globe, a fine breeze from the south filled our already expanded sails, and in forty-eight hours we had run four hundred miles.

On Tuesday, the 25th, an American brig showed us the stars and stripes; we returned the compliment, and passed on. On the 28th, we passed into the torrid zone, but still found the weather comfortably cool, the mercury standing at sixty-seven degrees in the shade. The small pox not appearing among us the tenth day out, we concluded that all had escaped without catching the disease. For this indication of Providential care, we felt to offer unfeigned thanksgiving.

The ocean which washes the western shore of the continent of North America, is pacific, both in name and nature. Nothing could exceed the pleasantness of our sailing for twenty-five days after leaving Valparaiso. The wind was constant from the south-east, never strong, and consequently the ocean was smooth; and, with little perceptible motion, we were borne along from one to two hundred miles per day.

On the 19th of March we re-crossed the equinoctial line at west longitude one hundred and sixteen degrees. We found the weather, in the region of the equator, not so warm as we anticipated, yet, at night, the heat in the cabin was somewhat oppressive; but during the day we were constantly fanned by the gentle and cooling breeze which wafted us onward towards our destination.

On the 23d, the monotony of our voyage was broken in upon by the capture of one of the monsters of the deep. Two uncommonly large sharks appeared on our stern, attended by pilot fish, and a number albicores. The pilot fish is the jackall of the lion of the deep, and it is said that the albicore usually follows in the train, for the purpose of sharing in the prey taken by the shark. We fastened a rope to a large shark hook, which we baited with a piece of pork, and cast it into the sea. The sharks were soon attracted by it, and one of them seizing the bait, the sailors drew upon the rope, and the hook fastened to his upper jaw, but it required several men to draw him up along side the ship, and it was necessary to rig a pulley before he could be hoisted over the bulwarks on to the deck. As this was the first view we had had of a shark, no little curiosity was excited on board by his appearance among us. This curiosity was not satisfied until even the physiology of his sharkship was thoroughly investigated by dissection. One claimed his back bone, one his jaw bone, one his teeth, one his fins, and another his tail; the remainder was cast back into the ocean, and soon devoured. In addition to the shark, there appeared, about the same time, two large sword fish, bounding out of the water, and showing their silvery sides, but we were obliged to be satisfied to view them at a distance, as they manifested no inclination to be captured.

On the 24th, having passed through the region of variables, we were favored with a strong north-east trade, and, during one week, we sailed the distance of thirteen hundred miles; but, on the morning of the 31st, the weather became squally. This was supposed to be occasioned by our contiguity to a number of small islands, which lay to the windward of us.

It had been the practice of some of the ministers on board, to preach occasionally to the sailors in the forecastle, and, apparently, considerable good had been accomplished in this manner. Many of them had become very serious, and a few had professed to experience a change of heart; but a circumstance transpired on the 24th, which was as afflicting to all on board as it was injurious to the sailors. Charley, the sail maker, a Dane by birth, being a pestilent fellow, though a favorite among the seamen, refused to perform, immediately, the pleasure of the mate, Mr. Farrington. The latter required Charley to carry a musket from the bow of the ship back towards the stern, but not doing it so soon as it was supposed he ought, Farrington drew his fist, and smote Charley back of the ear, and knocked him on the windlass, so that he received a severe wound in the head. The blood ran freely; the sailors became much excited, and resolved that there should be no more preaching among them, but subsequently recalled this resolution, and allowed us to continue our instructions.

They were a heterogeneous class, being composed of Danes, Prussians, Germans, English, Irish and Yankees.

On the 3d of April, we discovered a sail on our larboard quarter, about six miles off. She appeared desirous of speaking with us, and soon there appeared a speck on the water between the two vessels, which after a while could be distinguished as a whale boat approaching us. We luffed up to the wind, and waited for her to come along side. Soon she was under the lee of the Lausanne. She contained six men, two Americans, one of whom was the captain, one African, and three Sandwich Islanders. The captain came on board, and reported his ship as the whaler Fama, of Boston, seventeen months from home, and himself as Captain Sawyer. He appeared highly gratified to receive "news from home," though what we brought was nearly six months old. The Kanakas, or Sandwich Islanders, were stout, noble-looking fellows, and Mr. Dibble, the Presbyterian missionary, understanding the Hawaiian language, entered into conversation with them. He learned from them that both the king and queen of the Islands were converted, and had become members of the Church. He also learned that the king had removed his residence from Honolulu, on the island of Oahu, to Lahina, on Maui, in consequence of the temptation to drunkeness which beset him in the former place, he having been intemperate previous to his conversion. This is a fine example for converted drunkards. Let them remove as far as possible from the cause of their ruin. Captain Sawyer, after having obtained a few potatoes and other vegetables, which are always a great rarity to whalemen a long time out, left us to pursue our course, and returned to his hazardous employment.

Tuesday, the 8th, at eleven o'clock, the island of Maui presented its high bluffs to our view about forty miles to the south-west of us, making it forty-five days since we lost sight of the Chilian coast. We could also indistinctly see the high mountains of Owyhee, or Hawaii, which, however, were about seventy miles off.

Between these two islands is a channel thirty miles

wide. On Hawaii is a burning mountain, which is considered a great curiosity. In consequence of a succession of calms and squalls, we were detained off the islands longer than we anticipated. For several days the weather was dark and gloomy, the sea ran high, the rain fell in torrents, and we thought of the fate of the Lark, which was lost on the coral reef, which surrounds the island of Hawaii. In the evening of the 10th, however, we came in sight of Morokai, another of the group; but not considering it safe to run down the channel in the night, we tacked ship and lay to the wind. The following morning the island of Oahu could be distinctly seen in the misty distance. This island presents an excellent waymark for navigators, and is known by one of its high mountains, which appears to rise out of the ocean in the form of a sugar loaf. At twelve o'clock of the 11th, we had Diamond Hill in full view before us, and there appeared something across a large bay which Mr. Dibble informed us was the city of Honolulu. Presently, we were abreast of the city, though at the distance of four miles. The channel into the harbor being pointed out by Mr. Dibble, our course was directed towards it, and we were soon boarded by an old gentleman who acts as pilot for the harbor. In a few moments our anchor was dropped in the roads outside the coral reef which encircles the island of Oahu. We immediately received a visit from the U. S. consul, Mr. Brinsmade, and Captain Stetson. The latter is the son-in-law of the Rev. John Lindsey, of New York, and resided on the island of Kauai. He had been waiting for our arrival for five weeks. These two gentlemen, after paying their respects, returned to the shore, and provided accommodations for about twelve of the passengers for the following night.

The next day, the vessel was brought into the inner harbor, and provision was made for a number of other families, but some were under the necessity of continuing on board over the Sabbath. On Monday, however, our indefatigable friends, the consul and Captain Stetson, succeeded in procuring comfortable lodgings for all the passengers during their stay on the island. The consul is a member of the Presbyterian church, and Captain Stetson is a member of the M. E. Church. Both, by their unremitting attention to our wants, secured our warmest affection. The members of the Presbyterian mission, and many of the foreign residents, extended to us that cordial hospitality which is seldom exhibited to a company of strangers. It fell to my lot, with my family, to be entertained by Mr. and Mrs. Johnstone, the teachers of Oahu Charity School, whose dwelling commands a fine view of the mountain scenery, the rolling surf, and the city and harbor of Honolulu.

The Sandwich Islands are ten in number, Hawaii being the principal in extent and the number of its inhabitants, but Oahu first in point of commercial importance. They once contained several hundred thousand inhabitants, but of late years, their population has greatly decreased. This, doubtless, has been the result of their connexion with foreigners; and strange as it may appear, christian nations have introduced those means into the Sandwich Islands, that are destined to prove the destruction of the Hawaiian nation. Intemperance, with its concomitant evils, threatens the ruin of these islands, but thanks to an overruling Providence, with the seeds of death, a conservative influence has been introduced. The cross of Christ has been erected on these shores, and thousands have rallied around it. There are forty families of missionaries scattered over these islands, who are supported by the American Board of Commissioners for Foreign Missions, whose labors have been crowned with wonderful success. Of the one hundred thousand inhabitants which the islands now contain, seventeen thousand are members of the church, and Paganism has no existence in the group.

The island of Oahu is about sixty miles long and forty broad, and contains a population of about twenty thousand souls. The city of Honolulu is by far the most noted place on the island, as it is the commercial emporium for the whole group. It is delightfully situated on a beautiful plain, and surrounded with the most enchanting scenery, variegated with ocean, hills, cloud-capped mountains, and rich and fertile vales.

The climate is delightful, the mercury seldom rising above eighty-five degrees in the shade, nor sinking below forty. The number of the inhabitants at present is about ten thousand, four hundred of whom are foreigners. Here are English, French, Americans, Chinese, Africans, &c.; the most of the foreigners, however, are Americans. Some of them have large mercantile establishments, and are extensively engaged in the sugar business. The private dwellings of some of the citizens, both native and foreign, are well built, and richly furnished. The coral rock, which here abounds, is becoming extensively used for building, and makes an excellent material for that purpose. The buildings of the missionaries are principally of coral, well made, commodiously situated, and suitably furnished.

The next Sabbath after landing, we attended the native church in which the Rev. H. Bingham officiates, and, to our astonishment, found collected about two thousand Hawaiians, to hear the word of the Lord. These were, nearly all of them, decently clad; a few, however, were almost entirely naked, but they all behaved with becoming propriety, and the most strict attention was paid to the word dispensed. The preacher addressed them in the native language. The meeting house was built after the native style, being thatched with grass from the bottom to the top. The house, however, is getting out of repair, and another is being erected of coral, near this, which will seat, on the ground floor, when completed, three thousand persons.

Besides this, there is another native church in the city, of which the Rev. Lowell Smith is pastor. This has been built but two years, and the congregation numbers from twenty to twenty-five hundred.

There is also a Bethel chapel, commodiously situated, which was erected by the Seaman's Friend Society, and is under the pastoral care of the Rev. Mr. Diell, who was absent from his charge on account of ill health.

This was occupied every Sabbath by the Methodist missionaries during their continuance on the island.

Through the influence of Mr. Brinsmade, we were all favored with an introduction to the royal family. One hour previous to the time appointed for our interview, we collected at the American Consulate, which is situated about one half mile from the king's house, and, at the time specified, marched down through the city towards the fort, where we were met by a soldier, who conducted us to the audience chamber. We were introduced into a room of some twenty feet square, spread with Chinese carpeting, and well furnished with tables, chairs, sofas, &c., for the accommodation of visitors. The king and his suite were not present when we entered, but being informed of our arrival, the former soon made his appearance, attended by the governor of Oahu, and a very large and dignified woman who had been the wife of two kings, and who then officiated as his majesty's prime minister, and her little son, of some eight years of age, who was heir apparent to the throne. They received us with much grace and dignity, and bidding us welcome to their shores, assured us of their friendship. The object of our expedition being explained by the consul, and interpreted to the king by the Rev. Mr. Richards, both the king and his premier expressed their astonishment and admiration, and said that they ardently desired that we might be prospered in our enterprise. They pronounced our cause "good," and proffered their hospitalities while we were with them, and their continued aid in the prosecution of our work.

Our superintendent, the Rev. Jason Lee, addressed his majesty through the interpreter, relative to our mission in Oregon, and proposed an exchange of the produce of that country, consisting of flour, fish, beef, &c., for the products of the Sandwich Islands, consisting of sugar, molasses, coffee, indigo, &c., to which the king seemed heartily to concur, and said that he was very much pleased with the idea. This conversation being closed, the consul gave signs that it was time to retire, and accordingly we all arose, and passing round the room, one after another, shook hands with the king, his minister and her son, and departed, highly gratified with our interview with the royal family of the Hawaiian nation. Here were displayed none of the pomp and trappings of royalty, none of the parade and ceremony usually exhibited in the courts of kings. But every thing, the apartments, furniture, and apparel of the royal family, partook of that neatness and simplicity worthy the supreme head of an infant and dependent nation. The king was dressed in blue broadcloth, made up in the English style, with epaulettes on his shoulders and a miniature crown on the lapel of his coat. He is distinguished by the title of Kamehameha the Third.

On Monday, the 19th, the twentieth anniversary of the landing of the first missionaries on the island of Oahu, was celebrated at the house of Rev. H. Bingham, who was one of the pioneers in the business of evangelizing these islands of the ocean. The season was rendered interesting by many hallowing associations. A short history of the Sandwich Island mission was given by Mr. Bingham, and, in view of the astonishing results of missionary labor, as seen in the elevation of the Hawaiian nation, from the deepest degradation of heathenism, to the enjoyment of the blessings of christianity and civilization, surely we had reason to exclaim, in the language of Moses, "What hath God wrought!"

On Thursday, the 22d, we visited what is called, in the language of the country, the Para, about eight miles east of Honolulu. We were accompanied by the consul, Captain Carter, Captain Grimes, Dr. Judd and lady, and Mrs. Hooper. At half past nine we had all mounted our horses, which had been provided for our use, and, led by the consul, proceeded out of the city, like a troop of cavalry, on the round gallop; and taking a winding path, we soon found ourselves on a contracted plain, with huge mountains on our right and left, rising some thousands of feet high, their lofty heads being ornamented with caps of fleecy clouds.

Presently we entered a dark thicket, and found the path so narrow and difficult, that it was impossible to

4

proceed but by single file, and at a very slow pace. After descending and ascending a number of almost perpendicular banks, where some of the ladies found it very difficult to keep to their saddles, and fording a small rivulet which dashed through the thicket, we came into a small opening, overgrown with grass, and within a few rods of the Para. Here we dismounted, and leaving our horses in the care of some Kanakas, who had placed themselves here for that purpose, proceeded on foot to view the object of our curiosity. Soon we found ourselves on the brink of a frightful precipice several hundred feet high, and almost perpendicular, down which there are steps cut in the rock to enable persons to ascend and descend in safety. This is the only place where it is possible for persons to pass from one side of the island to the other without making the circuit of the shore, and this pass has been always considered remarkably difficult and dangerous. But in 1837, Mr. Alanson Beers, a blacksmith, who accompanied one of the former expeditions to Oregon, made an important improvement in this pass, by fixing firm into the rock, a railing of iron for some distance down the steepest part of the descent. This Para is six hundred feet above the level of the ocean, descending to the north-east abruptly until you arrive at a plain, which extends about three miles to the shore, and which supports a population of more than five thousand people. The appearance of this plain from the top of the Para, dotted with the adobe-walled cottages of the islanders, and near the centre of which was pointed out the dwelling of the Rev. Mr. Parker, and the church where listening hundreds are taught the way to heaven, is truly delightful; and, with the grandeur of the mountain and ocean scenery, is a full compensation for the labor and difficulty of visiting the place.

This Para is noted, not only for the sublime natural scenery by which it is surrounded, but also for its interesting historical associations. Here terminated one of the bloodiest wars that ever desolated these islands.

Having satisfied our curiosity, we remounted, rode

over the battle ground, stopped to take a view of a beautiful cataract, and returned to a house owned by the consul, and situated about two miles out of the city, where we sat down to a sumptuous repast. Here we spent a social hour, until the heat of the day had passed, and then, taking to our horses, galloped back to the city, well pleased with our excursion.

On Saturday, the 25th, rode up to Waiakiki, about three miles, where there is a beautiful cocoanut grove; from thence to the valley of Manoah, by way of the Chinese tombs, passing the country residence of the Rev. H. Bingham. This valley is exceedingly fertile, and much frequented by visitors, on account of its delightful mountain scenery. In this valley is situated the old palace, the residence of some of the former kings. It is a small thatched cottage, surrounded by a dense grove of fruit trees, resembling in appearance the apple tree. The building is in a very dilapidated condition, and constitutes the habitation of bats, mice, and other vermin. On returning to the city, we were informed that the vessel would leave the harbor of Honolulu for her destination on the morning of the 28th. This gave us but little time to extend our observations; but from the few we were able to take, we were favorably impressed with regard to the importance of the Sandwich Islands. Doubtless the prosperity of these islands has depended, and still depends, mainly upon the whale ships that annually flock to their ports.

The people of the islands, both native and foreign, had not recovered from a feverish excitement, into which they had recently been thrown by the belligerent attitude in which a French man of war presented itself before Honolulu. The principal offences against France, of which the Frenchman complained, were, first, that the Hawaiians had refused to admit French Roman Catholic missionaries to land on the islands, when Protestant missionaries had always been allowed that privilege; and, second, that the Hawaiian government had passed a law prohibiting the introduction of French brandy. For these *crimes*, France resolved to call the *wicked*

Hawaiians to an account ; and, consequently, so soon as the frigate arrived, which had been sent to compel the Hawaiians to submission, the French commander, Captain La Place, in the most menacing form, sent the king word that he had a certain number of hours to select between two alternatives. First, Roman Catholic missionaries must be admitted without restraint; the landing of French brandy in any quantities must be allowed ; and the Hawaiian government must pay to the French an indemnity of twenty thousand dollars ; or, second, the favorite town of the islanders must suffer all the horrors of a bombardment, with the prospect of an entire subjugation to the French. For awhile the king hesitated whether to be buried amidst the ruins of his country, or submit to the unjust and arrogant claims of the French, but, through the influence of his counselors, finally preferred the latter alternative.

The name of the frigate was the Artimese, and she was commanded by Captain La Place. This unhappy interview betwixt the French and Hawaiians left the impression on the minds of the citizens of Honolulu, both native and foreign, that France will take the first reasonable opportunity, to reduce the islands to subjection.

CHAPTER V.

Journal continued — Departure from Honolulu — Slow progress — Fresh breeze — Coast of Oregon — Old pilot — Captain delivers up the vessel — Crossing the fearful bar — Deep anxiety — Cast anchor in Baker's Bay — Rev. Daniel Lee — Chenook Indians — Clatsops — Ascend the river — Fort George — Run aground — Difficulty of ascending — Arrival at Vancouver — Meeting called — Missionaries receive their appointments — Sent off to their stations — First encampment in Oregon — Ascending the Wallamette in canoes — Tum Water — Portage — Champoeg — Horseback ride — Arrival at the Mission Station.

According to arrangements, on Tuesday morning, the 28th of April, at nine o'clock, we were all assembled at the United States Consulate, with many of our newly made friends of Oahu, who had endeared themselves to us by their unwearied kindness and hospitality, awaiting the preparation of boats to convey us to the ship. Soon all was in readiness, and taking an affectionate leave of our attendants, we were quickly on board the Lausanne. The winds were favorable, the sails were unfurled to the breeze, and we moved slowly out of the harbor through a winding channel, which the God of nature has formed through the mighty reef of coral nearly encircling the island.

For several days after leaving Oahu, we were obliged to run close upon the wind, and, consequently, made but slow progress. Our course was north-east from the islands to the mouth of the Columbia river, and consequently the north-east trade was a head wind. So soon, however, as we reached the thirtieth degree of north latitude, a fresh breeze from the west wafted us on at the rate of one hundred and fifty to two hundred miles per day.

In addition to the usual subjects of interest at sea, consisting of whales, sharks, porpoises, dolphins, albatroses, &c., the company were entertained, for a succession of evenings, by a course of lectures, delivered by the Rev. Jason Lee, on the subject of the Oregon mission, embracing its first establishment, and the proper course to be pursued to advance its future prosperity. While thus employed, the winds of heaven were propitious, and we were rapidly approaching the coast of Oregon. At ten o'clock on the morning of the 21st of May, the western coast of North America, which is washed by the great Pacific ocean, that land towards which we had been directing our course for upwards of seven months, presented itself before us. Cape Disappointment appeared on our leeward quarter, and Point Adams on our bow. Considering the direction of the wind, the vessel could not have been placed more favorably for entering the mouth of the Columbia river.

Wind and tide both favoring us, preparations were immediately made for crossing the dreaded bar of the Columbia. Captain Spaulding found an old sailor at Oahu, who had spent some time at the mouth of the Columbia, a number of years before, and who said he was well acquainted with the channel across the bar. This man the captain had taken the precaution to bring with him, to act as pilot on entering the river; and, accordingly, on approaching land, the captain surrendered the vessel into the hands of the old pilot. The latter went aloft, and issued his orders from the fore top mast head. All was anxiety on ship board, as it was cried by the man with the sounding line, "five fathoms and a half," for we then knew that we were passing over the fearful bar, and that very soon we should experience the fate of a number of vessels, which, years before, had pursued the same track but to rush to inevitable destruction, or, be quietly moored in the placid waters of the bay, behind the projecting cape. Soon the water deepened to seven and nine fathoms, and the captain observed, "We have reason to congratulate ourselves on having crossed the bar of the Columbia in safety, and are now steering our course for Baker's Bay." And surely all felt heartily to acquiesce in the sentiment, as we slowly passed around the point of Cape Disappointment, and dropped our anchor on American ground.

The English barque Vancouver, lay at anchor in the bay, waiting for a fair wind to put out to sea. So soon as we anchored, Captain Duncan, from the barque, came on board, and informed us that we had made at least one "hair breadth escape," as we came within a cable's length of running on to a sand bank, where the William and Ann were wrecked a few years before. He also informed us that he had just come down the river from Fort Vancouver; that Rev. Daniel Lee, and Mr. W. H. Wilson, who were members of the Oregon mission, were at the fort when he left, and that the people generally were anxiously awaiting our arrival. A few hours after we came to anchor, an Indian canoe appeared, coming down the river, with a number of persons in it, and seemed to be directing its course towards us. While several miles off we could see, through the telescope, that there was one white man, with about a dozen Indians, in the canoe, and when they approached so near as to determine who we were, they set up a loud shout for joy at our arrival. Soon they came along side, and to our great satisfaction, we were saluted by the Rev. Daniel Lee, who had left his station at the Dalls, and come down the river to visit the Chenooks, and preach to them. Though thirty miles above the mouth of the river, yet he discovered our sail, as we passed over the bar, and, supposing us to be the reinforcement expected, he resolved to hasten down and ascertain the fact.

Rev. Daniel Lee is a nephew of the Rev. Jason Lee. They had performed a perilous journey together across the Rocky mountains; had endured together the trials of missionary life in Oregon; and as they had been separated for more than two years, one remaining in Oregon, and the other recrossing the Rocky mountains, and then doubling Cape Horn, the circumstances of their meeting were of no ordinary interest. The sensations realized cannot well be described. The uncle and nephew embraced each other, and wept. Their tears were tears of joy, mingled with grief—joy, that after so long a separation, and the endurance of so many hardships, they enjoyed the privilege of seeing each other's face—joy, that a kind and merciful Providence had preserved us during our long and tedious voyage, and had brought us in safety to this distant shore—joy, that the Lord had poured out His spirit in Oregon, and that many of the Indians had been converted : but grief, that since their separation in Oregon, some of the pioneers of the cross in this land of darkness, had been taken from the scene of their labors and usefulness; a grief mitigated by the consideration, that they died as the christian dies, happy and triumphant.

Towards evening a number of Indians of the Chenook tribe came on board, among whom were some of the *nobility*, one of the principal chiefs, whose name was Chenamus, and his wife, whom they called the queen, being of the number. Most of them were very small in size, and very poorly clad, some of them not having sufficient clothing to cover their nakedness. The chief had nothing on but a blanket, which he wrapped around him, but the queen had on a calico dress, a neckerchief, and a red woolen shawl. Soon they were reinforced by the arrival of a band of Indians from the south side of the river, called the Clatsops, who were very savage in their appearance, some of them being painted in the most hideous manner. They collected together on the fore part of the deck, and commenced singing and dancing in the most fantastic style. Four persons engaged in the dance, and as one got weary and retired, another would step in and carry it on. They appeared to enjoy it exceedingly, and doubtless supposed that they were affording us the highest gratification in celebrating our arrival among them. Many of them continued on board during the night, and though it was very cold, some slept in their open canoes which lay along side the vessel, with nothing around them. Their appearance, as they lay shivering in the cold, was truly deplorable. These, we learned, were slaves, and were not allowed by their masters to come on the deck. Surely, thought we, if any human beings in the world need the sympathies of their fellow men, we have found them on entering the territory of Oregon.

The day after we crossed the bar, we were obliged to continue at anchor in Baker's Bay, on account of a severe storm from the south-east, which prevented our sailing up the river; but on the morning of the 23d, the wind became fair, and we prepared to ascend the majestic Columbia. A gentleman by the name of Birney, residing at Fort George, and belonging to the Hudson's Bay Company, came on board, and volunteered his services as pilot from Baker's Bay, to the place of his residence, the distance of thirteen miles. Weighing anchor, we were conducted along a winding channel quite across the mouth of the river, and passed within a short distance of Point Adams, where the principal village of the Clatsops is situated. Crossing the mouth of a bay lying back of Point Adams, called Young's Bay, we came to anchor for the night, within a stone's cast of Fort George, otherwise known as the "far famed Astoria, the New York of the Pacific ocean."

Fort George consists of three small block-houses, one of which is occupied by Mr. Birney and family, and the others for purposes of trading. Here we went ashore, and after examining the site of old Astoria, built a fire by the side of a cold spring, and cooked and enjoyed our supper again on "*terra firma*," where our table would stand still. Weighed anchor on the morning of the 25th, and before a fine breeze, proceeded about one mile and a half, and run the ship aground. All hands spent most of the day in endeavoring to work off the vessel, but could not succeed. The next morning we were favored with a high tide, and succeeded in clearing the bar, but had not run but a short distance before we struck another bar with considerable violence, and, at first, feared that if we ever got clear of it, it would be with great difficulty; but the still swelling tide of the next morning, again floated us, and sailing a short distance, again we ran aground, and were detained another day. We concluded that, either the navigation of the Columbia for vessels as large as ours, was exceedingly

4*

difficult, or our pilot was ignorant of the channel. However, we succeeded, after running aground several more times, in reaching that point of land on which Fort Vancouver is situated, to which we had been looking forward as the termination of our voyage to Oregon, and where, by the good providence of God, we were permitted to cast anchor the first day of June, 1840.

Dr. John McLaughlin, the superintendent of the affairs of the Hudson's Bay Company, though a Catholic himself, received us with much cordiality, and extended to us the hospitalities of the place, so long as we should find it convenient to remain.

Vancouver is the emporium of the Hudson's Bay Company in Oregon. This is the general depot for all the goods brought to the country, and also for the furs collected, until they are shipped for England.

Here we remained a number of days, receiving and storing our goods; but on the 13th of June, a meeting of the members of the mission was called, by Rev. Jason Lee, to consult in relation to fixing the appointments of the newly arrived missionaries. These took place as follows: J. P. Richmond at Fort Nez Qualy, on Puget's Sound; J. H. Frost at Clatsop, on the mouth of the Columbia; W. W. Kone and G. Hines on the Umpqua river, and A. F. Waller was left without an appointment for the purpose of assisting in the erection of mills on the Wallamette river. The lay members of the reinforcement were principally located in the Wallamette settlement, that being the place where the main business operations were carried on. There being a physician in the Wallamette settlement, Dr. J. L. Babcock was appointed at the Dalls, also H. B. Brewer as a farmer.

All the missionaries were immediately initiated into the Oregon mode of traveling, in getting from Vancouver to their respective appointments. Canoes were provided for us, and we all scattered away; some up the Columbia, some down; some up the Cowilitz, and some up the Wallamette.

It was in the evening of the 14th day of June, that Rev. A. F. Waller, Rev. W. W. Kone, myself, and our families, found ourselves floating on the surface of the great Columbia, in two small canoes, on our way up to the mission station in the Wallamette settlement, having taken nothing with us but blankets, and provisions to make us comfortable on our journey. It was in the season of high water, and the bottom lands, along the river, were all overflown. Conducted by our pilots, we crossed the main channel of the Columbia to the south side; and running our canoes in among the cottonwood timber, we crossed a point of land which lies fifteen or twenty feet above low water mark, but which was then several feet under water, and coming to a kind of promontory covered with a dense forest of fir, we ran ashore and made our first encampment in Oregon. By the aid of flint, steel, and powder, we soon had the forest illuminated; then the women prepared supper of fried meat and boiled potatoes, bread, butter and tea, and spread it out upon the ground, where all partook of it with great relish. Next our bedding was prepared, and after recruiting our fire, we prepared to sleep. The roar of the wind through the thick branches of the fir trees, whose tall tops were waving gracefully over our heads, the hoot of the large owl, and the howling of the wolf, frequently broke in upon our slumbers, but the morning found us unharmed. In preparing to leave camp, the business of the morning afforded each of us considerable amusement by our awkwardness, arising from unacquaintance with this manner of living; but we concluded that we should soon become initiated, and make very good soldiers.

Taking to our canoes at six o'clock, on the 15th, we proceeded a mile, and found ourselves in the Wallamette river, having saved a few miles of rowing, by crossing the point. Found the scenery along the river exceedingly wild as we ascended, the shores rocky, and lined with dense forests of fir, and but little land adapted to cultivation. At one o'clock we arrived at the Wallamette Falls, called by the Indians Tum Water. Here we found about one hundred and fifty of the most filthy and degraded looking beings in human shape, that our eyes ever beheld. Surely, thought we, it will require the labor of many years to elevate these Indians from the depth of their pollution into a civilized and christian people. The falls are about thirty feet perpendicular, beautiful indeed, affording almost unlimited hydraulic privileges, yet the Indians held the place in unmolested control. The Hudson's Bay Company, however, had built a small block-house on the left bank, as we ascend the river, for their accommodation, in passing up and down. Here we were obliged to make a portage of half a mile, which occupied us till nearly night; and we found it exceedingly fatiguing to carry all our things over the rocks, for half a mile, on our backs. We had accomplished it, however, at five oclock, and proceeding up four miles farther, we made our second encampment on Rock Island, having traveled but twenty-five miles since morning. The weather being fine, we enjoyed another comfortable night, and the following day, at one o'clock, P. M., arrived at Champoeg, which is the lower part of the settlement on the Wallamette river. The mission station was sixteen miles above, and, according to arrangement, horses were sent down to meet us. They arrived at three o'clock, and at four all were mounted, several of us taking children on before us, and the cavalcade started off upon a gallop over the plains. As we were well mounted, Mrs. Hines and myself took the lead, and passing over the most delightful country that we ever beheld, two hours and a half brought us into the midst of three little log houses which stood on the banks of the river, and known as the principal station of the Oregon mission.

Here we arrived in safety on the 16th day of June, 1840, and were cordially welcomed by the missionaries on the ground, and made as comfortable as their circumstances would admit.

Remaining two days in the family of Rev. David Leslie, I then took possession of a small room in a house about one mile from the station, built for a mission hospital, where we again commenced keeping house, and where I designed my family to remain until I had performed an exploring tour through the country of the Umpquas.

CHAPTER VI.

Exploring tour to the Umpqua — Preliminaries — Departure — Delightful country — Encampment — Amusing incident — Fording river — Mountain La Beache — Elk river — Umpqua fort — Indian fight — Frenchman in charge — Meeting with the Indians — Old chief's confession — Hostile Indians — Danger of going among them — Resolved to go — Voyage to the coast — Indians accompany us — Interesting encampment — Indians on the coast — Meeting with them — Speeches of the chiefs — Results of the meeting — Talk to God — Solicitude of our Protectress — Watching — Presents — Departure — Description of the country — Return to the fort — Story of the Frenchman's wife — Dangers we had escaped — Perilous adventures of the mountaineers — Tour continued — Mountainous country — Fording Elk river — Giant tree — Aromatic tree — Umpqua Indians — Head chiefs — Shocking story — Burst of heathen passions — Difficulty with guide — Settled — Fear of treachery — Confirmed — Request of We-We — Refused — Warning — An Indian can be honest — Unhappy results of not trusting him — Night — Lost in a forest — Sabbath — Indians again — Homeward route — Fine country — Delightful scenery — Home.

SOME time in the winter of 1837, before Rev. Mr. Lee left Oregon to return to the United States after a reinforcement, he visited the Umpqua tribe of Indians for the purpose of ascertaining their number and situation; but it being in that season of the year when it is next to impossible to explore the country, in consequence of the abundance of water which every where presents itself in the way of the traveler, he could not extend his own personal observations far, but was under the necessity of depending for information concerning the objects of his visit, upon the few Indians with whom he came in contact on his route, and a Frenchman who had charge of a trading post belonging to the Hudson's Bay Company, and situated on the Umpqua river. Such was the information given and the confidence reposed therein, that Mr. Lee, before going to the States, had come to the determination that, if the mission was again reinforced, he would establish a station somewhere in the vicinity of Umpqua fort. Accordingly Mr. Kone and myself were appointed to labor as missionaries among the Umpqua Indians. As Mr. K. was a millwright by trade, it was intended by Mr. Lee to retain him for some months on the Wallamette, to assist in the erection of the mission mills; and that I should proceed and explore the country, select a location for the station, and prepare for the removal of our families.

Hearing reports from that country of a discouraging character, Mr. Lee resolved to accompany me on the tour, and satisfy himself with regard to the propriety of carrying out his original design.

It should be understood that the Umpqua country lies to the south of the Columbia river, about two hundred and twenty-five miles. The river which gives its name to the country, rises in that ridge of mountains which divides the lower from the upper country, and after running about two hundred miles, empties into the Pacific ocean near the forty-third parallel of north latitude. It waters quite an extensive country, as yet to white men but little known. Having made arrangements for the comfort and safety of our families in our absence, we found ourselves prepared to start on our tour on the 18th day of August, 1840. Our party consisted of Rev. Jason Lee, Dr. Elijah White, myself, and an Indian guide, whom we designated by the name of "Captain." Dr. White, however, designed to accompany us no farther than the Umpqua fort, and then return. Our mode of traveling, of course, was on horseback; and, in addition to our riding horses, we had three for carrying our baggage, and four spare ones, that in case of the loss or failure of any, we might not be left destitute. This is a precaution indispensably necessary to be taken by all who would secure their ultimate safety in traversing the extended plains of this wild country. As this was the first prairie expedition with which I had ever been connected, it was necessary for me, at the outset, to learn the peculiarities of the mode of traveling; and, as Mr. Lee had performed two journeys across the Rocky mountains he was well qualified to be my instructor.

Watching Mr. Lee closely while he was packing our bedding, provisions and cooking utensils, on the backs of the horses, I soon observed that it required considerable skill and practice to wind the lash rope around the pack and the body of the horse, so as to secure the burden to the back of the animal in case of fright, stumbling, or running against any obstruction, all of which, in the process of binding the packs, it is necessary to guard against with the utmost precaution. Mr. Lee having magnified his office as our instructor, by packing the three horses himself, we all mounted, and each man with his gun athwart of the pommel of his saddle, our little cavalcade put off, on a moderate gallop, across the beautiful and fertile plain, lying in the rear and south of the mission premises. At noon we arrived at a place called by the Indians, Chemekete, where the Oregon mission have commenced erecting mills, and where it is in contemplation to establish the Mission Manual Labor School. This place is ten miles up the Wallamette river from the old mission station, and is one of the most delightful locations in the whole valley. The fertile plains surrounding it, the enchanting nature of its scenery, and the fine water privilege afforded by the beautiful rivulet that meanders through it, render it a place of considerable future importance. Having dined with the family of W. W. Raymond, who is employed in forwarding the saw mill, we proceeded on our course, being south, through a country beautifully diversified with rising grounds, varying from the gentle undulation to the majestic hill, fertile valleys, variegated with here and there a grove of a species of red-oak, and now and then a stately fir which had braved the fury of a thousand storms. Occasionally could be seen the fallow deer and prairie wolves, scampering in almost every direction, as we passed along the narrow Indian trail, which, in its serpentine course, led us farther and farther from our habitation. At nightfall we encamped near one of the tributaries of the Wallamette river, called "Santa Am's Fork." This is a fine stream of water, being several rods wide, and coming down from the mountains of the east, it is said to form a number of beautiful cascades, while the fine timber adorning its banks, and the extended plains of arable land on each side, hold out strong inducements to the emigrant to erect his cabin upon its fertile shores. However, the bottom lands along this river, though appearing exceedingly fine at this season of the year, when the water is low, give evidence that, in the winter, they are often overflown. Here we found a species of yellow pine, similar to the Norway pine, it being the first I had seen in the country, but we reposed for the night under the branches of a majestic fir, and our trusty horses cropped the wild grass of the prairie around us, while we slept. Six o'clock the next morning found us prepared to resume our journey, and at twelve we had traveled twenty miles, when we stopped for dinner, on one of the numerous streamlets which water the Wallamette valley.

Re-packing our animals, after resting two hours, we traveled, in the evening, about ten miles, and encamped for the night by the side of a small pool of water, in the centre of a large prairie. The country through which we passed during the day, was exceedingly flat. Some parts of it were quite low, and subject to inundation from the rapid rise of the Wallamette river. The prairies had been all overrun with fire a short time previous, and it was with difficulty that we could find sufficient feed for our horses. However, around the pool the grass was so green that the fire had passed it by, and this rendered it a suitable place to spend the night, particularly for our animals. There was something very peculiar about this pool. It embraced a superficial area of some ten rods of ground, with no visible inlet or outlet, and it was several miles from any other water, though the water in the pool was nearly upon a level with the surrounding land. It was also literally filled with frogs, there being at least five to every square foot.

We spread our bed where the grass was abundant, but soon after lying down we were disturbed by a somewhat novel circumstance. I began to feel a gentle stir directly under my back, though for some time I made

TOUR TO THE UMPQUA.   97

no mention of it, not yet deciding what it might be. But as the effort beneath me continued as though some living being was thrown into convulsions through suffocation, I at length cried out that there was some living creature under my blanket. The "Captain" understanding me, exclaimed, "A snake! a snake!" I sprang instantly to my feet, seized my blankets, and scattered my bed around the prairie, and, to the no small amusement of our party, out jumped a large bullfrog, and made his best leaps to get back into the pool.

August 20th. We arose in the morning invigorated by repose, and traveling twenty-five miles, at one o'clock we arrived at the place on the Wallamette river where we designed to cross, our trail having been on the east side of the river. In approaching the stream, we found the trail exceedingly difficult, especially for our pack horses, as it led us through a dense forest of cottonwood and swamp maple, but at length we emerged from it in safety, and found ourselves on the river's brink. Examining the ford, we found the river too deep, and the current too strong, to admit of our crossing our pack horses in safety, and discovering an Indian below us, in his canoe, we beckoned to him to come up to us, which he accordingly did. He appeared very shy at first, as he was entirely naked, not having so much clothing on as an apron of fig leaves, but after a while we induced him to take our things into his canoe, and carry them across the river. Dr. White accompanied him, while Mr. Lee, myself, and the "Captain," crossed over the horses. The water was up to the animals' backs, and the current so strong that we feared it would bear us down; but, with the exception of getting thoroughly wet, we gained the opposite shore without difficulty. Here we took some refreshments, and then continued our way over a delightful plain fifteen miles in extent, and at night stopped on the California trail, at a place which, by the numerous fires which had been built around, we judged was often used as an encampment. This is the great trail extending through from Upper

California to the Columbia river, and passes through the valley of the Wallamette, on the west side of the river.

Friday, 21st. After traveling about twenty miles over a rolling country, presenting almost every variety of scenery, we halted for dinner on a small stream called "Bridge river," on account of a log bridge having been thrown across it, by some California party. This stream runs in a deep cut, and, but for the bridge, would have been difficult to cross. In the afternoon we passed over the mountain "La Beache," (Elk mountain,) which consists of a vast assemblage of hills thrown together in wild confusion, and covered with a heavy forest of fir and cedar trees. The latter is the most stately and majestic timber of the kind I have ever seen. Some of the trees are from from ten to fifteen feet in diameter, and towering to an incredible height. On beholding them, one is reminded of the scripture account of the cedars of Lebanon. It required three hours to cross this mountain, and as we descended it to the south, we found the fire making sad havoc with the fine timber with which its sides were adorned. In some places it raged so hard along the trail, that it was quite difficult for us to pass; but, urging our way along, we arrived at sun down at Elk river, and camped on a beautiful plain on its south bank.

Saturday, 22d. Leaving the California trail we took a path that bore farther to the west, which followed the direction of the Elk river. During the day we passed over an exceedingly mountainous country. Some of the hills were rocky and precipitous, and it was with great difficulty that we were able to keep our balance on the narrow path among the rocks, that, in its zigzag course, marked our way up and down their almost perpendicular sides. Mr. Lee remarked that in crossing the Rocky mountains, there was nothing that would bear any comparison with the difficulty and roughness of our trail through the Umpqua mountains. But urging our way along, now plunging into the deep ravine, now scaling the high ledge of rocks, now climbing the precipitous mountains, now descending into the dark valley, and fording Elk river over the slippery rocks not less than five times, at two o'clock, p. m., we found ourselves on the banks of the Umpqua river, opposite of the fort. We stripped our horses of their packs and saddles, and turned them loose to roam at large on the north side of the river, until we performed a voyage to the coast; and, crossing over in a canoe, we were kindly received at the fort by an old Frenchman, having charge of it, by the name of Goniea. We were made welcome to all the comforts the place afforded.

This fort, or rather trading post, stands on the south bank of the Umpqua river, on a little plain comprising about two hundred acres of land, thirty of which are under cultivation. It is forty miles from the Pacific ocean, and advantageously situated for the purposes for which it was established, namely, the collection of beaver and other furs from the Indians along the coast and in the interior. The fort itself consists of three or four little log huts built on three sides of a square, and covered with cedar bark. These huts are stockaded by poles set in the ground, and rising twelve feet high; and at two opposite corners of the enclosure thus formed, there are two bastions commanding all sides of the fort, and containing means for the defense of the establishment against the attacks of the Indians who are frequently quite troublesome in this region. Not long since the place was attacked by a band of savages, outnumbering ten times the inmates of the fort, but after a long fight, in which no one was killed, and but two or three of the Indians were wounded, the latter were compelled to retreat.

The Frenchman in charge, it is said, belongs to a wealthy and honorable family in Montreal, and though frequent efforts have been made to reclaim him from his wanderings, and induce him to return to his family and friends, yet all have been unavailing. Such is the power of habit with him that he now prefers a life but little in advance of the wretched savages that surround him, to all the elegance and refinements of the most civilized society. He lives with an Indian woman whom he calls his wife, and who belongs to a tribe that reside on the coast, near the mouth of the Umpqua river.

Sunday, 23d. A good night's rest on a bed of Mackinaw blankets, and a liberal supply of boiled pork and potatoes, furnished by our Indian hostess, wonderfully recruited us after the fatigues of our journey. We found no Indians around the fort except a small band of twenty-five Calapooahs from the Wallamette valley. These we collected in one of the huts within the stockades, and Mr. Lee addressed them in the jargon of the country, concerning the things which belong to their peace, and the chief interpreted it to his people. They seemed to be much interested, and were ready to promise that they would all become good. The chief confessed that his people had formerly been guilty of adultery, but said he had stopped all that a year ago; that he allowed himself to have two wives still, but that he meant to put one of them away as soon as he returned. As we expected to pass through his country on our return, we engaged to meet him and his people on a certain day, and give them another "talk."

Monday, 24th. Dr. White and the "Captain" left us and returned to the Wallamette, and Mr. Lee and myself started in a canoe, to visit the Indians at the mouth of the Umpqua river. We had been informed by Mr. Goniea that there would be great danger in our going among them alone, and, indeed, he appeared to stand in the utmost fear of them. Of their hostility to the whites, and especially the Americans, we were ourselves aware, as they had in more than one instance attacked them, and at one time in particular they cut off an entire party of fourteen men who were coming through from California to Oregon, except three persons, who fortunately escaped to tell the story of the massacre of their companions. But Providence seemed to favor our design of going among them. On Sunday afternoon, a brother of the Frenchman's wife, with a small party of Indians from the coast, arrived at the fort, having come up the river in a canoe. After having an interview with them we proposed to the Frenchman that his wife, who, we learned, was a relative of the principal chiefs of the tribe, should take us under her protection, and with her brother and his party, conduct us to their people. To this the Frenchman consented, saying, "now the danger is small, before it was great." According to arrangement, at ten o'clock, A. M., we put out with our light canoe into the rapid current of the Umpqua. We ran a number of narrow shoots where the current is at least twelve knots an hour, and in some instances shot past the rocks which projected into the stream within six inches, with the velocity of an arrow. But our Indians —seven in number—showed themselves to be on their proper element by the astonishing dexterity with which they ran the dangerous rapids with which the river abounds. Fifteen miles below the fort, the river rushes over a ledge of rocks in a number of narrow channels, and falling about twenty-five feet in so many rods, forms a fine salmon fishery. Here we found, crowded into four small lodges, about one hundred Indians, exceedingly squalid in their appearance, and subsisting entirely on fish.

Our Indian protectress, who also officiated as interpreter, informed them who we were, and for what purpose we had come among them, with which they seemed to be highly pleased, saying it was good; and as we passed on, nine of them, five men and four women, jumped into a large canoe, for the purpose of accompanying us down the river.

Having thus increased our company more than half, we proceeded on our voyage, contemplating the barbarous appearance of both animate and inanimate nature around us, until the gathering shadows reminded us that night approached; and running our canoes in along the right hand shore, we at length found a place sufficiently broad, from the river to the base of the mountain, to admit of our encamping, and here we pitched our tent for the night. Our Indians soon struck up two good fires, one for themselves and one for us. Mr. Lee and myself prepared our supper, our female friend providing us with a choice piece of salmon which she had broiled, and which, with bread, butter, and tea, constituted our humble repast. Never did we partake of a supper with a better relish. While we were enjoying it, our neophytes prepared supper for themselves, and it was not a little interesting, to one who was not familiar with such scenes, to see them prepare their food. Their supper consisted of fresh salmon, and a species of hazel-nut, which is found in the country in great abundance. Having made a suitable fire, they commenced the operation of cooking their salmon. This was performed in the following manner: they all provided themselves with sticks about three feet long, pointed at one end and split at the other. They then apportioned the salmon, each one taking a large piece, and filling it with splinters to prevent its falling to pieces when cooking, and which they fastened with great care, into the forked end of the stick; then placing themselves around the fire so as to describe a circle, they stuck the pointed end of the stick into the ground a short distance from the fire, inclining the top towards the flames, so as to bring the salmon in contact with the heat, thus forming a kind of pyramid of salmon over the whole fire. One side being cooked, the other was turned to the heat, and speedily the whole was prepared for eating. Stones were then provided for the purpose of cracking nuts, and all being seated on the ground, the eating process commenced. The extreme novelty of their appearance, the nut cracking, the general merriment, the apparent jokes, ready repartees, and bursts of laughter, were sufficient to have excited the risibilities of even a Roman Catholic priest, however phlegmatic. And certainly a more jovial set of fellows than these sons of nature, I have never seen. They are as untamed as the elk they chase over their mountains; and feasted upon their fish and nuts with as much seeming satisfaction to themselves, as the most fashionable and refined party that ever graced the gay saloon enjoyed while regaling themselves from the most costly viands.

Supper being over, we called the attention of the

Indians, while we engaged in our evening devotions. I sang a hymn, and then we both engaged in prayer, the Indians all kneeling with us, and evidently manifesting a peculiar interest in what was passing before them. And, thought I, why should they not feel interested? Never before had the death-like silence, which reigned along this valley, been broken by the voice of prayer and praise. The sombre shades of moral darkness, which had ever cast a melancholy gloom upon the people, had never been penetrated by the rays of gospel light. The heralds of mercy who bring glad tidings of good things to those who wander upon the dark mountains, had never before set their feet on these hostile shores. And, while the Indians surrounding us appeared to be sensible of the nature and importance of our visit among them, the circumstances were such as to create in us feelings of the greatest solicitude. After our devotions were finished, Mr. Lee addressed the Indians through our interpreter in relation to the objects of our visit, and they listened as to a story calculated to excite the utmost wonder. We all retired in quietness, rested in peace, arose in safety, and proceeding on our way along the widening Umpqua towards the great Pacific ocean, arrived at noon among the Indians at the mouth of the river.

We found but little land along the river which holds out any inducements to emigrants, the country on both sides as we approached the coast, becoming more and more rocky and mountainous. Whatever the country may be back from the river, it is certain that along the stream it can never sustain much of a population. Hills upon hills, and rocks piled upon rocks, characterize almost the whole distance from the Umpqua fort to the Pacific ocean.

On arriving at the coast we found the Indians living in three small villages, the larger being on the south, and the other two on the north side of the river. The whole number, as near as we could ascertain, amounted to about two hundred men, women, and children, about one-third of whom were absent in the mountains, for the purpose of gathering berries. It was thought best, by our female guardian and adviser, to pitch our tent some half a mile distant from the larger village on the south side of the river, near which she told us the chiefs and their people would meet us to hold a "talk."

Though the news of our arrival quickly flew to all the lodges, yet none of the Indians came near us, until we sent them word that we had come, and desired to see them at our tent; then three chiefs and fifty-five of their people, mostly men, came out to see us. Seating themselves in the sand in a semicircle in front of the tent, they informed us, through our interpreter, that they were "ready to hear what we had to say." Mr. Lee then addressed them, describing the objects of our visit, and telling them whence we came; how long it took us to perform our voyage from our native land to their country; that we had many friends at home who desired us not to leave them; that a sense of duty had brought us to their country to tell them about Jesus Christ; that in coming to them, we had been exposed to a thousand dangers, but had been preserved in the midst of them all by the "Great Chief above;" that we had heard much about them, and that we were glad now to be permitted to see them for ourselves, and become acquainted with them. He then inquired whether they approved of our visit, and whether they desired to be instructed.

After a few moment's consultation among themselves, the chiefs, one after another, arose, and advancing to within six feet of Mr. Lee, addressed him in substance as follows, there being but little difference in their speeches: "Great chief! we are very much pleased with our lands. We love this world. We wish to live a great while. We very much desire to become old men before we die. It is true, we have killed many people, but we have never killed any but bad people. Many lies have been told about us. We have been called a bad people, and we are glad that you have come to see us for yourselves. We have seen some white people before, but they came to get our beaver. None ever came before to instruct us. We are glad to see you; we want to learn; we wish to throw away our bad things, and become good." They spoke very loud, and their gestures were remarkably violent. Sometimes they would rise upon tiptoe, with both hands stretched high above their heads, and then throw themselves forward until their faces almost touched the ground. Returning to their seats in the sand, they told us that they were now prepared to hear us more particularly.

According to Mr. Lee's request, I stepped out into an open space and struck into Heber's missionary hymn; and while singing the first verse, they all seated themselves on the sand, forming three-fourths of a circle around us, and then with the most fixed attention, listened to the remaining part of the hymn. We then joined in prayer, all the Indians kneeling with us, and invoked upon our enterprise the blessing of Almighty God. Though our congregation was totally ignorant of the nature of worship, yet the scene, to us, was deeply affecting. Never before had they thus bowed, never before had they heard the voice of prayer. We then preached to them the gospel as well as we could in the jargon of the country, giving them an account of the creation of the world, the fall of man, the advent, sufferings, death, resurrection, and ascension of Christ, to save mankind from sin, from death, and from hell, all of which was interpreted to her people by our female friend. They appeared very solemn, and manifested an ardent desire to understand what was said to them; but we scarcely dared to hope that they understood much, though they appeared exceedingly interested. Yet we cherished the fond belief that, for the first time in their history, a few rays from the Sun of righteousness pierced the gloom of the long and dismal night which had hung around. The chiefs expressed their approbation of what they had heard, saying it was all very good, and that they had never heard such things before. They all dispersed, and we prepared and took our supper.

After dusk they all returned for the purpose, as they told us, of "hearing us talk to God" previous to our going to bed. They built a large fire, and seated themselves around it. I then sang another hymn; after which we both engaged in prayer. As they still lingered around, Mr. Lee gave them another lesson from the word of the Lord, after which they reluctantly scattered away to their wigwams, leaving us to repose ourselves on our bed of blankets, spread upon the sand. Mr. Lee slept soundly during the night, but the scenes of the preceding day, the circumstances of the night, and the fact that we were lying at the mercy of those who had proved themselves among the most treacherous of savages, produced such an effect upon my nerves, as to destroy all inclination to close my eyes. I repeatedly drew aside the tent cloth, and cast a look around, and in every instance observed that our protectress and her brother, and an Indian who had lived among the whites, but had returned to his people, were keeping up a large fire in front of our tent, which threw its light back into the dense forest which lay in our rear. Sometimes they were in earnest conversation, then they would pile on the dry sticks until the flame would ascend to the height of ten feet, and enable them to distinguish every object within a circle of twenty rods. This they continued during the whole night, neither of them for a moment attempting to sleep.

Wednesday morning arrived, none of the Indians having, to our knowledge, shown any disposition to molest us during the night. After our breakfast was over, knowing that we intended to leave so soon as the tide had risen sufficiently to admit of our passing over the sand bar above, they all collected again and seated themselves on the sand, while we once more offered up our fervent prayers to the "Desire of nations" in their behalf. After prayer, they were again addressed a few words; and we were preparing to leave them, when one of the chiefs stood up on his knees, and began to speak. He said he was very glad that we had come to see them; that their hearts towards us were like our hearts towards them; that he wanted us to continue with them another day, and tell them about God; that they had heard about us, and had been told we were a bad people; that they were glad to see us for themselves, and were convinced that what they had heard was a lie; that they now believed us to be a good people, and that they meant to be good also. We asked them whether they would receive a man, and use him well, if one were sent to them alone? They replied, "We will let him come among us; we will give him food, and will not hurt him, but will do what he says." When they were informed that probably the next summer one of us would come and visit them again, they were exceedingly well pleased, and said, "It is very good."

Before leaving, we visited their lodges, and one of them presented us with a beaver skin, and the wife of the principal chief gave us a woman's dress, which was made of cedar bark. The bark was strung out fine about eighteen inches long, and woven together at one end, so as to admit of being tied around the person, thus constituting a kind of fringe. Two of these fringes made a complete dress; one was fastened around the body above the hips, and hung down to the knees; the other was tied around the neck, and formed a covering for the breast and shoulders; the arms and lower extremities being left perfectly unencumbered. All the women were dressed in this manner with the exception of our friend, and one who had been the slave of a Frenchman, but had run away from her master, and returned to her people. These were dressed somewhat in the style of a Swiss peasant.

Having fully satisfied ourselves with regard to the number, disposition, and accessibility of the Indians in this solitary region, we prepared to take our leave, and the people all assembled to witness our departure. Giving them a few presents, at nine o'clock, on Wednesday morning, carried forward by the stroke of the Indian paddle, we were rounding a high bluff situated on the south side of the mouth of the Umpqua river, and forming one side of a small bay, in the bosom of which the Indian village we had just left was situated, and which was fast disappearing behind the point of the projecting cliff. Crossing the mouth of the river, which is about one mile wide, we stopped a few moments on the north side to lay in a little provision, and gave ourselves an opportunity to take some observations of the surrounding country. The land on both sides of the mouth of the river presents a most forbidding aspect. On the south the mountains extend quite to the waters of the Pacific, and form a shore of the most bold and precipitous character. On the north is a low sandy beach extending back from the mouth of the river about three miles, in the form of a triangle, and appearing destitute of vegetation, except a small growth of cottonwood. From our brief stay at the place, and our limited observations, it was impossible for us to form a just estimate of the whole country; but it appeared to us, that little importance can be attached to this portion of Oregon, viewed with reference to either agricultural or commercial pursuits. However, as there is a snug little harbor in the mouth of the river, and a channel across the bar, which will admit of the ingress and egress of craft, drawing not more than six or eight feet of water, this will probably be the outlet for the extensive and fertile valley above.

Contemplating the probable period when the barbarism of both animate and inanimate nature along this river shall give place to civilization and christianity, we turned our backs upon the great Pacific, and by the combined assistance of the Indian paddle and the flood-tide, passed rapidly up the river, and at night encamped at the salmon fishery. Found the river to be affected by the tide nearly twenty-five miles from its mouth. We ascertained that the Indians at the falls are not of the tribe of those on the coast, though they speak a similar language.

Spreading our blankets upon a shingle beach, we slept without molestation though surrounded by treacherous savages. Next day we started at an early hour, and though having but fifteen miles to travel, yet on account of the numerous strong rapids we had to ascend, and the portages we had to make, we were till sunset in reaching the fort. We were again welcomed by the Frenchman, and refreshed with a supper of bread, made of pounded wheat, and roasted elk beef. During the evening Mr. Goniea came to us considerably excited, and warmly congratulated us on the safe guardianship his wife had exercised over us in our absence. He said that, in all probability, we should have been robbed of all we had, if we had not lost our lives, had it not been for the faithfulness of his wife and her brother. He told us that one of the chiefs of the clan we had visited, was at the fort on our first arrival, and saw us as we came in. Learning that we designed to visit his people on the coast, and excited with the utmost fear, he hastened down the river, and reported many evil things about us, intending thereby to instigate the Indians to prevent our going among them. Mr. Lee had brought a fowling piece with him, and had in his possession a patent shot pouch. This was the thing that had alarmed the chief. One story he told was that we had brought medicine in a bag that Mr. Lee wore on his neck, for the purpose of killing them all off; and, that if we were permitted to come among them, the fatal bag would be opened, and they would all be destroyed. This exasperated many of them, and Goniea's wife told him that we were in great danger the night we slept on the coast; that the Indians were lurking about us during the whole night, seeking an opportunity, when it was dark around our tent, to attack us; but that she and her brother kept a constant watch over us until morning. This explained to me the circumstances of that night, already described. But be this as it may, we were not, at the time, sensible that we were particularly exposed; and we felt ourselves safe under the protection of our Heavenly Father.

Notwithstanding the seeming favor with which we were received among them, the Indians along this river, and especially those on the coast, have often proved to be among the most treacherous of savages, and none have ever been among them, but have learned that they are capable of practising the most consummate duplicity. A story told by the gentlemen of the Hudson's Bay Company, concerning what transpired on this river, clearly illustrates the treachery and cruelty of these savages, as well as the perilous adventures of the Oregon mountaineers.

A company of fur hunters, known by the name of the Smith, Sublette & Jackson Company, was formed on the frontiers of civilization, and the plan proposed to accomplish their object was, to divide the company betwixt the three leaders, and the three portions to separate, each taking a given quantity of the Indian territory to explore. In this division, Smith was to take the country extending from the Platte river, by the way of Santa Fe, to California; thence turn north along the Pacific ocean, as far as the Columbia river, and thence back into the interior to join the other partners of the company.

The country was in its wildest state, but few white men having ever passed through it. But nothing daunted, Smith and his company marched through to California, and thence along the coast, north, as far as the Umpqua river, collecting in their progress all the valuable furs they could procure, until they had loaded several "pack animals" with the precious burden. On arriving here, they encamped on the border of the river, near the place where they intended to cross, but on examination, found that it would be dangerous, if not impossible, to effect the passage of the river at that place. Accordingly, Smith took one of his men and proceeded up the river on foot, for the purpose of finding a better place to cross. In his absence the Indians, instigated by one of the savage looking chiefs whom we saw at the mouth of the river, rushed upon the party with their muskets, bows and arrows, tomahawks and scalping knives, and commenced the work of death. From the apparent kindness of the Indians previously, the party had been thrown entirely off their guard, and consequently were immediately overpowered by their ferocious enemies, and but one out of the twelve in camp, escaped from the cruel massacre. Scarcely knowing which way he fled, this one fell in with Smith, who was on his return to the camp, and who received from the survivor the shocking account of the murder of eleven of his comrades. Smith, seeing that all was lost, resolved upon attempting nothing further than to do his best to secure his own personal safety, with that of his surviving companions, the Indians having secured all the fur, horses, mules, baggage, and every thing the company had. The three immediately crossed the river, and made the best of their way through a savage and inhospitable country towards Vancouver, where, after traveling between two and three hundred miles, and suffering the greatest deprivations, they finally arrived in safety.

Rehearsing the story of their wonderful escape and subsequent sufferings, to the members of the Hudson's Bay Company, the utmost sympathy was excited in their behalf, and a strong party was immediately fitted out to go and rescue the property from the savage robbers, and restore it to its surviving owners. The vigor and perseverance of this party, were equal to the promptitude with which it was fitted out. They proceeded to the scene of blood, and after committing the mangled bodies of Smith's murdered companions to the grave, compelled the Indians to relinquish the property they had taken, spread terror through the tribe, and returned in triumph to Vancouver. All this labor and expense were bestowed by the company gratuitously, and Smith and his friends, while at Vancouver, were fed and clothed without money and without price. In addition to this, Governor Simpson, who, at that time, was at Vancouver, proposed to take Smith and all his furs to England, where he could avail himself of the advantages of the London market, and obtain a higher price; but Smith replied that he had already been laid under too many obligations by the company, and could not consent to receive this last proffered favor. Accordingly he sold his furs to the company and went into the interior, where he found Sublette conflicting in his trade with the interests of the company, and induced him to leave that quarter. He then went into the country of the Colorado, and collected considerable property in furs and peltries; but in crossing that river, he was again defeated by the Indians, and lost all. Subsequently, he returned to St. Louis, and fitted out an expedition to Sante Fe. But this was his last journey among hostile tribes. Surrounded by the savage horde that beset his path, he was again attacked by his relentless foe, and miserably perished.

Having listened to the story of the ill-fated Smith, we prepared to continue our exploring tour farther into the interior, and up the valley of the Umpqua river. Through the assistance of Mr. Goniea, we procured an Indian guide of the Umpqua tribe, whom the French had designated by the name of "We-We," and who well understood the jargon of the country, and could officiate as our interpreter. The forenoon of Friday was spent in finding our horses, and preparing our pack. All being ready, betwixt twelve and one o'clock we started, with our guide in advance. Passing over a number of high hills, and fording the Umpqua three times, where the bottom was very rocky and the water up to our horses' backs, we camped at night on the bank of a small rivulet, under the shelter of a grove of fir. We had traveled about twenty miles. The country traversed that day, though mountainous, is tolerably well adapted to grazing purposes, the land on the hills, and in many of the valleys, being covered with a spontaneous growth of the most nutritious grass. The timber grows less and less abundant as we proceed up the river; some of the fir trees, however, are most magnificent. We measured one with our lasso as high up as we could reach, and found it to be thirty-six feet in circumference. We judged it to be three hundred feet high. In the lowest valleys next the streams, grows a kind of timber, the like of which I have never seen in any other country. It appears to be of the laurel family, and is so strongly scented, that the air in the groves where it is found, is strongly impregnated with its aromatic odors. The elk abound in this country, and afford a fruitful source whence the Indians derive a subsistence. No Indians appeared during the first day.

Saturday, 29th. Continued our toilsome way over mountains, and through valleys similar to those already described, and at noon arrived at the head quarters of that portion of the Indians of this valley, distinguished by the name of the river. Here the head chief of the Umpquas has fixed a temporary abode, and here one of those circumstances recently transpired, which, though of common occurrence in heathen countries, where the vicious propensities of depraved human nature are permitted to revel uncontrolled, are sufficient to freeze the heart's blood, even to contemplate at a distance. It is as follows: A report came to the ears of the chief of the Umpquas, that his wife had been guilty of infidelity towards her husband. This so enraged him, that, without knowing whether the report was true or false, he seized his musket, and went directly to the lodge where his wife was sitting, and deliberately shot her through the heart.

Soon after our arrival on the side of the river opposite to the village, this chief, with the few men that were with him, came over to see us. He delivered a long speech, which was interpreted to us by "We-We," in making which, one of his first objects seemed to be to justify the murder of his wife, and then to express his gratitude that christian teachers had come among them. While he was haranguing us, my attention was caught away from his speech by a terrible burst of heathen passions, which took place on the other side of the river, among the lodges. In the absence of the men, the women had a regular fight, scratching and biting one another, and tearing each other's hair, and squalling most frightfully. So tremendous was the explosion that even the chief paused in the midst of his address, and significantly remarked, "our *women* are *hias masicha;*" (very bad.) Such were the indications here, that we came to the conclusion that the sooner we were out of the place the better it would be for us, and so soon as we had taken a little refreshment from our scanty stores, we told our guide that we were ready to proceed; but he positively refused to go any farther that day, saying that it would be using his people very ill, and that the chief would be very angry with us, if we did not stop and sleep with them one night. The contention became

5*

quite warm, and we began to consider ourselves in rather critical circumstances. If abandoned by our guide, it was extremely doubtful whether we could find our way back to the fort, or forward to the great valley of the Umpqua. The whole country was rough and mountainous, and there was no visible trail but a small portion of the way.

But with all these difficulties, we showed that we were fixed in our resolutions to leave this suspicious horde of savages before darkness should favor them in the execution of any treacherous designs which they might entertain towards us. Discovering that we were ready to mount our horses, We-We became more pliable, and said that he would proceed with us, on condition that we would pay him an extra shirt, we having at first given him a shirt and a pair of pantaloons. Mr. Lee said he would give him no more, but, to get rid of the difficulty, I told We-We that if he would go, I would give him the additional shirt so soon as we should reach the great valley. Turning to his people, We-We addressed them a few words in the Umpqua language, and then told us he was ready to go. Accordingly, we left this group of wretched beings about three o'clock, P. M., and galloped swiftly over a little plain, towards a high mountain. Three hours' hard labor in ascending and descending, brought us to the foot of the mountain on the opposite side, and passing through a dense thicket, we found ourselves again on the bank of the river. We-We brought out a well known Indian "whoop," and was answered by another Indian, just below us, on the river. Immediately four Indians came in sight, with a canoe, and We-We told us we had better unpack our horses, and put all our things in a canoe to be taken up the river, a few miles beyond a place where the pass was very rocky, narrow, and dangerous. But the strange conduct of the Indians we had left, had excited our suspicions; and supposing that those in the canoe were some of the same party whom We-We had, perhaps, caused to come up the river for no good purpose, we resolved to keep what we had under our own eye as long as we could.

We told the guide that we should keep our things on our horses' backs. We-We hung his head, and told us we would be sorry for it before we got through. We proceeded, but found it as We-We had forewarned us. Our trail lay along a frightful precipice which towered far above us, and extended far below us, and in some places was so narrow and broken that a miss-step would have precipitated us headlong on the rocks below, or into the rushing waters of the Umpqua. In one instance my own horse fell from ten to fifteen feet down the rocks, but at length succeeded in gaining the trail without receiving much injury.

But we were not destined to make the pass, without considerable difficulty. In passing the last dangerous point, "old Pomp," our pack horse, lost his footing, and rolling down a rocky steep of some thirty feet, went backwards into the Umpqua river. We had fastened around his neck a long lasso, and the end of it remaining on shore, we succeeded, by drawing it around a tree, in raising and keeping his head above the water until We-We had relieved him of his pack. While We-We was at work among the rocks, where the water was up to his neck, trying to relieve the horse of his burden, he told us that we might have saved ourselves that difficulty, if we had trusted to the honesty of an Indian; and we ourselves began to suspect that our fears had been quite groundless. It required our utmost efforts to keep the horse from drowning; but after we had relieved him of his load, he managed himself a little better, and finding a place which was not quite so steep as the one where he entered the river, we succeeded, at that point, in getting him on the rocky shore. All our bedding, provisions, &c., were thoroughly soaked; but gathering up what was not spoiled, and putting some on the horses, and carrying some on our own shoulders, we started on, being informed by the guide, that it was not far to a fine prairie. Night began to set in, and as we left the scene of our disaster, we entered a dense forest of fir, and the gloom continued to thicken around us until we were enveloped in total darkness. We were leading our animals by the bridle, and feeling our way among the trees, in the midst of darkness, so dense that it was impossible to see a white horse, though within a foot of one's nose, when we became so entangled among the logs, ravines, and brush, that we found it was impossible to go either forwards or backwards, to the right or to the left, and colloquising a little through the darkness, we came to the conclusion to tie our horses to the trees, and make the best of the night we could. Having a few matches in my pocket, and the leaves and limbs under my feet being perfectly dry, I soon had the forest illuminated, and then was disclosed to our view a most horrible place. We sought for a spot on which to sleep, but could find none level and large enough to stretch ourselves upon. We must either bend over the top of a knoll, or double up in a ravine, or remain in a sitting or standing posture. We preferred the second, so wrapping ourselves in our wet blankets and rolling into a hollow, we *tried* to compose ourselves to sleep; but the cracking of limbs by the tramp of our horses, the howling of wolves, and the screech of an owl, frequently disturbed our repose. The morning sun, however, enabled us so to adjust our rather disarranged affairs that we could, quite comfortably, prosecute our journey. Next day was Sabbath, but we could not remain where we were, and we proceeded on a few miles, and came to a band of about thirty of the Umpquas, with whom we tarried for several hours. They behaved themselves quite orderly, and were anxious to render us all the assistance in their power. We preached the gospel to them as well as we were able, and they said they wanted very much to have a missionary come among them. Not desiring to sleep in the vicinity of their lodge, we made signs of wishing to leave, and the old men came around us, of whom there were several, and patting us on the shoulders, seemed to express great attachment. But we concluded that their love was not so ardent as to render it desirable, on our part, to stop with them over night, and, as our provision was growing scarce, we decided to set our faces towards the Wallamette valley. Gathering up the wreck of our pack, we again mounted, and traveling about twelve miles, encamped on the bank of a beautiful rivulet which is one of the tributaries of the Umpqua. We traveled during the whole day the distance of twenty-five miles, over as fine a country as can be found in any part of the world. An agreeable variety of hills, plains, and groves of pine, fir, and oak, constituted scenery of the most picturesque beauty, and the eye was never weary in gazing upon the ever varying picture. In addition to this, the soil is good, the grass abundant, and the country well watered; but as we proceeded up the valley of the Umpqua, the timber became scarce. A few pine on the hills, with a few scattering oak, are the principal kinds. Though the country is now destitute of inhabitants, except the wild beasts, and a few savages as wild as they, yet the day is not far distant, when it will be teeming with a civilized and christian people.

The Indians inhabiting the Umpqua valley, from the Pacific ocean one hundred miles into the interior, are very few. All that we could find, or get any satisfactory evidence as now in existence, did not exceed three hundred and seventy-five souls. These live in several different clans, and speak two distinct languages. They would be favorable towards the establishment of a mission in their country, but seem to think that the greatest benefit it would confer on them, would be to enable them to sell their beaver and deer-skins for a higher price. Temporal good is the sole object they would have in view. The most of them, residing as they do on the coast, are almost inaccessible, and the establishment and support of a mission among them, would be attended with immense expense. The best information we could obtain, from the Indians and others, led us to the conclusion that the time doubtless has been when the Indians of this valley were vastly more numerous than at present. The Umpqua tribe, but a few years ago numbering several hundred, by disease and their family wars has been reduced to less than seventy-five souls. Under the impression that the doom of extinction is suspended over this wretched race, and that the hand of Providence is removing them to give place to a people more worthy of this beautiful and fertile country, we arrived at the place of our encampment, and found ourselves again on the great California trail.

Having fulfilled his engagement in bringing us around to this trail, our guide left us to return to his people.

Monday, September 1st. We quickened our pace through a country well adapted to agricultural purposes, and abounding in every variety of scenery; and at noon, having traveled twenty-five miles, we stopped for dinner on Elk river, at the place where, on going out, we left the California trail. In the afternoon, we again passed over the Elk mountain, and found that the fire was still raging with increasing violence. A vast quantity of the large fir and cedar timber, had been burned down, and in some places the trail was so blockaded with fallen trees, that it was almost impossible to proceed; while now and then we passed a giant cedar, or a mammoth fir, through whose trunk the fire had made a passage, and was still flaming like an oven. Every few moments these majestic spars would come "cracking, crashing, and thundering" to the ground; but while the fire was thus robbing the mountain of its glory, we pushed on over its desolated ridges, and at sun-down arrived on a little prairie at its base, where we made our encampment. Several times during the night we were awakened by the crash of the falling timber, on the mountain, which sometimes produced a noise similar to that of distant thunder.

Tuesday, 2d. Homeward bound, at noon we arrived in the Wallamette valley, where, according to engagement, we met the Callapooah chief. He had collected about sixty of his people, and said that he had about forty more. We remained with them four hours, and endeavored to preach to them "Jesus and the resurrection." Many of them were sick, and they appeared wretched beyond description. Our bowels of compassion yearned over them, but it was not in our power to help them. Commending them to God, at four, P. M., we pursued our way; but finding no water, we did not camp till eleven o'clock at night. We were then obliged to strip our horses on the open prairie, and turn them loose without water, and lay ourselves down upon our blankets with our lips parched with thirst. Next morning, however, we found ourselves, like Hagar in the desert, within a short distance of good water. Here I roasted a duck for our breakfast, which the Callapooah chief had given us, and which we ate with neither bread nor sauce; but a cup of coffee, that "*sine qua non*" for prairie traveling, washed it down, and on the strength of it, we traveled forty miles, during the day, over a country of surpassing loveliness, on account of its enchanting scenery and amazing fertility. Surely, thought I, infinite skill has here been employed, in fitting up a country which requires nothing more than a population under the influence of the religion of Christ, to render it a perfect paradise. The last night we encamped within fifteen miles of our families and friends, and the next day, Thursday, the 4th, we arrived at home in safety, but found our families all prostrate with the ague and fever. Having been constantly in a healthy exercise in our absence, we returned in the enjoyment of good health, and were consequently able to render ourselves useful in taking care of the sick.

CHAPTER VII.

Tour to Vancouver — Reception at the fort — Preaching in the hall — Business completed — Expedient to keep warm — Cold weather — Difficult navigation — The rapids — Forest encampment — Strange visitor — Affecting intelligence — Death of Rev. James Olley — My Mohican guest — Return home — Meeting — Fruitless attempt to recover a dead body.

DECEMBER 7th, 1842. Left the Wallamette for Vancouver, for the purpose of procuring supplies for the Oregon Mission School, accompanied by five Indian boys.

Proceeded on horse-back about twenty-five miles to a place on the Wallamette river, called, by the French, "La Butte," this being the most convenient place to land our supplies. Here, after having slept beneath the wide spreading branches of a large fir tree, we took the canoe which is kept by the mission above the falls of the Wallamette, for the purpose of transporting goods up and down the river, and proceeded to "Tum Water," that is, the falls. We left our canoe above the portage, and taking a boat provided for us by Mr. Abernethy, the mission steward, we continued on about fifteen miles below the falls, and encamped one hour after sundown, having rowed our canoe and boat during the day the distance of thirty-five miles.

The night was very cold, but collecting a large quantity of fuel, we were able to keep up a good fire during the night, and in this manner kept ourselves comfortably warm. Started the next morning as soon as it was day, and, though for six miles we had to contend with the strong current of the Columbia, we arrived at Vancouver at two o'clock, P. M. I went directly to the fort, and had an interview with James Douglass, Esq., one of the commandants of the place, and ascertained that I should be able to accomplish my business early on Monday morning. I was received with all that courtesy and hospitality which usually characterize the gentlemen of the Hudson's Bay Company. It was Saturday, and in the evening I received a respectful invitation from Mr. Douglass, to preach in the hall, the following day. Accordingly, after the usual church service was read, I endeavored to explain and enforce the inquiry of the jailer—" What must I do to be saved?"

On Monday morning, the 11th, having completed my business, and prepared to return, we proceeded to our boat, and found the Columbia river filled with ice. The weather had been increasingly cold, and the ice came down the river in large fields, and threatened to put a stop, for the time being, to the navigation of the stream. However, it had not yet become very hard, and though there was some danger in the attempt, yet we launched forth into the stream, and breaking our way through the ice with our setting poles, we at length succeeded in getting safely into the mouth of the Wallamette.

This river being clear from ice, we proceeded up about seven miles, and encamped under a high bluff, which sheltered us from the piercing winds from the north-east. The ground being frozen, the weather exceedingly cold, and, withal, a scarcity of bedding, I took the following precaution to ensure a comfortable night: I built a large fire where I designed to make my bed, and after the earth became thoroughly warmed and dried, I removed the fire a little distance, and plucking some fir boughs, threw them upon the heated earth; then spreading my buffalo skin upon the boughs, I lay down upon it, and with a couple of blankets over me, slept comfortably during the night.

Next day at noon, we arrived at the falls, and on Wednesday, the 13th, made our portage. At two, P. M., we proceeded up the rapids above the falls, which, at that season of the year, are very difficult of ascent. They are ascended by cordeling, and it is frequently necessary to work for hours in the water among the rocks, in order to get up one boat load, an exercise any thing but agreeable when the mercury is nearly down to zero. We succeeded, however, with much toiling, and a *severe* wetting, in reaching the deep water above the rapids, without any serious accident, and at night encamped seven miles above the falls, in a dense forest of fir trees. I had preserved a few matches from getting wet, and succeeded, after awhile, in striking up a good fire, though the wood where we were encamped was very wet. I cooked me a supper of fresh salmon, not forgetting to make a good cup of tea; and after partaking of my humble repast from my ground table, with that peculiar relish which good health and hard labor always give to wholesome food, and offering up a tribute of thanksgiving to Providence for the blessings of the past, and invoking a continuance of his favors, I spread my skins and blankets upon the ground, and reclined myself to rest.

As I lay stretched upon my bed of skins before the fire, musing upon the good providence of God, which had been manifested in our preservation amid the dangers to which we had been exposed in ascending the fearful rapids, I was startled by the voice of a man from the river below us, inquiring, "What boat is that?" I replied, it belongs to the Oregon mission. "Then," said he, "I will come ashore." It was ten o'clock at night, and it was quite an uncommon thing for boats to remain upon the river to so late an hour. Consequently, I felt quite solicitous to know who the stranger might be. The sound of his oars, as they fell upon the water, grew louder and louder as he approached the shore, and in a few minutes he was along side of our boat, to which he fastened his small skiff. Clambering up the precipitous bank of the river through the thick underbrush, the light of our fire relieved me of some anxiety, as it shone upon the face of a "half-breed" Indian, direct from the place where I resided, which was forty miles above.

This half-breed was an educated man, and a sketch of his history may be found below. After giving me the gratifying intelligence that my own family were well, he inquired if I had heard the sad news. "What news?" said I, "I have heard nothing sad." "Then," said he, "I am the bearer of intelligence concerning the most afflicting event that has ever transpired in our settlement: *the Rev. James Olley is no more.*" Intelligence more unexpected could scarcely have been communicated; and when the circumstances of the removal of Mr. Olley from this stage of action were related, the effect upon my mind was quite overpowering.

Mr. Olley was a local preacher in the Oregon mission, and sailed from New York in the fall of 1839, with the large reinforcement in the ship Lausanne. He was a carpenter by trade, and after his arrival in Oregon, continued to serve the mission in that capacity, as he was able. He was making preparations to build himself a house, and desiring some better lumber than any he could obtain in the vicinity of the mission for the purpose of making window sash, he had employed a young man by the name of Eiken to accompany him up the Wallamette river about twenty miles, where there was pine timber, with the design of procuring a couple of logs and running them down the river to the mission saw-mill, where they could be cut into boards to suit his purpose. He proceeded to the pinery, and cutting two small sized logs rolled them into the water, but found that they were so heavy they would not float. He had designed to take them in tow, but finding that they would sink to the bottom, he resolved upon this expedient, to raise them to the surface, and lash a log to each side of his canoe. All being prepared they entered the canoe thus encumbered, and committed themselves to the rapid and treacherous current of Wallamette river. The weather was exceedingly cold, as it had been for a number of weeks previously, and the water in the river coming down from the snowy mountains of the east, was as cold as the ice itself.

As there had been but little rain during the fall, the river was not high, but there are places in it at all stages of the water, which are very rapid, and it requires great skill and dexterity to run them in safety even with an empty canoe. However, they proceeded down the current about ten miles, without accident, Mr. Eiken being in the stern, and Mr. Olley in the bow of the canoe, when they came to one of the fearful rapids with which the river abounds. At this place is a ledge of rocks extending across the bed of the stream, which rises out of the water in one place, forming a small island. The rapid commences a short distance above this ledge, and where the water breaks over the rocks it becomes exceedingly violent. Neither Mr. Olley nor Eiken had ever passed up or down this part of the river, consequently they were entirely ignorant of the dangers of the place; but there was no alternative, they were already in the strength of the current, and to make the shore on either side was impossible. Consequently they were carried with great violence on the rocks about fifteen yards from the little island, and about forty yards from the opposite shore. The bow of the canoe and logs first struck the rocks, and the stern swung so violently down that Eiken was thrown clear from the canoe into the strongest part of the current. But, being young, vigorous and active, he succeeded in making the shore about three hundred yards below, but he was so much exhausted through exertion, and benumbed by the cold, that when he reached the shore he was scarcely able to move; and while struggling in the icy water just before reaching the place where he could gain a foothold on the bottom, he was on the point of yielding to the fury of the current, and giving himself up for lost. But he escaped to tell a more solemn tale concerning the fate of his comrade. As soon as Eiken possibly could, he returned to the place opposite where the canoe and logs struck, and observed that Mr. Olley, having held fast to the raft, and now being on one of the logs, was looking round as if to contrive what course to pursue.

He called out to him and inquired, "what are you going to do?" Mr. Olley made no reply. Probably from the noise of the water rushing over the rocks, he did not hear him. Eiken thought he might have been bewildered. He directly sat down on the log and pulled off his shoes and stockings, and threw them into the river, keeping on his pantaloons, coat and cap. He then deliberately plunged himself into the stream, and was carried violently down the dashing current. Having learned to swim in his youth, he kept his head above the water for some time, and appeared to be nearing the shore. Eiken pursued him down as fast as he could, but could not keep up with him, such was the rapidity of the current. As he was borne downward a large log which extended into the stream, hid him from Eiken's view. Previously to this, his motion in the water became more irregular, and he appeared to have turned himself on his back, and to have thrown up his hands as in the attitude of prayer, or calling for help. He had then doubtless given up all hopes of making the shore, and was committing himself into the hands of his God. Be this as it may, when Eiken succeeded in getting round the log so that he could command a view of the river below, our beloved associate, friend, and father, had passed forever from the view of mortals.

These facts coming to my ears under the circumstances already described, for awhile weighed down my spirits, but a few hours of refreshing slumber after midnight, quieted my nerves, and the next morning found me prepared to resume my toils and exposures.

My visitor in camp, continued with me for a couple of hours, and after refreshing himself from my almost exhausted stores, observed that he was in a great hurry to get down to the mouth of the Columbia river to secure a piece of land which still remained unoccupied, and this explained his running in the night. He had been in the country about two years, and as there had been many reports in circulation concerning him, I resolved to avail myself of the opportunity thus afforded me to obtain from himself some facts in relation to his history.

"I once," said he, "saw a book which was entitled, 'The last of the Mohicans;' but I could tell the author a different story from that." In answer to my inquiries, I learned from him the following particulars. He was born in New England, and his father being a white man, he was therefore a proper yankee. His mother was an Indian woman, a relic of the Mohican tribe, and he was therefore a Mohican. He grew up to manhood in company with a brother of his, received a tolerably good English education, and was known by the name of J. L. M. Cooper. He and his brother, sick of the prejudices existing against them in their own country, resolved upon going to sea. They accordingly shipped on board a trading vessel bound to the Pacific, and after a voyage of several months, found themselves collecting Spanish hides, on the coast of California. Not liking the business very well, and finding themselves in a country where they would like to remain, they resolved, when the vessel was about to leave, to desert her, and take up their residence in California. They succeeded in their designs, but had not been long in the country before J. L. M. Cooper found himself involved in serious difficulties with the Californians. He treated some of them roughly, and they accused him also of using too great liberties with their property, particularly their horses, and finally became so enraged against him as to resolve upon taking his life. There was a Spaniard in particular, who, he believed, would take the first opportunity to carry this threat into execution. He accordingly secreted himself in a jungle, where his wants were supplied by his friends, and where he designed to wait until a company of trappers and hunters belonging to the Hudson's Bay Company, then in California, should start across the country for the Columbia river. By joining this company he hoped to escape the vengeance of the Spaniards. Betrayed by one in whom he had placed confidence, he would have lost his life but for a double betrayal. His place of concealment had been discovered by his determined foe, and the night fixed upon in which he was to die. In his turn Cooper's enemy was betrayed, and Cooper was informed that on a certain night he must prepare for a deadly encounter.

The night arrived; Cooper built a large fire; made up the form of a man; put his cap on his head, and laid it down before the fire as if to sleep. He had loaded his unerring rifle during the day, and examining it a little by the light of the fire to see that the percussion cap was in perfect order, he retreated a few steps from the fire, and hid himself in a place he had prepared for that purpose, in a dense thicket. At length he heard the stealthy footsteps of the vengeful Spaniard, as he cautiously approached his victim, whom he supposed he saw stretched in sleep before the fire. The Spaniard cast his dark eye along his rifle several times, and then would venture a little nearer, to make a surer aim. At length, *click, crack, bang!* went the rifle, and the report seemed to linger long amid the darkness of the night, and three balls had pierced the slumbering image before the fire. At this moment Cooper stepped out from his concealment; brought his rifle deliberately to his face, and the report rising upon the midnight air, the Spaniard was in eternity. The ball had pierced his heart.

The company of hunters were already scores of miles on their way to Oregon, and Cooper, securing one of the best horses he could find, perhaps without rendering an equivalent, soon placed himself beyond the reach of his enemies, on the south side of the Snowy mountains. This is Cooper's version of the story. Another is this: that he deliberately murdered a Spaniard in a gambling affray, and then escaped from California with the company above mentioned, upon a stolen horse. Be this as it may, the hour of midnight had arrived when my Mohican guest had finished his story, and then rising from the ground, he buckled his belt, from which dangled a large butcher-knife, a little tighter around him, and thanking me for his supper, said, "I must go." Splash, splash, splash, went the oars, as he glided away from the shore, and was lost amidst the surrounding darkness.

On Thursday, the 14th, arrived in safety at "La Butte," and landed our goods. I sent back the Indian boys with the canoe to the falls, to get a load of salmon and molasses, remaining myself with the goods over night, and sleeping between two large roots of a fir tree.

On Friday, according to arrangement, a team was sent to meet me at the Butte to receive the goods, and a horse to convey me home, where I arrived in safety at nine o'clock in the evening, after an absence of eight days. Found my family in good health, but the neighborhood wore a gloomy aspect. One of its prominent members, had, in a most afflicting manner, been called away, and all appeared to mourn, but not without hope

Sunday, 17th. Preached to a number of the missionaries and settlers, from the words of the Evangelist, "And beginning to sink, he cried, saying, Lord, save me."

On Monday, the 18th, in company with Rev. Jason Lee, procured a canoe, and a number of persons to assist in rowing it, and about sundown started up the river for the purpose of examining the place where the sad catastrophe, before related, transpired, and of searching for the body of our friend and brother Olley. We proceeded up the river about two miles and encamped for the night. Next morning continued slowly up the strong current, examining every nook, corner, and place where we supposed it to be possible for a body to lodge, and were encouraged to believe that we should succeed from finding one Mackinaw blanket, two coats, one bear-skin, and one paddle, all of which belonged to Mr. Eiken. At one o'clock, P. M., we arrived at the place where the fatal disaster occurred, and found that the current continued exceedingly strong about three-quarters of a mile below the place where the canoe struck the rocks. The river then widens into a kind of basin, broad and deep, and, judging from those places where it can be seen, with a very rough bottom. We examined the place as minutely as possible, but no vestige of the body could be discovered. This was the tenth day after the accident. Fatigued with the constant exertions of the day, at dark we drew our canoe ashore; cooked our supper upon the shingle beach, and cast ourselves down upon our blankets, to rest for the night. Repeating our examination the next morning, with as little success as the day previous, we came to the conclusion, however desirous we might be to rescue the body of our friend from a watery grave, it would no more be seen until that day should arrive when the seas, and the rivers also, shall give up their dead. As we descended the river towards the place of our embarkation, this passage of holy writ cheered our otherwise drooping spirits: "If we believe that Jesus died and rose again, even so also them which sleep in Jesus, will God bring with him."

CHAPTER VIII.

Another tour — Rock Island rapids — The Jesuit — Stormy encampment — Return — Hospitality — Story of our host — Mr. Cornelius Rogers — Party increase — La Butte — Lonely Sabbath — Arrival home — Mr. Rogers and party — Meeting at the hospital — Indian Messenger — Sad tidings — Great bereavement — Esq. Crocker — Call to civil duties — Thomas McKay — Great rain — Estate of Mr. Rogers — Return — Great freshet — Damages — Safe arrival home.

JANUARY 16th, 1843. Left home in company with L. H. Judson, for the purpose of performing another trip to Vancouver. We took a light canoe belonging to Mr. Lee, and shot out of a little cove which runs up within a half mile of our house, into the strong current of the Wallamette, and the water being high, we glided down with great rapidity, and at seven o'clock, P. M., encamped on a high bank on the left hand side of the river, having run the distance of forty miles.

Tuesday, the 17th, being favored with a good moon, we started, at five o'clock, and at daylight run the Rock Island rapids in safety. This place is considered dangerous at the present stage of water. Some accidents, though not of a very serious character, have recently happened here. Not long since a Jesuit priest, by the name of Blanchet, was passing up the river in a canoe manned with Indians and half-breeds, and loaded with mill-irons, as he was making arrangements to erect mills in the French settlement above. Arriving at this place, they attempted to ascend the rapids; but in doubling a point of rocks, around which the water rushed with great violence, they were borne down with fearful force to where they were in danger of being drawn under an immense raft, lying in the river. They struggled in vain to govern their canoe, and being greatly alarmed, in their eagerness to secure it, it was capsized, emptying themselves, mill-irons, and all into the river. Some of them struggled long in the water, but finally succeeded, some one way, and some another, in getting safe to land, happy in the consideration that the loss they had sustained could possibly be repaired. Though the followers of the "Padre" were sanguine in the belief that he possessed the power of working miracles, yet he has never been able to raise his mill-irons from the bottom of Rock Island channel.

Proceeded on our journey, and at sunrise arrived at the falls, and took breakfast with our good friend, George Abernethy, Esq. At eleven o'clock, continued our voyage, though with the prospect of bad weather. At twelve it became quite cold, and began to rain and hail. It continued storming without intermission, during the afternoon. This rendered it extremely disagreeable traveling, but there was no alternative; so we continued to ply the paddle, though iced with the falling sleet, until it began to grow dusk. Arriving at a small promontory covered with fir timber, twenty miles below the falls, we landed, and commenced making preparations for a stormy night. We were thoroughly drenched with rain, though, as good luck would have it, we had preserved our fire-works from getting wet. The storm beat upon us with violence, but we were twenty miles distant from human habitation, and had no choice; we must prepare to make ourselves as comfortable as possible during the night, though our prospects were exceedingly gloomy. The first thing to be done was to kindle a fire, no desirable task when every thing is as wet as rain can make it. However, selecting a place at the leeward of two large firs, that we might be the more sheltered from the wind and storm, after about half an hour, and when patience had performed "her perfect work," we succeeded in kindling a small blaze, which by extreme care we soon increased to a comfortable fire.

Having prepared our evening's repast, we partook of it with a keen relish, while the large drops from the spreading branches of the fir-trees, as they were shaken with the wind, fell in showers upon us.

Supper being over, we managed partially to dry our blankets and skins, and spreading them upon the wet ground, we lay ourselves to rest. I spread an umbrella over my head to shelter it from the large drops from the trees and the rain and sleet from the clouds, and, despite the storm, slept soundly until six o'clock in the morning.

Next day proceeded on to Fort Vancouver, and the following day accomplished our business and prepared to return.

Thursday, 19th. Left Vancouver in the morning, and after a day of hard toiling in a continued storm of snow and rain, arrived, late in the evening, at the house of Richard McCary, about five miles below the Wallamette falls. The night was excessively cold and stormy, and we were pleased to be sheltered beneath a friendly roof. Our host had spent the prime of his life in ranging the Rocky mountains, as a hunter and trapper, and entertained us with anecdotes of his hair-breadth escapes from the the hostile Sioux and Blackfeet. At one time, he, with seven other Americans, ventured far from the general rendezvous of the hunters, in the country of the Blackfeet, for the purpose of trapping beaver. The country was entirely destitute of timber, except here and there a small bunch of bushes, which grew in the swails. They pitched their tent on the banks of a small rivulet, on the open prairie, within a little distance of one of these thickets; designing, if they were attacked by the Blackfeet, to retreat to the thicket, and there defend themselves and protect their property.

One morning, as they went down to the stream to examine their traps, McCary being in advance of the rest of the party, a troop of Blackfeet warriors came dashing over a rise of ground, but a short distance in front of them, numbering, as they supposed, two or three hundred. As the Americans wheeled and ran towards their tent, the Blackfeet poured a volley of musket balls after them. McCary fell upon his face to the ground; a ball had entered the back side of his neck, and come out at one of his cheeks. No bone being broken, he soon recovered his senses, but as he could not instantly move, he expected to feel the scalping knife passing over his skull bone; but the Indians were kept at bay by his seven comrades, who, by this time, had secured their rifles and ammunition. Firing a round or two, and seeing some of the Indians fall, to their astonishment they saw McCary, whom they supposed to have been shot dead, rushing towards them to join them in their retreat to the thicket.

Here they continued the fight, the Indians with great bravery venturing up very near the thicket; but their musket balls and poisoned arrows took effect only upon the bushes and logs which formed the fort of the Americans; while the latter scarcely discharged a rifle but that an Indian was seen to lick the dust. The Blackfeet finding that they could not destroy the Americans without losing too many of their men, gave up the contest; and after securing their dead and wounded, and taking the property of the Americans, consisting of their tent, blankets, furs, traps and horses, they gave the shrill war whoop, and disappeared. After dressing McCary's wound as well as circumstances would admit, the trappers turned their faces back towards the rendezvous, where, after many days of suffering, they all arrived in safety. McCary, not relishing such adventures, and fearing that the next bullet might not be so merciful as to shun the vital organs, resolved to leave his dangerous business; and marrying a Nez Perse, he abandoned the Rocky mountains forever.

Our entertainment with this story far exceeded the refreshment we received the remaining part of the night, by sleeping on the bare floor.

Next morning proceeded to the falls, where we continued during the day.

Saturday, 21st. Left the falls at twelve, M., in company with two other canoes, and arrived at "La Butte" one hour after dark, cold, hungry, and worn out with fatigue. Mr. Cornelius Rogers was in one of the canoes, on his way up to the settlement to get his wife and her sister, a little girl two years of age. Mr. Rogers had entered into business at the falls, and having been married but a few months, had not yet commenced keeping house. Moving up and down the river is, for the want of other means, done in canoes, always a dangerous mode of traveling. The three canoes contained about twenty persons, and all slept at the "Butte;" and though the night was cold, many lay upon the ground without covering.

On Sunday morning, the 22nd, Mr. Judson and Mr. Rogers, being entirely out of provisions, left camp on foot, and proceeded to the mission, where they arrived in the evening, hungry and nearly exhausted. Having a few remnants of food left, I resolved to remain in camp during the Sabbath; and, to make myself as comfortable as possible, I collected a quantity of wood and bark, and building a large fire under the lee of the lofty furs that line the banks of the river, and being left entirely alone, spent the day in reading and meditation. Sunday night there was quite a fall of rain and sleet, and though I slept alone in the forest, and in the morning found that ice had collected in my hair, yet, by the blessing of Providence, I received no injury. At five o'clock on Monday morning, I left the "Butte" for my place of residence, where I arrived at noon, having traveled the distance of twenty-five miles.

On Thursday, the 2nd day of February, Mr. Cornelius Rogers left the settlement with his family, consisting of his wife and her little sister, to remove to the falls, where he expected to settle. Wm. W. Raymond, a member of the Oregon mission, residing at the mouth of the Columbia river, had come up with the large mission canoe that would carry about three tons, for the purpose of taking back supplies for the station; and not having enough to load the canoe himself, he proposed to take Mr. Rogers and his effects down to the falls. Mr. Rogers gladly accepted of the offer; and as Dr. Elijah White, sub-agent of Indian Affairs in Oregon, and Esq. Crocker, late of Lansingville, Tompkins Co., N. Y., were desirous of visiting Clatsop, they had obtained the privilege of accompanying Mr. Raymond down the Columbia river. These all repaired to the river's side, apparently in high spirits; embarked on the ill-fated craft; the Indians plied their paddles dexterously, and they glided away from the sight of their friends on the shore, upon the smooth surface of the treacherous element.

Sunday, Feb. 5th. I preached at the Hospital to a few of the missionaries, some of whom had been the subjects of severe affliction for a great share of the time since they had been in the country. I endeavored to encourage them from the words of St. Peter, " Think it not strange concerning the fiery trial which is to try you, as though some strange thing happened unto you, but rejoice, inasmuch as ye are partakers of Christ's sufferings." The sufferings incident to our residence in a heathen land, and the disposition with which we should bear them, were the subjects of the discourse.

The services had just been brought to a close, and I was about taking my leave to return to my family, ten miles up the river, when an Indian, almost exhausted with running, came into Dr. Babcock's, where I had stopped a few moments, bearing a small package of letters. The running of the Indian, the number of letters, the season of the year, and the storminess of the day, all conspired to excite our fears, and create a presentiment within us, that some unusual occurrence had taken place. I broke the seal of my letter from George Abernethy at the falls, and, most shocking to relate, the first words that met my eye were as follows :

" DEAR BROTHER :—

I have barely time to say that the mission canoe went over the falls yesterday evening with Mr. and Mrs. Rogers, Aurelia, and 'Squire Crocker and two Indians. We started immediately out with the mission boat, and reached within thirty yards of Mr. Rogers before he sank to rise no more."

It appears that they proceeded from the place of embarkation in safety, until they arrived at the head of the rapids, above the cataract. Here they all got out of the canoe, which they let down the rapids by a rope, and proceeded on foot down to a bluff rock which projects out into the stream, and is but a few steps from the place of landing. Here they all got into the canoe again except Mr. Raymond and three Indians, who remained on shore, for the purpose of holding on to the rope which was fastened to the canoe to enable them to drop below the point of rocks in safety. They passed the point, and brought the canoe along side of a large log which the high water had carried in along the shore, and which was used as a kind of wharf. The instant the canoe struck the log, Dr. White stepped one foot on it, and leaning towards the shore, held on to the canoe with the other foot, but before another one could step on the log the current took the bow of the canoe, which was up the stream, and in an instant they were drawn into the strongest part of the current. Mr. Raymond and the Indians exerted themselves in vain to hold on to the rope; they were drawn into the river, and forced to let go, to save themselves. All efforts were vain, all hope was lost. At this perilous moment two Indians sprang from the canoe, and darted like lightning through the rushing flood, and gained the shore. As the canoe approached the awful verge, Mr. Rogers threw himself upon his knees before his wife, who remained in her seat, holding her little sister in her lap. For a moment all was still except the rushing waters, then a wail was heard above the roar of the angry flood—they had made the fatal plunge. Some of their bodies were seen a short time, floating below the falls, but before they could possibly be approached with a boat, they had all sunk into their watery graves. Thus terminated the mortal career of Esq. Crocker, Cornelius Rogers, his wife and her little sister, and two Indians. The remains of the first two were subsequently recovered, and committed to the earth; the others have never been found. If by some awful convulsion in nature the whole city of New York were to be submerged beneath the waves of the Atlantic ocean, the shock to the State could not be greater than was felt in the colony of Oregon, when the mission canoe, with her precious cargo, went over the falls. This awful dispensation of Providence wrapped the whole country in gloom, and indeed there were many circumstances which combined to render it truly afflicting.

Mr. Rogers had formerly been a member of the Presbyterian mission in the upper country, and was regarded as a very efficient missionary; but becoming discouraged with the prospect there, he had asked and obtained a discharge from the mission, and for some time had made it his home in the Wallamette settlement. He had adopted Oregon as a place of permanent abode, and consequently asked and obtained the hand of Satira Leslie, eldest daughter of Rev. David Leslie, though she was but fifteen years of age. When Mr. Leslie took his departure from the country to the Sandwich Islands, and perhaps to the United States, the September previous, Mr. Rogers accompanied him down to the mouth of the Columbia river, in the brig Chenamus, Mr. Leslie having with him his entire family. It consisted of five interesting girls, he having buried his wife but a short time before. When the vessel was about ready to sail, and bear Mr. Leslie and two of his daughters away, the marriage of Mr. Rogers with Satira was duly solemnized on board the ship, as she lay at anchor in Baker's Bay. Dr. J. P. Richmond officiated on the occasion. It was arranged that Mr. Rogers and his wife would take back to the Wallamette the two youngest daughters of Mr. Leslie, and take care of them until Mr. Leslie could provide for them in some other way, while the remaining two were to accompany their father to the Islands, and perhaps to the States. Accordingly, they thus separated in Baker's Bay, about the 1st of September, 1842, fondly indulging the expectation that, after a separation of a few months, or years at most, they would again meet, and spend many happy years in each others' society. But an inscrutable Providence ordered it otherwise.

From the time that Mr. Rogers returned with his important charge from the mouth of the Columbia river, to the period of the fatal voyage down the Wallamette, he had been variously, though usefully employed; and desiging to spend his days in Oregon, his feelings and interests were bound up in the country. He was justly

*6

regarded as one of the most useful men it contained, and consequently his sudden removal was considered as a great loss to the rising settlement. His young and blooming companion was not only every way worthy of her husband, but the darling of a fond and doting parent, and beloved by all that knew her. She was at my house but a short time previous to her leaving the settlement to attend her husband to the falls, and informed us that she designed to take her youngest sister, Aurelia, a child two years old, with her, and leave the other, Helen, four years old, with Mrs. Gray. But for this arrangement, all three would have gone together; but Helen lived to bear to her afflicted parent the melancholy tidings of the awful death of his eldest and youngest daughters.

Esquire Crocker had been in the country but a short time. He performed the journey across the mountains for the benefit of his health. Liking the country better than he anticipated, he had come to the conclusion to send for his family and establish himself in Oregon; but by one stroke of Providence his designs were forever frustrated.

Having been appointed by the authorities of the country to secure and appraise the property of the late Mr. Cornelius Rogers, the principal part of which was at the falls, I started for that place on the 9th of February, in company with Mr. W. H. Gray. Traveled ten miles, and stopped at Dr. Babcock's, who was the Judge of Probate, to get our instructions, and continued with him during the night. Next morning at daylight, proceeded on horseback towards Champoeg, but as there had been a fall of snow the day previous, and the rain was then falling in torrents, it was almost impossible to make headway.

As we urged our way along, we found the streams and ravines so swollen, that the few bridges that had been made, were either carried away or afloat. However, by fording some of the streams where the water covered the saddles, and swimming others which were not fordable, we succeeded in getting to Champoeg, the distance of sixteen miles, at one o'clock, P. M., thoroughly drenched. As it continued to rain violently during the afternoon, we concluded to stop until morning.

Spent the night in a house or hut occupied by Charles Roe, an American, who was absent with his family from home. The wife of this man is the daughter of Thomas McKay, who was the son of the unfortunate man of the same name, who perished on the Tonquin, when she was blown up on the north-west coast. Her mother is a woman of the Nez Perce tribe. She is the sister of the three McKay boys who accompanied the Rev. Jason Lee from Oregon to the United States, in 1838. Her father has recently discarded the old Nez Perce woman, her mother, to whom he was never formally married, except after the Indian custom, and taken to himself a young half-breed, who becomes his lawful wife under the sanction of a Roman Catholic priest.

Rested as well as we could during the night on a naked plank, rose early in the morning, the rain pouring down with increasing violence. But our commission was one of urgency, so, turning horses loose upon the prairie, and borrowing a canoe, we struck out into the dashing current of the Wallamette. Already the banks of the river were full, and the rapidly increasing flood was rolling onward with fearful fury towards the Pacific, bearing upon its bosom immense quantities of floodwood, ever and anon undermining a large tree upon the shore, which would fall with a tremendous crash into the roaring flood; but keeping our cockle-shell craft in the centre of the stream, and carefully avoiding coming in contact with the numerous logs floating upon its surface, we proceeded down the distance of ten miles in about one hour. Fearing to attempt to run the dangerous rapids of Rock Island, we rowed our canoe into a little eddy some distance above, and fastened it to some trees. We then took our baggage on our backs, and proceeded on foot towards the falls, distant eight miles. A number of streams crossed our path, but passing some on logs, and wading through others, we arrived there at three o'clock, P. M.

Sunday, 13th. I preached to about twenty Americans of different ages, from the invitation of Christ to those who labor and are heavy laden, and rejoiced in the consideration that there is rest in Christ.

Monday, 14th. Attended to the duties imposed upon me in relation to Mr. Rogers' estate, in connexion with W. H. Gray and Robert Shortess. Found the estate to be worth fifteen hundred dollars, and the liabilities to amount to seven hundred. Ascertained that the heirs of Mr. Rogers reside in Utica, State of New York.

Tuesday, 15th. Having accomplished our business, we left the falls at two, P. M., and returned to our canoe, where we encamped for the night. The river had continued to rise until it was higher than it had been known for thirty years, and we knew it would be almost impossible to ascend with our canoe, yet there was no alternative. The banks were overflown, and we were obliged to pull ourselves up the river by the bushes and trees on the shore, as, the moment our canoe was outside the the bushes, in spite of the combined strength of six men with their paddles, she would run astern. Toiling for seven hours, without cessation, except to take two raccoons out of a hollow tree, where they had been driven by the flood, we found that we had ascended three miles only, and being above the mouth of Pudding river, we concluded to "*cache*" our canoe in the bushes, and try the rest of the way on foot.

We found ourselves in a dense forest, but striking a bee line towards the south-east, after traveling some miles we struck the trail leading from the settlement to the falls, and at dark arrived at the house of a Frenchman near the Butte, and about three miles below Champoeg.

Having no provision, I procured of the Frenchman a supper of fried venison, and a cup of tea, for which, with the privilege of furnishing a supper for ten thousand fleas, he charged me one dollar. It was the first bill of the kind I paid in Oregon, the people generally being quite hospitable.

Next morning procceeded to Champoeg and found our

trusty horses not far from where we turned them loose. The water had risen to an amazing height; farms were swept of their fences, and farmers suffered heavy losses in grain, the water rising several feet deep in some of their barns. Thomas McKay had recently built a large grist mill, and an old gentlemen by the name of Canning was tending the mill. In the morning when he awoke, as he slept in the mill, in the second story, the mill was standing in the centre of a large lake. Some persons at a distance, supposing that Canning must be in a perilous condition, procured a canoe, and sailing high over fields, fences, logs, &c., soon arrived at the mill, and running their canoe into the window of the second story, found Canning perched upon a high box, in one corner of the mill, awaiting some one to rescue him from his danger. No essential damage was done the mill, but several hundred bushels of wheat were lost. The flood coming so suddenly upon the valley, the herds on the bottom lands had not time to make their escape. Horses, cattle, hogs, &c., were swept away and drowned.

This was a high flood, but from the appearance of the country, I am persuaded that it is subject to still greater inundations.

Recovering our horses, we left Champoeg in the afternoon, and arrived at our homes the following evening, relieving our families from the painful anxiety into which they had been thrown for our safety in consequence of our exposure to the flood.

CHAPTER IX.

Panic — Indian troubles — Tour to the Interior — Causes — Precautions — Excitement increases — Mr. Brewer's letter — The Sub-Agent — Expedition resolved upon — Opposed by Dr. McLaughlin — Departure — A squall — Ascent of the Columbia — Mount Hood — Romantic scenery — Sabbath encampment — Reflections — Remarkable rocks — Cascades — How formed — Indian tradition confirmed — La Dallas — Canasissa — Negotiation — De Shutes — John Day — Sabbath Reflections — Arrival at Dr. Whitman's — Interview with the Kayuse chiefs — Excursion — Adventure of Mr. Perkins — Party proceeds — Snake river — Red wolf — Laperai — Accident — Grotesque exhibition — Temperance training — Rev. Mr. and Mrs. Spaulding — Return to Dr. Whitman's — Interesting negotiation — Closing feast — Homeward — Story of the Walla-Walla chief — Peter Ogden — Arrival home.

APRIL 14. This settlement has been thrown into a panic by intelligence which has just been received from the upper country, concerning the hostile intentions of the Kayuse, Nez Perce, and Walla-Walla Indians. It appears that they have again threatened the destruction of the whites. Some time in October last, Indian report said that these tribes were coming down to kill off the Boston people, meaning those from the United States. This intelligence produced considerable excitement at the time, and induced the sub-agent of Indian Affairs to go directly to the upper country and ascertain the truth of the report, and if possible settle all matters of difficulty. On arriving among the Indians, he ascertained that the report was not without foundation; but entered into such arrangements with them as appeared to give satisfaction. Thomas McKay contributed much to allay the excitement among them, and in connexion with the sub-agent, induced the Nez Perces to adopt a code of laws, and appoint a head chief and inferior chiefs, sufficient to carry the laws into execution. It had been the policy of the Hudson's Bay Company to destroy the chieftainship, cut the different tribes into smaller clans, and divide their interests as far as posssible so as to weaken them, and render them incapable of injuring the whites, by preventing them from acting in concert. But the sub-agent adopted a different policy. The individual appointed to the high chieftainship over the Nez Perces, was one Ellis, as he was called by the English, who, having spent several years in the settlement on the Red river, east of the mountains, had, with a smattering of the English language, acquired a high sense of his own importance; and consequently, after he was appointed chief, pursued a very haughty and overbearing course. The fulfillment of the laws which the agent recommended for their adoption, was required by Ellis with the utmost rigor. Individuals were severely punished for crimes which, from time immemorial, had been committed by the people with impunity. This occasioned suspicions in the minds of the Indians generally, that the whites designed the ultimate subjugation of their tribes. They saw in the laws they had adopted, a deep-laid scheme of the whites to destroy them, and take possession of their country. The arrival of a large party of emigrants about this time, and the sudden departure of Dr. Whitman to the United States, with the avowed intention of bringing back with him as many as he could enlist for Oregon, served to hasten them to the above conclusion. That a great excitement existed among the Indians in the interior, and that they designed to make war upon the settlement, was only known to the whites through the medium of vague report, until a letter was received from H. K. W. Perkins, at the Dalls, in which he informed us that the Wascopam and Walla-Walla Indians had communicated to him in substance the following information: that the Indians are very much exasperated against the whites in consequence of so many of the latter coming into the country, to destroy their game, and take away their lands; that the Nez Perces dispatched one of their chiefs last winter on snow shoes, to visit the Indians in the buffalo country east of Fort Hall, for the purpose of exciting them to cut off the party that it is expected Dr. Whitman will bring back with him to settle the Nez Perce country; that the Indians are endeavoring to form a general coalition for the purpose of destroying all the Boston people : that it is not good to kill a part of them, and leave the rest, but that *every one* of them must be destroyed. This information produced a great excitement throughout the community, and almost every man had a plan of his own by which to avert the impending storm. In the estimation of some, the Indians were to be upon us immediately, and it was unsafe to retire at night, for fear the settlement would be attacked before morning. The plan of the agent was to induce men to pledge themselves, under the forfeiture of one hundred dollars in case of delinquency, to keep constantly on hand, and ready for use, either a good musket or a rifle, and one hundred charges of ammunition, and to hold themselves in readiness to go at the call of the agent to any part of the country, not to exceed two days travel, for the purpose of defending the settlement, and repelling any savage invaders. This plan pleased some of the people, and they put down their names; but many were much dissatisfied with it, and as we had no authority, no law, no order, for the time being, in the country, it was impossible to tell what would be the result, if the Indians should attempt to carry their threats into execution.

April 14th. Information was brought to the settlement from the Klackamas tribe of Indians, who live three miles below the falls of the Wallamette, which served to increase the excitement occasioned by the reports from the interior. It appears that an Indian of the Molala tribe, connected with the Klackamas Indians by marriage, stole a horse from a man by the name of Anderson, and when asked by the latter if he had stolen his horse and rode him off, answered, "Yes, I stole your horse, and when I want another one I shall steal him also." To this Anderson replied, "If you stole my horse you must pay me for him." "Yes," said the Indian, "I will pay you for him, take that horse," pointing to a very poor horse which stood near by, with one eye out, and a very sore back. Anderson replied, "That is a very poor horse and mine was a very good one; I shall not take him, and if you don't bring him back I will report you to Dr. White." "I am not afraid of Dr. White," said the Indian, "let him come if he wants to, and bring the Boston people with him; he will find me prepared for him."

Anderson not being able to effect a settlement with the Indian, immediately reported him to the agent, whereupon the latter wrote to a man at the falls by the name of Campbell, to take a sufficient number of men armed with muskets, and go very early in the morning to the Indian camp, and take the horse-thief a prisoner, and bring him up to the falls. Accordingly, Campbell procured five men, and went to the camp as commanded, but found thirty or forty Indians painted in the most hideous manner, and armed with muskets, bows and arrows, tomahawks, and scalping knives, and determined at all events to protect the horse-thief, and drive back those that should come to take him. Campbell rushed on to take the rogue, but met with such resistance from superiority of numbers, and finding that the enterprise, if urged forward, would terminate in bloodshed, if not in the loss of all their lives, sounded a retreat, and extricating himself from the Indians, returned to the falls. He communicated the results of his attempt to Dr. White, and the Doctor started off immediately in company with G. W. Le Breton, resolved to capture the thief and bring the tribe to terms.

April 17th. The excitement still continued, former reports having been confirmed, and all were engaged in repairing guns, and securing ammunition. A report was in circulation that Dr. McLaughlin refused to grant supplies for any consideration to all those persons who subscribed the memorial praying the Congress of the United States to extend jurisdiction over Oregon. If this be so, the American population, as nearly all signed the memorial, will not be able to obtain ammunition, however necessary it may be, as there is none in the country except what may be found within the stockades of Vancouver. I think, however, that the report is false Report says, furthermore, that the Klikitat Indians are collecting together back of the Tuality plains, but for what purpose is not known. The people on the plains, consisting of about thirty families, are quite alarmed. There is also a move among the Calapooahs. Shoefon, one of the principal men of the tribe, left this place a few days ago, and crossed the Wallamette river, declaring that he would never return until he came with a band of men to drive off the Boston people. He was very much offended because some of his people were seized and flogged, through the influence of Dr. White, for having stolen horses from some of the missionaries, and flour from the mission mill. His influence is not very extensive among the Indians or we might have much to fear. The colony is indeed in a most defenceless condition; two hundred Indians, divided into four bands, might destroy the entire settlement in one night.

In the evening of the 17th, Dr. White arrived at my house bringing intelligence from the falls. He and Mr. Le Breton attempted to go to the falls on horseback, but in trying to ford Haunchauke river, they found the water so deep that they were obliged to swim, and the Doctor turned his horse's head, and came out the side he went in; but Le Breton, being the better mounted of the two, succeeded in gaining the opposite shore; and having the Doctor's letters in his possession, continued on to the falls. The Doctor returned to the settlement. Le Breton returned the following day, and brought information from the five men who attempted to take the Indian who had stolen Anderson's horse, that soon after their retreat the Indians became alarmed and broke up in great haste; but before they left, they informed Anderson that the horse they had stolen from him was worn out and good for nothing, and tying a good horse to a tree near Anderson's house, they told him that he must take that and be satisfied. They then hurried away, saying that they should not be seen in that region again. It was ascertained that the Klackamas Indians had nothing to do with the stolen horse; that it was a band of the Molalas, the very same rascals that stole a horse from me two years before, and after having him in their possession several weeks, brought him down within a few miles of my house, where they encamped, and where I went with one man and took him from the midst of more than fifty grim looking savages.

On the 20th of April, a letter was received in the settlement, written by H. B. Brewer, at the Dalls, which brings the latest intelligence from the infected region. This letter states that the Indians in the interior talk much of war, and Mr. Brewer urges Dr. White to come up without delay, and endeavor to allay the excitement. He does not inform us that the Indians design any evil toward the whites, but says that the war is to be between themselves, but that the Boston people have much to fear. As the Doctor, in his visit to the interior last October, left an appointment to meet the Walla-Walla Indians and the Kayuses, in their own country, on the tenth of May, and believing that a great share of the excitement originated in a misunderstanding of the Indians, he came to the conclusion at all hazards to go among them. At the solicitation of the agent, I determined to accompany him on the expedition.

The great complaint of the Indians was that the Boston people designed to take away their lands, and reduce them to slavery. This they had inferred from what Dr. White had told them in his previous visit; and this misunderstanding of the Indians had not only produced a great excitement among them, but had occasioned considerable trouble betwixt them and the missionaries and other whites in the upper country, as well as influencing them to threaten the destruction of all the American people. Individuals had come down from fort Walla-Walla to Vancouver, bringing information of the excited state of things among the Indians, and giving out that it would be extremely dangerous for Dr. White to go up to meet his engagements. Their opinion was, that in all probability he and the party which he might think proper to take with him, would be cut off. But it was the opinion of many judicious persons in the settlement, that the welfare of the Indians, and the peace and security of the whites, demanded that some persons qualified to negotiate with the Indians, should proceed immediately to the scene of disaffection, and if possible remove the cause of the excitement by correcting the error under which the Indians labored. Accordingly, **Dr.** White engaged twelve men besides myself, mostly French Canadians who had had much experience with Indians, to go with him; but a few days before the time fixed upon to start had arrived, they all sent him word that they had decided not to go. They were doubtless induced to pursue this course through the influence of Dr. Mc. Laughlin, and the Catholic priests.

When the day arrived for starting, we found ourselves abandoned by every person who had engaged to go, except Mr. G. W. Le Breton, an American, one Indian boy, and one Kanaka. With the two latter the Doctor and myself left the Wallamette settlement on the twenty-fifth of April, 1843, and proceeded on horseback to the Butte, where we found Le Breton in waiting for us. He had provided a canoe and a few pieces of pork and beef for our use on the vogage.

Here we met a letter from Dr. John Mc Laughlin, at Vancouver, discouraging us from our undertaking in view of the difficulties and dangers attending such an expedition; but we had counted the cost, and were not to be diverted from our purpose, though dangers stared us in the face. We supposed that if the Indians entertained any hostile intentions against the whites in general, there could be no better way to defeat their purposes than to go among them; convince them that they had no grounds of fear; and that the whites, instead of designing to bring them into subjection, were desirous of doing them good. Prevented by one thing and another from setting sail, on the night of the twenty-seventh we slept on a bank of sand at the Butte, and next day proceeded in our little canoe down to the Wallametie falls, where we continued until the twenty-ninth. Here we received another package from Dr. Mc Laughlin, giving us information that Rev. Mr. De Merce, a Catholic priest, had just come down from the upper country, bringing intelligence that the Indians are only incensed against the Boston people; that they have nothing against the French and King George people; they are not mad at them, but are determined that the Boston people shall not have their lands, and take away their liberties. On receiving this intelligence from Mr. De Merce, Dr. Mc Laughlin advised the Frenchman who had engaged to go with Dr. White, to have nothing to do with the quarrel, to remain quiet at home, and let the Americans take care of themselves. He alse expressed, in his letter, the opinion that all the people should remain quiet, and in all probability the excitement among the Indians would soon subside.

Not seeing sufficient reason to change our course, on the morning of the 28th, we left our hospitable friends at the Falls, and continued our course down the Wallamette towards Vancouver. At noon we had sailed twenty miles, and stopped for dinner within five miles of the mouth of the Wallamette, on a low piece of ground, overgrown with luxuriant grass, but which is always overflown at the rise of the Columbia, which is about the first of June. "Weighed anchor" after dinner, and at four o'clock, P. M., arrived at Vancouver. Called on Dr. Mc Laughlin for goods, provisions, powder, balls, &c., for our accommodation on our voyage up the Columbia, and, though he was greatly surprised that, under the circumstances, we should think of going among those excited Indians, yet he ordered his clerks to let us have whatever we wanted. However, we found it rather squally at the fort, not so much on account of our going among the Indians of the interior, as in consequence of a certain memorial having been sent to the United States' Congress, implicating the conduct of Dr. Mc Laughlin and the Hudson's Bay Company, and bearing the signatures of seventy Americans. I inquired of the Doctor if he had refused to grant supplies to those Americans who had signed that document; he replied that he had not, but that the authors of the memorial need expect no more favors from him. Not being one of the authors, but merely a signer of the petition, I did not come under the ban of the company; consequently I obtained my outfit for the expedition, though at first there were strong indications that I would be refused.

We remained at the fort over night and a part of the next day, and after a close conversation with the gentleman in command, were treated with great courtesy.

At two o'clock, P. M., of Saturday 29th, left, and continued our voyage up the Columbia. As we proceeded from the fort, mount Hood appeared directly before us. Though this mountain is twenty-five miles from the river, and more than forty from Vancouver, yet it appeared to be not more than five or six miles distant. There are few things, perhaps, in the world, that combine more grandeur and sublimity in their appearance than this stupendous glacier viewed from the surface of the Columbia river. The Alleghany and Katskill mountains are but mounds when compared with this astonishing pile of Basalt, whose head is lifted to the amazing hight of sixteen thousand feet, and whitened with perpetual snow. We feasted our eyes upon this sublime spectacle until the sun had bidden us good night, and the shades of evening had thrown a dark mantle around the enchanting scenery; then mooring our canoe in a little eddy, we made our encampment for the Sabbath on a small island about ten miles above Vancouver, which is evidently laid under contribution by the Columbia every succeeding June, but which, at this time, was fifteen feet higher than the waters of the river. A canoe containing seven Indians, left the fort with us, and as we were short of help, one of the Indians engaged, for the consideration of a blanket and one shirt, to take the stern of our canoe, and assist us up to the Dalls. These Indians belonged to the Wascopam tribe, and most of them profess to have been converted to christianity through the labors of Rev. Daniel Lee, and Rev. H. K. W. Perkins. We all encamped in the same place, and when the time for evening prayers arrived, the Indians all joined us with apparent sincerity and devotion, after which we committed ourselves to sleep on our blanket beds upon the ground.

TOUR TO THE INTERIOR. 151

After a comfortable night's rest, we arose and enjoyed our humble repast, consisting of ham, bread, butter and tea. We prepared to spend the sacred day as profitably as we could, though in the lonely solitudes of a dense forest of Cottonwood, on the banks of the Columbia. We engaged in a season of reading the scriptures, singing, and prayer, after which I endeavored to give our Neophytes a lesson concerning the things which belong to their peace. This done, I strolled along the banks of the river about one-fourth of a mile, for the purpose of being alone, and coming to a wild appletree which leaned its trunk over the smooth surface of the waters, I seated myself upon it, and a train of reflections, varying in their influence upon my feelings as they differed in character, passed through my mind.

I thought of beloved parents from whom I had not heard for years; of the tears they shed when last I saw them, and received the parting benediction, and of the anxiety they must still feel, if alive, for their wandering son. I thought of all my former associates, of brothers and sisters, and early school mates, and christian friends, with whom I had taken sweet counsel, and walked to the house of God, and who, if they had not forgotten me, would ask, "Where is he? and what is his employment?" I thought of everything of interest in my native land; of bustling cities, with wheels rattling and hoofs clattering over their pavements; of smiling villages and towns, with their splendid turnpikes and McAdamized roads; of railroad cars and steamboats; of temples erected to the God of heaven; the toll of chiming bells as they informed the waiting thousands that the time of worship had arrived; of crowded assemblies listening to the messengers of Jesus; and of saints rejoicing, and altars thronged with mourning penitents. Continuing these reflections until my mind experienced a kind of abstraction from the objects surrounding me, I fancied myself really amidst the scenes, the contemplation of which had produced this pleasing illusion, and starting up I found myself surrounded with the stillness of death, save the murmuring of the turbid waters of the Columbia that rolled beneath where I sat. Contrasting the land which had passed before my mental vision with that in which I felt myself a voluntary exile, I exclaimed, how changed the scene! This, thought I, is truly a land of darkness. Amidst the solitudes of these forests and plains the gospel is never heard except perchance the missionary of the cross may be passing through the land, and then to but here and there a small group of wretched Indians, who are alternately shivering with ague, and burning with fever, upon the brink of death. I was led to inquire, when shall this state of things give way to civilization and christianity? when shall "the sound of the church-going bell" be heard among these mountains and over these plains? When shall the banks of this noble river be studded with cities and villages, with the temples of Jehovah, whose steeples blazing in the sunlight, shall tell the traveler that God is worshiped here? And I fancied this response came back to my inquiries: not until the present race shall have gone to the graves of their fathers, and others shall rise to take their place.

Returning to the camp we sat down upon the ground to a dinner which the Doctor's Kanaka, John, and my Indian boy, Sampson, had prepared for us. Towards evening the Doctor and myself walked leisurly into the thickest of the forest, towards the centre of the Island, and seating ourselves upon a log, talked of by-gone days, raised a song of praise to the Redeemer, and upon our knees offered up a tribute of thanksgiving for the past, and invoked the Divine blessing on our future course.

Monday, May 1st. At sunrise proceeded on our voyage, and were much delighted with the magnificent scenery on the shores of the great Columbia. At eight o'clock passed the Prairie Du ———, which lies on the north side of the river. This is a low, wet prairie, with but little land which will admit of cultivation, but well adapted to grazing purposes. As we proceeded, the land next to the river became more uneven, the shores more rocky and abrupt, and at length we found ourselves crawling along at the base of a frowning precipice of rocks, rising more than three hundred feet perpendicular over our heads. A little farther on and huge masses of Basalt appeared thrown together in the wildest confusion, and these would be succeeded by another frightful precipice, causing one involuntarily to cringe while looking upward towards its dizzy height. From the top, as if to add beauty to terror, came leaping down a limpid brook, which lost itself in spray, long before it reached the bottom ; and then again large fir-trees, stuck upon the top of the rock three or four hundred feet directly over our heads, and leaning their waving tops far over the rolling waters, would seem to look down upon us with the most threatening aspect. Conical formations of rocks from thirty to one hundred feet high appeared, peering up out of the water, resembling in form the huge hay-stacks of a Connecticut farmer. As we passed along at the base of these grand abutments of nature, swarms of swallows far above our heads, were delightfully playing around the holes and crevices of the precipice, in which they had built their nests.

At twelve o'clock, we passed a low point of land which has received the name of Cape Horn, in consequence of the difficulty of the navigation of this part of the river arising from the strength of wind which generally prevails here. Often, when it is safe running on all other parts of the river, canoes, on arriving here, are obliged to lie by, sometimes for days, before they can possibly pass this point. Indeed, the Cape Horn of the Columbia is more difficult to double with the pigmy craft which is used on this river, than the stormy cape bearing the same name at the southern extremity of Terra del Fuego.

A few miles above Cape Horn, we came to a huge rock, which is justly considered a great curiosity. The mountains at this place retire about one half mile from the river, and this rock is situated midway between the river and the mountain. In form it is nearly round ; is about twenty-five rods in diameter at its base, and rises perpendicularly on all sides to the height of at least one hundred and fifty feet. It then assumes a conical form, and gradually diminishes in size till it rises some two hundred feet more, and then presents to the heavens a broken surface of several rods in diameter, beautifully ornamented with a luxuriant growth of variegated evergreens. Passing this stupendous monument reared by nature's hands in mockery of the works of art, we arrived at the cascades at sundown, and camped for the night, after having run a hair-breadth risk of losing our canoe and all our baggage, at one of the violent rapids below the cascades. Our men, consisting of two Indians and one Kanaka, were cordelling our canoe up the rapid; and coming round a point of rocks, it took a sheer out into the strongest part of the current, and began directly to fill with water. My Indian boy, Sampson, was the only one that had hold of the rope, and such was the strength of the current against the canoe, that he could not hold on to the rope with his hands ; and being about to be pulled from the rocks into the river, he grasped the rope between his teeth, and falling down upon the rocks, held fast to them with his hands, and in that manner succeeded in bringing the canoe back to the shore, with no other damage being done, than the wetting of our provisions and bedding.

When we retired to rest, wrapped in our wet blankets, we were reminded of a little incident in the experience of Mr. Townsend, a naturalist, who traveled down this river several years before. It had rained severely all day, and every article he had, bedding, wardrobe, provisions and all, were thoroughly drenched. He rolled himself in his wet blankets and lay down to sleep, thinking of the last words of his dying grandmother, "Be careful and never sleep in damp sheets."

Tuesday, 2d. From the effects of the wind upon the the water and the sand, filling the air with the latter as snow in a February storm in Western New York, and raising the former into high waves, we were obliged to lie quiet in our camp. Occasionally, however, we ventured out to the shore of the Columbia, contemplating her majesty, as she pours her exhaustless flood down the ledge of rocks which forms the beautiful cascades. The river here falls in continued rapids for three miles, not less than fifty feet. That portion of the rapids properly called the cascades, presents an appearance of grandeur and sublimity not inferior to that of the rapids of the Niagara river, above the great cataract. At this place the Columbia rushes through the cascade range of mountains, and the channel through which it pours its mighty torrent, appears not more than thirty rods wide, while each shore presents indubitable evidence that, by a vast accumulation of water above, these mountain barriers were torn assunder, and thus this mighty river found its way to the Pacific ocean. The Indians here have a tradition that, a long time ago, the mountain was joined together over the river, and that the river performed a subterraneous passage for some distance, with a slow current, and that their people used to pass up and down with their canoes without difficulty; but all at once the foundations of this mighty arch crumbled beneath their ponderous weight, and the whole mass came tumbling into the river, filling up the channel and quite damming up the stream, and thus were formed the beautiful cascades. The probability is that this tradition is true only in part. Doubtless the time was when there were no cascades here, and they were probably formed by the mountain's sliding into the river in tremendous avalanches, and thus filling up the channel. The land on each side of the river at this place is rough and sterile, and the scenery wild beyond description. The cascades are fifty miles above Vancouver, and one hundred and forty-five from the mouth of the Columbia.

At three, P. M., the wind lulling, we proceeded up ten miles and camped for the night, which was exceedingly windy, with some rain. Found the river wide above the cascades, with little current, and, from appearances, were convinced that the Indian tradition concerning the falling in of the mountain, is not without foundation. The original channel appears to have been very narrow, compared with the present width of the river. Forests which were situated on its former banks, have been overflown, and a vast number of stumps and trees which have not yet wasted away, stand in the present bed of the stream.

Wednesday, 3d. Continued our voyage, but at noon were obliged to lay by in consequence of the rise of the wind.

Anxious to make headway, we continued out after the wind had increased to a strong gale. We passed a number of dangerous points, where the shore was precipitous and "iron bound;" but the wind being directly astern, and having a blanket rigged for a sail, we darted past them like an arrow, though the waves ran so high that they threatened every moment to engulph us. In passing the last point before we came to shore, we run a very great hazard of losing our canoe and baggage, if not our lives. A canoe much larger than ours, with five Indians, had just passed the point, and barely escaped. Running their canoe into a little bay just above, they hurried back along the shore, and arrived at the point just as we did, expecting to see our little canoe driven against the shelving rocks, by the violence of the winds and waves, and dashed to pieces. But with amazing swiftness, and in fearful proximity, we shot by the dangerous point, realizing no other damage than a wetting, and a fright. As for myself, when we were tossed in our feather-like craft over these Atlantic waves, and driven with such violence so near the frowning rocks that I could touch them with my hand as we were shooting by, and my heart beating so violently that it sounded like the grunting of a black grouse in the top of a fir-tree, I thought I had much rather be on *terra firma*; so, mooring our canoe in a little cove, we waited for the wind to fall. Resuming our voyage towards evening, we ran a few miles, and camped for the night.

Thursday, 4th. Arrived at the Dalls, and found our friends well and prospering. Here reside Rev. Daniel Lee, one of the pioneer missionaries to Oregon, Rev. H. K. W. Perkins, and Mr. H. B. Brewer. They are laboring to establish a permanent mission at this place for the benefit of the Indians, but with doubtful success.

The country around is much better than I expected to find. In the vicinity of the mission the land is exceedingly fertile, and the scenery is most delightful.

Soon after we arrived, about twenty Indians came to

the house of Mr. Brewer, where we stopped, to have a talk with Dr. White. When he was up the winter before, he prevailed on these Indians to organize themselves into a kind of government. One high chief, and three subordinates were elected; laws were enacted, and the penalties annexed were whippings more or less severe, according to the nature of the crime. The chiefs had found much difficulty in enforcing the laws. In punishing delinquents some of the Indians resisting, even to the point of the knife.

The chiefs, who were appointed through the influence of Dr. White, were desirous that these regulations should continue, evidently because they placed the people under their absolute control, and gave them the power to regulate all their intercourse with the whites, and with the other Indian tribes. But the other influential men who were not in office, desired to know of Dr. White, of what benefit this whipping system was going to be to them. They said they were willing it should continue, provided they were to receive blankets, shirts and pants, as a reward for being whipped. They had been whipped a good many times, and had got nothing for it, and it had done them no good. If this state of things was to continue, it was all (*cultus*) good for nothing, and they would throw it all away. In reply they were told by the Doctor that we could not be detained to settle any of their difficulties now; that we were going farther into the interior, and were in a very great hurry; and that when we returned he would endeavor to make all straight. But he wished them to understand that they need not expect pay for being flogged, when they deserved it. They laughed heartily at the idea, and dispersed, giving us an opportunity to make arrangements for the continuance of our journey.

We left our canoe at the Dalls in the care of an Indian, and engaged eight horses of an old Indian, by the name of Canasissa, who was to bring them to us the following morning.

Friday 5th. Canasissa arrived early in the morning, and coming to us with a very long face, inquired what we were going to give him to accompany us, as he wished to see that the horses were well used. The Doctor replied, "You are a very old man; the journey is long, and the Indians are very *silex*, (angry); you may get into difficulty; you had better stay at home." Still Canasissa insisted on going, but was told that if he went he must go for nothing. He then said that he had brought but seven horses, and thought that we did not give only enough to pay for the seven, but he should have brought the eighth if he could have found it. He was told that we must have the eighth. "Yes," said Canasissa, "You may have the eighth, if you will give me one blanket more in addition to what you were to give me." But we peremptorily refused to take any without the whole, according to agreement; and went about negotiating with another Indian to supply us with horses. When Canasissa saw that we were about to succeed with the other one, he altered his tone, and came up to us saying that it was very good for us not to pay another blanket; that he would bring the other horse, and would go with us himself. Taking him at his offer, we made arrangements also with Rev. H. K. W. Perkins to accompany us.

Horses ready, saddles all on, and bridles, consisting of hide-rope, tied to the horse's lower jaw, with our baggage, provisions, &c., packed on the backs of two of the horses, we mounted, and left the mission at eleven o'clock. Four miles brought us to the great Dalls, and here Canasissa brought us the eighth horse, and acknowledged that the object he had in view in not bringing it to us in the first place, was to extort from us an additional blanket, a trick quite characteristic of these Indians, who seem instinctively to embrace every opportunity that presents itself, to overreach those who, in any measure, are dependent upon them. I was peculiarly struck, while we were negotiating with them, with their astonishing tact in cheating. As a matter of course, lying has much to do in their system of trade, and he is the best fellow who can tell the biggest lie, make men believe it, and practice the greatest deception.

A few years ago a great religious excitement prevailed among these Indians, and nearly the whole tribe, consisting of upwards of a thousand, professed to be converted, were baptized, and received into the christian church; but they have nearly all relapsed into their former state, with the exception that many of them still keep up the outward forms of religion. Their religion appears to be more of the head than of the heart, and though they are exceedingly vicious, yet doubtless they would be much worse than they are but for the restraining influences exerted upon them by the missionaries.

They are known by the name of the Wasco Indians, and they call their country round the Dalls, Wascopam. They claim the country extending from the cascades up to the falls of the Columbia, the distance of about fifty miles. "La Dallas," or the narrows, as the word signifies in English, are somewhat remarkable. Here the Columbia suddenly contracts into a very narrow channel, and then rushes through a mighty gorge or chasm in the rocks, with fearful violence, in its passage tumbling and boiling and roaring, and ever and anon forming the most tremendous whirlpools. Yet the Hudson's Bay Company's boats are frequently made to run these frightful narrows, and it is not uncommon for them to pay for their rashness with the loss of a boat, and a sacrifice of a number of their men.

Just below the Dalls, where the current continues to be strong, is a little island, used by the Indians as a place of deposit for the dead. There is something peculiar in their manner of sepulture. The dead are taken to a small house, built on this island for the purpose, and laid in a pile around the inside of the house, the head next to the wall, and the feet towards the center of the building. Here hundreds have been deposited, forming a pile several feet high.

The country around the Dalls is valuable, in consequence of its adaptation to grazing and farming purposes, and the extensive salmon fishery which might here be established. These Indians, with most of the tribes of Oregon, are destined to utter extinction, and the time is not far distant when their country will be occupied by the descendants of the Pilgrims.

At two o'clock, we left the Dalls, and seven miles brought us to the shoots, or falls of the Columbia, which at this stage of the water, are about ten feet perpendicular, but in June, when the river is high, the water sets back from the Dalls so that there are no falls to be seen.

Arrived at the river "De Shoots" at five, P. M., ten miles above the Dalls, and three above the falls of the Columbia. This river rises among the mountains which divide the Wallamette and the Walla-Walla countries, called the Cascade Range, and taking a north-easterly course and watering a fertile valley, it forms a number of beautiful cataracts and cascades. It falls into the Columbia one hundred and ninety miles from its mouth. Probably it derives its name from the fact that it possesses numerous falls, and finally rushes down a ledge of rocks into the Columbia with great violence. We found it very difficult to cross; but with the help of a few Walla-Walla Indians whom we found here, and a couple of scoop-shovel canoes, we succeeded in crossing without accident, though, to the inexperienced, it would have been considered an enterprise of great peril. But the crossing was not so difficult as it was to satisfy the Indians who assisted us. They wanted all we had, even the clothes on our backs; but we paid them what we pleased, and repacking our animals, continued on five miles farther, camping for the night beside a small rivulet and under the lee of a sanddrift thirty feet high. Sometimes, in the valley of the Columbia, the wind is so strong that the sand is driven about like snow, the air is full of it, and woe be to the eyes that are compelled to meet the beating storm.

May 6th. Journeyed on, and at eleven, A. M., came to a stream of water which has received the name of John Day's river. It is about twenty rods wide at its mouth, too deep to ford, but easily crossed by swimming, in consequence of its having but little current. It derived its cognomen from a remarkable circumstance in the history of the gentleman whose name it bears.

John Day was a native of Kentucky, and though a man of some fortune, and considerable talents, and might have lived in affluence and ease in his native country, yet, from choice, he abandoned all the endearments of civilized life, and became a rambler in the savage wilds of the Rocky mountains and Oregon. When Wilson Price Hunt performed his astonishing journey from Missouri to the mouth of the Columbia river, John Day was one of his most faithful and persevering companions, and suffered with him the most surprising hardships. Excelling in the qualifications of a hunter, and faithful to the trusts committed to him, responsibilities were thrown upon him during that perilous journey which proved more than he was able to bear. At Astoria he was appointed to accompany Robert Stewart back to Missouri, on business of importance, but had not proceeded far up the Columbia before he became restless and uneasy, and finally gave evident signs of insanity. On the evening of the second of July, 1813, he attempted to destroy himself, but being disarmed, he sank into quiet and professed remorse. He pretended to sleep, but just before daylight he sprang up, siezed a pair of loaded pistols, and endeavored to blow out his own brains, but he held the pistols too high, and the balls passed over his head. He was then secured so that he could not harm himself, and sent back to Astoria. This event happened in the vicinity of this river. He was taken back from this point in hopes that he might recover, but his constitution was entirely broken; he lingered for a number of months, and died, evidently from the effects of the hardships he had endured.

Dined on the bank of this river, and conversed on the perilous adventures of the mountaineers; then resumed our wearisome journey, but found little to interest us, or to break the monotony of the scenery along the Columbia. In the afternoon, however, we were entertained with the appearance of a flock of sandhill cranes, numbering, at least, two thousand, which passed directly over our heads, on their passage to the mouth. Two large rattlesnakes placed themselves in our path; we examined them for a moment, and then "bruised their heads." A few small trees also, the like of which I have never seen in any country, were objects of curiosity We passed a few score of Indians during the day, but they manifested no signs of hostility, and at night encamped for the Sabbath about midway between the Dalls and fort Walla-Walla.

Sabbath, May 7th, was an exceedingly windy day, and we found it much more pleasant to continue in camp, than it would have been to travel. Indeed, I have seldom looked for the day of rest more anxiously than I did the last part of the week past. Though we made only about one hundred and fifty miles during the week, yet, from the constant labor resulting from our mode of traveling, we had become exceedingly fatigued, and the day in which we are to perform no servile work, was most thankfully welcomed. Though we were doomed to spend it far from the abodes of civilized man, yet it brought with it the most delightful associations. It reminded me not only of the completion of the work of creation, when the morning stars sang together, and all the sons of God shouted for joy, but my mind was carried back to him, who, "though he was rich, yet for our sakes became poor, that we through his poverty might be made rich." I saw him in my contemplations amidst all the scenes of labor and suffering through which he was called to pass. The garden of Gethsemene, the judgment hall, the bloody summit of Calvary, and the crimsoned cross, passed in review before me. I heard the Saviour of men, while his blood was pouring forth as from a high and lofty altar to satisfy the demands of offended justice, when he looked around upon his murderers and cried out, "It is finished." It was not fancy; faith brought the Saviour near, and looked upon him when he bowed his head upon his breast and gave up the ghost. From the summit of the blood-stained mountains, I followed him to the sepulchre, and here I saw my Saviour under the dominion of the grave, a captive to the king of terrors. But the third morning drew near, and the sun that sat in blood, arose in glory. The crucified Redeemer, triumphant over death, and leading captivity captive, received gifts for men.

> "He rises who mankind has bought,
> With sweat and blood extreme,
> 'Twas great to speak a world from nought,
> 'Twas greater to redeem."

Monday, 8th. Arose invigorated in body and mind, and invoking the Divine blessing upon us in our future trials, packed our animals and wound our way along up the numerous turns of the Columbia. The trail runs in the deep valley of the river along the shore; this makes the route quite uninteresting. The prospect is entirely broken off by the tremendous walls of Basalt, which tower from four to seven hundred feet on both sides of the river. When this wall approached the river so as not to admit of the trail passing between it and the water, we were obliged to climb this stupendous ledge, traveling for awhile upon its top, then clambering down among the rocks till we regained the lower valley. While doing this we sometimes take alarm from the fearful crash of a detached mass of Basalt as it came leaping down from the summit of the precipice. This climbing, however, gave us an opportunity of seeing what the country is a little distance from the river. Nothing can exceed the barrenness of the land. Though the face of the country for a considerable distance from the river on each side, is agreeably diversified with hills and valleys, yet, as far as the eye can reach to the right and left, it is one continued desert of sand, gravel, and rocks. It is said that farther away from the river than we could see, the land is more fertile, and the grass abundant.

Having traveled thirty-six miles over this desert region, we stopped for the night on the banks of a beautiful stream called the Utilla. Here we found fifteen or twenty of the Walla-Walla Indians, exceedingly squalid in their appearance, and living on the fish they caught in the stream. These fish are a species of the salmon, and we succeeded in getting enough for our supper and breakfast. The land on this river is more fertile, and grows better as you go up the stream.

Next morning, at the rising of the sun, we left our attendants with the pack animals, and proceeded on ahead, determined, if possible, to reach the mission station at Waialetpu, on the Walla-Walla river, the same day. Passed Fort Walla-Walla at twelve, and arrived at Dr. Whitman's at five, having traveled fifty miles since we mounted in the morning. We were received with great cordiality by Mrs. Whitman and Mr. Giger, Dr. Whitman being absent on a tour to the United States. They had heard we were coming, and were looking for us with great anxiety. We soon learned that the reports in the lower country about war, that had produced such an excitement, were not without foundation: the Kayuse Indians, among whom this mission is established, had freely communicated to Mr. Giger, whom they esteemed as their friend, all they knew concerning it.

When the Indians were first told that the Americans were designing to subjugate them, and take away their lands, the young chiefs of the Kayuse tribe were in favor of proceeding immediately to hostilities. They were for raising a large war party, and, rushing directly down to the Wallamette settlement, cut off the inhabitants at a blow. The old chiefs were of a different opinion; they suggested more cautious measures. Taking into consideration the difficulty, at that season of the year, of marching a large party the distance of three or four hundred miles through a wide range of mountains, covered with snow, they advised all the Indians to wait until they should obtain more information concerning the designs of the Americans. They also thought that it would not be wisdom in them, in any case, to commence an offensive war, but to prepare themselves for a vigorous defence against any attack. They frequently remarked to Mr. Giger, that they did not wish to go to war, but if the Americans came to take away their lands, and bring them into a state of vassalage, they would fight so long as they had a drop of blood to shed. They said they had received their information concerning the designs of the Americans from Baptiste Dorio. This individual, who is a half-breed, son of Madame Dorio, the heroine of Washington Irving's Astoria, understands the Nez Perce langauge well, and had given the Kayuses the information that had alarmed them. Mr. Giger endeavored to induce them to prepare, early in the spring, to cultivate the ground as they did the year before, but they refused to do anything, saying that Baptiste Dorio had told them that it would be of no consequence; that the whites would come in the summer, and kill them all off, and destroy their plantations.

After Dorio had told them this story, they sent a Walla-Walla chief, called Yellow Serpent, to Vancouver, to learn from Doctor McLaughlin the facts in the case. Yellow Serpent returned and told the Kayuses that Dr. McLaughlin said he had nothing to do in a war with the Indians; that he did not believe the Americans designed to attack them, and that, if the Americans did go to war with the Indians, the Hudson's Bay Company would not assist them. After they got this information from the *hias* (great) Doctor, the Indians became more calm; many of them went to cultivating the ground as formerly, and a large number of little patches had been planted and sown, before we arrived at the station.

The Kayuses were principally encamped along the base of the Blue mountains, a few miles east of Dr. Whitman's house; and after we had obtained all the information we could from Mrs. Whitman and Mr. Giger, concerning the state of things among them, we sent them word that we had come, and desired to see them. We also sent the chiefs word that we desired them to make arrangements to have all their people meet us at the mission on the following Friday, to have a talk.

The chiefs came to see us at Dr. Whitman's, and told the story of their grievances, and said that they desired to have the difficulty settled. They said it would not be convenient for the people to come together so soon as we desired, as many of them were off among the mountains, hunting elk. As they must be informed of the meeting, it would be several days before the people could get together. We ascertained, however, that this was a mere pretence. They had been informed that Ellis, the Nez Perce chief, was coming down to meet us on their ground, and this had determined them not to have any meeting until Ellis should arrive. But as we had learned that Ellis was coming with his warriors, consisting of several hundred—for what purpose we could not ascertain, some saying to make war upon the Kayuses—we came to the conclusion that the meeting of the two tribes should, if possible, be prevented.

While considering this subject, we were solicited by the chiefs to take a ride among the Indian plantations. Accordingly, a party was made out which would have made all the sacerdotal order laugh to contemplate. The captain of the party was a Kayuse chief, by the name of Feathercap: and of all the Indians I have seen he has a countenance the most savage. But, with this, there is a dignity and decision manifested in his movements, which might put many a white man to the blush. He is about five feet ten inches high; has a voice of the stentorian order, and possesses all the native characteristics of an orator.

His dress was quite fantastical, being composed of skin breeches, a striped shirt, which he wore over his breeches, and a scarlet coat, gilted off very much in the fashion of the regimentals of a British general. His head-dress was composed, first of a cotton handkerchief thrown loosely over his head, then a cap made of otter skin over the handkerchief, and on the top of the cap, fastened with savage taste, the long hair of a white horse's tail, which hung in ringlets down the backside of his neck. Thus rigged, he was prepared to guide us on our tour of pleasure. An Indian woman and her daughter joined our party, of whom mention has been made in another part of this narrative. The old woman lived many years with Thomas McKay, but he finally cast her off, and she is now the wife of an old half-breed

Iroquois, by the name of Jo-Gray. Her daughter is the wife of Charles Roe. They both live in the lower country, but were up on a visit to their relatives among the Indians. Their dresses were an imitation of the Boston fashions, but were much defiled by the smoke, dirt, and grease of wigwams. They were both astride their horses, the younger carrying her little son before her.

There were also three other Indians, without noteworthy peculiarities. Mr. Giger, who is a small man, mounted a donkey which was about the size of a Newfoundland dog, and exceedingly antic, just having recruited from a journey across the Rocky mountains. In addition to these, Mrs. Whitman, Dr. White and myself made up the party. Feathercap led us about one mile, across a low piece of fertile ground, when we arrived at the nearest plantations. We ascertained that about sixty of the Kayuses had commenced cultivating the ground. They each have fenced around a small piece of ground, from one-fourth of an acre, to three acres, and each one is entitled only to what he raises himself. They had in the ground wheat, corn, peas and potatoes. Many of the places were well fenced and well cultivated, and the crops looked flourishing. The Indians appeared highly pleased that we went out to see their farms, and told us they were very glad that they had been learned to till the ground. They have already learned that their livelihood, which previously was very precarious, by their little farms, is fully secured to them. This, they say, makes their hearts glad.

Our motley party proceeded in high glee, alternately conversing in the English, Chenook, and Walla-Walla languages, and remarking upon whatever presented itself before us. The little man on the *hias tenas* (very little) mule, was the subject of much amusement with the Indians; and in the novelty and excitement of our little excursion, the subject of war and blood was entirely forgotten. We passed pleasantly along, now crossing a beautiful plain, blooming with flowers, which sent forth their rich odors upon the breeze; now penetrating the small thickets of servill, chokecherry, thorn and rose bushes; and now fording little brooks of pure, limpid water, which came leaping down from the blue mountains, until we had traveled the distance of eight miles in a circuitous route. We then found ourselves very unexpectedly back to the point whence we started, all prepared for a consultation concerning the Indian war.

As there was a large party of the Kayuses and Walla-Walla Indians encamped on the head waters of the Utilla, about fifty miles from Dr. Whitman's, embracing some of the principal chiefs, Mr. Perkins was desired to go out, and invite them to come in so as to be at the meeting, subsequently to be held at the mission station. Not knowing the way, he procured an Indian guide, and started off with no other person to accompany him. Traveling through a beautiful country, well adapted to pastoral pursuits, towards evening he arrived at the Utilla, where he expected to find the Indians, but they had removed to another place about twenty miles farther off. Inasmuch as he had no provision, and no means of kindling a fire, and there being no signs of Indian habitations in the vicinity, he resolved to proceed to camp, though in doing so, he was obliged to cross the stream. He asked the guide where the crossing place was, and was told that it was just before him. He tried to get the Indian to go in first and see how deep the water was, but the Indian refused, saying he was afraid. Mr. Perkins then rode his horse in, but soon found the water so deep that the horse was obliged to swim. But now it was as easy to go ahead as to turn about, and urging his horse a little, he was borne through the rapid stream in safety, to the opposite shore.

His guide, frightened at the idea of passing the stream in the same manner, could not be induced to follow, and making an excuse that he did not know the way, deserted him, and went back. Luckily, however, Mr. Perkins discovered an Indian not far distant, driving some horses, and of him he learned where he should find the trail that led to the Indian camp. He pushed on at full speed, and arrived there just after dark, having rode since ten o'clock in the morning, the distance of seventy miles. Here he found three chiefs by the name of Tauitau, Yellow Serpent, and Five Crows. The last has recently professed conversion to the protestant religion, and the first has become a Catholic. Yellow Serpent is favorable to the Protestant missions, but does not give as good evidence of conversion as Five Crows. Yellow Serpent is the principal chief of the Walla-Walla tribe, the other two are brothers, and chiefs of the Kayuse.

The son of Yellow Serpent was also with him. He has spent a number of years in the Methodist mission school, on the Wallamette river, where he received the name of Elijah Hedding, and where he acquired some knowledge of the English language, and professed conversion to christianity. Mr. Perkins put up for the night at Yellow Serpent's lodge. Supper was served of dried salmon, after which prayer was proposed by Elijah. They sang a hymn, and Mr. Perkins led in prayer, and was followed by Elijah, who, after he had concluded, requested his father to pray. This ended, they sung another hymn, and prepared to sleep. Mr. Perkins having wet his blankets in swimming the river, had none to sleep in, but Yellow Serpent, taking his own blanket from his shoulders, gave it to him, saying that he had no blankets, but would make him as comfortable as he could. Wrapped in the Indian's blanket, he composed himself to sleep.

The next morning, quite early, he called at Tauitau's lodge, and was informed, on entering, that they had not yet had their morning prayers. The chief caused a bell to be rung, at the sound of which all his band came together for devotion. Tauitau then said to Mr. Perkins, "We are Catholics, and our worship is different from yours." He then fell upon his knees, all the rest kneeling and facing him. The chief had a long string of beads on his neck, to which was attached a brass cross. After all were knelt, they devoutly crossed themselves, and commenced their prayers as follows: "We are poor, we are poor," repeating it ten times, and then closing with,

"Good Father, good Son, good Spirit," and then the chief would slip a bead on the string. This was continued until all the beads were removed from one part of the string to the other. When their devotions closed, Tauitau said, "This is the way in which the priest taught us to worship God," but Elijah said that "Tauitau and his band prayed from the head, but we pray from the heart. Bidding them good morning, Mr. Perkins mounted his horse, and at evening arrived in safety at the mission.

Friday, 12th. As the Indians refused to come together unless Ellis and his men came down to meet them, we informed them that we should go up and see Ellis in his own country, but being suspicious that we intended to prevent his coming down, they were much opposed to our going. Explaining to the chiefs the object of our visit, they seemed to be satisfied, and we went about preparing for the continuance of our journey.

At five, P. M., all were ready, and we started off on a round gallop in a northeasterly direction, and the sun went down beneath the waters of the Pacific. The light of the moon enabled us to keep along the winding trail as it led us over a beautifully undulating country, till eleven o'clock at night, when we camped on a small rivulet called the Toosha, forty-five miles from where we started. Next morning at sunrise proceeded. At noon encamped on another little stream, having traveled thirty-five miles. Rested for an hour, and continued our course through an exceedingly romantic country. At five, P. M., arrived at the Snake or Lewis river, where a portion of the Nez. Perse tribe reside, headed by one whom they call "Red Wolf."

The village is situated on a small inclined plain, quite fertile, but the country round about is very rocky and mountainous. The valleys, however, afford abundant grass to supply the numerous horses owned by the Indians. Red Wolf, in more than one instance, has proved himself a friend to the Americans. When Capt. Bonneville was in this country, many years ago, in his trade with the Indians, he met with violent opposition from the Hudson's Bay Company, and was compelled to leave that portion under the control of the company. But, in his attempt to do, he lost his way, and wandered about until he and his men were reduced to a starving state. Fortunately, he struck a trail that led him to the lodge of Red Wolf, and he immediately told the chief of his great distress. Red Wolf was moved by the story, and ordered a horse to be butchered without delay. Bonneville and his men feasted themselves to their entire satisfaction; and when they were ready to leave, they were supplied with a guide, and provision for their journey.

From Dr. Whitman's to Red Wolf's place it is one hundred miles; and having traveled it in one day, our horses were leg weary. Consequently, we turned them loose among the hills to remain till we returned, and obtained fresh ones of Red Wolf, for the prosecution of our journey. It was twenty-five miles from Red Wolf's to the mission station among the Nez Perces, under the care of Rev. Mr. Spaulding and the sun was two hours high; the trail was difficult in some places but the horses were as light-footed as antelopes. Red Wolf had volunteered to accompany us, and crossing the river, swimming our horses in the rear of our canoe, we each one mounted the animal designated by the chief, and himself taking the lead, we measured off the ground with wonderful rapidity. We passed a number of small villages, and found the vallies which were fertile, astonishingly filled with horses. From one eminence could be seen not less than one thousand. But Red Wolf led us on with such astonishing swiftness that we had scarcely time to cast a glance at the Indians, horses, rivers, mountains, &c., by which the scenery of our route was diversified, and which we left one after another in quick succession far in the rear. Just as the sun was setting we brought up on Clear Water River, on the side opposite the house of Rev. Mr. Spaulding. We had traveled twenty-five miles in two hours, and sixty miles since we dined at twelve o'clock. Hailing across the river, Mr. Spaulding came over in a small canoe, and took us and our baggage over, and, with his wife, and Mr. and Mrs. Littlejohn, gave us a most cordial and hearty welcome to their isolated home.

Sunday, 14th. Some two hundred Indians, of all ages, met in the rear of Mr. Spaulding's house for religious worship. They behaved with great propriety, and some of them gave good evidence of genuiue conversion. Mr. Spaulding had received three of them into church fellowship, two of them chiefs, by the name of Joseph and Timothy; and thirty others stood propounded for membership. According to arrangement, these were to be received on the Sabbath after our arrival. Being examined according to the order of the Presbyterian church, and giving satisfaction as to their religious experience, they and their children received baptism, and they became members of Christ's visible church.

In the evening it fell to my lot to preach to the few Americans who providentially had been thus thrown together. This is evidently the most promising Indian mission in Oregon.

Monday, 15th. Climbed to the top of a mountain, twenty-two hundred feet high, which overlooks the valley of Sapwai, and enables one to trace the windings of Clear Water, for several miles. We started a number of large rocks down the precipitous sides of the mountain towards the river, but on descending found that our sport was not gratuitous. Some Indians had just come up the trail on horseback, and a fragment of one of the rocks had struck a horse's leg and broken it. But the horse being not very valuable, the matter was easily adjusted.

When we arrived, Ellis, with some hundreds of his people, was fifty or sixty miles off, and a letter was sent to him to come down and meet us.

Tuesday, 16th. Joseph, who is second to Ellis in the chieftainship, made a martial display of his band, in a little plain in the rear of the house, where he entertained us with a sham fight. We estimated the number under Joseph at seven hundred. Arrayed in their war dress, they made a very savage, not to say imposing, appearance.

Wednesday, 17th. Joseph called out his band and awaited the arrival of Ellis. We were requested to take our places in the front ranks of Joseph's band, in the centre, and soon appeared, coming over the mountain, behind which had been waiting, a cloud of Indians, that spread itself over its sides. The mountain seemed alive, as hundreds of Indians came moving towards the valley. They were all mounted on their best horses, and these were ornamented with scarlet belts and head dresses, while tassels dangled from their ears. They arrived on the borders of the plain, and the two bands were separated from each other about fifty rods, and now the scene that presented itself beggars description. A thousand savages rushed into all the manœvers of a deadly fight, while the roar of musketry, the shrill sound of the war whistle, the horrible yelling, and the dashing too and fro upon their fiery steeds, which continued for half an hour, and approached us nearer and nearer until the froth from their horse's nostrils would fly into our faces as they passed—these, with the savage pomposity with which they were caparisoned, and the frightful manner in which they were daubed with paint, their fiery visages being striped with red, black, white, and yellow, were all calculated not only to inspire terror, but a dread of savage fury in the mind of every beholder. At the very height of the excitement, when it appeared that the next whirl of the savage cavalry would trample us all beneath their feet, Ellis stretched himself up to his utmost height upon the back of his splendid charger, and waving his hand over the dark mass, instantly all was quiet, and the terrifying yell of the savage was succeeded by profound silence. All dismounted, and the chiefs and principal men, shook hands with us, in token of friendship. All again mounted, ourselves joining the troop on horses provided by the Indians for our use, and they marched us back over the hill to a little plain beyond, for the purpose of entertaining us with a still farther exhibition of their customs.

Connected with Ellis's band were some braves whom the whole nation delight to honor. The Blackfeet

Indians have always been the deadly enemies of the Nez Perces, and of all the braves, none are honored so much as those who have killed Blackfeet. One of them then present, has killed twelve with his own hands, taken their scalps and muskets, and brought them as trophies to his lodge. This he had done to revenge the death of an only brother, who, according to his story, was treacherously murdered by the Blackfeet. A large circle was formed around this brave, he occupying the centre of the circle, bearing on one arm the muskets he had captured from the enemy, and hanging on the other the scalps he had taken. He displayed these trophies before the multitude, and at the same time, gave a history of the manner in which each one was taken. Ellis said he was the greatest brave in the nation, and they always honor him in this way. A terrible battle had been recently fought by a party of the Nez Perces with a party of Blackfeet, in which the former were victorious. This battle was acted to the life, with the exception that no blood was shed. The scene then closed with a war dance, conducted by a chief whom the whites designate by the name of " Lawyer," and in whom is combined the cunning and shrewdness of the Indian, with the ability and penetration of the statesman.

Though this savage "training" was more exciting than any martial display I had ever witnessed, yet it closed up quietly and peacefully, and as it had been conducted upon strictly temperance principles, all retired from the scene perfectly sober. At dark, of the thousand Indians present during the day, scarcely one was to be seen outside of his lodge.

Ascertaining from Ellis that he designed to go down to meet the Kayuses when we returned, with some of his men, for the purpose of inducing them to accept of the laws which the Nez Perces had received, and with which they were well pleased, we waived our objections against his going, and on Thursday, the 18th, prepared to take our departure.

Here I would take occasion to observe, that the Rev. Mr. Spaulding and his worthy companion are laboring faithfully for both the spiritual and temporal good of this people, and in no place have I seen more visible fruits of labor thus bestowed. There are few missionaries in any part of the world more worthy of the confidence of the church that employs them, than these self-sacrificing servants of Jesus Christ. Far away from all civilized society, and depending for their safety from the fury of excited savages, alone in the protection of Heaven, they are entitled to the sympathies and prayers of the whole christian church. Bidding them farewell, we re-crossed the Clear-Water, where our horses were in waiting, rode back to Red Wolf's place, and slept.

Next morning sent an Indian out among the hills to hunt for our horses, and as we were finishing our breakfast, which our boys had prepared for us, Red Wolf came out of his lodge and rung a large hand-bell, to call the Indians from the other lodges to their morning prayers. All assembled to the number of one hundred, an exhortation or harangue was given them by one of the chiefs, and then singing a hymn in the Indian tongue, two engaged in prayer. I was greatly surprised, in traveling through the Indian country, to find that these outward forms of christianity are observed in almost every lodge. The Indians generally are nominally christian, and about equally divided betwixt the Protestant and Catholic religion.

At eight o'clock, a hallooing upon the side of the mountain indicated that our horses were found, and would soon be at our camp. Packing, saddling, and bridling were done in short order, and, Mr. Spaulding joining our party, we soon left the valley of the Snake River behind us. Examining the country more critically on our return than when we went out, we found it to be indescribably beautiful and picturesque, sometimes rising into the romantic and sublime, and generally well adapted to all pastoral purposes. No timber of any consequence appeared, except on the banks of the streams. Crossing the Tookanan, and Toosha, we stopped for supper on a beautiful brook, called Imaispa. We found we had barely provisions enough for this meal, and two of us resolved to proceed, rather than go hungry all the next day. Letting our horses crop the grass for an hour, we traveled on; Mr. Perkins and Mr. Spaulding preferring to remain where they were till morning. At daybreak we arrived at Dr. Whitman's, having set upon our horses all night.

During our absence the Kayuses had all collected within a few miles of Dr. Whitman's, and were preparing for the great meeting with the Nez Perces, on our return.

On Saturday, 20th, Ellis, with three hundred of his people, arrived, and camped within a short distance of the mission. Wearied out by excessive labor, we put off the meeting of the two tribes until the ensuing week.

Sunday morning about one hundred Indians assembled at the mission for religious worship, and were addressed by all the missionaries present. In the afternoon I walked out on the plain a short distance, and soon found myself on a little rise of ground, where were two graves, one of which was inclosed in a picket. Inquiring who was buried there, my attendant replied, "The grave inside the picket is that of the only child, a little daughter, of Mr. and Mrs. Whitman, who was drowned in that creek which passes near the house. That on the outside incloses the remains of Joseph, the Hawaiian, who lived with Dr. Whitman a number of years, and served him faithfully while he lived." This Hawaiian was a converted man, and possessing considerable talent, he was very useful to the mission. Though he was a great lover of the Indians, and would do all he could for their welfare, yet, when he died, not one of them could be prevailed upon to assist in carrying him to the grave; but Dr. Whitman, and Mr. Pombrun, of Fort Walla-Walla, bore him upon their shoulders to the house appointed for all the living.

I returned from this excursion reflecting upon the severe trials of missionaries, many of whom are compelled to bury their offspring with their own hands.

Preached in the afternoon to seven Americans, two

of whom came in from their camp, three miles distant, where they were preparing to cross the mountains to the United States. One of these, Wm. C. Sutton, is truly "a brand plucked from the burning." For three years he has been a living witness of the power of the gospel to save even the chief of sinners. He lived for many years in the Rocky mountains, and contracted all the vices common to the mountaineers; but abandoning the trapper's life, and coming down among the missionaries in the lower country, he was powerfully awakened to see the folly of his former course, and after struggling for days on the brink of despair, was brought "from darkness to light, and from the power of Satan to the living God."

Monday, 22d. We were visited by a number of Indians in the morning, among whom was one by the name of Jacob, whose history is a clear exhibition of the cunning and wonderful credulity of the Indians. By some means he obtained a large picture from the whites, which he was told represented the devil, and Indian shrewdness at once suggested to him that he could use the picture greatly to his advantage among his people, who had always believed that an evil spirit existed, and had much to do in inflicting misery upon the Indians. Taking good care to keep his picture concealed, and preparing the way for the people to receive him in his supernatural character, by spending much of his time alone, apparently in solemn thought, and in performing his conjurations, he at length gave out that he had *Diabolus* under his control, and could bring him up at any time, in the sight of the people. To prove his assertion, he left the camp, charging the people to watch him, and as he went behind a little breastwork, several rods off, which he had prepared for the occasion, to keep their eyes fixed upon the top of the breastwork. Performing his incantations awhile, at length *Diabolus* appeared to the terrified Indians, rising slowly above the breastwork. Jacob had accomplished his object, proved himself master of the Devil, and by this manœuver secured to himself unbounded influence among his people.

During the day, Nez Perce Indians continued to arrive, until six hundred people, and a thousand horses, appeared on the plains. The Kayuse and Walla-Walla bands united, forming a troop of three hundred men, all mounted. These met the Nez Perces on the plain in front of Dr. Whitman's house, and then a scene similar to that at Lapwai, presented itself. The Indians worked themselves up into a high state of excitement, and Ellis said afterwards that he thought the Kayuses were determined to fight in good earnest. Tauitau, the Catholic chief, as he approached us, appeared quite angry, and disposed to quarrel. Seeing the excitement increase, and fearing that it might end seriously, unless the attention of the Indians could be drawn to some other subject, Mr. Spaulding gave notice that all would repair to Dr. W.'s house, for the purpose of *tallapoosa*, (worship). But Tauitau came forward in a very boisterous manner, and inquired what we had made all this disturbance for. We repaired to the house, followed by several hundred Indians, and after engaging in a season of prayer, found that the excitement had died away, and the Indians were scattering to their lodges for the night.

Tuesday, 23d. The chiefs and principal men of both tribes came together at Dr. Whitman's to hear what we had to say. They were called to order by Tauitau, who by this time had got over his excitement, and then was placed before them the object of our visit. Among other things they were told that much had been said about war, and we had come to assure them that they had nothing to fear from that quarter; that the President of the United States had not sent the Doctor to their country, to make war upon them, but to enter into arrangements with them to regulate their intercourse with the white people. We were not there to catch them in a trap as a man would catch a beaver, but to do them good; and if they would lay aside their former practices and prejudices, stop their quarrels, cultivate their lands, and receive good laws, they might become a great and a happy people; that in order to do this, they must all be united, for they were but few in comparison to the whites; and if they were not all of one heart, they would be able to accomplish nothing; that the chiefs should set the example and love each other, and not get proud and haughty, but consider the people as their brothers and their children, and labor to do them good; that the people should be obedient, and in their morning and evening prayers they should remember their chiefs.

Liberty was then given for the chiefs to speak, and Ellis remarked that it would not be proper for the Nez Perce chiefs to speak until the Kayuse people should receive the laws. The Kayuse chiefs replied, "If you want us to receive the laws, bring them forward and let us see them, as we cannot take them unless we know what they are."

A speech was then delivered to the young men to impress them favorably with regard to the laws. They were told that they would soon take the places of the old men, and they should be willing to act for the good of the people; that they should not go here and there and spread false reports about war; and that this had been the cause of all the difficulty and excitement which had prevailed among them during the past winter.

The laws were then read, first in English, and then in the Nez Perce.

Yellow Serpent then rose and said: "I have a message to you. Where are these laws from? Are they from God or from the earth? I would that you might say, they were from God. But I think they are from the earth, because, from what I know of white men, they do not honor these laws.

In answer to this, the people were informed that the laws were recognized by God, and imposed on men in all civilized countries. Yellow Serpent was pleased with the explanation, and said that it was according to the instructions he had received from others, and he was very glad to learn that it was so, because many of his people had been angry with him when he had whipped them for crime, and had told him that God would send him to hell for it, and he was glad to know that it was pleasing to God."

Telaukaikt, a Kayuse chief, rose and said: "What do you read the laws for before we take them? We do not take the laws because Tauitau says so. He is a Catholic, and as a people we do not follow his worship." Dr. White replied that this did not make any difference about law; that the people in the States had different modes of worship, yet all had one law.

Then a chief, called the Prince, arose and said: "I understand you gave us liberty to examine every law—all the words and lines—and as questions are asked about it, we should get a better understanding of it. The people of this country have but one mind about it. I have something to say, but perhaps the people will dispute me. As a body, we have not had an opportunity to consult, therefore you come to us as in a wind, and speak to us as to the air, as we have no point, and we cannot speak because we have no point before us. The business before us is whole, like a body we have not dissected it. And perhaps you will say that it is out of place for me to speak, because I am not a great chief. Once I had influence, but now I have but little."

Here he was about to sit down, but was told to go on. He then said,—"When the whites first came among us, we had no cattle, they have given us none; what we have now got we have obtained by an exchange of property. A long time ago Lewis and Clark came to this country, and I want to know what they said about us. Did they say that they found friends or enemies here?" Being told that they spoke well of the Indians, the prince said, "that is a reason why the whites should unite with us, and all become one people. Those who have been here before you, have left us no memorial of their kindness, by giving us presents. We speak by way of favor. If you have any benefit to bestow, we will then speak more freely. One thing that we can speak about is cattle, and the reason why we cannot speak out now is because we have not the thing before us. My people are poor and blind, and we must have something tangible. Other chiefs have bewildered me since they came; yet I am from an honorable stock.

Promises which have been made to me and my fathers, have not been fulfilled, and I am made miserable; but it will not answer for me to speak out, for my people do not consider me as their chief. One thing more; you have reminded me of what was promised me sometime ago, and I am inclined to follow on and see; though I have been giving my beaver to the whites, and have received many promises, and have always been disappointed. I want to know what you are going to do."

Illutin, or Big Belly, then arose and said, that the old men were wearied with the wickedness of the young men. That if he was alone, he could say yes at once to the laws, and that the reason why the young men did not feel as he felt was because they had stolen property in their hands, and the laws condemned stealing. But he assured them that the laws were calculated to do them good, and not evil.

But this did not satisfy the prince. He desired that the good which it was proposed to do them by adopting the laws, might be put in a tangible form before them. He said that it had been a long time since the country had been discovered by whites, and that ever since that time, people had been coming along, and promising to do them good; but they had all passed by and left no blessing behind them. That the Hudson's Bay Company had persuaded them to continue with them, and not go after the Americans; that if the Americans designed to do them good why did they not bring goods with them to leave with the Indians? that they were fools to listen to what the Yankees had to say; that they would only talk, but the company would both talk and give them presents.

In reply to this the Doctor told them that he did not come to them as a missionary, nor as a trader.

It was now nearly night, but just before the meeting closed a gun was fired in one of the lodges, and directly John, the Hawaiian, came running to the house with his hand up to his head, and the blood running down his face, and as he came into the assembly he cried out with great agitation, "Indian, he kille me! Indian, he kille me!"

John had been to the lodge for the purpose of trading with the young Indians, and the Indians became angry at John and threatened to shoot him. John told them that they dare not do it, and one of them instantly seized a musket and lodged the contents of it in the side of John's head. Fortunately there was no ball in the gun, consequently the results were not serious, though a hole was cut to the bone, an inch in diameter.

In the evening Ellis and Lawyer came in to have a talk. They said they expected pay for being chiefs, and wished to know how much salary Dr. White was going to give them. Ellis said he had counted the months he had been in office, and thought that enough was due him to make him rich. They left at a late hour without receiving any satisfaction.

Wednesday, 24th. Some hundreds again assembled to resume the business relative to laws; but the first thing investigated was the shooting of John. The Indian, immediately after committing the deed, had fled, but the chiefs took summary measures to bring him back. He was brought before the assembly and found guilty of the crime, but the sentence was postponed until they received the laws.

The Indians then continued to speak in reference to the laws, and their speeches were grave, energetic, mighty and eloquent, and generally in favor of receiving the laws. After all had spoken it was signified that they were ready for the vote whether they would take the laws or not, and the vote was unanimous in the affirmative. Having adopted the laws, it was now necessary to elect their chiefs, according to the provisions of the law; and Tauitau was nominated to the high chieftainship. Some were opposed; a majority were in favor, and while the question was pending Tauitau rose and said: "My friends, my friends, I rise to speak to you, and I want you all to listen." He then adverted to their past histories, and told them how much they had suffered in consequence of their divisions and quarrels, and then inquired if they would lay aside all their past difficulties, and come up and support him, if he would accept of the chieftainship.

It was now time to close for that day, and the vote being put, Tauitau was declared duly elected to the high chieftainship of the Kayuse tribe. Before the meeting adjourned, Dr. White presented the Indians with a fat ox which he bought of the mission, and Mrs. Whitman gave them a fat hog. These they butchered directly, and feasted upon them till ten o'clock at night, when all was consumed.

Thursday, 25th. A number of the chiefs came early in morning at our request, to settle a difficulty concerning some horses which they gave to Rev. Jason Lee, when he first came to Oregon, Mr. Lee having requested us to come to an arrangement with them, if possible. After a long talk, we succeeded in settling with them by proposing to give them a cow for each horse that they had given Mr. Lee. We found that the Indians always expect to be well paid for a present.

After this the Indians again assembled, and Tauitau came forward and certified that he had made up his mind that he could not accept of the chieftainship in consequence of the difference of his religion from that of the most of his people. He was accordingly excused from serving, and Five Crows, his brother, was immediately nominated. When the virtues and firmness of Five Crows were spoken of, the people exclaimed, "our hearts go towards him with a rush." His election was nearly unanimous, and highly pleasing to the whites, of whom he is a great friend, particularly of the Americans. He was so affected when his appointment was announced, that he wept. It required but a short time to elect the subordinate chiefs, after which Mr. Perkins and myself addressed the meeting on the subject of the discovery of the country by Americans, their settling in it, and the necessity of living together on friendly terms; and then the meeting, which had been continued for four days, and at some stages of which the utmost excitement had prevailed, came to a peaceful conclusion, and all went about preparing for the closing feast.

A second ox was butchered, cut into small pieces and boiled. It was then spread out upon the grass, and cut into mouthfuls, put on to plates, pans, pail covers, and pieces of boards, and placed along in the centre of a large temporary lodge, made of skins, and about seventy-five feet long. The people were then all called together, and took their seats on the ground, ourselves being conducted by the chiefs to some seats of skins prepared on the windward side of the lodge, so that we would be secure from the smoke, all, when seated, forming a lengthened ring around the food, three and four persons deep. Five Crows called the table to order, when a blessing was asked; then several Indians passed around the meat to all present, the number, as near as we could judge, being six hundred, embracing men, women and children. Fingers were used instead of forks, and the clattering of teeth and smacking of lips served as music while the process of mastication was going on. All seemed intent upon the business before them; laws, speeches, and war, were lost sight of, and the eating of the ox absorbed every other consideration. It was only necessary for each person to eat one pound, and all would be consumed. In twenty minutes the ox which, three hours before, was peacefully feeding on the prairie, was lodged in the stomachs of six hundred Indians. After the feast Ellis arose and said that it was fashionable among the Indians for all the chiefs to unite with the whites at such a time as this, in smoking the pipe, in token of their alliance and friendship. Accordingly, the pipe of peace was brought forward. Its stem was one inch in diameter, and three feet long, and the bowl four inches long and two in diameter, and made out of a species of dark free-stone. Ellis passed it around, to the chiefs first, and then to the whites, after which speeches were delivered by Five Crows, Ellis, Lawyer, Brothers, Tauitau, and Yellow Serpent; a season of prayer followed and the scene was closed. Next morning the Indians all came to give us the friendly hand before we parted; and the chiefs informed us that they had sentenced the Indian who shot John to a punishment of forty lashes on his bare back. Thus closed our negotiations, and the immense crowd of Indians, taking their leave, returned to their homes in the utmost order. In the evening all was still, and, walking out to the camping ground where the fires were still blazing, I found but one solitary old Indian, who was boiling up the feet of the ox for his next day's supplies.

Saturday, 27th. The forenoon was employed in preparing to return home; and at one, P. M., took our departure from Waialetpu. Mrs. Whitman accompanied us back to the lower country. Traveled fourteen miles, and encamped for the Sabbath on a branch of the Walla-Walla River, called the Toosha, near its mouth. The land along the Walla-Walla and its tributaries is generally very fertile, except in those places where it is strongly impregnated with sal soda. The face of the country is truly beautiful.

Monday, 29th. Moved camp, and proceeding a few miles, met the Rev. Mr. Eells from Tshimkain, a mission station among the Spokan Indians. He was on his way to Waialetpu and Lapwai, and thence home. He gave us an account of his mission, rather discouraging upon the whole, from the opposition arrayed against him from the Catholics. Leaving him to pursue his journey alone, we continued on to fort Walla-Walla, and dined with Mr. McKinley, who has charge of it. Here Mrs. Whitman decided to stop for the arrival of the Hudson's Bay Company's brigade of boats from the upper forts, which was expected in a day or two, preferring that mode of conveyance to riding on horse-back. After dinner we crossed the Walla-Walla river, and desiring to make some observations in the vicinity, encamped for the night. Towards evening I walked out alone to take a view of the burying ground of the Walla-Walla tribe. It was whitened with the bones of horses that had been slain over the graves of their owners, while here and there could be seen a human skull lying by the side of a horse's head. One of the most singular cases of volun tary interment recorded in the annals of heathen superstition, took place in this burying ground some twenty-five years ago. There resided in this vicinity a man belonging to the Walla-Walla tribe, who, rising by his own merits, became the most successful warrior, and renowned chieftain of which the Walla-Wallas could ever boast. During his life, his people were the terror of all the surrounding tribes; and wherever he led them out against the enemy, he was sure to bring them back in triumph, bearing the numerous trophies of his victories in the form of scalps, muskets, shields, &c. These he hung as so many ornaments, to the sides of his lodge. Years of uninterrupted prosperity passed, and the old man saw his five sons grow up by his side. As they arrived to manhood, they strikingly resembled himself, not only in their tall, athletic and commanding forms, but also in their astonishing bravery and indomitable will. His word was the law of his tribe, and he had learned even his own people to tremble at his nod. His voice of command was never disobeyed, whether raised amidst the tumult of battle, the quiet of his village, or at the fire side of his own wigwam. He was justly proud of his sons, and saw, in the changeless affection they bore to their father, their love to one another, and their unrivaled talents, not only his own comfort and support in old age, when he would become useless, but also the continued prosperity of his beloved tribe.

But a cloud was rising to darken the prospects of the aged chief. His eldest son, the glory of the tribe, the heir to the chieftainship, was slain in battle, and the old man's grief was inconsolable. But he had other sons, and around them clustered his hopes. His eldest living one was now the heir, and every way qualified to succeed him, but he had not ceased wailing for the eldest before the second was cut down; and then the third, and the fourth, some in battle, and some by disease. Now his youngest, Benjamin, alone was left; and the cup of the old man's grief was nearly full. Bitterly did he complain of that cruel fate that had bereft him of his sons, and he found consolation only in the reflection that they had been great warriors, and every way worthy of their father. But now they were dead, and all his affections centered in his youngest boy. Surely, thought he, my only remaining son of five, as noble as ever father could boast, will live to be my support in my declining years; he will be my staff when my palsied limbs can scarcely bear me in and out of my wigwam; he will close my eyes when I lie down to die; he will mourn over my grave when I am buried; he will heir my property when I am no more, and as chief of the Walla-Walla nation he will follow in the footsteps of his father.

But disease was already preying upon the vitals of that beloved son, and the father felt his last prop crumble beneath him, as his son expired before his eyes. Like a person under the influence of some desperate resolution, he left the wigwam where lay the wreck of his hopes, and went to fort Walla-Walla, which was commanded by Englishmen, and told them of the death of his last son, and requested them to make arrangements to have him buried according to the English custom. Complying with his request, the dead body was put into a coffin, the funeral service read, and the dark procession moved to the grave, the people showing the sincerity of their sorrow by bitter wailing and tears; but the old man's grief was too deep thus to find relief. The coffin was lowered into the deep dug grave, and the bearers were about to fill it with earth, when the old man stepped upon the grave's mouth and examined the dark abode of his son, then commanded them to desist until he had delivered a message to the people. With a countenance indicating a settled purpose of soul, he looked around upon his beloved people, whose wailings had already given place to a death-like silence, and commanded them to listen to the trembling voice of their old chief, while he delivered to them his last speech. He then rehearsed before them the history of his life, painting, in glowing colors, the successes which had invariably attended him in the numerous wars in which he had been involved, with the surrounding tribes; the splendid trophies taken from the enemy with which his lodge was adorned, and the elevated position to which he had raised the Walla-Wallas, by the prowess of his arm; and then with a heart throbbing with emotion he traced the history of his doting sons. He had sustained them in infancy; he had taught them to love and to obey him; he had trained them to be warriors; he had seen them rush bravely into the deadly fight, and bear off the palm of victory; and he had fondly hoped that they would have long survived him. But a cruel fate had robbed him of his boys; his last hope had perished, the sun of his prosperity had set, and left him surrounded with the darkness of despair; and he was now like a tree whose branches had been broken off, and whose trunk had been shattered to pieces by the successive strokes of the thunder-bolt. And then assuring them that no entreaty should prevent him from accomplishing his design, he announced to them the startling fact, that he had resolved not to survive the burial of his youngest son; and rushing into the grave he stretched himself upon the coffin of his son, and commanded the people to bury him with his beloved boy. A general burst of lamentation from the multitude surrounding the grave rose upon the breeze as the last command of the mighty chief was as promptly obeyed as any he had ever issued in the day of battle. Thus perished the glory of the Walla-Walla nation.

Fort Walla-Walla is situated on the left bank of the Columbia, just above the mouth of the Walla-Walla River. It may more properly be called a trading post, as it looks but little like a fort except that two or three small buildings are enclosed in an adobey wall, about twelve feet high. The company and some private individuals met with considerable loss, not long ago, from the burning of this fort, which was supposed to have been fired by the Indians. The land around is very barren, though the face of the country is good. The company cultivate a farm about three miles from the fort, on the banks of the Walla-Walla.

Tuesday, 30th. Rode sixty-five miles, but on the 31st, both man and beast were so fatigued that we were unable to travel more than twenty-five miles. During this day I proceeded on in advance of the party about one mile, and stopping my horse, dismounted, and took my blanket from my saddle, threw it upon the ground, lay down upon it, and instantly dropt into a sound sleep. There I should doubtless have remained for hours, if one of the party, who had fallen in the rear, had not awakened me, the others having passed within a few feet without my knowing it.

Thursday, June 1st. Arrived at the mission station below the Dalls, where we met with news from the lower country, ships having arrived in the Columbia River, bringing letters, goods and passengers for Oregon. As Dr. White expected to be detained some time at the Dalls, I resolved to proceed homeward the first opportanity. Fortunately the brigade of boats for which Mrs. Whitman awaited at Walla-Walla, arrived at the Dalls a few hours after we did; and applying to Mr. Ogden, who had command of the brigade, I obtained a passage in his boat down the Columbia River to Fort Vancouver. The boats were nine in number, each capable of carrying five or six tons; all loaded with furs which had been collected in the vast interior, and now on their way to the general depot at Vancouver, where they were to be examined, dried, packed and shipped for London. Associated with Mr. Ogden were Mr. McDonald, and Mr. Ermatinger, the two former being chief factors in the company, and the latter a chief trader, both honorable and lucrative offices. Sixty men were required to man the boats, and these were all French Canadians, and half-caste Iroquois.

We all remained at the Dalls over night, and on Friday, the 2d of June, moved down the river a few miles, and were met with a head wind, which soon blew to a gale, compelling us to put to shore, which we succeeded in gaining with some difficulty, breaking one of our boats against the rocks, in the attempt. Here we were detained for some hours, during which Mr. Ogden related some of his wonderful adventures among the Indians with whom he had resided for more than thirty years.

He was an eye witness to a remarkable circumstance

that transpired at the Dalls, during one of his voyages up the Columbia. He arrived at the Dalls on the Sabbath day, and seeing a congregation of some three hundred Indians assembled not far from the river, he drew near to ascertain the cause, and found the Rev. H. K. W. Perkins dispensing to them the word of reconciliation, through a crucified Redeemer. There was sitting in the outskirts of the congregation an Indian woman who had been, for many years, a doctress in the tribe, and who had just expended all her skill upon a patient, the only son of a man whose wigwam was not far distant, and for the recovery of whose son she had become responsible, by consenting to become his physician. All her efforts to remove the disease were unavailing, the father was doomed to see his son expire. Believing that the doctress had the power of preserving life or inflicting death according to her will, and that instead of curing she had killed his boy, he resolved upon the most summary revenge. Leaving his dead son in the lodge, he broke into the congregation with a large butcher-knife in his hand, and rushing upon the now terrified doctress, seized her by the hair, and with one blow across her throat, laid her dead at his feet.

The wind continued to blow until nearly midnight, when a loud call from the pilot warned us that we must leave camp. Though it was very dark, the *voyageurs* were well acquainted with the river, and continued to ply the oars until three o'clock in the morning, when they brought up a few miles above the cascades, to wait for daylight. In the morning proceeded to the cascades, where we were detained for several hours, while the *voyageurs* carried their boats and furs across a portage of half a mile.

The portage was made, and the boats again loaded, but still there were fearful rapids below, which they designed to run. Mr. Ogden preferring to walk across a point of land down to the foot of the first rapid, I volunteered to accompany him, and coming to an eddy below the point, we awaited the arrival of the boats.

Soon the first came, booming around the point, and

thrown violently up and down by the rolling current, then the second, and the third, and so on, till the whole nine appeared in sight. Only two of them gained the eddy, in one of which was Mrs. Whitman; all the others were borne down the tumbling torrent with fearful fury, and it appeared to us on shore, that they must inevitably be lost. One only was capsized, and its crew of eight men struggled hard in the mighty current, until they were all picked up by the other boats, some of them being quite exhausted, and one so far gone that it was with considerable difficulty that he was restored. The boat also, with all its cargo, was saved. After this we were highly favored with respect to wind and current, and on Sunday, at two o'clock, P. M., we arrived in safety at Fort Vancouver.

Monday, the 5th. Procured a passage in one of the company's barges to the Wallamette Falls; and the following day a ride on horseback of fifty miles brought me back to my own dwelling, having, since I left home, performed a journey of one thousand miles.

CHAPTER X.

Homeward bound — Departure from Oregon — Lost in a fog — Vancouver — Unexpected meeting — Night running — Labor lost — Dreary encampment — Sabbath — Pillar Rock — Fort George — Clatsop Plains — A whale — Entertainment - Embarkation — Detention — Great cave — Weigh anchor — Remarkable escape from shipwreck — Driven back — Second trial successful — Voyage — Mani — Night danger — Arrival at Oahu — Shipping — English fleet — News from home — Rev. Jason Lee — "Hoa Tita" — Affecting separation — Admiral Thomas — Great alarm — Detention — How improved.

LATE in the fall of 1843, information was received on the Wallamatte that the English barque Columbia was about to sail from Vancouver to the Sandwich Islands, and would take a certain number of passengers. Accordingly, Rev. Jason Lee, John Ricord, Esq., of New York, and myself and family, engaged passage; Mr. Ricord at three dollars per day, and the rest of us at two and a half each, the half dollar being deducted in consequence of our being missionaries. Mr. Lee and myself designed, after arriving at the Sandwich Islands, to take the first opportunity to proceed to the United States, but Mr. Ricord designed to remain at the Islands.

Having made the necessary arrangements, and put all our baggage into one of the company's batteaux to take to the vessel, we took a small boat in tow, in which we intended to proceed from Vancouver down the Columbia. At dark we took leave of our friends, who stood on the banks of the river to witness our departure. There being a good moon, we did not apprehend much difficulty in running in the night, as we were well acquainted with the river, and we were willing to venture a little to get our baggage on board, before the vessel dropped down the Columbia. Proceeding on till a late hour at night, we lost ourselves in a dense fog, and supposing that by some unaccountable twist we had got turned about, and were going the wrong way, we resolved as soon as posisble to make the shore. Finding a place where we could fasten our boats we remained quiet until morning. At nine o'clock the fog had disappeared, and thereby disclosing the shores to our view, enabled us to ascertain our position. Moving forward, we labored hard with our oars during the day, and at dark came along side of the vessel which lay in the Columbia a short distance above the mouth of the Wallamette. Leaving all our baggage, except such as we should need on our trip down the Columbia, we passed on, and at nine in the evening arrived at Vancouver; but as the gates of the fort were closed, we were obliged to encamp on the beach for the night.

Having accomplished our business, on the 6th we took our leave of our hospitable friends at Vancouver, but the tide being against us, we made slow headway. At seven o'clock, P. M., however, we came up with the ship, and being invited by Captain Humphries, we spent a comfortable night on board. Next morning proceeded on in our small boat, and as there was no wind to favor the ship, we soon left her behind. At two o'clock, P. M., passed the mouth of the Multnomah, and landed a short time at the point where, in 1835, Capt. Wyeth attempted to establish a trading post, but failed, as every other such attempt has done, from coming in contact with, and meeting the opposition of, the Hudson's Bay Company. A little below this point we stopped to dine, on a fine gravelly beach, and while preparing our dinner, several canoes appeared below us, moving up the stream. Discovering our smoke, they made for the point, and on coming to the shore, we found, in one of the canoes, Mr. W. W. Raymond and his family, who were on their way from Clatsop, at the mouth of the river, up to the Wallamette. Mr. Raymond was employed as a farmer at a mission station established on the Clatsop plains. With them we spent a pleasant hour, during which we regaled ourselves upon an unusual variety for such a time, our dinner consisting of beef, pork, potatoes, bread, butter, pie, cake, and raspberry preserves; but we feasted with the expectation of suffering hunger before we arrived at Clatsop, if the winds and weather did not favor our progress. Taking leave of our friends, we departed from our delightful encampment, and with the tide in our favor, proceeded on our voyage. Night came on, and a dense fog rendered it difficult to run; nevertheless we concluded there could be little danger of our going wrong so long as we felt the force of the tide bearing us downward; but we soon found that we were missing our way, and running in behind an island, at the lower end of which a sand-bar had formed across the channel, on which the water was so shallow that we could not pass with our boat. Backing around, we rowed hard for an hour, when we found ourselves again at the head of the island, and by this time the darkness was somewhat dispelled by the rising moon, and we ventured to run on until midnight.

Mooring our boat in a little bay among the rocks, we clambered up on the side of a mountain, covered with a dense forest, where we spent the remainder of the night. Our place of encampment presented a striking contrast to the one we had just left, being among the rugged and precipitous cliffs which overhung the river on the left-hand shore, and as everything around had been thoroughly soaked with rain we found it exceedingly difficult to light a fire.

But after burning my fingers to a blister, scorching my face, and singing off my eye-brows, by flashing powder, I at length accomplished my object, and our dreary encampment assumed a more cheering aspect.

On Saturday, the 8th, proceeded down as far as Oak Point, which is about thirty miles above Astoria, and encamped for the Sabbath under a precipice of rocks on the opposite side from the point. This precipice, which rises several hundred feet, is composed of different layers or strata of irregular, massive amigdaloid and basalt, and, contrasted with the low flat shore on the opposite side, presents a very imposing appearance.

Here, amidst the solitude of rocks, forest, and water, we experienced the truth that devotion is not confined to the damask desks and cushioned seats of refined civilization, but cheers with her presence the lonely and wandering exile.

Monday, 9th. Ran down to Pillar Rock, fourteen miles above Astoria, where, being met by the flood-tide, we were obliged to camp. This rock is a great natural curiosity. It is a mighty column of basalt standing alone in the midst of the river, and though not more than fifteen or twenty feet in diameter at its base, it rises perpendicular on all sides to the height of more than one hundred feet. Remaining here over night, the next morning we crossed the river diagonally from Pillar Rock to Tongue Point, the distance of eleven miles, without serious accident, though the wind was high, and the boat took in considerable water. At twelve arrived at Astoria, where we met with a very cordial reception from Mr. Birney and his family, whose hospitalities we shared until the following day. This gentleman is an officer in the Hudson's Bay Company, and one of its pioneers. In common with all the English and Scotch magnates of the forest, he possesses the disposition to entertain strangers, both with the comforts his house affords, and by narrating his different campaigns, trials, sufferings, contests with the Indians, and hair-breadth escapes.

This place is now called Fort George by the English, but doubtless will resume the name of Astoria when it is settled that the country belongs to the United States.

In the afternoon of the 10th, Rev. J. L. Parrish, who is employed as a missionary among the Indians on the Clatsop Plains, came from Point Adams across the mouth of Young's Bay in a canoe, and met us at the fort, designing to proceed up the river to visit some Indian clans in the vicinity of the Katlamette Islands; but falling in with us, he resolved to return, and the next morning took us all in his large canoe safely to Point Adams, though the bay was quite rough from the effects of a strong east wind. From Point Adams south to a high promontory called Kilemook's Head, the distance of twenty-five miles, is a broad sand beach, which at low-tide constitutes a splendid road.

On our landing on the point, an Indian was dispatched with a note to inform Mrs. Parrish of our arrival, and to procure a horse and cart to carry us and our baggage down the beach, the distance of seven miles, to their residence. At sunset our transportation was accomplished, and we found ourselves comfortably situated with our kind friends, Mr. and Mrs. Parrish, on what is called the Clatsop Plains.

It is only necessary for one to walk up from tide water about one hundred feet to the top of the first ridge, to become convinced that these undullating plains have been formed by the constant accumulation of sands, deposited by the ceaseless action of the waves of the Pacific ocean. They are about twenty miles long, and from one to two and a half miles broad, and contain about forty square miles. There is a tract of timbered land lying between the prairie and Young's Bay, containing twice the amount of land there is in the plains. The timber is of a very good quality, and comprises fir, spruce, pine, cedar, hemlock, and alder. There is little doubt but that all this tract of land, which now lies only a few feet above the level of the ocean, was once entirely submerged; that from Cape Disappointment to Kilemook Head, the distance of thirty miles, and from the present mouth of the Columbia to Tongue Point, the distance of fifteen miles, it was once a large bay, and that the level tract of country back of Point Adams, comprising Clatsop Plains, and the tract of woodland above mentioned, have been formed by the sand and various vegetable substances that, from time immemorial, have washed down the Columbia River, and have been deposited here by the continued action of the tide. The evidences of this are, first, the fact that the soil is of the same alluvial character that is found on the shores of the river above; and, second, there are several ridges, or undulations, which extend the entire length of the plains, and curve precisely with the shore, and which all appear to have successively formed the boundary of the Pacific ocean. Some of these ridges appear in the woods, and large trees have grown on the top of them, which proves that this tract has been forming for hundreds of years. The soil, if we may judge from the immense growth of grass and weeds on the plains, is of a superior quality. The location is delightful, the scenery of ocean and mountain on a grand scale, and evidently this will be one of the most valuable portions of Oregon. At present, there are six American citizens settled on the plains, and as many more have taken claims.

On Thursday, the 21st, we received a note from Captain Humphries, informing us that the ship had arrived at Fort George; and taking leave of our friends on the Clatsop Plains, we proceeded up the beach towards the mouth of the Columbia.

On our way we fell in with a fin back whale that had been driven ashore by the fury of the south-west gales. Though this is a common occurrence, more or less being driven up every year, yet it is considered by the settlers and Indians on the plains, as a very lucky event. It is a rule among both classes, that when a whale is driven ashore, each one is entitled to all he can get. When we discovered the object, Mr. Lee, Mr. Ricord and myself, were in advance of the rest of the party, and in our rear were a number of Indians, who were going up to row us across Young's Bay to Fort George, and Mr. Solomon Smith, an American who resides on the plains, and who had kindly taken Mrs. H. and the children into his cart to carry them up to point Adams. When Smith first discovered the object, he exclaimed, "Who knows but that Providence has sent me up out of the ocean fifty dollars? Yonder is something that looks like a whale." We were all speedily up with the object, Smith and the Indians manifesting as much joy at their good luck as a man would feel who had unexpectedly received an immense fortune; and they all seemed instantly to forget that they were going to assist us up to fort George. Smith having no other instrument than a jack knife, and fearing that the Indians who were just behind, would get more than he, left his horse and cart standing in the centre of the wide beach, sprang nimbly on to the carcase of the huge monster, and with his knife traced that portion of the animal to which he intended to lay claim. It was somewhat pleasing to observe that the Indians, in their selections, paid the utmost respect to the pre-emption right of Mr. Smith. Here was no jumping of claims, but as one after another arrived, all were satisfied to select from that part of the vast surface of the whale around which lines had not been run. We witnessed the dividing of the spoil a short time, and not being able to get either Smith or the Indians to proceed any farther till they had secured all the blubber, I took the cart in charge. At sundown we encamped on Point Adams, contenting ourselves with the idea that when the southeaster, which by this time began to rage, had abated, and the whale had all been removed from the beach by its despoilers, we should be able to cross Young's Bay to fort George, where the barque Columbia lay at anchor. The storm continued until the 23d, when Mr. Parrish came up with a number of Indians and took us across the bay. We were entertained over the Sabbath in the house of Mr. Birney, where I preached the gospel to some twenty-five persons, embracing the crew of the barque, the passengers, and the residents of Fort George. On the 25th, we were required, by the Captain, to embark, but as the wind was contrary, we were obliged to remain until the 26th, when we weighed anchor and ran down to Baker's Bay. This bay is the common anchorage for ships after coming into the river and before going out.

On leaving Fort George we were in hopes immediately to pass over the bar of the Columbia, but on arriving at Baker's Bay the wind became adverse, and, with the prospect of a violent and tedious storm from the south and west, we came to anchor snug under Cape Disappointment, that we might be sheltered from the fury of winds and waves.

Though at present it is a most dreary and barbarous looking region around Baker's Bay, yet, as Cape Disappointment must always be the guide of the mariner into the mouth of the river, and as the bay is the only safe anchorage, and vessels are always more or less detained in passing in and out, this must eventually become a place of considerable maritime importance. This is the only entrepot of the country, and consequently all supplies must pass either way through this channel. This river is the thoroughfare on which must be conveyed everything that goes to and from the interior, and, judging from the rapidity with which the country is filling up, the time is not far distant when steamboats will be flying up and down this river, as they are now seen on the Hudson and Mississippi. Three places offer facilities for the establishment of the grand depot for the country, which must be located somewhere near the mouth of the river. These are the shore of Baker's Bay, back of Cape Disappointment, the east side of Point Adams, and old Astoria. One of these places may doubtless be contemplated as the location of some future splendid commercial city, say the New York of the west.

While in Baker's Bay we experienced a very disagreeable detention of forty days, during which the storm from the south and west, continued to rage, with unceasing violence. Day after day Captain Humphries and myself would climb to the top of Cape Disappointment, and look off on the broad expanse of the Pacific, and contemplate the majesty of the ocean as she rolled her mountain billows, and dashed them successively against the base of the mighty rock on which we stood. The huge swell, rolling in from the south-west, would break with fearful grandeur the entire width of the channel across the bar of the Columbia, and the thick haze darkening the horizon corroborated the indications of the barometer, that the storm had not yet abated.

Occasionally, however, we were able to extend our walks along the shore north of the Cape, and view whatever of interest presented itself. Here is a cave extending into the rock one hundred and fifty feet, and containing the bones of animals, trunks of trees, and other substances, which the tide has there deposited. The country around presents an aspect wild beyond description.

On the morning of the 31st of January, the wind blew fair from the north-west, and having been detained already beyond all endurance, the Captain resolved to make an effort to get to sea, though from the top of the Cape the mountain swell could be seen breaking across the channel. Accordingly, we weighed anchor, and soon passed Cape Disappointment, and steered for the channel across the dreaded bar. The Captain took his position on the foretop, and had not proceeded more than one mile and a half before he was convinced that he was premature in leaving the bay, as the bar was still too rough to attempt to cross. The anchor was immediately let go, and the Captain determined to remain where he was for an hour, in hopes that the ebb tide would run down the high sea on the bar, so as to admit of our crossing in safety. Again the anchor was raised, and the Captain resumed his position on the foretop, but as we approached what are called the north breakers, he came running down with great perturbation, and informed us that the huge sea was still breaking entirely across the channel, and that there was no prospect, if we attempted to cross, of saving either the vessel or our lives.

To cast anchor where we were would be imminently dangerous, but there was no alternative, as it was impossible for us to get back into the bay. Accordingly, we hauled to, and dropt our anchor within a few cable's length of the north sands. The wind was blowing a gale, and a tremendous swell came rolling over the sand bar, and threatened instantly to overwhelm us, while the vessel was tossed about with the greatest violence. As if to add terror to the gloomy prospect before us, night came on, and enveloped us in total darkness. Loud nowled the wind, and the mighty breakers, rolling in majestic grandeur over the sand bar at the north of the channel, angrily shook their white locks around us during the whole night. If the vessel had dragged her anchor, or parted her cable, she must inevitably have been destroyed, and all on board have perished, as no small boat could have lived in that sea for a single moment.

In addition to the miseries of seasickness, during that dismal night, the horrors of shipwreck were vividly portrayed before us as we thought of the ship Isabelle, which was cast away upon a sand-bar but a short distance from our stern, of the William and Ann which was wrecked on the same bar in 1838, with twenty-six persons on board, not one of whom was left to describe the circumstances of the lamentable catastrophe; and of the United States' ship Peacock, which was lost on the north sand-bar, but a little distance from where we lay. But an ever watchful Providence interposed in our behalf; the wind lulled about daylight, and hauled around a few points; the sea became measurably pacified, and at sunrise we stood back for Baker's Bay, where we again let go our anchor, to await a more propitious time to make our exit.

We had not to wait long, for on the 3d day of February, the mouth of the river being exceedingly smooth, and the wind from the north-east, Captain Humphries and myself went once more to the top of Cape Disappointment to take a view of the fearful bar, and pronouncing it passable, at one o'clock, we weighed anchor, and spreading our sails to the breeze, passed beautifully and majestically over the spot where two days before our gallant barque would have been driven to the bottom by one break of the rolling surge.

A voyage of twenty-four days, during which we experienced a succession of violent gales unusual on this part of the ocean, brought us in sight of the island of Mauie, which we first saw forty miles distant at two, P. M., of the 26th of February. At five we made the island of Oahu, and though during the day we had been sailing before a reefed topsail breeze, when we came up with the north end of the island, the wind suddenly fell, and we found ourselves plunging and rolling over an exceedingly heavy swell occasioned by a strong south wind, which for some time had prevailed in the vicinity of the islands. During the night we were drifted some distance towards the island of Oahu and began to fear lest we might be driven ashore, and the absence of wind prove more destructive than the gales we had experienced. In the morning, however, the regular trade set in, and as it was a fair wind, we were carried quickly past Diamond Hill, when the city of Honolulu presented itself to our view. A white flag was raised to the top of the mast to announce that no epidemic prevailed among us, and soon after, we were boarded by an old pilot, who, taking the ship in charge, conducted us along the narrow zig-zag channel leading through the Coral Reef which, with this exception, surrounds the island of Oahu, and bringing the vessel up within a few rods of land, gave orders to "let go the anchor."

We found a variety of shipping in the harbor, American, English, French, Spanish and some others.

The Dublin line of battle ship lay in the roads the night previous to our arrival, but so violent was the motion of the vessel in consequence of the tremendous swell that rolled in from the south, that she parted both her cables, and it was with the utmost difficulty that she was prevented from driving on the coral reef. A timely breeze enabled her to remove from her dangerous proximity to land, and after laying off and on until the swell subsided, she finally came again to anchor in her former position. The Dublin was the flag ship of a small English fleet under the command of Rear Admiral Thomas, the hero of the Chinese war, who had been sent from China by the British government to settle the difficulties occasioned by the outrageous conduct of Lord George Paulet in capturing the Sandwich Islands, and to restore them back to his Hawaiian majesty.

Soon after we came to anchor, Dr. J. L. Babcock, of the Oregon mission, who had been on the island for some months with his family, for the benefit of their health, came on board, and invited us ashore. They were stopping at the house of John Colcord, where, for the time being, we also took up our abode.

Immediately after landing, we learned from Dr. Babcock that news had arrived from the islands that Rev.

George Gary had been appointed to supersede Rev. Jason Lee in the superintendency of the Oregon Mission, and was expected at the islands on his way to Oregon, in a few weeks. This information caused us to hesitate whether to proceed, if we had an opportunity, or remain until Mr. Gary's arrival. Inquiring whether there would be any opportunity soon to take passage to the States, we ascertained that, in all probability, no vessel would leave the islands for that destination under several months; but that a small schooner belonging to the Hawaiian Government, called the "Hoa Tita," would sail the next day for Mazatlan, on the coast of Mexico. Mr. Lee and myself proceeded directly to the consul to ascertain whether it would be possible to procure a passage to the coast, but found that one only could be accommodated on the small craft, and that it would not be practicable to take a family across the continent. Thus baffled in our purposes to proceed together to the United States, we held a council in which Dr. Babcock participated, and came to the conclusion that, under the circumstances it was our duty to separate; Mr. Lee to take the "Hoa Tita" to Mazatlan, thence take the route through Mexico to Vera Cruz, and thence to New York, and myself and family to take the brig Chenamus, which would be ready to sail in a few weeks, and return to Oregon.

With reference to Mr. Lee, no time was to be lost in preparing for his embarkation, but with the assistance of the acting consul, Wm. Hooper, Esq., and Mr. Ladd, everything was soon made ready. Now came one of the severe trials of missionary life. Mr. Lee had buried his second wife in Oregon, and was left with a tender infant, a little girl of three weeks old. Mrs. Hines received the child from the bed of death to take care of it so long as Mr. Lee should desire, and after the burial of its mother he also came to reside in our family. Mr. Lee looked upon this his only child, as his earthly all, and no personal consideration would have induced him to leave her in the care of others, on an island in the Pacific ocean, and perform a hazardous journey to the other side of the globe, with but little prospect of ever again beholding his beloved daughter.

But with a heart as affectionate as ever beat in the breast of a man, Mr. Lee never allowed his personal feelings to control his conduct, when they opposed themselves to the calls of duty. In his opinion it was the voice of duty that called him to tear himself away from all he held dear upon the earth and return to his native land. Accordingly, at three o'clock, P. M., of the 28th of February, after tenderly committing his motherless child to the care of the writer and his companion, he was conducted to the "Hoa Tita," which lay at the wharf, and which, with a fair wind, was soon wafted from the shores of Oahu towards the Mexican coast.

On the 2d day of March, Rear Admiral Thomas, having accomplished his mission to the Hawaiians to the entire satisfaction of both natives and foreigners, took his leave of Oahu, and amidst the roar of cannon which saluted him from the fort and from the ships of war in the harbor, he steered his course for the Society Islands. The following day his majesty Kamahamaha III, arrived at Honolulu from Maui, where he has resided for some time.

Though it was the Sabbath, yet he was saluted with many guns as his crown flag was seen flying at the entrance of the harbor. He is now to take up his residence in the city of Honolulu.

In the evening of the 7th of March, the bells of the churches and of the ships in the harbor, rung an alarm, and the whole city seemed at once in an uproar. The cry of fire was heard in every direction, and as no fire could be seen from where we were, I concluded that it must be in some ship in the harbor. I accordingly ran down to the wharf, and found that the brig Chenamus was indeed on fire in her hold, and no one could tell to what extent. A report was at once circulated that she had on board a vast quantity of powder, some said three hundred barrels. This alarmed many exceedingly, and but few would go down to the wharf for fear the vessel would blow up immediately. The utmost confusion and disorder prevailed until Captain Couch, who was absent from the ship when the fire was first discovered, arrived. He immediately corrected the mistake in reference to the amount of powder, and also informed the people concerning the probable position of the fire, which he supposed to be in the lower hold forward of the mainmast, and as the powder was in the after run, the danger was not so imminent as had been supposed. The fire, however, had so far progressed that it was considered exceedingly dangerous to take off the hatches for fear it would break forth, and destroy not only the ship itself, but also the other ships lying near. The hatches had become hot, and the quarter-deck, as far back as the companion-way, was too warm to stand upon, when the captain gave orders to scuttle her. Three holes were accordingly made in her hull, and when the captain left her deck there were already several feet of water in her hold. She continued filling and sinking until morning, when her upper deck was level with the water. Soon after daylight divers were procured to go down and stop up the scuttle holes, and cork up the cabin windows, to prepare for pumping her out. Thirty-six hours' labor of fifty men, sufficed to get the water all out, and as soon as possible the cargo was on the wharf, when it was ascertained that the ship had received but little or no damage from the fire, and but a small portion of the cargo had been injured except by the water. The fire had been principally confined to some fanning-mills, which were stored under the main hatchway. On the Monday following, the damaged goods were sold at auction for the benefit of the underwriters, and the captain went about repairing his vessel in order to proceed on his voyage to the Columbia River. The Chenamus is a fine brig, built expressly for the Pacific trade, and owned by Captain Cushing, the father of the Hon. Caleb Cushing, the present minister from the United States to China. He has established a commercial house in Oregon, and carries on an extensive trade with the settlers in that new and rsing country.

In consequence of the unfortunate accident to the Chenamus, we were detained for five weeks, during which we had an opportunity of extending our observations on the missions, government, commerce, &c., of the Sandwich Islands.

CHAPTER XI.

View of the Sandwich Islands — How formed — Volcano — Coral Reefs — Names of Islands — When discovered — Singular tradition — Cook's death — Population — Previous condition — Long and bloody war — Results — Missionary statistics — Effects of Missionary labor — Seaman's Chaplaincy — Romanism — Kamahamha III — Reformation — Singular custom — School for young chiefs — Influence of Missionaries — The King's Cabinet — Important history of two hundred and seventy-six days — Increase of Cabinet — Paper King — Protection — Commerce — Whale Fishery — Productions — Society — Temperance — Destination of the Islands.

The Sandwich Islands, in common with a vast number of others in the Pacific Ocean, have doubtless been formed by volcanic action, in connexion with the operations of the coral worm. Doubts may reasonably be indulged in relation to the causes which have produced the present form of many other portions of the globe, but there can be none concerning the manner in which the Sandwich Islands first emerged from the bosom of the deep. That they have been thrown up by volcanic eruptions is evident, from the numerous old craters which appear on all parts of the islands; from the vast quantities of congealed lava everywhere observable; from the nature of the soil, it being nothing more nor less than decomposed lava, and from the present existence of an active volcano on the principal island of the group. This burning mountain, known by the name of the volcano of Kilawea, is situated on the island of Hawaii, or Owyhee, as it was formerly called; and from its continued action in casting up immense quantities of lava, stones, and dirt, which in some instances have been known to roll down the sides of the mountain in such vast quantities, as, in their progress, to fill up the deep ravines washed in the sides of the mountain, and sometimes to bury up the cottages of the natives with their occupants, and extending quite to the ocean, enlarging even the island itself, must be viewed as disclosing the principal cause of the formation of this interesting collection of the Pacific Isles. Though the crater of this mountain is the only flue now open through which the subteranean fires discharge themselves, yet doubtless all the old craters have, in their turn, served the same purpose; and from their appearance one is led to suppose that many of them may have been in action at the same time.

There are different opinions entertained concerning the formation and continued enlargement of the coral reefs by which all the islands are surrounded. The prevailing opinion is that they owe their origin to the constant action of what is called "the coral worm." Though it appears evident that the above mentioned two causes have produced the Sandwich Islands, yet, after all, perhaps these are mere speculations, and they may have existed nearly in their present form since the period when the waters of the deluge were gathered to their original bed, and the ark rested on Mount Ararat.

Be this as it may, there are ten of these isolated spots of earth embraced in the group known by the name of the Sandwich Islands. They are distinguished by the names of Hawaii, Maui, Oahu, Kawai, Molokai, Lanai, Niihau and Kahoolame. The two I have not mentioned are of no note, being small and barren, and containing no permanent inhabitants.

The existence of these islands first became known to the civilized world in 1778. Captain James Cook, the celebrated English navigator, is entitled to the credit of the first discovery of this interesting group, to which he gave their present name, in honor of Lord Sandwich, his principal friend and patron in the British government. He was on one of his voyages to the north-west coast of the American continent, for the purpose of searching for a north-west passage from the Pacific to the Atlantic ocean, when he fell in with these islands. On a subsequent visit to them, it is generally known that he fell a victim to the barbarity of the savages, the existence of whom he had revealed to the world. When Captain

Cook first arrived at the islands, he was received by the natives with great veneration as a supreme being. This, in part, arose from the following singular tradition. The Hawaiians have, from time immemorial, entertained a belief in a deity, or goddess, which they called Pele. She, they believed, had the control of the volcano of Kilawea.

Lono, one of the chiefs, was the friend of Pele, but when once he happened to insult her, she was angry and began to pursue him. He fled in great terror, and passing his home in his flight, he cried, " Aloha, Aloha," to his wife and children, but could not stop, for Pele was near in pursuit. Shortly he came to the shore where he found a man just landing in a fishing canoe, and, to escape the vengeance of Pele, he immediately siezed the canoe and pushed out to sea. When Captain Cook first arrived he forthwith received the name of Lono, the people supposing him to be the same personage who had left in a canoe, now returned in a much larger vessel. But the reverence which they manifested for Cook did not long continue. From an unrestrained intercourse with them, they found him to be a man like themselves; and conceiving a strong dislike for him on account of some supposed injuries which he and his men had inflicted upon them, they resolved upon his distruction, and accordingly he fell beneath the weight of a Hawaiian club, near the village of Kadmaloa, on the shore of Kaalakekua Bay, and on the island of Hawaii. A stick of cocoa set up in the fissure of the rocks a few feet from the water's edge, marks the place where the gallant navigator met his untimely fate.

The population of the Islands, when first discovered, as estimated by Captain Cook, was four hundred thousand. If this was a correct estimate, during the forty-five years following Cook's discovery, we find a decrease in the population of two hundred and fifty-seven thousand nine hundred and fifty; for in 1823 we find a population of only one hundred and forty-two thousand and fifty. A census was taken in 1832, and it was found that the decrease for the nine previous years amounted to eleven thousand seven hundred and thirty-seven, leaving a population at that time of one hundred and thirty thousand three hundred and thirteen. Another census was taken in 1836, which revealed the astonishing decrease of twenty-one thousand seven hundred and thirty in four years. One of the missionaries, the Rev. W. P. Alexander, in 1838, calculated that there were annually, in all the islands, six thousand eight hundred and thirty-eight deaths, and only three thousand three hundred and thirty-five births. I have frequently conversed with missionaries who have been for many years upon the islands, and they all agree in stating that the yearly deaths at the present time bear about the proportion to the yearly births of seven to three; and that only about one-half of the marriages lead to offspring. Allowing that there has been twenty thousand decrease from 1836 to 1846, and it will not fall short of this, there is now a population of eighty-eight thousand five hundred and seventy-nine. This brings us to the lamentable result, that since the discovery of the island in 1778 there has been an average annual decrease of four thousand five hundred and eighty. The astonishing rapidity of the decrease of Hawaiian population, is, perhaps, without a parallel in the history of nations, not excepting the ill-fated Indians of North America.

In beholding the downward career of the Hawaiians in respect to population, one is led to inquire for the causes which have produced these astonishing results. These are numerous, and among the principal are the sweeping pestilence which raged with singular fatality during the years 1803 and 1804, the destructive wars of Kamehameha the first, and the almost universal prevalence, and uncontrolled progress of a disease said to have been introduced by the vicious crew belonging to the vessel of Captain Cook, and as fatal in its ravages, as it is loathsome to contemplate. The laxity of native morals, which has always existed among the Hawaiians, is a sufficient cause why this disease should prevail among them to an unusual extent; and this very cause adds to the effect of the disease in preventing offspring. Hitherto all the efforts of the missionaries and the medical men in the islands to stop the ravages of the disease, have been ineffectual, and it is extremely doubtful whether any means can be devised sufficient to roll back the tide of death which threatens the destruction of the Hawaiian nation.

Great changes had taken place in the political and religious history of the Hawaiian nation previous to the arrival of the first missionaries. Many of these resulted from the free intercourse of the people of other nations with the islanders, so soon as their existence became known to the civilized world. When they were first discovered, the islands were governed by a number of independent chiefs, and all the people were held under the iron control of a system of idolatry, called the Tabu system. After a few years' intercourse with foreigners, beholding their vast superiority over themselves, arising, as they supposed, from the difference of their religion, there arose a party among the natives who rejected their ancient Tabu, and embraced in theory so far as they understood it, the religion of the foreigners. At first this party was small, but continuing to increase, it at length embraced nearly one half of the nation. Kamehameha was the first chief to declare himself openly against the Tabu system. At that time he was a petty chief, controlling but a small portion of the island of Hawaii. But being more enlightened than his countrymen, and withal ambitious and enterprising in his habits, he resolved to attempt the accomplishment of a revolution in both the government and religion of his country. But the cruel system of idolatry against which Kamehameha had arrayed himself, strengthened as it was by ages of uninterrupted growth, was not to be destroyed without a powerful struggle, its friends and supporters still being more numerous than its enemies. The most violent enmity had grown up betwixt the two parties, and at length Kamehameha found himself involved in the most bloody war. All the principal chiefs were upon the side of the Tabu, and it became necessary for Kamehameha to fight them successively. He first turned his attention to the subjugation of his own native island of Hawaii, and meeting the chiefs with their forces in battle, his own superior skill and prowess prevailed, and he soon found the island of Hawaii, containing then more than one hundred thousand inhabitants, prostrate at his feet. Here establishing his authority by the wise use of every necessary precaution, he prepared for the invasion of the other islands. He met the adherents of the Tabu on the islands of Maui, Kauai, Lanai, and Morokai, in battle, and in every instance triumphed over them. Those of his enemies who escaped took refuge on the island of Oahu. Here an army of men as large as that which Kamehameha had drawn to his standard, had collected, and resolved to make one more desperate stand, to support their favorite Tabu. At length the conquering chief effected a landing on the island of Oahu, and the opposing forces met in the rear of the city of Honolulu, and fought the last and bloodiest battle of the whole war. The victory of Kamehameha was complete, his enemies were annihilated, and he was forthwith proclaimed king of the Hawaiian nation.

Providing for the government of Oahu, Kamehameha returned to Kailue on his native island, and in a proclamation to the nation announced that the old Tabu system was at an end. Thus fell idolatry on the Sandwich Islands, and thus all the group were connected together under one government. At the head stood the victorious chieftain who had effected the revolution, under the title of King Kamehameha the First.

It was in this condition that the first missionaries found the islands on their arrival. Providence had prepared the way for them in the destruction of the bloody system of idolatry which had reigned over the islands for ages, and accordingly the first news that saluted them on approaching Hawaii, was, "Kamehameha is king, and the Tabu is destroyed."

It was on the 4th day of April, 1820, that the brig Thaddeus, from Boston, with seven male and seven female missionaries came to anchor in the bay of Kailua, and on the 8th the king and chiefs consented to their landing and residing on the island.

Three years afterwards a reinforcement arrived, consisting of seven males, and six females. A second reinforcement of six males and ten females, arrived in the spring of 1828; a third, of four males and four females, in the spring of 1831; a fourth, of ten males and nine females, in the spring of 1832; a fifth, of two males and two females, in the spring of 1833; a sixth, of three males and five females, in the spring of 1835; a seventh, fifteen males and seventeen females, in the spring of 1837; an eighth, of four males and four females, in the spring of 1841. In January, 1842, one male and one female joined the mission at the islands from the Oregon Mission. A ninth reinforcement, of two males and two females, from the United States, arrived in September, 1842. This makes an aggregate of sixty-one males and sixty-seven females who have been employed on the mission since its first establishment twenty-six years ago. Of these a number have died, some have returned to the United States, some have become disconnected with the mission and remain at the islands, and others continue their labors as missionaries in behalf of the Hawaiian race.

The greatest number of laborers in the field at one time, has not exceeded about eighty adults, or forty families, and this has been near the average number for the last ten years. Of course, to sustain so large an establishment, the expenditures must have been very great. These have been incurred in supporting the missionaries, and providing them with dwellings; in the printing and binding of books for the seminary and other public schools; in the erection of churches and schoolhouses, and in the circulation of books. The entire amount expended, from the first establishment of the mission up to 1844, according to the report of the financial agent, amounted to six hundred and eight thousand, eight hundred and sixty-five dollars. Fifty thousand dollars of this was furnished by the American Bible

Society; nineteen thousand seven hundred and seventy-four dollars by the American Tract Society, and five hundred and thirty-nine thousand and ninety dollars by the A. B. C. F. M.

Eighteen mission stations have been established, and continue to be occupied; six on Hawaii, four on Maui, four on Oahu, three on Kauai, and one on Morokai. In addition to two printing offices and a bindery, a commodious seminary, school-houses, and churches, forty permanent dwelling-houses have been erected for the accommodation of the missionaries, that in appearance would not disgrace any of the villages of Western New York.

The results of all this immense labor and expense are sufficient to establish in every reflecting mind, the utility of christian missions. The great object held in view in the missionary enterprise, is the conversion of the heathen to the Lord Jesus Christ, and their final salvation in the kingdom of heaven. As it regards the first, by missionary effort, christianity has been introduced into the Sandwich Islands, and adopted as the religious system of the nation. Twenty-three christian churches have been gathered, and embraced, on the first of April, 1843, twenty-three thousand eight hundred and four members in regular standing. In addition to this, the Hawaiian language has been systematized and reduced to writing; fifty thousand copies of the New Testament and twenty thousand of the Old Testament have issued from the Hawaiian press; seventy different works, scientifical, historical, and religious, have been translated and published; one-half of the adult population have been taught to read, and nearly all of the children of the islands, are now gathered into the schools. A mission seminary where the higher branches are taught, has been in operation for years, and usually numbers about one hundred and thirty students. A female seminary of a similar character numbers about eighty pupils. These are on the island of Maui. A boarding school for boys numbering sixty scholars, and one for girls of about twenty-five, are in operation on Hawaii. A boarding school for the young chiefs, and a number of select schools at the various stations throughout the islands, and under the care of gentlemen and ladies belonging to the mission. Reading, writing, geography, arithmetic, astronomy, geometry, trigonometry, mensuration, surveying, navigation, algebra, history, phylosophy, &c., are taught in these schools, some of which are already beginning to rank with the academies of New England.

These are some of the direct benefits resulting from missionary efforts, as they exhibit themselves on the Sandwich Islands; and in viewing them we can form some conception of the value of those efforts which have accomplished this work, considered with respect to time. But who can estimate the value of a soul, the redemption of which cost the infinite price of a Redeemer's blood? When I take a view of the small amount of money and labor expended, the little suffering endured, and the few lives sacrificed in the missionary cause, and connect them as instrumentalities with the eternal salvation of souls as the object, I am led to exclaim, my God! how trifling are the means used in comparison to the great end accomplished! And yet thousands from the Sandwich Islands will share in the blessedness of the first resurrection, because these instrumentalities have been used in their behalf, and the Divine blessing has accompanied the efforts which have been made.

In addition to the results of these efforts, as already stated, it may be proper to remark that the government has assumed a much more stable and consistent character than it formerly possessed. Written laws have been enacted by which the people are better secured from oppressive exactions on the part of their rulers, and encouraged to cultivate industrious and virtuous habits. The security, stability, and value of property have been greatly enhanced. Diplomatic intercourse has been opened with other and greater nations, among which are England, the United States, and France, all of which have acknowledged the independence of the islands, and express an interest in their prosperity. Indeed, a great change for the better has taken place, and, though it is true that, still Hawaiian society is in a very crude state, and is susceptible of vast improvement, it is not the less true that the wonderful change through which it has passed since the cross was first planted upon the islands, is without parallel in the history of ancient or modern times.

There are few subjects presenting themselves to the visitor at the islands, more interesting than the Seaman's Chaplaincy, at Honolulu. The fact that the American Seaman's Friend Society, in addition to many other places in the world, have directed their pious benevolence to the greatest seaport of the Sandwich Islands, should be regarded as evidence of the importance of the place as well as of the discrimination of the managers of that society. They have here erected a chapel on a most eligible site, which is conveniently fitted up to accommodate two or three hundred hearers. In the basement there is a depository for Bibles and Tracts, which may here be found in English, German, French, Danish, and most other European languages, and are carefully and liberally distributed. The Bethel Flag floats from a staff elevated from the top of the steeple, inviting the mariner to the house of prayer. Public worship is performed every Sunday morning and evening; there is a meeting every Thursday evening for prayer and religious conference, and a monthly seamen's concert for prayer; both held in the vestry, and well attended. The chaplain also invites all seamen to his private residence, where he instructs, advises, reproves, and exhorts, as occasion may require, and distributes Bibles, Tracts, &c., to those who attend, with great assiduity, as they are received with many thanks by the sailors, and open sources of unspeakable consolation to many of them, while prosecuting their hazardous employment.

The society has been peculiarly fortunate in their choice of chaplains for this important post. The present incumbent is the Rev. Samuel C. Damon who has officiated since the death of his predecessor, the Rev. John Diell. Mr. Damon is well qualified for the place he is called to fill, and his performances in the pulpit are alike creditable to himself as a clergyman and man of letters, and well adapted to the varied circumstances of his hearers. His audience is frequently composed of English lords and knights, consuls and consul generals, admirals and rear admirals, the king of the islands and his suite, the ardent votaries of wealth in the character of merchants and sea captains, naval officers of different nations, common seamen and Kanakas. His subjects are well chosen to arrest the attention of all these, nor does he shun to declare unto them all the counsel of God. In addition to his ordinary labors as chaplain, which alone are very arduous, he is the editor of a very interesting and useful paper called "The Friend of Temperance and Seamen." About four hundred seamen annually visit him at his study, to receive religious instruction, and advice. From a consideration of these facts, I am led fully to the conclusion that the seaman's chaplaincy at Honolulu is every way worthy to be sustained.

Since the French compelled the Hawaiians to receive with their brandy, Roman Catholic missionaries, Catholicism has been making rapid advances among the natives, and thereby presenting a great obstacle in the way of the final success of the Protestant missionaries. According to the best information I could obtain, there were nine Catholic priests on the islands, and the baptized members of the church amounted in all to about twelve thousand five hundred, besides those who were under preparatory training.

They have one hundred schools established, containing upwards of three thousand scholars. These are under the direction of priests, sisters of charity, and native teachers. The catholic cathedral is by far the most *sightly* looking church in Honolulu, and is under the charge of the Rev. the Abbe Maigret, of the Society of Picpus, in Paris. In connection with the cathedral there is a school of three hundred scholars, of both sexes, under the superintendence of the Abbe himself, whose services are without charge to those who belong to his communion. Some time in 1842 a vessel sailed from France, containing a bishop for the islands, seven priests, and twelve sisters of charity; but she has never been heard of since she left the coast of Brazil, and is supposed to have been lost in the vicinity of Cape Horn.

King Kamehameha III. and his small court have for several years resided chiefly at Lahaira, in the island of Maui, but in June, 1844, they removed their residences to the city of Honolulu, on the Island Oahu. At this place a palace has been recently erected in a conspicuous part of the city, and when the public grounds surrounding it are properly improved and ornamented, will present an imposing appearance, and constitute a suitable residence for the royal family.

Until recently, it has been extremely doubtful whether the Hawaiian government would continue in existence for any length of time, but now his majesty Kamehameha III, is recognized as belonging to the family of independent sovereigns, and efforts are being made by his ministers to place his court, and organize his tribunals on a footing corresponding with his present situation. As the ministers of the king are principally Americans, and of course unaccustomed to the forms of ceremony observed in royal palaces, it may be expected that the code of court etiquette which they have adopted, may be somewhat defective. If by some strange metamorphosis, a republican is transformed into an aristocrat, he generally surrounds himself with an excess of ceremony, and on this ground fault has been found with the code of etiquette which the ministers of Kamehameha III. have thrown around the court. Formerly the king was approachable on all occasions, and by every body; now a routine of ceremony must be observed before even a sea captain can gain an audience. This is peculiarly trying to those English and American residents who have formerly had free access to the royal presence. Though this privilege is now denied the people generally yet, on proper application being previously made, the representatives of foreign powers, are, at all times, admitted to a personal interview with the king, for the purpose of submitting to his majesty any case of well founded grievance which any of their countrymen may have against the authorities of the land.

The character of the king since he came to the throne, has undergone a very great change. Formerly he was adicted to low and degrading vices, among which intemperance was one of the most prominent, but some ten or twelve years ago, a thorough reformation took place in his majesty, and he is now not only a consistent temperance man, but also a member of the church of Christ. Though there are a few individuals at Honolulu who are disposed to censure, and find fault with everything and everybody in the islands, yet none seem inclined to complain of his majesty Kamehameha III. The general testimony is favorable to the goodness of his disposition, the uprightness of his intentions, and his clemency and kindness to his subjects. None accuse him of cruelty or tyranny, and many, qualified to judge, concur in ascribing to him considerable native talent, and much acquired information. His majesty is an example of sobriety to his subjects, regular in his attendance at church, and zealous in the discouragement of all Pagan rites, and the establishment of the Christian religion in the nation.

He is now thirty-three years of age, and was married in 1837 to Kalama, by whom he has no offspring. In the probable event of his having no lineal successor, the crown will devolve on Alexander Liholiho, whom the king has adopted for that purpose. He is an active and promising lad, now in the twefth year of his age.

A very singular custom prevails in the Hawaiian monarchy of appointing a female prime minister of the kingdom. It is said this custom originated in the will of Kamehameha I, which declared his son Liholiho his successor in the throne, but that Kaahumanu, his favorite queen, should be his minister. The present premier is Kekauluohi, who is about fifty years of age, very dignified in her appearance, and much respected by all classes.

Her prerogatives are nearly equal to those of the king, and whatever she does in the realm, is to be considered as executed by his authority; but the king has a veto on her acts, while, on the other hand, his own are not binding unless approved of by her. She has an interesting son, William Charles Lunalilo, about twelve years of age, but his sex disqualifies him from being her successor; consequently, Victoria Kamamalu, who is eight years of age, is the reputed heir to the premiership.

Alexander and Victoria are both the children of Kekuanaoa, the present governor of Oahu, by Kaahumana the former premier of the kingdom. These children, with all the other young chiefs of the realm, are under the care of Mr. and Mrs. Cooke, who are members of the mission, and who spare no pains to fit them, through a proper education and training, for the high functions which they are destined to fill. To the missionaries belongs the merit of having excited the king and chiefs of the islands to desire a school for the systematic education of those children into whose hands would fall the future destiny of the government. By the request and concurrence of the king and chiefs, in 1839, Mr. and Mrs. Cooke were selected by the mission as suitable persons to undertake the education of the young chiefs. The building occupied by this school of the chiefs, is situated in a retired part of the city of Honolulu, and, though it cost but two thousand dollars, being constructed of sun-dried adobes, is commodiously arranged to secure the purposes of its construction. It contains seventeen rooms in all, of various dimensions, opening into a court in the centre thirty-six feet square, the outside of the building being seventy-six feet square. The school room is very conveniently arranged, and books, maps, stationery, and globes terrestrial and celestial, are at all times accessible to the scholars, and there is also an excellent apparatus to illustrate the movements of the planets which compose our solar system. The scholars are fifteen in number, seven males and eight females, and each of them has from two to six native attendants in the character of grooms, tailors, washers,

&c., according to the rank, age, and sex of each. These attendants are all under the direction of John Li and his wife, who are both very respectable natives, and who co-operate with Mr. and Mrs. Cooke in excluding these attendants from any intimacy with the young chiefs which might prove prejudicial to their welfare. Reading, writing, spelling, arithmetic, geography, history, drawing, music, vocal and instrumental, are the principal branches of education which these future rulers of the islands are receiving at the hands of Mr. and Mrs. Cooke. These interesting youth, in every department of education, show a tractability quite equal to any other children of the same ages, and under similar circumstances; and it is quite evident that, under the excellent government and tuition of Mr. and Mrs. Cooke, these young chiefs will be prepared to go forth into the world and fill their respective stations, with a fund of knowledge vastly superior to that of their predecessors; and it is equally obvious, that the administration of these future rulers, must be immeasurably more enlightened than any that has ever before existed in the islands. Yet the tongue of calumny has represented the appointment of Mr. and Mrs. Cooke to their responsible station, as a measure having no higher object, than the selfish policy of *priestcraft*.

As might be expected, the missionaries, from the position they have occupied, have exerted a controlling influence in the councils of the Hawaiian government, for many years, but the first appointment from among them to any office in the government was that of the Rev. William Richards in 1838 to the office of teacher or counsellor of the chiefs. This appointment was made in accordance with a request of the king and chiefs, and accepted by Mr. Richards at first, but for one year. Subsequently he received a higher appointment, and filling the different offices of privy counsellor, secretary of state, and embassador to a foreign court, he has been one of the principal actors in the government since his first appointment.

Another appointment to a responsible office in the

government took place from among the missionaries in 1842, which became a matter of much serious controversy in the islands, and perhaps of some willful misrepresentation. This was that of Dr. Gerritt P. Judd. This gentleman was solicited by the king to accept of the office of interpreter, and giving up his connexion with the mission, he identified himself with the Hawaiian government. Some of the foreign residents, and particularly the English, took occasion from this, to charge upon the missionaries a disposition to domineer over the king and people for the benefit of themselves and of the American residents. If it was necessary to appoint a foreigner to this office, doubtless Dr. Judd, from his thorough knowledge of the native language and character, was as well qualified as any man; and from his having voluntarily officiated, and possessing a high reputation among the natives, it was natural that the choice of the king should fall on him. In his new functions, the Doctor appears to have given great satisfaction, at least to the king, for during the troubles of the government with the English, he was appointed by the king to represent his person, and after the restoration of the islands from British rule, he was elevated to the high and responsible office of secretary of state for foreign affairs.

A third appointment from among the missionaries took place in 1845. This was that of the Rev. Mr. Andrews to the office of supreme judge. As these three appointments were made from among themselves through the influence of the missionaries, it has been charged upon them by the enemies of the mission, that, forgetting their appropriate calling, they had used the extensive influence they had acquired in the nation to arrogate to themselves all the important offices of state, and the emoluments arising from such offices. But, as it is the business of the journalist to state facts, and neither to condemn nor attempt a justification of the important transactions narrated, it will not be expected that I shall appear on either side of the unhappy controversy which has proved the source of so much disquietude to the foreign residents on the Sandwich Islands.

In accepting the reins of government, when proffered to them, doubtless the missionaries acted under the influence of a justifiable fear for the safety of the Protestant faith, which they had been instrumental in establishing in the islands; and it was natural for them to prefer a *Christian Protestant* to either an *immoral* or a *Catholic* domination.

The history of the Sandwich Island government during the short space of two hundred and seventy-six days, in 1843, presents three of the most remarkable and important events that ever transpired in a nation, in the same length of time.

The first was the cession of the islands, by his majesty Kamahamaha and the Premier, on the 25th day of February, 1843, to the Right Hon. Lord George Paulet, on the part of her Britanic Majesty, Victoria, Queen of Great Britain and Ireland; the second was the restoration of the islands to their native sovereign, on the 31st of July, 1843, by Rear Admiral Thomas; and the third was the united declaration of Great Britain and France, dated on the 28th Nov., 1843, acknowledging the islands as an *independent State*, and mutually engaging never to take possession, neither directly nor under the title of protectorate, or under any other form, of any part of the territory of which they are composed. Kamehameha III. was driven to cede his sovereignty to Great Britain provisionally, in consequence of charges being preferred against him by British subjects which he was utterly unable to meet, and which in fact were founded in great injustice. Under the influence of wise counsel the king preferred to lay aside his crown rather than act a disgraceful part by complying with the exorbitant demands of the British Lord, and await for the final decision of Great Britain to announce that the Hawaiian government had passed away, or that the crown was still on the brow of Kamehameha III. While the question of the life or death of the Hawaiian government was pending, the British ensign was waving over the islands, and the reins of government were siezed by Lord George Paulet in the name of her majesty, Queen Victoria. His Lord ship had the nonor of standing at the head of the government of the islands during one hundred and fifty-six days; but on the arrival of Rear Admiral Thomas, in the Collingwood line of battle ships, and the investigation of the grounds of the difficulty by the Admiral, the course pursued by Lord George was unceremoniously condemned, and the decision of the British government was anticipated by Rear Admiral Thomas. The king was restored to his just rights on the 31st of July, in a way calculated to preserve the respect due to royalty and restore confidence and good feeling among all the foreign residents. On the issuing of his proclamation, declaring that Kamehameha III. still reigned, Rear Admiral Thomas was hailed as the deliverer of the nation, and the people were as loud in his praises as they were vociferous in their reproaches of Lord George; and the 31st of July was registered as a day to be observed as a national festival, to commemorate the restoration of Kamehameha to the throne of the Sandwich Islands, from which he had been unjustly driven.

Since the settlement of these troubles and the acknowledgement of the independence of the islands by three great nations under an unusual engagement, the king appears to submit the government principally into the hands of his foreign ministers. The cabinet, with the exception of the premier, is composed of foreigners, three of whom were formerly members of the American mission, and two arrived at the islands as mere private gentlemen. One of them, John Ricord, Esq., was a young adventurer from New York, who crossed the continent by the way of St. Louis and the Rocky Mountains, and came down to Oregon in the fall of 1843, professing that his sole errand to the Pacific was to seek a fortune. Not finding it readily along the coast of the Pacific, he resolved to commit himself to its winds and waves. Confined in Baker's Bay by a succession of storms which lasted forty days and forty nights, he at length began to suspect that "Old Neptune" was suspicious that his motives for invading his dominions, were not of the purest kind; but finally his doubts of the favor of Neptune subsided, as the angry elements were hushed to silence, and the gentle breeze wafted him through the gateway across the bar of the Columbia. Twenty-four days brought him along side of Oahu, the sight of which he hailed with transport, as he felt that confidence which is the harbinger of success. Remaining in a voluntary quarantine for a day or two, in consequence of the dilapidated state of his wardrobe, which he found it necessary to repair before appearing in public, he at length received an introduction to some of the members of the cabinet as a qualified member of the bar, from the Empire State. Possessing the advantages arising from a gentlemanly appearance, ready wit, and considerable suavity of manners, he succeeded immediately in ingratiating himself into the good will of the members of the government, and on the ninth day after his arrival he took the oath of allegiance to Kamehameha III, and received the insignia of his appointment to the honorable and responsible office of Attorney General of the Sandwich Islands, with a salary of two thousand dollars per annum.

The other was a Scotchman by the name of Robert Crichton Wyllie, who came to the islands in the company of General Miller, her Britanic Majesty's Consul General for the islands of the Pacific. Probably Mr. Wyllie owes his promotion to his present distinguished office to the interesting "Notes" on the population, religion, agriculture and commerce of the islands, which he published soon after his arrival. In these notes the missionaries are very highly commended, and some very wise suggestions are made concerning the future policy of the Sandwich Islands' government.

The cabinet of Kamehameha III, at present stands as follows: Dr. G. P. Judd, Minister for the Interior, Rev. Mr. Richards, Privy Counsellor, Rev. Mr. Andrews, Supreme Judge, Hon. John Ricord, Attorney General, and Robert Crichton Wyllie, Secretary of State for Foreign Affairs. These five functionaries constitute the government of the Sandwich Islands, for every thing goes according to their direction. In all the great transactions of the nation in its intercourse with other nations, and also in most of its internal affairs, the king in reality has no more power than one of his inferior chiefs. He says himself, that he is a mere "paper king," that his foreign ministers do the business, and bring him the papers to sign, and all he has to do is to obey them. In consequence of this apparent assumption of power on the part cf the foreigners connected with the government, it has been charged upon them by some, that they are actuated by motives of selfish ambition; that they artfully dupe the king and his native suite, by filling them with a sense of their own importance, when in reality they are mere cyphers, and in this way succeed in promoting their own aggrandizement. But the truth is that, with all the improvement the islanders have made, they still remain grossly ignorant, especially on the great principles of government; and, so extensive is their intercourse with other nations, and so complicated the business to be transacted, that the king finds it indispensibly necessary to put the helm of government into the hands of enlightened foreigners; and thus far he has been peculiarly fortunate in the selections he has made, judging from the course which has been pursued. For while his ministers have been careful to guard their own reputation, they have acted as though they believed, that their success in this depended on their faithfulness in guarding the honor and interests of the king.

As a matter of course, since the recognition of the Sandwich Islands as belonging to the great family of kingdoms, the ministers, and all the public functionaries are putting on much of the dignity and importance of royalty, but on some of them who have been altogether unaccustomed to such high honors as result from their offices, the garments of court etiquette hang but loosely; nevertheless they may be considered as skillful politicians if they steer the government ship so as to escape the Sylla on the one hand, and Charybdis on the other, to which she is continually exposed. Now that the three greatest naval powers on earth have entered into a mutual understanding never to take possession of the islands under any pretence whatever, the safety and perpetuity of the government depend upon the course which shall be pursued with other nations. So long as no just grounds of hostility are afforded, the engagement betwixt the three great powers would lead them to remonstrate effectively against any aggression which might endanger the existence of the government. If the astonishing mortality which has prevailed so long among the natives, can by any means be checked, and the fountains of life be purified, so that children shall again be multiplied in the islands, and the decrease of numbers be effectually staid, then may we expect to see, in the future history of the Sandwich Islands, a satisfactory proof of the ability of the copper-colored race to govern themselves, and to become truly civilized. But if the tide of death shall continue to sweep on for fifty years to come, the Hawaiian nation will be numbered among the things that have been.

In connection with this view of the government, it may be proper to consider their means of protection.

Commanding the anchorage is a fort mounting seventy guns, varying in calibre from the long brass thirty-two pounder down to the four pounder. The fort is nearly a quadrangle, with the guns pointing on all sides, and consequently few in proportion, pointing to seaward. A small naval force would be sufficient to silence the guns of the fort, in a short period. As the fort affords no adequate means of protection from an attack by sea, the money laid out for its erection and the purchase of the guns mounted upon it, one of which cost the Hawaiians the sum of ten thousand dollars, was very foolishly expended. So far as their being able to defend themselves by this fort is concerned, they may as well melt down their *big guns* and cast them into poi-pots as to continue the fort as it now is. It will probably soon be demolished, and another one will be erected on the reef, seaward of the present one, which, under the direction of a skillful engineer, will serve a much better purpose.

There is a remarkable hill in the rear of Honolulu which overlooks the city and harbor, called by the natives Puawana, and by foreigners *Punch Bowl Hill.* The top of this hill is concave, the center of it being from forty to fifty feet lower than the outer edge. It is one of those extinct volcanoes, whose former active operation is satisfactorily established, by the different strata of vitrified lava descending from the top of the hill on all sides, at the depth of from four to six feet from the surface of the soil. On the almost circular edge of this hill, on the side next the city, are planted eleven large guns, pointing different ways ; but lying on the ground, and being at too great a distance from the harbor, they are entirely useless as a means of defence. Of this the government are fully aware ; but they continue the guns in their present elevated position for the purpose of firing salutes on the king's birth-day, and on other great occasions. These being all the visible means of protection which the Hawaiians have, it is obvious that they will owe their safety, not so much to any martial array they can muster, whether on land or water, as to an impartial administration of justice to all nations with whom they have intercourse.

The prosperity of the islands is entirely dependent on their commerce, and the annual visits of whalers and ships of war. The commerce of the port of Honolulu, in 1843, was as follows, viz : twenty-five American vessels, nine British, four French, one Spanish, and one German. During the same year the port was visited by one hundred and nine whalers, and ten ships of war. The merchant ships left goods to the amount of upwards of one hundred and fifty-six thousand dollars, and the whale ships to twenty-one thousand eight hundred dollars. It is estimated that the visit of every whaler is worth to the islands from eight to fifteen hundred dollars, and every ship of war considerably more. Besides the amount of vegetables, &c., sold to the various ships touching at the port, there was exported, in 1843, in the produce of the islands, consisting of sugar, molasses, Kukui oil, bullock-hides, goat-skins, arrow-root, and mustard-seed, the amount of ninety-one thousand two hundred and forty-five dollars.

The net revenue of the kingdom in the same year, embracing duties, harbor dues, &c., amounted to fifty thousand dollars. But, as the islands depend mainly upon the whale ships that annually flock to their ports, for their prosperity, it is obvious that, were the whale fishery to fall off, or were the vessels engaged in it to abandon the islands for some port on the main land, the Sandwich Islands would relapse into their primitive insignificance.

The diversion of whalers to some other port has been a subject of alarm to the Hawaiian government, especially since it has been obvious that Upper California, with its splendid bay of San Francisco, would soon become the property of the United States. So long as this noblest harbor of the Pacific coast is blockaded against whalers by the enormous port charges enforced by the mistaken policy of Mexico, the Sandwich Islands have nothing to fear; but, when Mexico shall relinquish her hold on California, and a large commercial city shall adorn the shore of San Francisco, whose quiet harbor, free of charges, shall invite the weather beaten whaleman, then a fatal check will be given to the prosperity of the islands, and much of their present importance will disappear.

The great value of this fishery to those places where the ships are under the necessity of putting in to procure supplies, will appear if we consider its amazing extent. Take for instance one single year. Of six hundred American whalers that were in active operation on the different oceans, three hundred and sixty-seven visited the two ports of the Sandwich Islands, Lahaira and Honolulu in 1843, some of them twice in the same year. Surely no nation ever sent out such an immense fleet of whalers as now sail from the ports of the United States. Bold and adventurous, the Americans carry this enterprise into every portion of the world frequented by the object of their perilous search. There is no sea that is not whitened with their canvass, and no climate that does not witness their toils. While we look for them among the icebergs of the arctic regions, they are seen crossing the antarctic circle, and hovering around the south pole. They explore the vast extent of the Atlantic, Pacific and Indian Oceans, while the Carzette Islands, New Holland, and New Zealand are witness to their hardy and persevering industry. And as the immense fleet of whalemen sailing from the United States around Cape Horn have been dependent upon the Sandwich Islands for their supplies, so they have given to the islands much of the importance which they now possess; and if the inhabitants of the islands wish to preserve the valuable trade arising from this fishery, they will find it necessary to remove all the disadvantages of port charges under which whalemen now labor, in visiting their harbors.

Few portions of the world afford a greater variety of productions than the Sandwich Islands. As the temperature in the different parts varies from forty to ninety degrees in the shade, so nearly all the productions of the temperate and torrid zones, here come to maturity. In the Hawaiian markets of their own production, may be found arrow-root, sugar-cane, Kukui oil, castor oil, mustard seed, coffee, indigo, cotton, cabbages, pineapples, pumpkins, melons, oranges, bananas, figs, grapes, sweet potatoes, Irish potatoes, onions, taro, Indian corn, wheat, rice, tobacco, beef, pork, goats, turkeys, fowls, cocoanuts, mangoes, and bread-fruit. Though the productions are thus various, the staff of life amongst the natives is the *taro-root*. This root is cultivated on patches of ground wholly covered with water, so that the plant is wholly immersed, excepting the large green leaves. It grows to the size of a large potato; is boiled by the natives; prepared in the form of paste, and eaten either alone or with dried fish. It is considered a wholesome food, and exceedingly nutritious. When thus prepared it is called poi, and being almost indispensable to the subsistence of the natives, it forms one of the principal articles of traffic among them.

Society in Honolulu becomes a subject of interest to all, whether transient visitors, or residents. Though there are some jealousies existing betwixt the subjects of different nations concerning the degree of favor which they respectively enjoy under the government, the British complaining that the Americans have more than themselves, and the Americans, that the privileges enjoyed by the British, are much greater than theirs, and the French, that they are much worse off than either the British or Americans; yet all visitors agree in attributing to the foreign residents at Honolulu a degree of hospitality and good feeling not often enjoyed in any other part of the world. This virtue is not confined to the missionary families, but is a general characteristic of the foreign society. Strangers who come well recommended, are immediately introduced into society of a highly intellectual and polished character, consisting of consuls and other resident officers, naval captains and merchants, and American and English ladies, many of whom are highly accomplished, and possess greater personal charms than usually falls to the lot of even the fair sex. Embracing the missionary ladies, there are about thirty in Honolulu, whose presence would add polish to the very best society our country affords.

One characteristic of Hawaiian society is peculiarly striking. It is the almost universal regard paid to the Sabbath. Whether this arises from a deep religious feeling or from custom, I cannot say; but certainly there are few places of the same extent where more decency and order are observed on this day than are apparent in Honolulu. With the exception of a few of the oldest residents, who have always habituated themselves to the license and misrule of heathenism, all the foreign residents are regular in their attendance at the house of God. Indeed, it is very seldom that the quiet of the Sabbath is broken, either by strangers or the natives themselves.

Though there is a class in Honolulu that "look into the cup when it is red, that continue till night, till wine inflame them," yet I should not be doing justice to the society of the place, if I did not bear witness to the general prevalence of temperance. During the three months which I have spent on the islands, I have seldom seen a drunken man, either native or foreigner. There are no *beggars* parading the streets, few petty thefts committed, no robberies, seldom an assault or act of violence, unless provoked by a white man. Yet, notwithstanding all this, and all that has been done for their benefit, the state of the native Hawaiians is still truly deplorable. To call them a christianized, civilized, happy, and prosperous people, would be to mislead the public mind in relation to their true condition. All these terms when applied to the Hawaiians, should be greatly qualified. Their state appears to be that spoken of by the prophet Zechariah as a day which should be neither light nor dark, with this difference, perhaps, that in the case of the Hawaiians, there is still more of night than of day, more of darkness than of light. To an inquiry which I made of the Rev. Lowel Smith, one of the missionaries in Honolulu, concerning the prosperity of the natives, I received this reply: "The evident tendency of things is downward." Downward it is rapidly, in point of numbers, and if the ratio of decrease shall continue the same for only a few years, it does not require the eye of a prophet to see what will be the result.

The epitaph of the nation will be written, and Anglo Saxons will convert the islands into another West Indies.

CHAPTER XII.

Return to Oregon — Embarkation — Passengers — Horace Holden — Thrilling story — The whaleman — Voyage — Arrival in the Columbia River — Disagreeable navigation — Yearly meeting of the Missionaries — Appointments — Arrival of Rev. George Gang — Reasons for his appointment — Great changes — Mr. Lee — George Abernethy — Powers of the new Superintendent — Special meeting — Voyage — Laymen dismissed — Miscellaneous — Transporting supplies — Another meeting — Oregon Institute — Finances of the Mission brought to a close — Number of Missionaries returned — Number remaining in the field.

On the morning of the 3rd day of April, it was announced by Captain Couch that the Chenamus was again ready for sea, and that the passengers were expected to be on board at nine o'clock. According to the arrangement before Mr. Lee's departure, we had secured our passage, and were ready to obey the summons to embark, and the following evening we had lost sight of the beautiful "Isles of the South," and were dancing northward over the waves of the great Pacific. Among our fellow passengers were Dr. J. L. Babcock and family, who were returning to Oregon, to resume their places in the mission, and Mr. Horace Holden and family, who had resided some time on the island of Kauai, where they had been employed in the manufacture of sugar. He had formerly been employed in the whaling business, and on one of his voyages his vessel was wrecked, and he was cast away, with a few of his companions, on one of the Pelew Islands.

Nearly all his fellow sufferers were cruelly murdered by the savages before his eyes, and he saved himself from the same fate only by submitting without resistance, to all the indignities and cruelties that savage ingenuity could invent to torment a man without killing him. They stripped him of his clothing, and then, with

10*

a kind of pinchers, pulled every hair from his body; they bound him down to the ground, and then in a most cruel manner, tattooed upon his breast and arms, the most hideous and indelible figures, and then pronounced him worthy to live and be their slave. Remaining with them for more than a year, at length, to his inexpressible joy, a vessel visited the island, and he was released from his intolerable wretchedness. Returning to Boston, he published a brief narrative of his shipwreck and captivity, and soon after married, and with his wife sailed for the Sandwich Islands. With an interesting family he now goes to Oregon with the intention of spending the remainder of his life.

The third day from Oahu we were boarded by Captain Sawyer, a whaleman, whose vessel had sprung a leak so that it required the constant exertions of his men at pumping, to keep her afloat. The Captain told us that if the leak increased it was doubtful whether he succeeded in getting her into port, but said he should do his utmost to accomplish it. He said he had pumped out of her "all of the Pacific Ocean," and when he left he requested us to report him the first opportunity, that if he failed in getting her in, it would be known what had become of him.

After this nothing especial transpired on our voyage demanding notice; the wind and weather were favorable so that we made fine progress every day, and on the twentieth, after leaving port, we made the high lands north of the mouth of the Columbia River.

Crossing the bar in safety, in a few hours we came to anchor in the river off Fort George, where we found it exceedingly pleasant again to set our feet on *terra firma*. Weighing anchor the following day, we ascended the Columbia, but owing to the intricacy of the navigation, we did not gain the mouth of the Wallamette River, until three days after. So slow was our progress in the brig that Dr. Babcock, Mr. Holden and myself, requested and obtained the use of the barge, to ascend the river to the Wallamette Falls. Taking our families with us, we labored with the oar until towards evening, when we arrived at the foot of the strong rapids, one mile below the falls. Unable to ascend the rapids with the use of our oars, we were obliged to get into the river where the water was up to our waists, and almost as cold as ice, and draw up the boat by main strength. In doing this we were obliged to remain in the water for more than an hour, and, until we became so benumbed that we could scarcely stand upon our feet. However, we gained the head of the rapids in safety, and in a half an hour after, were comfortably seated by the fireside of our good friends, Mr. and Mrs. George Abernethy, of the Oregon mission.

The mission had been left by Mr. Lee, under the superintendency of Rev. David Leslie; and as the yearly meeting of the missionaries took place soon after our arrival, it was arranged for me to supply Oregon City and Tuality Plains with preaching, while Mr. Leslie supplied the Wallamette settlement, and Mr. Waller was to preach to the Indians along the Wallamette River, Mr. Parrish to supply the station on Clatsop Plains, and Mr. Perkins still to remain at the Dalls.

Four missionaries had returned to the United States, the station at Puget's Sound had been abandoned, and the four appointments mentioned above connected with the mission school and the various secular departments, constituted the Oregon mission, when the Rev. George Gary, the newly appointed superintendent, arrived at Wallamette Falls on the 1st day of June, 1844.

Mr. Gary had been appointed to supercede Mr. Lee in the superintendency of the mission in consequence of the dissatisfaction of the Board in New York with the latter, arising from the supposition founded in the statements of missionaries, oral and written, that they "had been misled as to the necessity of so great a number of missionaries in Oregon," and from the to them, "unaccountable fact that they had not been able to obtain any satisfactory report of the manner in which the large appropriations to the late reinforcement had been disbursed." These objections, however valid in the estimation of the Board, should not be considered as any disparagement to the character of Mr. Lee. Changes inconceivably great with respect to the Indians of Oregon took place betwixt the time the great reinforcement was called for, and the time of their arrival in the Columbia River. The natives were wasting away during the time, like the dews of the morning, so that Mr. Lee himself, on his return to Oregon with the reinforcement, was not among the least disappointed.

Other persons have fallen into the same mistake with respect to the Indians. The Rev. Mr. Parker, in his exploring tour, which took place only the year previous to Mr. Lee's first return, according to his representations, found the Indians very numerous, and everywhere desiring missionaries to come among them. For instance, the Callapooah tribe in the valley of the Wallamette, where Mr. Lee established his mission, Mr. Parker represents as numbering, in 1836, over eight thousand souls; and in 1840, six hundred were all that could be found in that valley. Similar changes had taken place in other tribes, changes that no human wisdom could possibly have foreseen. Besides this, at the time the call was made for the great reinforcement, there were but very few whites in Oregon, and the missionaries had been obliged to devote much of their time to manual labor for the purpose of procuring a subsistence, and as no one could have imagined that the country would have been so soon supplied with an industrious population of Americans, it was judged essential and important by Mr. Lee and his coadjutors in the work, that the mission should be supplied with a variety of secular men, embracing farmers, mechanics, accountants, &c., whose labors would relieve the missionaries from temporal pursuits, and enable them to devote their time to the spiritual interests of the people. It is by no means certain that the Missionary Board, with all its foresight, placed in the same position that Mr. Lee and his brethren occupied in Oregon at that time, would not have come to the same conclusion.

With regard to the objection against Mr. Lee, arising from his not furnishing the Board with the desirable report concerning the disbursements of the large appropriation, it should be observed that no such charge of delinquency appears against him up to the time of the appointment of the great reinforcement. Every thing with respect to the use of money appears to have been done to the entire satisfaction of the Board, and resolutions were passed, and articles published in the Christian Advocate and Journal, and other papers, commendatory of the character and course pursued by our "excellent superintendent;" but when the business of the mission became more complicated, in consequence of the appointment of a large number of men of a variety of pursuits, it was found necessary to appoint a financial agent, or mission steward, whose business it should be to keep an exact account of the manner in which the funds of the mission were expended, and to prepare the annual reports of the disbursements. Mr. George Abernethy, of New York, than whom but few men could be found better qualified to bear its responsibilities, was appointed to this important post. I am aware that Mr. Lee, as the superintendent of the mission, was the responsible man, but after the accounts of the mission were committed to the keeping of Mr. Abernethy, it was impossible for Mr. Lee, or any other man, to make out the reports, except Mr. Abernethy himself. To him every thing was clear, and the manner in which every dollar of the mission's money was expended could be accounted for, by a reference to his well kept books. If the Board was disappointed in not receiving a satisfactory report, it is doubtless chargeable upon the unsettled state of the mission for the first two years after the arrival of the large reinforcement, and the multiplicity of business upon the hands of the superintendent, and the missionary steward. Be this as it may, the Missionary Board, at a regular meeting held July 19th, 1843, recommended to the bishop having charge of foreign missions, either the appointment of a special agent to proceed to Oregon and investigate the financial concerns of the mission, or supercede Mr. Lee by a new superintendent. The latter course was decided upon by the bishop, and in the September following it was announced that the Rev. George Gary of the Black River Conference was appointed to the superintendency of the Oregon mission.

The instructions to the new superintendent were few, but he was clothed with discretionary power, and had the destiny of missionaries, laymen, property and all, put into his hands. With this unlimited authority Mr. Gary on arriving in Oregon, entered at once upon the delicate and responsible duties which devolved upon him.

On the 5th of June, Mr. Gary, myself, and our families left the falls and proceeded up the Wallamette River in a canoe, for the purpose of attending a meeting of the missionaries, called by the superintendent at the house of Rev. David Leslie, in the upper settlement. The distance to travel was about fifty miles, twenty by water, and thirty by land. We had made arrangements for persons to meet us at the Butte with means of land traveling, and expected to get through in a day, and therefore had not prepared for camping out; but opposed by the strength of the current, and our horses failing to arrive in time, we preferred to make ourselves as comfortable as possible under the wide spread branches of a majestic fir, to traveling during the night. This was Mr. and Mrs. Gary's first encampment in Oregon. Though we had no bedding to keep our bodies warm during the night, yet, fortunately for our hungry stomachs, we had left of what we had provided for the day a a quarter of a large fresh salmon. This I filled with splinters to prevent its falling to pieces while cooking, and then fastening in the forks of a stick, roasted it before the fire. This, with tea and bread, constituted our supper. As the night was not cold we enjoyed a comfortable rest, though our bed was mother earth, and our covering the canopy of heaven.

On the 6th, arrived at the house of Mr. Leslie, and the following day the missionaries were all collected, with the exception of Mr. Perkins and Mr. Brewer, at the Dalls. The meeting was called for the purpose of consultation concerning the various departments of the mission, and though commenced at an early hour of the day, such was the interest involved that the investigation continued until daylight the next morning. Some important changes in the mission were agitated, and it was decided to sell the mission property at Clatsop, near the mouth of the Columbia River, consisting of a farm, buildings, and stock. Mr. Gary informed the laymen connected with the mission, that he intended to dismiss them, and proposed to defray their expenses home, if they wished to return, or pay them an equivalent in such property as the mission possessed, in Oregon. With the exception of one, they preferred to remain in the country, and accordingly mission property was disbursed among the different families to the amount of from eight hundred to a thousand dollars each. The course adopted by Mr. Gary in disposing of the laymen belonging to the mission, was as satisfactory to the latter, as it was just and honorable in the superintendent. All the secular members of the mission were thus honorably discharged, except Mr. Brewer, the farmer at the Dalls. It was thought the interests of that station required his continuance. The appointments of the missionaries which took place at the yearly meeting before Mr. Gary's arrival, were confirmed.

On Sunday, 9th, preached at the mission school-house to upwards of thirty persons, a good congregation for Oregon; also at the house near the saw-mill. These houses have been erected since the arrival of the large reinforcement. They occupy a beautiful location, and the school-house is by far the most sightly building in Oregon. It is seventy-five by forty-eight feet on the ground, three stories high, and cost eight thousand dollars.

On Wednesday, the 12th, left the mission school to return to the falls, leaving my family behind for the time being, intending to return and get them after a few days. As it had been settled that I should remain at the falls for at least one year, I purchased a couple of cows with their calves for the purpose of furnishing my family with the luxury of milk and butter. The distance from the mission school to the falls by land, is fifty miles, and about one-third of the way is forest. Towards evening of the first day, while urging my animals along the narrow zig-zag Indian trail leading through the dark forest which skirts the Molala River, the piteous and well known cry of a panther but a few rods from the path, brought man and beast at once to a stand. Remaining for a moment, and discovering that the beast of prey was disposed to let us pass, I pushed on as fast as possible, desiring to get as far as I could from the haunts of my troublesome neighbor, before dark, for fear my animals might be attacked during the night. Arriving at nine o'clock on a little prairie between the Molala and Harchauke Rivers, I tied my calves to a small oak tree with a lasso, built a fire in a small hut which one of the settlers had built some time before, and abandoned, and rolling myself in my blanket, lay down to sleep. In the morning I found all safe, the panther had kept his distance. Loosing my animals I proceeded on, and at night arrived in safety at the falls.

Friday, 14th. Returned to the upper settlement, and preached the following Sabbath again at the mission school.

Wednesday, 19th. Having procured a quantity of supplies, consisting of wheat, beef, potatoes, &c., I hired it conveyed to the Bute, and thence took it in a canoe down to the falls. This is the manner of transporting provisions in the country—a very laborious and dangerous method.

Spent a few days in forwarding my house, which I had purchased in Oregon City soon after we returned from the islands, being quite solicitous to occupy it as soon as possible. Mr. Gary and his wife have decided to reside with us in preference to keeping house. They are still in the upper settlement, where Mr. Gary is arranging business with the lay members preparatory to their dismission.

Sabbath, 23d. Preached to a congregation of about forty persons in the Methodist Church at the falls, and proved the truth of the Saviour's promise, "Lo, I am with you."

Tuesday, 25th. Returned to the settlement above, to attend a meeting of the Methodist Society at the mission school, the following day. The meeting was called by Mr. Gary, and related to the Oregon Institute.

Ever since soon after the arrival of the large reinforcement in 1840, the people of Oregon had been endeavoring to establish a literary institution bearing the name of the "Oregon Institute." They had so far succeeded as to secure a very eligible location about three miles from the Oregon Mission school, and build a house which was nearly completed, at an expense of about three thousand dollars. It was now proposed by Mr. Gary to sell the Oregon Mission school house and premises, and disband the school; and though he had an opportunity to sell it to the Roman Catholics for a high price, he preferred to sell it to the trustees of the Oregon Institute for much less. It was exceedingly desirable on the part of the trustees, to secure this property, as, from the location of the farm, embracing a mile square, it was very valuable, and the house itself cost the mission not less than eight thousand dollars. Having an opportunity to sell the first mentioned premises without much sacrifice, they were disposed of, and the Oregon Mission school-house and farm were purchased at an expense of four thousand dollars, and are hereafter to be known as the Oregon Institute. For the promotion of the interests of the church, and for the welfare of this rising country, a more judicious appropriation of the property of the former mission school could not have been made. By selling it to the Catholics, Mr. Gary could have taken more money for it, but it would have been converted into a nunnery. Every Protestant will say, "Rather give it all away, than desecrate it to so impious a purpose."

The institution stands upon an elevated portion of a beautiful plain, surrounded with the most delightful scenery, and at a point which, at some future day, is destined to be one of considerable importance.

The building is beautifully proportioned, being seventy-five feet long and forty-eight wide, including the wings, and three stories high. When finished it will not only present a fine appearance without, but will be commodious, and well adapted to the purposes intended to be accomplished within. It is already so far advanced that a school is now in successful operation, under the tuition of one well qualified to sustain its interests. Already it numbers more students than did either the Cazenovia Seminary or the Willbraham Acadamy, at their commencement, and who can tell but that it may equal, if not exceed both those institutions in importance, as well as usefulness. Though I cannot say that it is the only hope of Oregon, for whether it lives or dies, Oregon will yet be redeemed from the remains of Paganism and the gloom of Papal darkness by which she is enshrouded; but the sentiment forces itself on the mind that the subject of the Oregon Institute is vital to the interests of the Methodist Episcopal church in this country. If it lives, it will be a luminary in the moral heavens of Oregon, shedding abroad the light of knowledge after its founders shall have ceased to live. But if it dies, *our* sun is set, and it is impossible to tell what will succeed. Perhaps a long and cheerless night of Papal darkness, but more probably, others, more worthy of the honor than ourselves, will come forth to mould the moral mass according to their own liking, and give direction to the literature of Oregon.

After the transfer of the premises of the Oregon Mission School to the trustees of the Oregon Institute, all the remaining financial departments connected with the mission, were disposed of principally to those laymen who had been dismissed from the mission, and the property thus sold, amounted to upwards of twenty-six thousand dollars. The finances of the Oregon Mission were thus summarily brought to a close, and the mission was not only relieved of a ponderous load, but assumed a decidedly spiritual character.

Previous to the arrival of Mr. Gary, four of the preachers, besides Mr. Jason Lee, namely: W. W. Kone,

J H Frost, J. P. Richmond, and Daniel Lee, had returned to the United States; consequently, after the dismission of the laymen, there remained connected with the mission five preachers, namely: George Gary, the superintendent, David Leslie, A. F. Waller, H. K. W. Perkins and G. Hines. H. K. W. Perkins in the latter part of the summer of 1844 also returned to the United States, leaving but few regular preachers in the country.

These, disencumbered from all financial embarrassments, addressed themselves to their work in the various portions of the country assigned them, A. F. Waller filling the place made vacant by the departure of Mr. Perkins at the Dalls, David Leslie in the upper part of the Wallamette settlement, and G. Gary and G. Hines at the Wallamette Falls and Tuality Plains. The Dalls was the only Indian Mission now sustained, and both here and among the white settlements, it was necessary for the missionary constantly to expose himself to fatigue and dangers in hunting up the people to give them the word of life. Fording, and swimming rivers, sleeping on the ground and in the rain, and going without food, were no uncommon incidents in the life of the Oregon missionary.

CHAPTER XIII.

Final departure and voyage home — Notice of Captain Sylvester — Arrangements to leave — Mode of departure — Vancouver again — Clatsop Plains — On board the brig Chenamus — Difficult navigation — Danger — Get into the Bay — Fair breeze — Exit — Fellow passengers — T. J. Hubbard — Wave and Devenport — Mode of taking a porpoise — Scarcity of men — Scarcity of incident — Pilot fish — Make land — Spoken by the English brig Frolic — Shipping — Arrival at Oahu Reception — Review of the Mission.

On the 10th of August, 1845, notice was given by Captain Sylvester, that the Brig Chenamus would sail from the Wallamette River for Boston by the way of the Sandwich Islands about the 1st of September, and that a few passengers might be comfortably accommodated on board. Mr. Gary began already to consider that his work in Oregon was accomplished, and he felt quite solicitous to avail himself of the opportunity offered, to return home; but kindly proposed to leave it altogether with the writer, to say which, whether the latter, or himself, should be the favored one, at the same time assuring me, that if he left, and I should remain in the country, he should leave the superintendency of the mission with me. This, after a night of the utmost solicitude, brought me to the conclusion to close up my missionary labors, and leave the scene of toil and danger, and set my face towards my native land. Rev. Mr. Gary, as the superintendent of the mission, made arrangements with the Captain for my passage, and that of my family, consisting of Mrs. Hines, her sister, Miss Julia Bryant, her sister, and Lucy Anna Maria Lee, the daughter of Rev. Jason Lee, who had already returned to the United States.

The amount required was one hundred and fifty dollars from Oregon to the Sandwich Islands, and five

HOMEWARD VOYAGE. 245

hundred and twenty from the Islands to Boston, by the way of Cape Horn.

Through the kind assistance of Mr. and Mrs. Gary, and Mr. and Mrs. Abernethy, we found ourselves prepared to leave Oregon City at the Wallamette Falls, on the 29th of August, 1845. The brig had already dropped down the river, and it was necessary for us to descend to the mouth of the Columbia in an open boat. Procuring a skiff which belonged to the mission, I loaded my baggage into it, leaving a place in the centre for the accommodation of my family. After dining with our kind friends, Mr. and Mrs. Abernethy, we repaired to the boat to take our departure. Adjusting the family in their place, I gave one oar into the hands of Kana, my Hawaiian servant, and the other to James Hemingway, an Indian boy who had resided with us for some time, and myself took the stern oar. We waved a farewell to our friends who stood on the top of the bluff above us, and silently, but not without the deepest emotion, glided off into the strong current of the river. Quickly the beautiful cataract and its flourishing village were hidden from our view by the dark point of fir timber which we had left behind us.

Rowing twenty-eight miles, we arrived, late in the evening, within two miles of Vancouver, but not wishing to disturb the gentlemen of the fort at so late an hour, we encamped for the night. Next morning went up to the fort to complete our preparations for sea; were very kindly received by James Douglass, Esq., who by his friendly attentions, and acts of benevolence, paved the way to render our voyage to the islands much more agreeable than it otherwise would have been.

Saturday, at two, P. M., left Fort Vancouver, and descending the Columbia ten miles, encamped in a grove of willows near the margin of the river, where we remained quietly, during the Holy Sabbath.

Monday, the 2nd, we continued our voyage, and after three days of excessive labor and fatigue, accompanied with imminent dangers and exposures, during which we knew not the luxury of eating or sleeping under the cover of a roof, we arrived in safety at the house of Rev. J. L. Parrish, on Clatsop Plains, about seven miles in the rear of Point Adams at the mouth of the Columbia. Here we remained until Saturday the sixth, when we were informed by Captain Sylvester that the brig lay in Young's Bay, and was ready to receive us on board. Taking an affecting leave of our old friends Mr. and Mrs. Parrish, with whom we had lived on terms of intimacy in our native land, and with whom we had suffered the perils of a voyage of more than twenty-two thousand miles, as well as the dangers and deprivations of a residence among the most savage of men, we were conducted through a forest of fir to a landing on the Scapanowan Creek, the mouth of which forms a good harbor for small craft. Here a boat was sent to take us off, and at four o'clock, P. M., we found ourselves comfortably situated on board the brig Chenamus, with our things nicely packed away in our state rooms, waiting for a favorable wind and tide to take us to sea.

Sunday, 7th. In the morning the Calapooah, a small sail-boat, came along side from shore, bringing vegetables and beef for the Chenamus. With her I expected Kana, my Hawaiian, but he had absconded during the night, choosing rather to remain in Oregon than to go back to his native island.

Monday, 8th. Weighed anchor in the morning before sunrise, with the wind in the north-east, and a strong ebb tide. Soon the wind died away, and we found we were drifting fast on to Sand Island, and were obliged to come to anchor about one mile and a half from Point Adams. While we lay here the Cadboro, a small schooner from Vancouver, bound to Vancouver's Island with furs, passed us, but finding herself approaching too near the point of Sand Island, she also came to anchor. The wind breezing up a little more fresh, the Chenamus made another attempt to get across to Baker's Bay, but failing, again came to anchor, and found herself worse situated than before. The wind was fair, but the tide bore us out of the channel. After dinner made a third attempt to get to the usual anchorage, in Baker's Bay; but being baffled by the tide, we were again obliged to anchor in a very exposed position, where we lay during the night.

The evening of the 10th was exceedingly pleasant, the wind in the north-west, and the prospects quite fair for getting out the next day.

Tuesday, 9th. The tables were all turned, the wind was in the south-east, with the prospect of a gale, the vessel in no desirable position, but the captain determined if possible to get into the bay. Accordingly, we weighed anchor, but made another ineffectual effort to gain our moorings, as we were obliged to anchor about one mile and a half from the proper ground. After waiting a few hours for the tide to favor us, we raised anchor again, and after tacking about two or three times between Sand Island and Chenook Spit, we came to anchor only one half mile nearer the desired haven.

Wednesday, 10th. In the afternoon we succeeded in getting down into the bay, and anchoring in a suitable place to take the breeze from the north, which is the only wind that will serve us in crossing the bar of the Columbia, and for which we made up our minds to wait patiently, remembering that, in this very place three years before, we were detained by adverse gales that lasted as long as the storm of the deluge.

On the 11th and 12th the wind was south and west, which forbade our leaving the bay, consequently we had another opportunity of climbing to the top of Cape Disappointment, and surveying the surrounding scenery. During our detention, at the solicitation of Mrs. H., we enjoyed a pic-nic of muscles, which we found here in abundance, with bread, butter, and tea.

Saturday, 13th. In the morning a fresh breeze sprung up from the north, and it was evident that we should bid the dark mountains of Oregon "Good bye," before night. On shipboard, all was bustle and anxiety, and about noon the command of the captain was to "Heave short." Accordingly, the windlass was manned, the passengers assisting, and quickly the chain cable was shortened, so that the brig was directly over the anchor. We waited a few minutes longer for the proper state of the tide, which is half-ebb, and then, at about one o'clock, the bows of the brig, yielding to the already freshened breeze, turned towards the dreaded bar, and the rolling deep. The schooner Cadboro' took the lead, and though the bar was exceedingly rough, and the mountain swells broke near us as we passed through the contracted channel, yet the wind was fresh and fair, and we soon found ourselves entirely free from all the sand-bars of the Columbia, and before a seven knot breeze, passing beautifully on our course over the deep dark waves of the Pacific Ocean.

Tuesday, 16th. This is the third day since we crossed the Columbia bar, and as we have been constantly favored with a fair wind, we have made fine progress on our voyage. Five gentlemen are our fellow passengers, whose names are, Wave, Devenport, Teck, a Prussian naturalist, Stewart, and T. J. Hubbard. The last came to Oregon with Captain Wyeth and Rev. Jason Lee in 1835, and having resided in Oregon since that time, is well acquainted with the history of the country. He was himself connected with a tragical occurrence, the like of which is quite too common in an Indian country. The cause of the difficulty was an Indian woman, whom Hubbard had taken,. and was living with as his wife. Previously, she had looked with favor upon another man by the name of Thornburgh, and the latter resolved to take her away from Hubbard, even at the expense of his life. For this purpose he entered Hubbard's cabin in the dead of the night, with a loaded rifle, but Hubbard, having knowledge of his design, had armed himself with loaded pistols, and discharging one at Thornburgh as he entered the door, the ball took effect in the breast of the latter, and he fell, and expired. A self-constituted jury of inquest, after a thorough examination of the case, brought in a verdict of "Justifiable homicide."

The manner in which Hubbard and the rest of our fellow passengers spend ther time on the voyage indicates that they have neitheir become wise nor virtuous from the history of the past. They seem incapable of interesting themselves, save at backgammon or the card table, nearly all the time not consumed in eating or sleeping being employed at one or the other of the two games.

Wednesday, 17th. Ware and Devenport were suffering exceedingly from seasickness, and proposed to give the captain one hundred and fifty dollars to set them off on the shore of California; but as a matter of course, this was inadmissible, and the two gentlemen were doomed to enjoy the pleasures of one sea voyage. But one of them declared that he had rather pack a mule across the Rocky Mountains, than to go to sea; and that, if he ever sets his foot on *terra firma* again, he will never be caught on another vessel.

In the evening backgammon and seasickness were both forgotten a short time in the excitement of taking a large porpoise. This is generally considered a great treat by seamen, especially those on merchant vessels. The manner of taking them is as follows: a rope is passed through a block or pulley, which is fastened to some part of the rigging near the bow of the vessel, one end of which is tied to a harpoon prepared with a handle six or eight feet long, so as to render it convenient to throw. A sailor then fixes himself on the martingal under the bowsprit, while a few others at the other end of the rope, stand by to haul in. The reason for their taking their position at the forward end of the vessel is this; the porpoise always plays around the bow more than any other part, and the rigging under the bowsprit will admit of a sailor's fixing himself directly over the porpoise in his frequent approaches to this point. When thus prepared, and the porpoises hover around the bow, the harpoon is cast with great force and precision into the selected victim, and instantly the water is crimsoned with his blood. When the "throw" has been a sure one, the word "haul" is given, and the fish, or animal, is immediately raised above the water, and brought upon deck. The taking of a porpoise is one of those exciting events which occasionally break in upon the monotony of life at sea. It was judged that the one we took would weigh two hundred and fifty pounds. It afforded several gallons of oil, and meat enough to last the sailors for a number of days.

Thursday, 25th. Thus far on our voyage we have had the most beautiful weather, there having been no head wind to speak of, and but about four hours calm. We have generally been favored with a gentle breeze from the north-west, which has wafted us on our direct course to Oahu at the rate of five and six knots an hour. This has been exceedingly favorable to us on account of the weakness of our crew, six of the men having run away from the brig in Oregon, and could not be recovered, leaving but three efficient men on board of her, beside her three officers. But the Lord knoweth how "to temper (or regulate) the winds to the shorn lamb."

We are cheered with the prospect of a speedy passage to the islands, as we seem to have secured the north-east trades; but of this there is no certainty, as the trades are not very regular, and at sea above all other places, "we know not what a day may bring forth."

Monday, 29th. We were interested in the discovery of a sail on our starboard bow, which appeared to be steering the same course with us. She was a barque, probably a whaler from the northern ocean, bound to the Sandwich Islands, and thence home. Incidents of interest on this voyage thus far have been exceedingly scarce, a very great uniformity having characterized the days we have been at sea. However, the monsters of the deep, whales, sharks, &c., have from time to time attracted our notice, while the dark albatros, mother Carey's chickens, a small sea gull, and the boatswain's mate marlinspike, or man of war bird, as he is indifferently called, are all of the feathered tribe we have seen. The last mentioned is a very interesting bird, snow white, and appears very beautiful as it flits around the vessel on its wings of light, as if desiring to find a place of rest among the moving spars. It is principally found between the tropics, and must therefore be considered a lover of warm weather.

On the 30th crossed the Tropic of Cancer, and as the wind was very light, we found the heat quite oppressive. By a very good observation on the 1st of October, we found our latitude to be twenty-two degrees forty-four minutes, longitude one hundred and fifty-three degrees, fifty minutes; twenty four hour's sail from Oahu before a seven knot breeze. The captain walks the deck whistling for a breeze, and in the evening, behold it comes, and the sailing is delightful. Those who have been sick are getting well, and all unite in pronouncing the voyage thus far, as it regards wind and weather, an unusually pleasant one.

Thursday, 14th of October. The trades have freshened up to a strong breeze, and all were delighted with the prospect of seeing land before night. Borne onward prosperously, according to expectation, at four o'clock, the tops of the mountains of the island of Maui, towering above the clouds, burst upon our view. At sundown Morotoi, could also be seen, but both soon disappeared amidst the darkness of night. We continued our course until four o'clock in the morning, when we could distinctly see the land but a few miles distant, and not knowing whether we were exactly right in our calculations, we lay to for the light of day to discover unto us precisely our condition. At six o'clock, A. M., we found ourselves about six miles from Morotoi, with Oahu on our starboard bow, about thirty miles distant. Soon after sunrise a sail appeared on our stern, and evidently neared us very fast, while two other sail appeared on our bow, and seemed to be steering directly towards the harbor. While we were passing around Diamond Head, and the harbor and shipping, with the town of Honolulu, were breaking upon our view, the vessel which had been coming up on our stern, passed us so near that our yard arms were but a few feet from hers. She proved to be her Britanic Majesty's Brig Frolic of sixteen guns. Her commanding officer hailed us as she passed, and inquired if we had seen the British Frigate America on our way down. We answered no. He replied that she left England with the design of visiting Oregon. The brig was a beautiful craft, but probably would not consider it much of a "Frolic" to take a turn-a-bout with an American "Wasp."

The patriotic American very naturally calls to mind under such circumstances the triumph of the "Wasp" over the "Frolic" in the last war, and is led to wonder why a "Wasp" has not been continued in the American Navy.

As we drew near the shipping in the outer harbor we discovered a number of men of war, one of which was the British line of battle ship the Collingwood, Lord Seymour, Admiral, with which the Frolic passed a number of signals, and approaching her, gave her salute of sixteen guns, which was returned by the Admiral.

It was an exciting time on board of our little brig as we so suddenly emerged from the solitudes of the ocean into such interesting and noisy scenes.

As a number of vessels were before us, it was necessary for us to come to anchor in the roads, soon after which we were boarded by the pilot, with whom the Captain went directly to the shore, promising to send off a boat to take the passengers ashore before night. This he accordingly did, and at sundown we landed on the wharf near the American Consulate, where we found servants waiting with a small hand wagon to convey Mrs. H. and the children to the house of Mr. Rogers, one of the Presbyterian missionaries, where we were kindly invited to take up our lodgings for a day or two. or until we could make other provisions.

This is the third time I have visited the Sandwich Islands during the last six years, and having mingled several months with both foreigners and natives, I have had an opportunity of making observations of no very superficial character; and as the result, I am compelled to entertain the opinion that the public generally, and particularly the christian world, entertain very erroneous views in relation to the true condition of the aborigines of these islands. Great changes have indeed been effected, and vast improvements made among the Hawaiians through the instrumentality of missionary labor, yet, after all, the amount of real good accomplished, I fear, is not so great as the christian world has been led to believe. Religion, in every department of Hawaiian society, however genuine the system which is taught them may be, is of a very superficial character. Of this the missionary residing among them, is more sensible than any other man can be, and one of them, in answer to the inquiry, " how many of your people give daily evidence of being christians?" replied "none, if you look for the same evidence which you expect will be exhibited by christians at home." Indeed, it is a source of the greatest affliction with the missionaries, that all their efforts are ineffectual in eradicating that looseness of morals, which attaches itself so adhesively to the Hawaiian character, and which is every where exhibiting itself in the gambling, thievish, and adulterous habits of the people of all classes, from the hut of the most degraded menial, to the royal palace.

One fact will show the astonishing extent to which promiscuous intercourse prevails. Relationship is always traced from the mother, and not from the father, as in all civilized countries, and indeed it is not an easy matter for a Hawaiian to tell who his father is.

The practice of promiscuous assemblages of males and females in the streets of Honolulu, is as common as it is odious and demoralizing. Crowds of this description may be seen at all times of day and night, where conduct may be witnessed, and conversation heard, of the most reprehensible character.

In attending the native churches one is struck with the listlesness and inattention which prevail in the congregation. No matter how important the truths, or how impressive the manner of the speaker, he seems scarcely to gain the hearing of the ear; and seldom do the worshippers give any satisfactory evidence that they feel any of the soul hallowing influences resulting from an evangelical waiting before God. The Islanders are far behind the Indians of Oregon in paying attention to the preaching of the gospel. If once you can get an Indian to consent to hear you, you are sure of his attention till your speech is closed. But as to the effect produced, there is little to boast of in either case.

There are the same cold and callous nature, the same unaccountable stupidity and brutal insensibility to contend with, in both, and these array themselves against all the efforts made to overcome them, with disheartening effect. Notwithstanding these things, which the faithful chronicler of facts cannot pass over without mentioning, there are, on the other hand, evidences sufficient to establish the vast importance and utility of the missionary cause. For a particular account of the islands and of the mission, the reader is referred to the notes of a former visit.

CHAPTER XIV.

Voyage to China — Change of calculations — Embark on board the Leland — Accident — Departure — Cabin associates — The Captain — Rules to judge of character — The Island of Grigan — The Ladrones — Dangerous reefs — Gale — Bashu Islands — Spanish Possessions in the Pacific — Formosa — Chinese Sea — Ship Montreal — Ty phongs — The contending Pilots — Appearance of the coast of China — Arrival at Hong Kong — Reception of Keying — Review of the British troops — Sabbath disregarded — The Rev. Charles Gutslaff — Island of Hong Kong — City of Victoria — Population — Schools — Morrison Education Society — Morrison Hill — Success of the School — Rev. S. R. Brown — Churches — Missions — Where established — Missionaries — Climate of Hong Kong — Soldiers' Burying Ground — Wesleyan Methodists — Short voyage — City of Macao — Grand Prior — Bazaar — Temple — Camoen's Cave — Voyage to Canton — Description of the "Provincial City" — Adventures in the city — Temple of Honan — Dr. Parker — Dr. Devan — Proclamation of Keying — Counter Proclamation — Flower Garden — Dr. Bridgeman — Great excitement — Danger of an outbreak — Thrust out of the city — Night excursion — On board the Leland — Things that strike the foreigner — Boat population — Pirates.

Friday, October 10th. I was informed by Captain Sylvester that the Chenamus, in which we expected to take passage to the United States, would not be ready to sail under two or three months, and there being several vessels ready to sail for the States by the way of China, 1 resolved, if possible, to obtain a passage in one of them. Applying to Mr. Finlay, the supercargo of the ship Leland, which had just arrived at Honolulu from Callao, and was designing in a day or two to continue her voyage to China, and thence direct to New York, I was at first informed that all the staterooms but one were occupied, and there being four of us he could not make us comfortable in that. At first we relinquished the idea of sailing in that ship, but ascertaining that a young gentleman had taken the room adjoining the spare one who expected to leave the vessel at Hong Kong, I concluded that, if Mr. Finley would allow me the privilege of sleeping on the sofa or floor of the cabin, Mrs. H. and the two girls could, for the short space of thirty days, get along with the one room, and after that, the disembarkation of the young gentleman would give us the privilege of the occupancy of both. This I suggested to Mr. Finlay, and readily obtained a proposal from him to take us to New York by the way of Canton for eight hundred dollars. As it would have cost me one hundred dollars per month to have remained at the islands, and five hundred and twenty for passage on the Chenamus, I concluded that the expense of the latter course would be nearly, if not quite, equal to the passage by the way of China. This, connected with other reasons which involve the character of the Chenamus, both as it regards her accommodations, and the morals which prevailed on board, had the influence to bring me to the conclusion to accept of the proposal of Mr. Finlay, and return to my native land by the way of the Celestial Empire.

Accordingly, on Wednesday, the 15th of October, at two o'clock, P. M., we embarked on board the Leland, and as the wind was fair, had a prospect of going to sea before night.

Twenty-two vessels had been waiting for the southern gales to subside, and the northern breeze to come to enable them to put to sea, and by good luck ours was the fourth on the pilot's list. A little accident came well nigh detaining us in the harbor over night. As our anchor was raised our vessel was driven by the strong trade wind directly down to another ship, stern first, doing but little damage however, but rendering it necessary for us to warp up against the wind for some distance, before we could get clear of the ships that lay in our track. Extricating ourselves from this difficulty, just as the sable curtains of the evening began to render it difficult for us to discern the outlines of the interesting island of Oahu, our pilot, Captain Penhollow, who had conducted us out of the inner harbor through the narrow winding channel that opens a passage through the coral reef with which the island is environed, wishing us a happy and prosperous voyage, returned towards the glimmering lights of the city of Honolulu, while to the command, "square away the yards," our ship's prow was pointed to the westward, and before the silent hour of twelve, the fast receding island had disappeared amidst the gloom of surrounding darkness. On leaving this delightful Oasis of the ocean, where we had spent so many hours of unmingled enjoyment, we could but feel those sensations which moved the heart of the poet to sing as he left his island home,

> " Shades of evening close not o'er us,
> Leave our lonely bark awhile!
> Morn, alas! will not restore us
> Yonder dim and distant isle;
> Still my fancy can discover
> Sunny spots where friends may dwell;
> Darker shadows round us hover,
> Isle of beauty, Fare thee well!"

A gale had long been blowing from the south, and consequently the sea was very high, and for two or three of the first days the passengers were nearly all confined to their births with sea sickness, but the 20th found us on a comparatively smooth sea, gliding along before a gentle breeze from the north-east, in the enjoyment of health, and consequently qualified to take observations in regard to the ship, officers, crew and passengers, with whom we were to be so intimately connected, and with the interests of whom our own were to be so closely blended, during a voyage encompassing three-quarters of the globe.

Our fellow passengers consisted of Rev. A. B. Smith, wife, and three orphan children, the daughters of the late Mr. Lock, of Oahu, Mrs. Hooper, the wife of Wm. Hooper, Esq., acting Consul at Oahu, two children, and Mr. Sheliber, the young gentleman mentioned above. Besides these, Mr. Finlay, the supercargo, occupied a state room in the cabin, and this constituted our cabin society, as the Captain stopped principally in the round house, on deck. Our first impressions regarding our associates in the cabin, were quite favorable, but the Captain we found to be a surly jack tar, well acquainted with Biliingsgate vocabulary, and ready to draw upon its resources on all occasions. Indeed, it appeared from the amazing facility with which he could call to his aid the most vulgar kind of swearing, that he must have taken his regular gradations in the high school of his Satanic majesty himself. Mr. Finlay, who had control of the business of the vessel, showed at the outset, a desire to render his passengers comfortable, in the abundant provisions, consisting of vegetables, pigs, poultry, &c., with which he caused the ship to be supplied.

As the Leland was built in packet style, we found the cabin fine, and the state-rooms quite commodious; and after a few days' experience we were obliged to admit that the table of the Leland was better furnished than that of any other vessel in which we had sailed.

We were favored with gentle breezes from the northeast and east which carried us along from five to seven knots an hour, without anything in particular to break the monotony of the voyage until the 6th of November, when at three, P. M., we made Grigan, the northernmost of the Ladrone Islands. The appearance of this island, as we passed along by it about six miles off, was exceedingly interesting, perhaps more so to us in consequence of our not having been for many days entertained with the sight of any object but the sky over our heads, the boundless expanse of waters, around us, and the little world in which we were floating. This island is very high, nearly round, and rising gradually from its margin, it hides its summit above the clouds. It appeared remarkably green as if covered with timber, or with other vegetation of a luxuriant growth.

The island was visited two years ago by Mr. Dwight from the United States, and some twenty or thirty persons, some of whom were white men, and some natives were found upon it. The white men appeared to be of the sailor class, but could not give a very good account of themselves.

The Ladrone Islands are numerous, and the entire group belongs to the once famous, but now crumbling kingdom of Spain. The two southernmost are now principally occupied by Spaniards, and are used by Spain as a kind of Botany Bay, or place of banishment for state prisoners. Though their climate is delightful and some of them are fine fertile islands, yet they are of but little consequence to the world; and this is doubtless owing to the weakness and indolence of their possessors. Since they were first discovered by Magellanni, 1521, they have been inhabited by a set of thieves and pirates, and hence they are called "Ladrone (pirate) Islands."

West of the Ladrones are a number of dangerous reefs, which have been seen by several navigators; and it was our fortune to get directly among them. However, Providence smiled upon us, and we passed them all in safety, though while exposed to them, we were visited by a tremendous gale from the south, which not only prostrated us with seasickness, but threatened to drive us into the caverns of the deep. The waves rolled in mountains, and dashing around us in frightful pyramids, and commingling their deafening roar with the howling of the fitful blasts, struck terror into the brave hearts of the sons of the ocean, and admonished all to fear and tremble before Him who rideth upon the wings of the wind. After four days of incessant gales from every point of compass, the wind subsided, a calm succeeded, a breeze followed from the north and brought with it the blessings of health to the sick, and prosperity on our voyage.

On the 14th of November the appearance of strange birds, and now and then an object floating upon the surface of the water, gave signs that we were approaching land. On the evening of the 15th, we passed through between the north Bashee Islands, and the Tobal, Tobago, and Hima. The Bashee Islands all belong to Spain. Many of them are thickly settled, and are said to be very fertile. All the Spanish islands in this part of the Pacific Ocean are governed by a captain general, whose residence is at Manilla, on the island of Luconia. His government is exeeedingly despotic, and he is only responsible to the ministry in Spain.

Luconia, or Luzon, as it is laid down on some maps, is said to be a splendid island, vieing in natural resources with the far famed island of Java; but from the despotic nature of its government, and the indolence and jealousy of the Spaniards, it is of but little consequence to the crown of Spain.

On Sunday morning, the 16th, the island of Formosa was descried from the quarter deck. This island, with the Bashees and Luconia, form a chain which separates the Chinese Sea from the Pacific Ocean. Formosa was the first land we saw over which the Emperor of China sways his sceptre. It is a large island, with many fertile valleys, but the highlands from our vessel appeared exceedingly barren. It contains a number of large cities, and the population is exceedingly numerous. There is no direct business carried on betwixt them and foreigners, as this is a part of the Celestial Empire which barbarians are not allowed to visit.

On the day before we entered upon the Chinese Sea, it was exceedingly dark and gloomy, but we had no sooner passed the islands above mentioned, than the clouds disappeared, the sun arose in indescribable splendor, a fresh and invigorating breeze sprang up from the north, and we were wafted most delightfully over the sea of China, at the rate of nine miles an hour, towards our destination. Early in the morning we discovered a vessel fifteen miles astern of us, and at evening she passed us about three miles to the leeward, and proved to be the American ship Montreal, which left the harbor of Honolulu four hours before us. She formerly belonged to a line of London packets, is reputed a fast sailor, and should have beaten us at least six days to China.

On the morning of the 17th, the water changed from a deep blue to a light green, which indicated that we were already on soundings, though two hundred and sixty miles from port.

The Chinese Sea is regarded as the most dangerous waters to navigate in this part of the world, owing to the numerous shoals and currents, and to the winds called "ty phongs," which prevail in this region. The name rendered into English is literally great-winds, ty, signifying great, and phong, wind. They often come without giving any warning of their approach, and woe to the luckless vessel on which their fury is poured. Sails, spars, and rigging fly in fragments before the blast, and happy is that ship whose dismasted hull still floats upon the surface of the agitated deep after the storm has expended its violence. Many vessels, with their entire crews, have foundered in these storms, and not a vestige of them have ever been seen afterwards.

On the morning of the 18th, we passed the rock called "Pedro Branco," and at sunrise Chinese fishing boats appeared on every side, and the rough outlines of the coast of China presented themselves before us. Presently two boats bearing the pilot's flag, approached us, and an amusing strife took place betwixt them to see which should get on board of us first. They both came along side at once, and the two pilots sprung on to the side of our ship at the same time; but one of them in his effort to jump, stumbled, and fell into the sea. We were passing through the water with great rapidity, and the unlucky pilot, struggling in the water for life, and frightened so that his eyes stood out of his head like those of a craw fish, shot astern of us with the velocity of an arrow. But, accustomed to such adventures, his comrades in the boat immediately cast off a couple of long Bambo sticks, which the unfortunate man seized, and with the assistance of them kept himself above the water. A few hours afterwards he was picked up by a small boat which was sent out for his relief.

On approaching the coast, fishing and other boats are seen in every direction, even far out of sight of land, and one is impressed with the idea of the vast population of the Chinese Empire, long before he mingles with the countless throngs on *"terra firma."* As the land, with the light of morning, burst upon our view, there was disclosed a succession of barren mountains, exceedingly irregular in their outlines, and with the numerous islands of rocks; and the bays and gulfs which abound along the shore, present the most formidable barriers to the vast interior. The striking dissimilarity of this coast to all others, as well as the treacherous and piratical character of the inhabitants, may explain in part the reason why maritime nations have been so tardy in gaining access among the Chinese. But this coast is getting now to be well understood. Since the war with England, two vessels have been constantly employed in surveying its numerous islands, intricate channels, and deep indentations.

At ten o'clock, A. M., of the 18th of November, we rounded the west point of the island of Hong Kong, and came to anchor in the beautiful bay, which reflects, as from a liquid mirror, the flourishing city of Victoria. We were immediately invited on shore by the Rev. S. R. Brown, who is in the employment of the Morrison Education Society, as conductor of a school for the benefit of Chinese boys, and to whom we had letters of introduction, and with whom we spent an agreeable week. On the following Sabbath evening I was invited to preach in a chapel recently built, and known as the "Union Chapel," though it is principally under the control of the missionaries of the London Missionary Society. The congregation consisted of English residents, soldiers, Americans, and native Chinese, and numbered about one hundred persons.

We arrived at Hong Kong just in time to witness the arrival and subsequent public entertainments of the celebrated Chinese statesman, Keying, who is the governor general of the province of Canton, and imperial commissioner to transact the business of the government relating to the intercourse of China with other nations. His visit had been long expected, and from the great popularity of the statesman, both in China and among the British, it was contemplated with a great degree of interest. Splendid preparations had been made for his reception, and to render his visit not only interesting to himself, but conducive to the extension of British influence in China.

He was conducted from Whampo to Hong Kong in a

British steamboat, and recollecting the immense destruction of Chinese occasioned by a similar vessel in the late war, he closely examined every part of her on his passage down; and while passing around among the men, he scattered his gold and silver with the most princely liberality. The boat arrived before the town of Victoria on Thursday evening, and his excellency received a salute from the guns of the batteries and from the ships of war in the harbor, which was returned after the Chinese custom. His excellency landed amidst the roaring of cannon and the strains of martial music, and was conveyed in a splendid palanquin to the house which had been fitted up with great care, for his reception; and where, during the remainder of the evening, all the public functionaries and grandees of Hong Kong paid their respects to their illustrious visitor.

On Friday evening Keying and his suite, Lord Cochran, Lord Seymour, with all the grandees of the place, dined at the house of Sir John Francis Davies, the governor of Hong Kong, and from the representations of an eye witness, the evening wound up with a bacchanalian revel. Towards the close of the following day, a review of the British troops on the island, was to take place, and Keying was to appear in public, and give an opportunity for those to see him who were not allowed to mingle in the gay saloons of lords, knights, and barons.

They were not disappointed in their expectations; for as the high mountains of Hong Kong began to cast a cooling shade upon the city of Victoria, Keying and his suite were carried in sedan chairs to the house of Sir John Francis Davies, and soon after both their excellencies, with their attendants, accompanied by the Rev. Charles Gutslaff, as Chinese interpreter, repaired to a high bank beside the road, and located themselves upon it for the purpose of reviewing the troops as they were marched before them. We had the good fortune to place ourselves within a few feet of the bank, where we had a fine view of this titled group, as also of the soldiers. The latter consisted of two regiments, one of

Irish, and one of Sepoys, from India, numbering about two thousand in all. They were marched after two splendid bands of music, and from the strict discipline manifest in their manœuvres, as well as from the wonderful display of gunnery with which the review terminated, doubtless Keying was impressed with a sense of the superiority of the tactics of British soldiers over those of his imperial master.

At seven o'clock in the evening their excellencies, with their suites, the officers of the army, and others entitled to the distinguished privilege, repaired on board the line of battle ship Agincourt, to dine with the admiral, Lord Seymour. Dinner, as usual among the English on such occasions, was followed with music and dancing, but it was said that an English lady refused to dance with Keying, which so chagrined his excellency that it was thought proper to break up the party at an early hour.

On the Sabbath, Gov. Davies, Keying, and their suite, accompanied by the Rev. Charles Gutslaff, performed on a small English steamboat, a voyage of pleasure around the island of Hong Kong. Perhaps Gov. Davies was influenced thus to desecrate the Holy Sabbath by the examples set him by some of the lords and dukes of England, who have been in the habit of using the Lord's day for their public dinners; but, be this as it may, such a course of conduct by the authorities of a colony professedly Christian, in such a country as China, is not only a public outrage upon Christianity itself, but is directly calculated to destroy the good effects of years of missionary labor. While the servants of God in China are endeavoring to impress the people with a sense of the sacredness of the Holy Sabbath, the public authorities, sanctioned by the presence of Rev. Charles Gutslaff, by thus openly desecrating the day, do much to nullify all that missionaries can possibly do. If the above were a solitary instance of a violation of the day in this public manner, the evil influence resulting from it, would perhaps soon die away. But the Sabbath is scarcely known in Hong Kong, judging from external appearances. All ranks, from the governor downwards, habitually profane the holy day; while the public works, such as the erection of government buildings and fortifications, are prosecuted on the Sabbath the same as on other days. This is a source of great grief to the missionaries in this part of China, and may be regarded as one of the greatest obstacles in the way of success, with which every missionary to this country must come in contact. True, English service, in a most sickly manner, is performed twice on the Sabbath, but there are but few who attend regularly, while the vast majority of English and other foreigners at Hong Kong, use the Lord's day as a day of business or recreation.

December 10th. Dined at eight o'clock in the evening with the Rev. Charles Gutslaff, who is now a resident of Hong Kong, having recently received an appointment from the Colonial Government as Chinese Secretary. Perhaps there are few men in the world who have excited more interest in a missionary point of view, than this reverend gentleman. He is a Prussian by birth, is about fifty-five years of age, and has been in China thirty years, most of which have been employed in missionary labors in various parts of the empire. Though he has lost much of his influence as a Christian minister, both among the natives and foreigners, yet he is laboring to sustain himself as a missionary in the country, as well as a civilian.

He informed me that twenty-five native preachers who belonged to a society which he had organized for the propogation of the gospel in China, came to him for counsel and direction in their work; and that they were circulating through every part of the Chinese Empire, and were preaching from ten to fifteen sermons each per day. After the death of John Morrison, Jr., who filled the office of Chinese Secretary for a few years, Gutslaff, from his thorough knowledge of the different dialects of the Chinese language, was appointed to this lucrative station. His salary is £1500 sterling per annum, considerably more than that of the Vice President of the United States, while the salary of the Governor of the little petty colony of Hong Kong, amounts to three times as much as that of the President of our Union. Gutslaff appears to have made it one object of his residence in China, to accumulate wealth, and it is said that his efforts in this respect, have been successful. Report affirms that he has £15,000 deposited in the bank of Australia which he has accumulated while employed as a missionary, and probably some of the prejudice existing against him, arises from this circumstance, but it would be doing him great injustice not to admit that his unwearied labors for the benefit of China have been productive of good. In addition to his other labors he has recently published a Chinese Dictionary, which, with those previously published, will afford missionaries great facilities for the acquisition of the language. To form a correct estimate of this original character doubtless requires a most intimate acquaintance, while a short interview with him cannot fail to leave the impression upon the mind of the stranger, that the most singular compound of the gentleman and the clown, the divine and the civilian, the scholar and the novice, the sage and the humorist, the christian and the worldling, enters into, and forms the character of the Rev. Charles Gutslaff.

The island of Hong Kong, as the fruits of an unjust war, was ceded by China to Great Britain at the close of the late unhappy contest, and now constitutes a part of that empire upon which it has become the boast of her statesmen that the sun never sets. It is very irregular in its outlines, both as it regards its coast and its surface. It is not far from eight miles long, and varying in its width from one to four miles. On approaching it in a vessel, it presents a very forbidding aspect. It rises abruptly from the water, and its most elevated points are about three thousand feet above the level of the sea. Originally it was one huge mountain of granite, but for many ages this primitive rock has been decomposing, and the present soil of the island consists of decayed granite, with a small portion of decomposed vegetable matter. There are several vallies in the island through which meander small brooks, and being green and fertile, give the name to the island; Hong Kong signifying an island of green and fertile vallies.

The city of Victoria, embracing both the Chinese and English portions, stretches along the eastern side of the island nearly three miles. Its greatest depth is not more than one-fourth of a mile, and the abruptness of the mountains behind the city, will not admit of extending the buildings far in that direction. Though it is but about five years since the city was commenced, yet it has grown up so rapidly, and contains so many magnificent buildings, that one of the learned Chinese Mandarins who accompanied Keying, on leaving the place, composed a poem in honor of the city, in which he entitled it "the city of splendid palaces." The city, however, is in a very unfinished state, and the sound of the hammer and trowel is heard in every part of it during seven days in a week, and it is therefore rapidly improving; and doubtless, from its favorable location, and by the assistance of British wealth and influence, it is destined to become a place of great commercial importance.

The population of Hong Kong amounts to about thirty thousand persons, most of whom are Chinese. There are about four hundred English residents on the island, besides the soldiers, and not more than ten Americans. These, with the regiment of Irish soldiers already referred to, constitute all the white people embraced in this colony. The Chinese population, numbering more than twenty-five thousand, are exceedingly industrious in their habits, and accomplish a great share of the retailing business of the city. In consequence of the unhealthiness of the climate the English residents have fixed themselves here but temporarily, and design, after having amassed a fortune, to return to old England to enjoy the fruits of their labors. Many of them, however, fall victims to the malignant fevers which here prevail, and their dreams of worldly aggrandizement vanish with their lives.

The schools of Hong Kong require to be noticed. Here are no public schools for the benefit of white children, consequently they are growing up, as in other new colonies, in comparative ignorance. The school which is supported by the Morrison Education Society is one of great importance to the interests of China, as the influence it exerts at present, and the objects it contemplates, sufficiently prove. The circumstances which led to the formation of the Morrison Education Society, was the death of the Rev. Robert Morrison, D. D., who, in connection with his unwearied labors as a missionary, officiated many years as translator in the service of the Hon. East India Company in China. The friends of this great and good man in China, having been deeply interested in the success of his labors while living, and wishing to cherish a grateful remembrance of him when dead, resolved to erect a monument worthy to perpetuate his memory, and calculated to assist in carrying forward that work, in the promotion of which he had fallen a sacrifice. Dr. Morrison died on the 2d of August, 1834, and on the 9th of November, 1836, the society which took his name, was organized at Canton, having a fund of six thousand dollars.

The objects of the society, as expressed in its constitution, are, " to improve and promote education in China, by schools and other means." Chinese youth were to be taught to read and write the English language, in connection with their own; and by these means the society designed "to bring within their reach all the instruction requisite for their becoming wise, industrious, sober and virtuous members of society, fitted in their respective stations in life, to discharge well the duties which they owe to themselves, their kindred, and their God." The trustees of the society designed to employ two teachers, one from England, and one from the United States, and made application accordingly. From England they received no reply, but a favorable one from the States, and on the 23d of February, 1839, Rev. Mr. and Mrs. Brown, from Massachusetts, arrived in China, but the war immediately breaking out, rendered it necessary for them to take up their residence at Macao. Here, by the advice of the trustees, Mr. Brown commenced operations, but the Chinese were so slow in appreciating the effort, that in September, 1841, the school numbered but thirteen scholars.

Catholic influence, and Chinese exclusiveness, rendered Macao almost as undesirable a location for the school, as Canton; and as Hong Kong had fallen into the hands of the British, application was made to Sir Henry Pottinger, her British Majesty's plenipotentiary, for the privilege of locating the school on that island.

This application resulted in the appropriation of a hill which overlooks the city of Victoria, as the location for the buildings, and which from that time has been known as "Morrison Hill." Extensive buildings were immediately erected, the number of the pupils increased, an assistant teacher employed, and from that time the school has been progressing in every way correspondent to the expectations of its warmest friends. At present the school numbers thirty students, all boys, and many of them have made great improvement. A circumstance which was related to me by Mr. Brown, shows in what light the Chinese first viewed the school, and the influence it is beginning to exert. An aged Chinese, who had finally consented to send three of his boys to the school, observed one day to Mr. Brown, "we could not at first understand why a foreigner should wish to feed and instruct our children for nothing. We thought there must be some sinister motive at the bottom of it. Perhaps it was to entice them away from their parents and country, and transport them to some foreign land. At all events, it was a mystery. But I understand it now. I have had my three sons in your school steadily since they entered it, and no harm has happened to them. The oldest has been qualified for the public service as interpreter. The other two have learned nothing bad. The religion you have taught them, and of which I was so much afraid, has made them better. I myself believe its truth, though the customs of my country forbid my embracing it. I have no longer any fears—you labor for other's good, not your own."

Preparations have recently been made for the enlargement of the school; as many more had applied for admission during the last year, than could possibly be accommodated. A fortunate appropriation of fourteen thousand dollars to the institution, with a recent subcription of several thousand dollars more, will enable the trustees suitably to enlarge it, and to place it upon a firm basis.

The above appropriation was made by the persons who had the settlement of the estate of the lamented J R. Morrison, son of the late Dr. Robert Morrison.

That gentleman, while living, was deeply interested in the welfare of the school, and it was thought proper, by those upon whom it devolved to dispose of his pro perty, to associate his name with that of his father, by bestowing fourteen thousand dollars of his estate upon the institution as a permanent fund, and thus to raise a noble monument to perpetuate the memory of both of these benefactors of the Chinese nation.

The conductor of this school, the Rev. S. R. Brown, is every way entitled to the confidence of the community which employs him, and of the Chinese, for whose benefit he is devoting his life. His interests are blended with those of this institution, and his whole soul is enlisted to promote its advancement. And, in the rapid improvement of the students in the arts and sciences, in the correctness of their moral deportment, and in the satisfactory evidence which some of them give of genuine conversion and a qualification for future usefulness, he already witnesses the happy results of his labors. As this institution was established upon a broad basis, and is conducted according to the most enlarged views of benevolence, its supporters and directors are among the benefactors of mankind.

There are two churches in Hong Kong, which have been erected for the accommodation of foreigners; one of which is the "Union Chapel," and the other is an Episcopalian church. In the former, the missionaries officiate alternately, and the latter is supplied by the chaplains from the army and navy. Some of these latter *divines*, after spending Saturday evening in card playing and wine drinking, will enter the sacred desk on Sunday, and preach, not as messengers of God, but as "one that playeth skillfully on an instrument"—and their hearers, as destitute of religion as themselves, will flatter their vanity by informing them that they have preached an admirable sermon. A few of these chaplains, however, are evangelical men, and when they preach, they hesitate not "to decalre the whole counsel of God." It fell to the lot of one of these to preach on a Sabbath when a number of the great men of the island were present; and knowing the viciousness of their characters, like a man of God he enforced upon them the important truth, that, "without holiness, no man shall see the Lord." At the close of his sermon he was informed by the general of the army that his "preaching was not acceptable; that they came to church to be comforted, not to be condemned to hell."

After the island of Hong Kong had been wrested from the Chinese by the English, the missionaries in this part of China, generally collected at this place. Formerly, Macao was the only place where foreigners with their families could reside. But as Macao was under papal influence, and Canton was yet inaccessible, Hong Kong was judged to be the most proper place for the establishment of the missions. Accordingly, missionaries of the London Missionary Society, and also of the American Board of Commissioners for Foreign Missions, and the Baptist Foreign Board, fixed their residences in this place. They built their dwelling houses, churches, and school-houses for the Chinese, with the design of constituting this place the center of their operations.

Some of these buildings were quite expensive, especially the mission house of the American Board.

At the conclusion of the war, Hong Kong becoming English ground, and Canton accessible to missionaries and their families, all the American missionaries resolved at once to abandon the former, and establish themselves in the latter place. This subjected them to a great pecuniary loss in the buildings and other property, which they were obliged to sacrifice at Hong Kong. But they considered it to be their duty to enter the opening which British cannon had made into China, believing that the advantages, in a missionary point of view, of a location in Canton, would more than counterbalance all the pecuniary losses to which such a course would subject them.

Consequently, Dr. Bridgeman, Dr. Parker, and Dr. Ball, of the A. B. C. F. M., and Dr. Devan, of the Baptist Board, have retired from Hong Kong, and have taken up their residence in the Provincial city. Whether they have acted wisely, remains to be decided; but be this as it may, the three or four Chinese houses of worship which they erected at Hong Kong, are nearly deserted, and the fruits of their labors are rapidly disappearing.

Dr. Legg and Mr. Gallaspie, of the London Missionary Society, are establishing themselves permanently in Hong Kong. Dr. Legg, however, is now on a visit to England, but designs to return and resume his labors in this place. They have recently erected a large and splendid mission house, which appears from a distance more like the palace of a prince, than the house of the humble missionary. They have here collected a school of boys, whom they are endeavoring to instruct, and, though the fruits of their labors are tardy in exhibiting themselves, yet, by various means, such as the printing of books in Chinese, and preaching by their Chinese assistants, they are casting their bread upon the waters, and are expécting to be able to gather it after *many days*.

It is difficult to tell what amount of good has been accomplished by missionary labor in Hong Kong, doubtless much more than the enemies of missions are willing to admit. But it is evident the work at this point, as well as in some other portions of the mission field, has been greatly injured by the publication of reports furnished by missionaries of too flaming a character. Missionary reports always return to the places they are designed to represent, and if they are not strictly true, they always create prejudice against the cause they are designed to promote.

The climate of Hong Kong is very unsalubrious, particularly during the prevalence of the south-west monsoons.

The monsoons are winds which blow one-half of the year from the south-west, and the other half from the north-east. The north-east monsoon prevails during our fall and winter months, and while it continues, the island is considered a comparatively healthy location; but after the winds set in from the south-west, the atmosphere becomes exceedingly oppressive. The heat of the sun becomes almost unendurable, and both natives and foreigners enter into every possible precaution to guard against the deleterious effects of the sun's burning rays.

Notwithstanding the extreme care exercised by foreigners to preserve health, this climate proves fatal to many of them. It is peculiarly debilitating to the female constitution, and a number of the wives of missionaries, have here fallen as martyrs in their work. The Hong Kong fever has become notorious wherever the name of the place is known; and while all who come to this country are more or less exposed to this most malignant of all fevers, perhaps the soldiers quartered here are the greatest sufferers. Such is the astonishing mortality that reigns among them, that it is necessary to reinforce them annually with a fresh regiment from home, in order to keep ready for effective service one thousand men. Indeed, in view of the unhealthiness of its climate, Hong Kong is no desirable place of residence for foreigners, and there are but two motives sufficiently powerful to induce either Europeans or Americans to continue here a great length of time: These are the love of money and the love of souls.

Having heard much concerning the soldiers' burying ground, on the 14th of December, curiosity led us to take a walk over this depository of the dead. About one mile and a half from the town, the old barracks were situated, where the soldiers were quartered immediately after the conclusion of the China war, and during the unhealthy part of the season.

But a few score of them had fallen before the prowess of their Chinese enemies, but while quietly lying in their barracks, and recounting the victories they had won, they were attacked by an enemy before whom kings turn pale, and the valor of the bravest soldier falters.

The Hong Kong fever brought death into the warriors' camp, and during the short period of six weeks, more than five hundred men were laid in the dust by this fearful scourge.

Walking in company with our friend Rev. Rowland Reese, we came to the ground where these half a thousand, together with several hundred, who had died previously, were buried, and the first thing that attracted our attention was the coffin of a small child, which lay partly embedded in the ground, its lid broken off, and disclosing some of the bones of the infant which the hungry dogs of the Chinese, in robbing the coffin, had allowed to remain. In viewing this, we recollected that British soldiers were sometimes allowed to take their wives and children with them, and they are consequently liable to share the fate of the soldier. Going a little farther, we found ourselves surrounded with coffins on every side, some of them partly covered, others entirely above ground, and many of them robbed of their contents by hungry dogs and swine, while ghastly skulls and other bones lay bleaching far and near. Our hearts sickened while we looked around upon this modern Golgotha, and we fancied we heard from the numerous skeletons which whitened the ground around us, the bitterest imprecations uttered against that cruel war system, which was relentless in its claims upon them while living, and in death cast them beyond the common sympathies of humanity.

We left this scene of desolation, indulging the reflection that those great ones of the earth, who, from motives of ambition and cupidity, entail so much misery upon their fellow men as results from the practice of war, will have a fearful account to render at the bar of God. Surely, thought we, this is the glory which multitudes who enter the field of strife, secure to themselves; they die like the brute, and are denied the rights of sepulture, but an eternal weight of glory awaits every christian warrior.

During our stay at Hong Kong we became acquainted with several Wesleyan Methodists from England. Some of them are soldiers in the army, and when there has been a sufficient number of them, they have formed themselves into classes, and as far as their circumstances would permit, they have in other respects enjoyed the institutions of Methodism. The Rev. Rowland Reese, who resides at Hong Kong, and has been for several years in the employ of the government, as a civil engineer, is a local preacher from England, and takes a very decided stand in the place where he lives in favor of that form of christianity called Methodism, which he considers to be not only the purest in the world, but the most efficient in its "*modus operandi.*"

Under this conviction, he has frequently addressed the British Conference on the subject of sending missionaries to China, proposing to give towards the support of one, one hundred dollars per year, though his income is quite limited. He has at length gained an assurance from the president of the conference, that measures have been taken to grant his request, and he is now looking for the arrival of the missionaries. He appears to be an excellent brother, and is certainly entitled to the blessing of those who entertain strangers.

Our continuance at Hong Kong was four weeks, three of which we spent at the house of Mr. Reese. Though the expense of living at Hong Kong is great, yet this truly benevolent man furnished us with all the comforts his house afforded, without money and without price.

On the 15th of December we took leave of our newly formed acquaintance at Hong Kong, and taking what the Chinese call a "fast boat," proceeded through a perfect labyrinth of islands, across the mouth of Pearl river to the city of Macao, the distance of thirty miles.

It was late in a very dark evening when we arrived in the inner harbor, and as our baggage must all pass through the Custom House on landing, we must necessarily leave it in the care of the Chinese on the boat, during the night, as there were no conveniences for our continuing on board. This arranged, we committed ourselves to the guidance of the captain of the boat, having given him the name of the individual whom we wished to find, and by the way of a narrow avenue, on each side of which the towering walls of the buildings were rendered scarcely visible by the glimmerings of a Chinese lantern, we entered the densely populated city of Macao. Winding along the crooked lanes, and traveling as fast as we could for thirty minutes or more, we at length entered a gloomy mansion, situated near the centre of the city, where our guide told us our friend lived.

Here we were cordially welcomed by the Rev. Dr. Happer, a missionary of the Presbyterian Board, who had kindly invited us to make his house our home while we desired to remain in the city.

Dr. Happer has been in China but little more than one year, and consequently has not made a great impression. He has established a school of twenty-five Chinese boys, and is teaching them the English language, while a person employed for that purpose is instructing him in the Chinese. He feels encouraged to prosecute his work, though the prospect of accomplishing much, is dark before him.

Macao is a Portuguese town, containing forty thousand inhabitants, thirty-five thousand of whom are Chinese, and five thousand Portuguese. Of the latter there are but a few hundred native Portuguese, they being mostly of the half-caste population. The Portuguese pay an annual tribute to China for the privilege of remaining here, and indeed Macao is under the control of the Chinese, though for purposes of mutual advantage, the Portuguese have been allowed to continue in possession.

The Portuguese first established themselves here more

than three hundred years ago, and during the first hundred years, Popish missionaries from this point, had penetrated into every part of the Chinese Empire, even into the very palace of the Emperor himself. But, intermeddling with the affairs of government, the priests were banished from Pekin. This checked the prosperity of the Papists, and though unwearied efforts have been made ever since that time to establish Popery permanently in the Empire, yet they have resulted in giving it but a doubtful footing.

Macao, however, being under the domination of Portugal, is papistical in its character, and contains several splendid cathedrals and convents; and the priests, from the snowy-headed "padre" down to the boy of ten years, may be seen perambulating the streets in every part of the city, almost without number. Here Catholicism exists in its grandeur and magnificence, as well as in its disgusting forms and nameless mummeries. But it may be remarked, in favor of the Catholics of Macao, that they are more tolerant in their principles and practice than any other Catholics in the world. During the celebration of high mass on Christmas eve, we took the opportunity of visiting three of the most splendid churches in the city, and in neither of them were we obliged to kneel, even at the elevation of the Sacred Host.

During the short but sanguinary contest betwixt the English and Chinese, Macao, as a matter of course, remained neutral; and as a consequence of the war, and during the short period of six years, she made more rapid improvements than ever before : but when the articles of peace were signed under her walls, the death blow was given to her prosperity.

English capital and English influence have already placed her rival, Hong Kong, or Victoria, far above her in point of wealth and commercial importance, though it is but five years since the latter sprang into being ; whereas Macao boasts of an antiquity of more than three hundred years. The houses of some parts of Macao are built after the European style, though the streets are very narrow and dirty, while in some places, as you pass along, the buildings present the appearance of dismal prisons. Other parts of the city are peculiarly Chinese, and these are by far the most extensive, and give one a very correct idea of the large cities of the Chinese Empire.

There are a number of places of interest in and about the city of Macao, which, from the satisfaction a visit to them is calculated to afford, are well worthy the attention of travelers. The first in order is that of the Grand Prior.

The portion of the city around the Grand Prior, on landing from the outer harbor, is the most interesting part of the Portuguese division of the town. It is built round the borders of the beautiful bay which constitutes the harbor in the form of a semi-circle, and the Prior forms an elegant promenade, not only for all the fashion and elite of the town, but for all such as desire to enjoy the invigorating breeze which comes in from the bosom of the Chinese Sea. Here may be seen almost every day, Portuguese, Englishmen, Frenchmen, Spaniards, Americans, Germans, Chinese, Indians, Parsees, Hawaiians, &c., mingling in one common troop along this beautiful Prior, and all apparently delighted with the surrounding scenery.

Passing from the Prior to the north, partly through the town, you come to a second place of interest, which is the Bazaar, or market, of the city. This is situated in the Chinese portion of the town, and contains all kinds of fruits, vegetables, and provisions peculiar to the country. Among the fruits, oranges and bannanas are the most prominent kinds; the former being more abundant than apples in New York, and four large fresh oranges can be procured for one cent. One is astonished in passing through the Bazaar to see the immense variety of meats, fish and fowl, with which it abounds. In addition to the common kinds, such as beef, pigs, mutton, capons, geese and ducks, may be found an astonishing variety, among which dogs, cats, rats and frogs, are the most prominent. These may be had either alive, dressed, or cooked, so that the most fastidious can easily be accommodated.

The Chinese Heathen Temple, situated within the precincts, and at the east end of the city, is another object of curiosity to all strangers who visit this part of China. This temple was principally hewn out of the solid rock, and its appearance reminds one of the Bible accounts of the idolatrous practices of the nations of antiquity; several majestic banyan trees extending over it their huge branches, cast a sombre shade upon its different departments, while its walls of blackened granite, and the hideous images which appear on every hand, as the gloomy nature of the worship there paid to heathen gods, are calculated to make impressions upon the mind of the beholder at once solemn and affecting. Here we witnessed, for the first time, the priests of Budha in humble prostration before their idols, and while witnessing their devotions, our fervent ejaculations were ascending to heaven that the long night of death which has reigned over them, unbroken, may soon pass away, and the devotees of this cruel system of idolatry, become the true worshipers of the living God.

There are several beautiful gardens within the walls of the city, among which the Casser Garden, at the western end of the city, is the most popular as a place of resort.

This is celebrated on account of the beauty of its shaded walks, the variety of the plants and shrubbery by which it is adorned, the enchanting nature of its scenery, but principally from its containing within its enclosure the celebrated grotto known by the name of Camoen's Cave.

This cave procured its cognomen from the following circumstance: Camoen was appointed by the crown of Portugal to an important office in the colony of Macao, and while residing in this place, he spent a great share of his time in the solitude of this cave. It was here that this most celebrated of all Portuguese poets composed his "Lusiad," a poem which has rendered his name immortal. The cave is interesting as a natural curiosity, but it has been materially injured by an attempt to adorn and beautify it by artificial works. It contains a bust of the celebrated man who has given it a name that it will probably bear to the end of time. In connection with this it might be proper to observe that after he left Macao, Camoen and his manuscript poems were both singularly and providentially preserved from unmerited oblivion. The vessel in which he sailed from Macao, was wrecked in the Chinese Sea; fortunately, however, not a great distance from the shore. When it appeared evident that the vessel was lost, and there being no other means of saving himself, forgetting every thing else as comparatively worthless, he seized his manuscript in one hand, and cast himself into the sea. Presently, the few who had gained the shore before him, discovered Camoen struggling in the briny element, and bearing in one hand above the surface of the agitated waters, the poem that was destined to give him an earthly immortality. At length a fortunate wave came to his assistance, and he was borne in triumph to the shore, happy that, with the loss of his wealth, he had saved what he esteemed of infinitely more value, the instrument which was destined to attach to his memory an enviable and enduring fame.

There are also a number of eminences in and about the place, which overlook the entire town and harbor, and which are very strongly fortified. Some of the guns by which the battlements are mounted, are of astonishing calibre, and bear date as ancient as 1625.

From the hill on which the "Central Fort" is built, the view of the city, harbor, roads, and the adjacent islands, is sufficiently interesting to pay one for the labor of climbing to its summit. From this spot was pointed out to us the precise place where the English and Chinese embassadors signed the preliminaries of peace at the conclusion of the late war. On the ramparts of the "Central Fort" I counted fifty of the engines of death ready to pour ruin upon invading foes.

Having visited every thing of interest in and around the city of Macao, we prepared to take our leave; de siring to spend as many days in Canton before embarking for the United States, as we possibly could. We had received a pressing invitation from Dr. Devan, a missionary of the Baptist Board, resident in Canton, to make his house our home so long as we desired to remain in the place. Accordingly, on Wednesday, the 7th of January, accompanied by Mrs. Hooper, one of our fellow passengers on the Leland, we embarked on a "fast boat," and with a fresh breeze proceeded up the Canton river.

These "fast boats" are always manned by Chinese, and, though differing from any other water craft which I have seen in any other part of the world, are quite comfortable for the conveyance of passengers; and as they are propelled by oars when the wind does not serve, they usually perform their passages with considerable dispatch; passengers always furnishing themselves with bed and board.

It was near sundown when we left the Grand Prior, and before we had proceeded far, darkness had shut from our view all surrounding objects, and reposing on the beds we had spread for our temporary use, we fell asleep, and the next morning found ourselves above the Bogue, or Bocca Tigris, and gliding along past the villages, paddy fields, and Pagodas, by which the banks of the river are adorned. Before passing Whampoa, we stopped a few moments along side the Leland, which had already commenced receiving her cargo, and leaving some of our baggage on board, we proceeded on through the multitude of boats which thronged the river, and which seemed to multiply in a ten-fold proportion as we approximated the "Provincial City." It was nearly dark when we arrived off the place of landing, and we found the wharf so thronged with boats that it was impossible for us to approach it nearer than fifty yards. We began to fear that we should be under the necessity of spending the night on the boat; no very comfortable prospect in view of the piratical propensities of the thousands by which we were surrounded. And as for confusion, Babel itself could not have presented a worse

12*

state. However, I hastened to dispatch a short note to Dr. Devan, by one of the officers of the boat, and fortunately the note found him. At eight o'clock he and his most amiable wife gave us a hearty welcome at their house, which is situated in one of the densest portions of the suburbs of the great city of Canton, and on one of the principal avenues leading to one of the gates of the city proper.

Here we are then, brought by a succession of favorable providences, and placed in the midst of the great and wonderful city of Canton. Every thing surrounding us is new and striking. The people, the costume, the buildings, the streets, and every thing the eye beholds, present an aspect totally different from any thing existing in any other portion of the world; and to give a minute and intelligible description of the almost infinite variety which this one city presents to the view of the stranger, if it were possible to accomplish it, would require volumes, and cannot therefore be expected in this journal. It will be impossible even to carry out the design of the traveler to Rome, who observed that he should "give a description of the Rome which he saw;" but it must suffice the reader to be introduced to a few subjects important to be understood, and interesting to contemplate relating to the celebrated city of Canton.

The Chinese write the name of their city, Kwangtung Sang Ching, "chief city of the province of Kwangtung," but in conversation they usually call it "Sang Ching," the "Provincial City." Doubtless Canton is a corruption of Kwangtung. This city is situated on the north side of the Choo Keang, or Pearl river, and about sixty miles from the great sea. It is in the twenty-third degree of north latitude, and one hundred and thirteenth east longitude from Greenwich.

The scenery around the city, though beautiful, and to some extent diversified, presents nothing bold or romantic. On the north and north-east sides, distant a few miles, may be seen a range of hills or mountains, but in every other direction the prospect is unobscured. The rivers, channels and canals, are very numerous, and are covered with a vast variety of boats, which are continually passing to and from the neighboring towns and villages. Southward the water covers nearly one-fourth of the whole surface. Paddy fields and gardens occupy the low lands, and occasionally may be seen little hills and groves of trees rising here and there, to diversify the scene.

Canton is one of the most ancient cities in the world, at least among those that have survived the revolutions of time. We have pretty satisfactory evidence that it existed several hundred years before the Christian era, and, according to Chinese classics, one of the ancient emperors, four thousand years ago, commanded one of his ministers to repair to the southern country, and govern the city, which was then called the Splendid Capital, and the country surrounding it. If this be true, a large city occupied the site of the present city of Canton more than one hundred and fifty years before the time of Abraham.

The city of Canton may be considered as divided into two parts; the city proper, or that portion within the walls, and the portion without the walls, or the suburbs, which differs in its buildings, streets and extent of population, very little from that within the walls. That part of the city enclosed by a wall is built nearly in the form of a square, and is divided into two parts by a wall running from east to west.

The northern, which is the largest part, is called the old city, and the southern, the new city. The entire circuit of the wall, including both divisions of the city within, is variously estimated at from six to eight English miles. The walls rise nearly perpendicularly, and vary in height from twenty-five to forty feet. They are about twenty feet thick, and are composed of stone and brick. A line of battlements is raised on the top of the walls at intervals of a few feet around the whole city. Leading through the outside wall are twelve gates bearing different names, some of which are very significant: Wooseen Mun is "the gate of the five genii." Yungtsing Mun is "the gate of eternal purity." This is the gate that leads to the place where criminals are publicly decapitated. Yungan Mun is "the gate of eternal rest." At each of the gates a few soldiers are stationed to watch them by day, and close and guard them by night.

The principal part of the suburbs are situated on the south and west sides of the city. They are much less extensive on the east than on the west; and on the north there are very few buildings, owing probably to the fact that the city proper in that direction extends on to the sides of a range of hills. This fact is poetically expressed by a Chinese writer, who observes that, on the north "the city rests on the brow of a hill."

It is said by good authority that there are from six hundred to a thousand streets in the city of Canton. Some of them are long, but most of them are short and crooked. The broadest street in Canton is sixteen feet wide, and there are hundreds not more than two feet. These are all flagged with stones, mostly large granite slabs.

It will be impossible to give any idea of the immense motley crowd that daily throngs these narrow lanes. The stout, half-naked, vociferating coolies, bearing every description of merchandise on their backs, the noisy sedan-bearers, together with the numerous travelers, retailers, pedlars, barbers, tinkers, beggars, &c., presents a scene before the spectator which puts all his powers of description at defiance.

In the suburbs, near the south-west corner of the city, are situated the foreign factories, of which there are thirteen. They occupy a plot of ground extending sixty rods from east to west, and forty from north to south. The factories present a very firm and substantial appearance, being but two stories high, and with the exception of two narrow streets, forming one solid block, each factory extending in length, the whole breadth of the block. They are owned by the Chinese Hong merchants, and are occupied by the Dutch, English, Swedes, Americans, French and Danes. The different factories may be distinguished by the flags of their respective nations, which constantly wave over them.

In the afternoon of Friday, the 9th, Dr. Devan proposed to conduct Mrs. H. and myself to those parts of the city where it was safe for ladies to go, with which we readily acquiesced, as we desired to learn as much as we possibly could concerning one of the great cities of the Celestial Empire. It is but a short time since foreign females have been allowed to approach nearer to the city of Canton than Macao. The ladies are indebted to the bloody gallantry of British soldiers, for the privilege of walking the crowded streets of this wonderful city. But even now, though the recent treaties with other nations provide for such a privilege, yet a very large portion of the wealthy Chinese population are violently opposed to foreigners penetrating far into the city, especially to pass through the gates. Notwithstanding this, according to arrangement, we set off on our tour, first taking the hongs and the factories, where the foreign merchants, and the missionaries of the A. B. C. F. M. reside. After calling on some of the latter, we continued on some half mile or more direct towards one of the gates opening into that part of the city, yet too sacred to be polluted by the feet of barbarians. As we penetrated farther and farther into the city, beyond the common walks of foreigners, it was astonishing to us to observe the great curiosity that was excited among the countless multitudes of Chinese through which we passed, by the appearance of a foreign lady walking by the side of a gentleman, in the thronged avenue, where never a Chinese lady is allowed to go except as carried by her servants, inclosed in her palanquin. We could not stop for a single moment for fear of being so thronged as not to be able to extricate ourselves, but found it necessary to urge ourselves onward as fast as we possibly could walk, while the excited mass poured after us in wild confusion, and every now and then a stalwart form rushing through the crowd, would thrust himself before us for the purpose of getting one fair peep into the face of a foreign lady before she had passed beyond their reach.

At length we came to what Dr. Devan told us was the gate of the city proper, but we did not dare to enter it, nor even to stop near it, such was the excitement that prevailed wherever we appeared; but casting a passing look within the walls, we continued walking for an hour, until we had explored a number of the principal streets, and at almost every step we were saluted by the name of "Fan-qui," (barbarian), and some times Dr. Devan told us they would call us "evil spirits."

Before closing our perambulations, we visited the Ningpoo Exchange, which is a famous building, so far up in the city that strangers seldom visit it. It contains almost countless apartments, and at every turn and corner is placed a brazen idol before which the smoke of burning incense is continually rising. In this Exchange a vast amount of business is performed by commercial men from all parts of China. Impressed with the novelty of every thing we had witnessed, we returned to Dr. Devan's in safety, and on Saturday, the 10th, found ourselves prepared to visit the celebrated Temple of Honan.

This most popular heathen temple in the Province of Kwangtung, is situated on the opposite side of the Choo-keang river from Canton. Accompanied by our friends, Dr. and Mrs. Devan, and a Chinese interpreter, we engaged a boatman to row us across the river to this splendid "Jos-house" of the Chinese. On entering the temple and casting an eye around upon the objects within, here, said I, idolatry must appear in its most magnificent aspects. As we entered the gateway leading to the inner court, there were two colossal figures, images of deified warriors, stationed, one on the right and the other on the left, to guard the entrance to the sacred palaces. Further on we came to the palace of the "four great celestial kings," images of ancient heroes. Still further on we were conducted along a broad pathway to "the great powerful palace." Enter ing this we found ourselves in the presence of "the three precious Budhas," three stately and magnificent images representing the past, the present, and the future Budha. The hall or palace where these images are placed, is one hundred feet square, and contains numerous other images of deified heroes, real or imaginary, before which altars are erected and incense is kept constantly burning. The temple is vast, and the buildings embraced within the sacred inclosures are numerous, and contain large numbers of Chinese gods. Some of the idols are truly splendid specimens of the works of art, and as they are arranged in perfect order around the walls of their respective and spacious halls, all of bronze work, and measuring from eight to twenty feet in height, they present a very imposing appearance. In addition to these shining images, there were several rough stones pointed out to us as being numbered with Chinese gods.

We were led by our conductor to the apartments containing the sacred hogs and geese, and were assured that it was an uncommon privilege for strangers to be allowed to behold these squalling and grunting divinities.

In "the great and powerful palace," which contains "the three precious Budhas," is hung a very large brass bell, which is used by the priests at the hour of worship to wake up the slumbering deities and to call their attention to the oblations of their devotees. One of the party, taking hold of the huge tongue of the bell, drew it up at one side and let it fall back against the other with such force as to cause the whole temple to ring with its vibrations. Some of the priests started back as with fear, but so soon as the sound had died away they came forward and reproached us for such a gross violation of the sanctity of the place. In addition to this we were guilty of another sacrilegious act in taking some of the incense which was smoking before the idols, and bringing it away with us; much, however, to the diversion of our Chinese attendants. As it was not the hour of worship we did not witness the devotions of the priests, but ascertained that at five o'clock, P. M., every day, they celebrate their vespers in the palace of the precious Budhas.

Parallel with each other on the right and left, are long lines of apartments, one of which is a printing office, and others are used as cells for priests, stalls for pigs and fowls, a retreat for "the king of hades," the chief priest's room, a dining hall, a kitchen, &c., and beyond these is a spacious garden, at the extremity of which there is a mausoleum wherein the ashes of burnt priests once a year are deposited. Here also was pointed out to us a furnace wherein the bodies of dead priests are burned, and a little cell where the jars containing their ashes are kept until the time for depositing them in the mausoleum arrives.

We ascertained that there were connected with this one heathen temple nearly two hundred priests; and judging from the immense expense of sustaining this establishment, we could but come to the conclusion that it costs China more to support idolatry than all Christendom pays to propagate the Gospel of the Son of God.

In connection with this it may be proper to subjoin a brief history of the temple of Honan as given by the Chinese, and which has been furnished in English by Dr Bridgeman of Canton: "It was originally a private garden; but afterwards, several hundred years ago, a priest named Cheyue, built up an establishment which he called 'the temple of ten thousand autumns,' and dedicated it to Budha. It remained an obscure place, however, until about A. D. 1600, when a priest of eminent devotion, with his pupil Ahtsze, together with a concurrence of extraordinary circumstances, raised it to its present magnificence. In the reign of Kanghe, and as late as A. D. 1700, the province of Canton was not fully subjugated; and a son-in-law of the emperor was sent hither to bring the whole country under his father's sway. This he accomplished, received the title of 'Pingnan-wang, king of the subjugated South,' and took up his head quarters in the temple of Honan. There were then thirteen villages on the island, which he had orders to exterminate for their opposition to the imperial forces. Just before carrying into effect this order, the king, Pingnan, a blood-thirsty man, cast his eyes on Ahtsze, a fat happy priest, and remarked that if he lived on vegetable diet he could not be so fat; he must be a hypocrite, and should be punished with death. He drew his sword to execute with his own hand the sentence; but his arm suddenly stiffened, and he was stopped from his purpose. That night a divine person appeared to him in a dream, and assured him that Ahtsze was a holy man, adding, 'you must not unjustly kill him.' Next morning the king presented himself before Ahtsze, confessed his crime, and his arm was immediately restored. He then did obeisance to the priest, and took him for his tutor and guide; and morning and evening the king waited on the priest as his servant.

"The inhabitants of the thirteen villages now heard of this miracle, and solicited the priest to intercede in their behalf, that they might be rescued from the sentence of extermination. The priest interceded, and the king listened, answering thus: 'I have received an imperial order to exterminate these rebels, but since you, my master, say they now submit, be it so; I must, however, send the troops round to the several villages, before I can report to the emperor; I will do this, and then beg that they may be spared.' The king fulfilled his promise, and the villages were saved. Their gratitude to the priest was unbounded; and estates, and incense, and money, were poured in upon him. The king, also, persuaded his officers to make donations to the temple, and it became affluent from that day.

"The temple had then no hall for celestial kings, and at the outer gate there was a pool belonging to a rich man who refused to sell it, although Ahtsze offered him a large compensation. The king, conversing with the priest one day, said, 'this temple is deficient, for it has no hall for the celestial kings.' The priest replied, 'a terrestrial king, please your highness, is the proper person to rear a pavilion to the celestial kings.' The king took the hint, and seized on the pool of the rich man, who was now very glad to present it without compensation ; and he gave command, moreover, that a pavilion should be completed in fifteen days ; but at the priest's intercession, the workmen were allowed one month to finish it ; and by laboring diligently night and day, they accomplished it in that time."

Such is the history of the temple of Honan, which is said to be the largest and best endowed establishment of the kind in this part of China.

The reader can form some idea of the extent of this temple when he is informed that its buildings and gardens occupy from eight to ten English acres of ground. We left this gloomy scene not without indulging the hope that the time would come when a church of the living God would supplant this temple of Budha, and the great bell be used to call devout worshipers to the house of prayer.

Sunday, 11th. Attended worship at the house of Rev. Dr. Parker, in the morning, and heard a good sermon by the Rev. Mr. Wood, of the Episcopal church. This gentleman recently came from the United States as a missionary to the Chinese, but, for reasons doubtless satisfactory to himself, he returns home after a residence of two months.

Dr. Parker, in addition to his missionary work, superintends the English service, which is conducted at his own house every Sabbath day.

At two o'clock, P. M., attended Chinese service at Dr. Parker's hospital, and heard a celebrated Chinese preacher deliver a discourse in the native language.

This man has officiated as a kind of evangelist among the Chinese for several years, and from his ardent zeal, and continued sufferings in his work, has given evidence of great sincerity. He has been violently persecuted by his countrymen at different times, and once was under the necessity of flying his country to save his life. However, at the present time, he travels wherever he pleases, and preaches without molestation.

At three o'clock, attended Chinese service with Dr. Devan, in one of the densest portions of the city. The *place* where the Doctor preaches he calls the "Dispensatory." It is about twelve feet square; opens at one side to the street, which is constantly thronged with passers by. Occasionally one is attracted by the voice of the preacher, and either stops in the street, or walks into the dispensatory, and listens a short time. Very few, however, give their attention to a whole discourse. The utmost confusion prevailed in front of the dispensatory, or preaching-place, while, but from six to ten occupied the benches during service, and these were mostly in the pay of the missionary, as assistant preachers, teachers, or servants. Though an ardent friend of the missionary cause, I could but think that, if the labors bestowed here were productive of much good, it would certainly be against all human probability. Dr. Devan, and all other missionaries here, are in the habit of distributing testaments and other religious books, at the conclusion of divine service.

The missionaries themselves, from the difficulty of acquiring the language, preach but little, but are in the habit of employing Chinese assistants. Doubtless some credit is to be given for the genuineness of the conversion, and the sincerity of some of these Chinese assistants; but from the best information I have been able to obtain I am led to the conclusion that, in China, as well as in some other heathen countries, in nine cases out of ten, the converts, in identifying themselves with the missionaries, are governed mainly by motives of self interest. And, indeed, nearly all of them receive pay from the different churches to which they belong. They are generally hired as preachers, teachers, tract distributors, or servants, and generally relapse into their former habits on being dismissed from their employment. In view of these things, it is not strange that visitors, and the merchants that reside at Canton, generally, express it as their opinion that the missionary labor performed among the Chinese, is entirely useless. But persons forming such an opinion, are generally ignorant of that principle which stimulates the servant of God to sow his seed in the morning, and in the evening not to withhold his hand, namely, that faith which believes, even against hope.

Monday, 12th. We resumed our exploration of the city of Canton. Strangers have not the freedom of the city, though there is much more liberty now than formerly. However, up to the present time, foreigners venturing too far up into the city, are frequently robbed, and ratanned through the streets. The recent treaties which other nations have made with China since the late war, provided that the city gates should be thrown open to foreigners, but as yet the people of Canton are violently opposed to such a desecration of their ancient customs. Keying, the imperial commissioner and governor general of the province of Kwangtung, caused a proclamation to be posted up in the city, on the night of the 12th, informing the people that the time had come when the conditions of the treaty in reference to the freedom of the city, must be fulfilled, and cautioning the people against molesting any foreigners that were disposed to enter within the walls. But the populace, supported by a large majority of the wealthy inhabitants of the city, on discovering the proclamation on the morning of the 13th, tore it down with great violence, rent it in pieces, and stamped it in the mud. Another proclamation, purporting to be from the wealthy and virtuous citizens of Canton, was put up in its place, which threatened death to any foreigner who should dare to enter within the gates. Notwithstanding the excitement which these opposing proclamations produced, we resolved to improve the short time we had to stay, in seeing whatever was interesting, within the undisputed range of the barbarians.

Tuesday, 13th. Visited the "Fatee," or flower-garden, on the opposite side of the river, and above the temple of Honan. This is a most magnificent garden, and the plants are all grown in earthern pots. Here are almost an infinite variety of flowers, and several kinds of oranges, which are also grown in pots, and which line the different alleys, and tempt the visitor to violate the rules of the garden, by disburdening the loaded plants of some of their golden fruit. The Chinese, better than any other nation, perhaps, understand the art of dwarfing trees and plants, and causing them to grow in any shape they choose. Here may be seen orange trees from one foot to three feet high, standing in large earthern pots, and so filled with fruit that every expedient possible is entered into to prevent them from breaking down. Here, also, is a shrub, in appearance similar to the hawthorn, which the Chinese cause to grow in the exact shape of a pagoda, a junk, an elephant, a bird, or any thing else, according as their fancy leads them. Nothing can exceed the regularity and beauty of the Fatee, or flower-garden; and it was some hours after we entered, before we were able to break away from the charm which the multiflorous productions of this delightful garden cast around us. Leaving this garden, which the ingenuity of the Chinese has rendered so interesting, we re-crossed the Chookeang, and visited the palace of Houqua, situated about two miles above the city of Canton. The house is splendid, purely Chinese, the furniture magnificent, and the walls of the rooms adorned with fine Chinese paintings. It was in this house where all the recent treaties with other nations were signed.

Wednesday, 14th. Called on Drs. Bridgeman and Parker, who are missionaries of the American Board. The latter has accepted an appointment under the United States' government, as Chinese interpreter, with a salary of three thousand dollars per annum. He has been in China twelve years; has established a hospital for the benefit of the Chinese, and from almost innumerable and successful surgical operations, has earned an enviable reputation in his adopted country. With the former I had considerable conversation concerning the success of missionary operations in China, and found him to be any thing but sanguine in his expectations, but hoping to see the results of his labors after *many* days. He is not one of those fiery spirits, who, from the excitement of the moment, are in the habit of blazing forth their high wrought accounts of the work of God in heathen lands, which frequently recoil back upon their authors, and the cause they are designed to represent, much to the injury of both, but he appears to take a sober, candid view of the great work in which he is engaged, and realizes the fearful responsibility that rests upon him. He has obtained considerable celebrity by publishing several important Chinese works. In the evening called on Dr. Ball, who is likewise a missionary of the American Board, and appears to be much devoted to his work.

Thursday, 15th. Explored various parts of the city and found the Chinese very much excited on account of the proclamation of Keying, in which he ordered that the gates of Canton, which had been closed for ages, should, for the first time, be opened to the barbarians of Europe and America.

There seemed to be a great commotion among the populace, and it was anticipated by the foreigners that the night would not pass away without some outrage. Those who are opposed to the order of the governor call themselves "patriots," and declare that the barbarians shall not enter their city gates, but the man that dares to attempt to pass the sacred inclosure, shall lose his head. At midnight a portion of the old city was illuminated by the burning of the house of the mayor. A mob of more than two thousand gathered around the house of this functionary with the design of consuming him and his property together. Leaving the house through a private passage, he escaped their fury, and in a short time all that remained of his princely mansion was a heap of smouldering ruins.

Friday, 16th. The excitement continued to rise, and early in the morning the foreign factories, particularly those occupied by the English, were invested by vast throngs of the angry Chinese, and the English were hourly expecting an attack. What contributed to increase the excitement was, the expected arrival of an English steamboat from Hong Kong, to receive the last payment of the indemnity. The whole amount of the indemnity was twenty millions of dollars, and this last payment was two millions. The patriots declare that it shall not be paid, and that if the authorities attempt to convey it out of the city, they will seize upon the money and burn down the English factories. I was in the factories a number of times during the day, and found the people preparing for a vigorous defence, expecting that they would be attacked the following night, and more so in consequence of the approach of the Chinese new-year, when the people are exceedingly desirous to obtain money, and always become greatly excited. About noon we received a letter from the gentlemen to whom the Leland was consigned, (Wetmore & Co.), advising us, as our vessel would be ready for sea Saturday evening, to join her without delay, for fear an immediate outbreak would greatly endanger, if not entirely close the communication between Canton and Whampoa, where our vessel lay. With much effort, in the midst of great excitement, we succeeded in getting ready to leave at sundown, and consequently we had the pleasure of a night-excursion on the Chookeang from Canton to Whampoa, the distance of twelve miles.

Though there is considerable danger in navigating these waters in the night time from thieves and pirates, which here abound in vast numbers, yet, at ten o'clock we arrived along side the Leland without accident, and, though we were literally thrust out of the city, yet we were glad to find ourselves once more on board the vessel destined to convey us to our native land.

Sunday, 18th. Had an engagement to preach on board the Rainbow that had just arrived from New York; but was prevented from going on account of the rain. When vessels are ready for sea, the captains never wait for Monday; consequently in the afternoon our ship weighed anchor, and dropped down the river a few miles; but at dark, again came to anchor to await the arrival of Mr. Finlay from Canton. About midnight Mr. Finlay arrived, and reported that the excitement still continued at Canton, and that the foreigners were hourly expecting a furious outbreak; but we congratulated ourselves, that before it took place we should be "far away on the billows."

Monday, 19th. Before a fine breeze we sailed down

the Canton river, passing the United States frigate Vincennes, and the line-of-battle ship Columbus. These vessels have recently arrived in China, and the commanding officer, Commodore Biddle, is authorized, on the part of the United States, to act as minister to the Chinese government. These vessels are both moving up the river for the purpose of being ready to act in defence of any American interests which may be involved in the insurrectional movements at Canton. It is also said that Gov. Davies, in case of any outbreak, will send the soldiers who are quartered at Hong Hong, up the river, to assist the Chinese authorities against the insurgents.

Captain Skillington, of the Leland, having discharged his steward and cook, we found it necessary to return to Hong Kong, for the purpose of supplying their places. Accordingly, at six o'clock, P. M., we cast anchor again in the bay of Hong Kong, about four miles from shore. It was impossible for the captain to accomplish his objects here without spending the whole of Tuesday, and this gave us an opportunity to take a more formal leave of our newly made friends in this place.

Before taking our final departure from the coast of the Celestial Empire, it will be proper to make some observations concerning a few things which have not yet been exhibited, but which cannot fail to strike the foreigner with considerable interest.

The first I shall mention is the antiquated appearance of every thing that presents itself. While the nations of Europe and America are moving onward from one improvement to another, with unexampled celerity, and attracting universal admiration as well as conferring incalculable good upon the world, the Chinese seldom advance a step beyond the customs, habits and fashions which characterized their remotest ancestors; and they have been equally slow in adopting any of the usages and improvements of "distant foreigners." Architecture, agriculture, costume, and all the arts and sciences, remain in China, as the lawyers say, "*in statu quo;*"

and this inertia of every thing is not only a prominent characteristic of the Chinese, but constitutes a subject in which they glory.

Another thing which strikes the foreigner is the astonishing contrariety to what he has been taught as proper, which appears in the habits and occupations of the Chinese. We have considered the right, as the place of honor, but the Chinese give precedence to the left. Black is considered by the nations of the west as the appropriate badge of mourning, but in the estimation of the Chinese, there is nothing so proper as white.

The Chinese do not number the cardinal points in our order, but always mention the south before the north, and the west before the east; thus,—south, north, west and east. And instead of saying north-west, south-west, as we do, they say west-north, west-south, &c. The compass of the Chinese, instead of pointing to the north, is so constructed as to point to the south. This contrariety appears in many other particulars, and the fact of its existence brings one to the conclusion that we are not to estimate the Chinese by the criterion of European taste and usage.

A third subject of interest to foreigners on entering the cities of China, is the numerous manufactories and trades in operation, wherever he goes. Properly speaking, there is no machinery in the country; consequently no such extensive manufacturing establishments as in Europe and America. In consequence of the absence of all kinds of machinery calculated to lessen the amount of manual labor, the number of hands employed in carrying forward the different trades is truly immense. A great proportion of the manufacturing business required to supply the commercial houses of Canton, is performed at Fuhshan, a large town situated a few miles westward. Still, the amount accomplished in Canton, is by no means inconsiderable. There are from fifteen to twenty thousand persons engaged in Canton in weaving silk; fifty thousand in manufacturing cloth of different kinds; five thousand shoemakers; from seven thousand to ten thousand barbers, besides an unnumbered multitude who work in wood, brass, iron, stone, and various other materials, too numerous to mention.

Those who engage in each of these respective occupations, form a separate community,—each community having its own laws and regulations to control their business.

On ascending the Chookeang river from Macao to Canton, nothing interests the foreigner so much as the vast number and almost endless variety of boats by which he is constantly surrounded; every boat forming a habitation for one family, or more, according to its dimensions and the wealth of the occupants. There are officers appointed by the government to regulate and control this portion of the inhabitants; consequently all the boats, of the various sizes and descriptions which are seen here, are registered. The number adjacent and belonging to the city of Canton is eighty-four thousand. A large proportion of these are what the Chinese call Tankea (egg-house) boats. These are very small, varying from ten to fifteen feet long, and from four to six feet broad. In large coops lashed to the outside of these boats, are reared large broods of ducks and chickens, designed for the city markets, while within them whole families live and die. These, together with the passage boats, ferry boats, canal boats, pleasure boats, cruisers, &c., complete the list of these floating habitations, and constitute a permanent dwelling place for a population of three hundred thousand souls!

Another subject of interest to the stranger visiting China, is found in the piratical character of many of the Chinese inhabiting the numerous islands, which constitute an extensive archipelago along the coast of the Chinese sea. Among these islands, piracies and robberies are of frequent occurrence. During our stay at Canton, an English vessel was attacked, almost within hailing distance of Macao. The pirates boarded her, after having cleared the decks of her crew, by killing one and causing the others to take refuge in the hold, and rifling her of all that would be valuable to them, made their escape. These pirates often combine in large numbers, and attack large commercial houses; nor are they discriminating, but fall alike upon those belonging both to Chinese and foreigners. The schoolhouse belonging to the Morrison Education Society, situated on Morrison Hill, and occupied by Rev. S. R. Brown and family, was, a short time ago, captured by a band of them in the night, the family escaping from one side, while the robbers were entering on the other. They were in possession of the house for several hours, and finally escaped with their booty to their island fastnesses. Soon after this occurrence they made an attempt upon an English house situated at the west end of the city of Victoria. Prepared with their scaling ladders, as their habit was, they mounted the building in large numbers, and while in the act of removing the tiling so that they could descend into the building, a charge of grape from a six pounder mounted on a neighboring eminence, was poured into them, and two of their number rolled like logs from the roof to the ground, and the remainder took to flight.

CHAPTER XV.

Voyage from Hong Kong to New York — Chinese Sea — Islands — Strait of Gasper — Java Sea — Strait of Sunda — Perilous condition of the Leland — Loss of cable and anchor — Ship saved — Sumatra and Java — Pulo Bassa — Malays — Indian Ocean — Cape of Good Hope — Cast anchor in Table Bay — Cape Town — Colony — Vineyards — Produce — Missionary labor — The responsibility of churches — Difficulty on board — Captain fined — His character — The supercargo — Mrs. Hooper — Adieu to Africa — Cleansing the ship — Man overboard — Splendid eclipse of the sun — Reflections — The Gulf stream — Coast of New Jersey — New York.

On Wednesday morning, the 21st of January, at four o'clock, our sails were again spread to the breeze, and bidding adieu to the granite mountains of the Celestial Empire, we shaped our course towards the Cape of Good Hope. We had a remarkably pleasant time in sailing down the Chinese Sea, though this is reported as the most dangerous navigation in the world. Multitudes of vessels, through the effects of the ty-phongs, have either been foundered in this sea, or dashed to pieces on some of the numerous shoals with which these waters abound. But happily for us, this is not the season of ty-phongs, but the north-east monsoon blows steadily, in a seven knot breeze, and renders the sailing most delightful.

We made several islands on our passage down the sea, some of which are inhabited by Malays. The islands appeared beautiful, being mostly covered with verdure; and surrounded by the watery waste, resembled the oasis of the Arabian desert.

Arriving at the entrance of the Strait of Gasper in the evening, we were obliged to come to anchor, and wait for the light of morning to conduct us through it. This strait connects the Chinese with the Java Sea, and is full of rocks and shoals, which render the navigation dangerous, especially in the night.

It was on a rock in this strait, where the Alcesta, an English frigate, was wrecked, with Lord Amherst on board. The vessel was a total loss, but the people took to the boats, and all succeeded in crossing the Java Sea to Batavia, on the island of Java, the distance of three hundred miles. In passing through the strait we were not conscious of a very great proximity to danger, but delighted ourselves with the beautiful prospect presented by the numerous islands, rocks, and birds upon the wing, by which the scenery was diversified.

A fine breeze wafted us quickly across the Java Sea, and on Sunday, the first of February, we entered the strait of Sunda. Having a fair wind, we attempted to run directly through, though the captain was aware that we would have to contend with counter currents. Suddenly the wind left us, and we found ourselves drifting broad side on to an island which was but a little distance from us. Before the men could get the anchor ready for letting go, such was the rapidity of the current, that we had approached within a few rods of the shore, and some of us expected every moment that the vessel would strike, as she was carried towards the point of the island at the rate of five knots. Our only hope was in the anchor, which fortunately was let go just in time to prevent the vessel from running aground. Chain was "paid out" freely, to prevent the anchor from dragging, and when we found that the anchor held, and had time to view the place, the captain observed that we might think ourselves well off if we got away from that spot by losing our anchor and cable. The current dashed past us with astonishing force, and would have carried us to inevitable destruction, if our anchor had not held us fast.

Though the weather was calm and pleasant, we passed here an uncomfortable night, in consequence of our dangerous position. We were within a stone's cast of the shore, and as our vessel swung to the current, it was but a short distance from our stern to where the water rushed furiously on to rocks which were imbedded below the surface, and formed eddies and whirlpools truly frightful to contemplate. But our cable was strong, and our anchor held firm, so that on the following morning we had changed our position but a few rods, the current having caused the anchor to drag but a short distance towards the land. Happily for us, a breeze sprung up on Monday, quartering from the shore, and against the current; but, though thus favored, we did not dare to raise the anchor; consequently, a spring was fixed upon it, and it was determined to make all sail, slip the cable, and leave the anchor where it lay. This appeared to be the only alternative, and, at all events, it succeeded. The vessel, after trembling a few moments against the current, began gradually to move before the freshening breeze, and as we turned partly across the current to get away from the land, the spring cable snapped asunder, and we were quickly borne by the timely breeze to a safe distance from our dangerous moorings.

Again in the centre of the strait of Sunda, steering our course towards the island of Pulo Bassa, which lay in sight, we felt called upon to offer up a tribute of thanksgiving to that merciful Providence who had delivered us from the imminent danger by which we had been surrounded.

Navigators, in passing through the strait of Sunda, have to guard against shoals, rocks and currents; and often head winds detain vessels here for many days before they can get through. At the entrance of the strait, we overtook two English vessels, which appeared to be feeling their way along, with the utmost care. One of them came to anchor near the islands called the Twin Sisters, and while we lay in our dangerous position, she weighed anchor, and showed us her English colors as she passed.

This strait divides the islands of Sumatra and Java. The former is inhabited by Malays, and is the scene where the missionaries, Lyman and Monson, met their tragical death. The coast is low and flat in some places, in others, hilly. The island presents the appearance of great fertility.

Java presents a more uneven surface, and, as seen from the strait, does not appear so fertile. The Dutch are its possessors. Batavia and Algier are places of considerable importance. This island is well situated for commerce, and, but for its deathly climate, it would doubtless prosper more rapidly.

Beside these, are several small islands about the strait, which altogether present a very agreeable prospect.

As the wind did not favor us for clearing Java Head, on the second, we put in towards Sumatra, and came to anchor under the lee of Pulo Bassa, which is a high circular island, and, with two or three other islands of the same character, and the highlands on the island of Sumatra, forms a good shelter from the north-west winds. On coming to anchor, the wind, which had been hardly sufficient to enable us to gain our harbor, entirely died away; and, as the sea was smooth, we were here permitted to spend a quiet night, which is a great luxury at sea.

The islands around us were inhabited by Malays, a number of whom came off with shells, turtles, banannas, &c., to trade with us. We purchased all they brought, and found that money was the object of their principal desire, and that they well understood its value. Those that came to us were very brown, dwarfish and filthy objects, and their teeth were as black as ebony, occasioned, probably, by their use of beetle-nuts, as an article of food.

On the morning of the 3rd of February, we weighed anchor, and were soon out of sight of land, amidst the solitudes of the Indian ocean.

For a few of the first days, after leaving the islands, we made but slow progress, on account of baffling winds. On the fourth day, however, we secured the south-east trade, which continued, with little variation, until we approached the Cape of Good Hope.

On our leaving China, it was the intention of Mr. Finlay, the supercargo, to stop at St. Helena, to procure water and fresh provisions; but, through the recommendation of the captain, it was finally determined to stop at Cape Town. Consequently, on approaching the latitude of the Cape, we hauled up towards land, and the eastern coast of Africa, with its high mountains and barren sands, appeared on our right, about one hundred miles north of the southern extremity of the continent. The most southern point of land is not the Cape of Good Hope, as is generally supposed, but a low point about thirty miles south-east of the Cape of Good Hope, called Cape Lagullus. Hence the soundings, which here extend far into the ocean, are called "Lagullus Banks."

We reached these banks the day before we made land, and the appearance of the grampus, cape geese, and other aquatic animals, which there abound, presented an agreeable diversion from the tedious monotony of a voyage of five thousand miles across the Indian ocean.

During thirty-five days there was scarcely an object appeared to attract attention, though we were sailing over that part of the great deep where some of the principal scenes of the "Flying Dutchman" were laid. However, we were gravely told by our captain, that, even to this day, there occasionally appears a full-rigged ship, hull and all, above water, in the vicinity of the Cape of Good Hope, answering to the description of the Flying Dutchman; and he averred, that he had often seen it himself, notwithstanding the assurance of Captain Marryatt, that the "Phantom Ship is no more."

The day we doubled the Cape of Good Hope was a remarkably pleasant one, and we sailed along in full view of the coast during the whole day. When we arrived off the Cape, we were within three miles of land, and every object on shore could be distinctly seen from the ship's deck. We had a splendid breeze in passing around, and we left in our rear, in quick succession, Cape Point, Gurner's Coin, and English Point, and rounding to, to enter the harbor of Cape Town, we fell under the lee of the high lands of the coast, where we lost our wind, and within sight of the town, harbor, shipping, light-house, and the American Consulate, where the stars and stripes were fluttering in the breeze, we lay in a dead calm till the following morning. A gentle breeze arose with the sun, and bore us into the quiet bosom of Table Bay, on the shore of which is situated the beautiful and picturesque city known by the name of Cape Town.

Our stay here was only a day and a half, but we improved the time in examining every thing interesting in and about the place. The town is quite beautiful, and seems to be more active and animated than any other English town I have ever seen.

It is built on an inclined plain, which extends from the base of Table Mountain to the waters of the bay, the distance of one mile and a half.

The streets are broad and regular, crossing each other at right angles, but without side-walks; a singular deficiency in a town where walking seems to be fashionable with all classes. Coaches appear to be numerous, and it is here that a stranger can judge of the quality of an individual, and the amount of his income, from the splendor of his riding equipage. Here may be seen the rough cart, drawn by a mule, the common buggy, coach and one, coach and two, coach and four, coach and six. I saw some of the latter class, with the coach and harness mounted with gold; but as I heard the sound of weeping issue from one of the coaches, I was reminded that misery is closely allied to opulence and grandeur.

To make up for the deficiency of suitable walks in the city, the Anglo Africans, a little distance out of town, have a number of the most beautifully shaded promenades, which, for all the elite of the place, are very fashionable as well as very pleasant resorts. Doubtless the present occupants of Cape Town are indebted to the Dutch for a great many of the comforts and luxuries which they now enjoy; particularly the delightful gardens and shaded walks, which render Cape Town a very pleasant place.

There are a number of elegant buildings in the city;

but there appeared to be but few now being erected, which shows that the place is at a stand. Churches abound, and the principal are the Episcopal, Lutheran and Wesleyan. There are three or four of the latter, but, from the shortness of our stay, I could not particularly inform myself in regard to the state of religion in the colony.

The number of inhabitants in Cape Colony, embracing all ranks and colors, is about fifty thousand; thirty thousand of whom reside in Cape Town.

As in all foreign countries that have been colonized by Europeans, where the native inhabitants are colored, the people of Cape Town present all possible shades of complexion. Those, however, who share in the blood of the Hottentot, it is presumed, are not admitted into the higher classes of society, but many of them, especially among the brunettes, possess remarkably fine forms and features, and, in the streets of Cape Town, and on the different promenades, present a very respectable appearance.

It is well known that the Dutch were the first Europeans that gained a footing in south Africa; and Cape Town, as well as the surrounding country, presents many evidences of the taste and enterprise of their first civilized inhabitants. The beautiful groves already spoken of, some of which are a mile in extent, are all artificial, and composed of a species of black oak. The trees have been collected with great labor, and planted in regular rows, and so near together that their boughs intermingle over head, so as to form a dense shade at all times of day. Doubtless the naturally destitute condition of the country, as it regards timber, and the desire to screen themselves from the burning heat of the sun, prompted the first settlers to form these artificial forests.

Be this as it may, they are used by the present population as a great luxury. We had an opportunity to judge of their utility from personal experience. As we rambled through the town, we found the heat of the sun exceedingly oppressive; but coming to a gate which opened into one of these retreats, we walked in, and found ourselves in an atmosphere truly refreshing. In the centre of the grove which we explored, and which is about one mile long, is the residence of the governor of the Colony, and, as we passed, we observed that the gateway leading to the palace was guarded by two huge lions. Nothing can appear more rural than the governor's seat, though within one-half mile of the tumult of the busy town.

Within the precincts of the town, as well as round about, vineyards abound. The raising of grapes appears to be one of the principal pursuits of the people, the Dutch portion of the population in particular. The grapes are of various kinds, and exceedingly fine, some of them comparing in size with the green gage-plum. They are used, as in other countries where they abound, for the manufacture of wines and raisins. These articles of commerce are sent to Europe and America, annually, in great abundance, and are known as Cape wines and Cape raisins. We were in one of the establishments where they are manufactured, and from the specimens of wines which were there shown, it is not difficult to believe that nine-tenths of the stuff sold and drank, in the name of wine, in civilized countries, are entirely spurious. The raisins, though of a good quality, will not compare with the Malaga, and some other kinds. We were conducted to a room where the negroes were packing raisins, and observed that they would first fill the boxes, and then spread a piece of cloth over the raisins and trample them in with their feet. Apples, also, and pears, abound in the city, and are of a good quality. They grow mostly in the interior, but are always to be found in the market, as also potatoes, onions and other vegetables, for the accommodation of ships.

As it regards the civil state of the country, all was quiet and prospering around the Cape, but in consequence of the threatening aspect of things among the Bushmen, the soldiers that were quartered at Cape Town have all been sent off to the frontiers, and it is expected that their presence in that region will keep every thing quiet.

The American Consul, who appears to be truly a religious man, gave us the following information, with respect to the results of missionary labor in Cape Colony: Large numbers of the native inhabitants, in various places, had professed to be converted, but very few had continued, for any length of time, to give evidence of a genuine change of heart. Indeed, it appears to be the case in Africa, as well as in other heathen countries, that it is much easier to get the people converted than it is to keep them so. Though the good accomplished for the natives may be limited, yet missionary labor, in such a place as Cape Colony, is vastly important, in securing the well-being of foreign residents, and in giving a correct tone to the moral state of society.

However elevated human nature may become through the influence of science, truth and correct example, it has a natural tendency downwards, which will always exhibit itself in proportion as the restraints of religion cease to be felt. Governments seldom supply their colonies with that kind and amount of religious influence necessary to preserve a wholesome moral atmosphere in society. This must be done by the church of Christ; and it is only necessary for Christians to understand the true condition of those countries which are being redeemed from barbarism by the settlement of colonies from civilized and Christian nations, to induce them to use their best endeavors to supply them with all the necessary means for religious instruction.

Foreigners, Europeans and Americans, are found in all heathen countries, where they have settled for the purpose of accumulating money; and, generally, the missionary will succeed with the heathen in proportion to the degree of influence he is able to throw around the conduct of foreign residents. Vicious foreigners, residing among the heathen, may, by a few weeks or even days of wickedness, destroy the religious efforts of many years; and these are the characters with whom the missionary must come in contact in all parts of the world; and this may be regarded as one of the greatest hindrances to his success.

The ship having procured its supplies of fresh provisions and water, and ourselves having purchased a suitable quantity of apples, pears and fresh grapes, for our own private use, on Friday evening, the 14th of March, we weighed anchor, to resume our homeward voyage; but, for the want of a breeze, we did not succeed in getting out of Table Bay, until the following morning. Before leaving, a circumstance happened illustrative of the character of the captain, under whose rule we lived for nearly one hundred and fifty days. He had shipped a sailor at Hong Kong, but in consequence of a disagreement about the price, the sailor, who was a smart, active Italian, had not signed any bonds, and consequently considered that he had a right to leave the vessel at the Cape, if he was so disposed. He accordingly informed the captain that he wished to settle with him, as he designed to leave. The captain, having had a grudge against him ever since the first difficulty, became now exceedingly enraged, at what he called the "——— scoundrel's insolence," and, seizing a belaying-pin, struck the sailor in the forehead, and, but for the rigging, the latter would have fallen to the deck. He gathered himself, however, and, rising upon his feet, with his face covered with blood, very properly upbraided the infuriated captain, for the cruelty of his conduct.

The captain had had a similar difficulty with a seaman at Hong Kong, whom he chased all over the deck of the vessel, unmercifully pounding him with a belaying-pin, subsequently causing him to be put in irons, and flogged. The seaman, after being discharged, entered a complaint against the captain, before the Consul, and, (as the captain told Mrs. Hooper,) recovered damages of him to the amount of one hundred dollars, which, the captain said, he "walked up and paid like a man." For fear of meeting with a similar retribution at Cape Town, for his cruel treatment of the defenceless Italian, he detained a boat along side, and kept the sailor on board of the vessel till we were well under way; and when he supposed that we were so far away that there was no danger of being pursued, he sent the sailor into the boat, to be taken ashore. As the Italian was leaving the deck, his comrades saluted him by saying, "there goes the best sailor we had among us."

Notwithstanding these objectionable traits in his character, our captain is an excellent navigator; he appears perfectly at home on the vessel, and is more laborious than any other captain I have ever seen. While I have no occasion to find fault with his course in reference to myself and family, I can speak in high commendation of his conduct towards Mrs. Hooper and her children. He was particularly attentive to *their* wants, while he was liberal with all the passengers on board; and but for strong drink, that great spoiler of humanity, he would be one of the safest captains that sail upon the "great deep."

From our experience on this vessel, I am fully persuaded that, where passengers and ships' crews suffer, as is often the case, for the want of suitable provisions, it is owing, in nine cases out of ten, to the penuriousness or carelessness of owners and captains. No word of complaint, however, can be preferred against the Leland, for the quality of the fare which she afforded. Every thing was in good time, and in good order; and the variety of meats, vegetables and sauce, with which the table was furnished, was truly surprising to us, who, on other vessels, had been accustomed to such different fare. Besides his attention to the wants of the passengers, Mr. Finlay proved himself to be a very agreeable cabin companion. He is very much of a gentleman, and having followed the seas for more than twenty years, as supercargo, he has collected a vast fund of general information.

It is often necessary to be subjected to a close connection with others, for some length of time, in order to be able to form correct opinions concerning them. Mrs. Hooper, we found to be, not only a very benevolent person, but an agreeable associate in the cabin. We shall often call to mind the many hours at sea which have been rendered more endurable by her intelligent conversation and cheerful deportment.

Saturday, the 15th of March, the mountainous coast of southern Africa disappeared in the dim distance.

For the first few days after leaving Table Bay, we made but little progress, in consequence of adverse winds, but the fourth day, we took the south-east trades, and began to indulge the pleasing reflection, that the next land we saw would be the shores of our own native country, though there were checks thrown upon our happiness by the consideration, that there were still many dangers to pass, and storms to buffet, before we should reach the desired haven.

The south-east trade-winds are not very strong, and the ocean, in the region where they prevail, is generally smooth, and the weather pleasant; consequently, it is in passing over these latitudes that vessels, homeward bound, prepare for entering port. The vessel is to be scrubbed, inside and out; the decks are to be scraped, holy-stoned, and varnished; the spars are to be cleansed and painted, and the bulwarks, masts, round-house, chains, guns, casks, buckets, and binacle, are all to be scoured and painted. The rigging is to be overhauled and tarred down; empty boxes, barrels, and all unnecessary lumber, are to be cast overboard; rent sails are all to be mended, and put in perfect order, and every thing, even to the anchor, is to put on, at least a clean outside, so that the ship will make as good an appearance when she enters port as when she left. As the Leland had been out nearly eighteen months, and in that time having performed a voyage round the world, she required much cleansing, and the seamen were busily employed in accomplishing this object, for several weeks.

While this work was going on, an accident happened which produced a great excitement on board. We were sailing before the wind at the rate of five knots an hour, and a sailor boy, who was on the outside of the bulwarks, scraping the fore chains, and was held to his place by a rope tied around his waist, and fastened to a belaying-pin, from carelessness, lost his hold, and, as the rope slipped upon the pin, he fell into the ocean. As he was falling, he hallooed as loud as he could roar, for his comrades to haul in the slack of the rope. As they did not understand him, a cry was raised, that resounded from the after cabin to the forecastle, that "a man was overboard." The ladies in the cabin heard the cry, and Mrs. Hooper thought it was her little daughter, as she heard the word "child," and Mrs. Hines thought I was the unfortunate one, as she heard my name mentioned in connection with "overboard."

Which of the two were most frightened, it is difficult to tell. Mrs. Hooper was actually thrown into a fit, and Mrs. Hines fainted, and neither of them, two weeks afterwards, had entirely recovered from the shock.

As soon as the cry was raised, the mate seized a hen-coop containing nine chickens, and cast it overboard, for the drowning man to hold upon until other relief could be sent. But this was not necessary, as the rope did not slip far on the pin before it held; and as it retained its hold on his body, the frightened tar, by the assistance of his comrades, was soon again brought on deck.

We were twenty-six days from the Cape of Good Hope, to the equinoctial line, and had the good fortune to pass from the south-east to the north-east trade, with very little detention. In the region of the equator we experienced numerous showers of rain, but as they were accompanied by favorable breezes, we were soon out of the rainy latitudes, and, by the assistance of a strong north-east trade, were passing up into the regions of the north, at the rate of two hundred miles per day.

We crossed the equator in longitude thirty-six degrees, and consequently were not far from the coast of Brazil. In north latitude, twenty degrees, we approached so near the Island of Trinidad, as to discern its whereabouts, and witness the immense columns of clouds which hung around its lofty and volcanic summit. From this our course lay along, about two hundred miles to the windward of the West India Islands. While passing these, we experienced a succession of squalls and calms which continued until we entered the twenty-fifth degree of north latitude. While in latitude twenty-four degrees forty-one minutes, and longitude sixty-one degrees forty minutes, on the 25th of April, we had a splendid view of a solar eclipse. It was a remarkably clear day, and the eclipse was so nearly total that it became quite dark. At the greatest obscuration the south side of the sun presented the appearance of the moon at thirty-six hours old, and the light preceeding from it was not, in appearance, unlike to the light of the moon on a clear winter's night. However common the phenomenon of an eclipse of the sun may be to us, far away upon the sea, it was a source of real entertainment; and we cheered ourselves with the idea that many of our friends on land were perhaps gazing at the same object.

A number of severe squalls while we were passing the Bermudas, brought to mind the quaint lines of the sailor:

> "If Bermuda let you pass,
> Look ye out for Hatteras;
> If Hatteras you pass by,
> Look ye out for Cape Henry."

Bermuda, however, "let us pass" on the 25th of April, and we began to flatter ourselves that our voyage would soon be over.

When a person first leaves his native land and goes to sea, the wonders of the deep are contemplated by him with a great degree of interest. The monsters that inhabit it—the whale, the shark, the porpoise—and the various kinds of fish that explore its boundless extent; together with the albatros, petrel, and other birds which live almost perpetually on the wing, and are seen alike in calms and storms in all latitudes, become, successively, the objects of his curious observation. The manner in which the ship is managed, the peculiar phrases which salute his ear, the tacking ship, the making sail, the shortening sail, and a thousand other things, conspire to interest and divert him. And, indeed, to the curious, the sea does not present that dull monotony of which so many voyagers have complained.

However, subjects contemplated with great interest on an outward voyage, do not claim the same attention when one is bound for home, after an absence of seven or eight years. The absorbing topic with us on approaching our native coast, was the distance we were sailing from day to day, and the probable time we should reach our much desired haven. We had been absent nearly seven years; and while approximating our native shores, a thousand thoughts revolved in our minds in reference to the circumstances in which we might find those persons and things that were interesting to us before subjecting ourselves to our voluntary exile. We had left a large circle of friends, and from many of them we had heard nothing for seven long years. As we had been situated in the most isolated country on the globe, the information we had received concerning the state of our own religious denomination, had been very limited, and usually more than one year old when obtained.

The numerous changes which must have taken place in the different localities and social circles in which it had been our privilege to move, had been kept from our knowledge. Indeed, a pall of darkness had long since fallen upon most of those things which were particularly interesting to us as private individuals; and from the uncertainty of every thing before us, we scarcely knew whether to be elated or dejected—to indulge in feelings of joy or those of sorrow—when we reflected that in a few more days the hills and valleys of our own New York would appear before us, and we should be permitted again to visit those places rendered dear to us by many hallowing associations. Whether we were to be greeted by our friends on our arrival, or whether we were to learn that they were dead, was altogether problematical, and we began to indulge the melancholy reflection that we might find ourselves strangers even in our own native village.

While the different changes which might have taken place in the various departments of church and state, and in the families with which we had been acquainted, were passing before our minds, our gallant vessel was bearing us rapidly onward towards our native shores, and on the 30th of April we entered the Gulf Stream in latitude thirty-six degrees north, and found this terror of the American coast in a remarkably quiet state, as it usually is when westerly winds prevail. We were sixteen hours in crossing the stream, and on the 1st day of May found ourselves on soundings, off the Capes of Virginia.

It is a singular fact often eliciting remarks from voyagers, though it is none the less remarkable on that account, that the water in the Gulf Stream is fifteen degrees warmer than it is on either side. Before reaching it from the south, the water for a great distance was full of an aquatic plant called the gulf-weed. As every object at sea commands the notice of the voyager, the sea-weed was observed with no small interest.

On getting past the stream, in the evening we were permitted to see a grand display of Nature's fire-works. The clouds that hung over the stream in dense masses, were lighted up by the continued flashes of electricity, with the most magnificent illumination. Sometimes it would appear as if the whole ocean in our rear was in one general conflagration.

After leaving the stream we were favored with remarkably pleasant weather and fair winds, and on the morning of the 2d day of May, at three o'clock, we made the lighthouse of Barnegat, on the coast of New Jersey. Soon after daylight we received a New York pilot, at which time our voyage was considered as terminated; making one hundred and two days from Hong Kong. After receiving the pilot, a dense fog enveloped us, through which we had to feel our way, and in the midst of which we were hovering around the entrance to New York Bay. At length the fog was removed by a friendly wind, and at dusk the Leland dropped her anchor inside of Sandy Hook, and within a stone's cast of the spot where lay the Lausanne the night previous to taking her departure in 1839.

We were detained at the Hook by dense fogs until the 4th of May, when we proceeded up the Bay to New York city, where we landed in safety on the evening of that day.

CHAPTER XVI.

Oregon Territory — Its geography — Boundary and extent — Harbors — Capes — Face of the country — Snow Mountains — Rivers — Mouth of the Columbia — Columbia Bar — Channel — Kinds of fish — Timber — Climate — Summer and Winter — Fertility of the soil — Clatsop Plains — Bottom lands — Puget's Sound — The garden of Oregon — Middle region — Upper region — Capabilities of the country.

That portion of the vast extent of country lying west of the Rocky Mountains, which has acquired, by universal consent, the name of Oregon, lies within the following boundaries: Commencing at the north-west corner, in the centre of the Strait of Juan De Fuca, at its mouth, consider the north line as extending along said strait, at an equal distance from the main land on the south, and Vancouver's Island on the north, eastward, the distance of one hundred and twenty miles, thence northward till it strikes the forty-ninth parallel of north latitude, thence due east along said parallel the distance of five hundred and fifty miles, to the Rocky Mountains; on the east by the Rocky Mountains, extending from the forty-ninth parallel of north latitude, to the forty-first, the distance of four hundred and eighty miles; on the south by the Snowy Mountains, which extend, in a continuous range, from the Rocky Mountains to Cape Mendocino, on the Pacific, the distance of seven hundred miles; and on the west by the Pacific ocean, from Cape Mendocino, five hundred and twenty miles due north, to the mouth of the Strait of Juan De Fuca, near Cape Flattery, the place of beginning. Since the dividing line between the two governments which have an interest and have exercised a controlling influence in the country, has now been defined, and the forty-ninth parallel is hereafter, forever, to separate the two nations, it remains no longer a subject of discussion; but any one, in casting his eye over a correct map of the country west of the Rocky Mountains, will discover at one glance, that a more natural division than the one which has been established, would have been a line extending from Puget's Sound north-eastwardly along the summit of the highlands, which separate the waters of the Columbia from those of Frazer's river, to the Rocky Mountains, so as to embrace in Oregon all the territory drained by the Columbia river. This would have given a natural boundary to the country on all sides, while the forty-ninth parallel is a very unnatural one, because, in crossing the great valley of the Columbia, it puts asunder that which the God of nature has joined together.

The boundary as defined, gives Oregon about six hundred and forty miles of coast on the Pacific ocean and Strait of Fuca. The shores of the strait are composed of beaches of sand or stones, overhung by sandy and rocky cliffs, and from these the land ascends gradually to the foot of the mountains, which rise abruptly to a great height within a few miles of the ocean. The coast along the Pacific is nearly straight from north to south, in some places iron-bound, and in others composed of low beaches of sand.

The harbors, or places of refuge for vessels along the Oregon coast, are very few, and, if we except Puget's Sound, with its numerous arms stretching far inland, there are none of the first quality. At the mouth of the Umpqua river there is a tolerable harbor for small craft, and the channel across the bar will admit of the entrance of vessels drawing eight feet. Bulfinch's harbor, discovered by Captain Robert Gray, of Boston, in 1792, is situated forty miles north of the mouth of the Columbia, and by artificial means may be constituted a safe anchorage. Port Discovery, situated near the south-east angle of the Strait of Fuea, is pronounced perfectly safe, and convenient for ships of any size. It is defended from the violence of the waves by Protection Island.

The most important harbor on the coast is that formed by the mouth of the Columbia river, as it constitutes a port of entry to the most important portions of Oregon. This harbor, though difficult of access in the winter season, when the prevailing winds on the coast are from the south and east, may, at other times, be safely entered by vessels drawing not more than sixteen feet, particularly if the navigator is acquainted with the intricacies of the channel. But this river, with its mouth, will be more particularly described hereafter.

There are but few Capes along this coast, and none that project far into the ocean; the shores being generally straight, bold and unbroken. The principal are Cape Blanco, which is a high point of land extending into the ocean between the Clameth and Umpqua rivers, and nearly under the forty-third parallel of latitude; Cape Disappointment, on the north side of the mouth of the Columbia river, and Cape Flattery, on the south side of the mouth of the Strait of Fuca. Cape Disappointment, however, does not properly class with the important Capes along the Pacific coast, as it does not extend into the ocean, but is, at least, three miles inside the bar of the Columbia. But it holds a prominent place on all our maps and charts, as, from its peculiar location and the appearance of the majestic fir-trees upon its top, it forms an unerring guide to the storm-beaten sailor, who is desirous of seeking shelter in the quiet and peaceful waters of Baker's Bay.

There are no islands of importance between Capes Mendocino and Flattery. One is found, however, lying about forty miles south of Cape Flattery, and named, by the Spaniards, the "Isle of Grief," in commemoration of the loss of some of their men, who were destroyed by the natives on the adjacent coast.

The face of this country is wonderfully diversified, and presents every variety of scenery, from the most awfully grand and sublime, to the most beautiful and picturesque in nature.

The country, in the vicinity of Puget's Sound, to a considerable extent, is level and beautiful, with the exception of which, all along the coast, it is broken and mountainous. On approaching the coast, at the mouth of the Columbia river, ridges of high lands appear on either hand, as far as the eye can reach, while the more elevated points serve as land-marks, to guide the mariner across the dreaded bar. The most remarkable of these elevations is one, called by the Indians, "The Swallalahoost," and celebrated by them as the place where one of their mighty chiefs, who, after death, assumed the form of a monstrous eagle, and taking wing, flew to the top of this mountain, and subsequently became the creator of the lightning and the thunder. From this tradition, as well as from the appearance of the mountain, it is supposed by some, that it might possibly have once been an active volcano. Captain Wilkes, on his exploring visit to the country, gave it the name of "Saddle Mountain," from the resemblance of its top to the shape of a saddle. With but little variation, the country south of the Columbia, from thirty to fifty miles back from the ocean, and extending the whole extent of the Oregon coast, presents the same rough, wild and mountainous aspect. Doubtless, this region is destined to be occupied by civilized man, but not until there is no room left in the numerous valleys of this wide-spread country.

Having passed over this range of high lands along the coast, you descend, on the north side of the Columbia, into the valley of the Cowilitz, and on the south, into that of the Wallamette river, and still farther south, you come down on the plains which lie on the Umpqua and Clameth rivers. The valley of the Cowilitz is about forty miles in length, and varying from ten to twenty in breadth, and extends east to the foot of that range of mountains of which "St. Helen's," the Mount Adams of Americans, is the highest peak. The Wallamette valley is more extensive, being from fifty to eighty miles broad, and more than two hundred miles long. The plains on the Umpqua, which commence about forty-five miles back from the ocean, are quite extensive, and, with those on the Clameth, and the Wallamette valley, extend east to that range of mountains, which, crossing the Columbia river, form the Cascades, and are therefore called the "Cascade Mountains."

Throughout these valleys are scattered numberless hillocks and rising grounds, from the top of some of which, scenery, as enchanting as was ever presented to the eye, delights and charms the lover of nature, who takes time to visit their conical summits.

The whole extent of country from the Cascade mountains to the Pacific ocean, varying in breadth from seventy-five to one hundred and twenty miles, is called the Lower Country.

The Cascade mountains extend in one continuous range, parallel with the coast, quite to California, and have therefore some times been called "The California Mountains."

Those whose highest observations have been limited to the Catskill and Alleghany mountains, can form no just conception of the grandeur and magnificence of this stupendous range. Some of its loftiest summits are more than fifteen thousand feet above the level of the ocean, and Mount Olympus, near Cape Flattery, and St. Helen's, near the head of the Cowilitz river, and fifty miles from the coast, can both be seen for some distance at sea.

These highest points are covered with eternal snow, and, presenting their rounded tops to the heavens, appear like so many magnificent domes, to adorn the temple of nature. From one elevation near the Wallamette river, and at the distance of from sixty to one hundred and fifty miles, the writer has counted eight of these snow-topped mountains, without moving from his tracks. Surely, no scenery can be more enchanting. One of these mountains, St. Helen's, requires a more particular account, from a phenomenon which it presented a few years ago. In the month of October, 1842, it was discovered, all at once, to be covered with a dense cloud of smoke, which continued to enlarge, and move off, in dense masses, to the eastward, and filling the heavens in that direction, presented an appearance like that occasioned by a tremendous conflagration, viewed at a vast distance. When the first volumes of smoke had passed away, it could be distinctly seen, from various parts of the country, that an eruption had taken place on the north side of St. Helen's, a little below the summit, and from the smoke that continued to issue from the chasm or crater, it was pronounced to be a volcano in active operation. When the explosion took place, the wind was north-west, and on the same day, and extending from thirty to fifty miles to the south-east, there fell showers of ashes, or dust, which covered the ground in some places, so as to admit of its being collected in quantities. This last phenomenon has been of frequent occurrence, and has led many to suppose that volcanic eruptions are not uncommon in this country.

St. Helen's is the most regular in its form and the most beautiful in its appearance of all the snow-capped mountains of Oregon; and though on the north side of the Columbia, it belongs to the Cascade range. Mount Hood, or Mount Washington, as it is sometimes called by Americans, is on the south side of the Columbia, and being larger, and more elevated than St. Helen's, presents a magnificent object, on which the eye can gaze without weariness, from innumerable points more than one hundred miles from its base. But any description of these gigantic piles of basalt and snow, must fall far below the reality; and indeed, the person desiring to realize all the delightful sensations produced by the scenery of these mountains, must fix himself on some eminence in the Wallamette valley, where all of them at once come in contact with his vision, and he will want no farther proof that the works of art sink into insignificance, when compared with the stupendous works of nature.

Descending these mountains to the east, you come into the valleys, successively, through which the river "De Shoots," John Day's river, the Unatila, and the Walla-Walla flow, before emptying into the Columbia;

and on the north side of the latter river, you come down into the valley of the north branch of the same river. On the north, this middle region is comparatively level, until you approach the northern ridges of the Blue mountains; but on the south side there are innumerable hills between the small rivers already mentioned, as also many plains of greater or less extent. As you approach the Blue mountains on the south, particularly on the Unatilla and Walla-Walla rivers, the hills disappear, and you find yourself passing over a beautiful and level country, about twenty-five or thirty miles broad, on the farther borders of which rise with indescribable beauty and grandeur, that range which, from its azure-like appearance, has been called the "Blue Mountains." This valley, extending from the Cascade to the Blue mountains, is about one hundred and seventy-five miles broad, and the traveler in passing through it, meets with a continued succession of rocks, hills and plains of all dimensions, but generally he is well pleased with the face of the country.

The Blue mountains are steep and rocky, and many of them also volcanic. Some are covered with perpetual snow.

They run nearly parallel with the Cascade mountains, though at the south branches of them intersect the latter range. They are about midway between the Pacific ocean and the Rocky mountains.

The face of the country east of the Blue mountains is, if possible, more varied than it is west. The southern part of this third region, or upper country, so far as its surface is concerned, is distinguished by its steep and rugged mountains, deep and dismal valleys, called *holes*, by mountaineers, and wide granite plains. It wears a forbidding aspect. But the north part is less objectionable in its features. The plains are more extensive, the mountains less precipitous, and the valleys not so gloomy. Many portions of this upper region are volcanic, and some of the volcanoes are in constant action.

On the eastern limits of this region, rise the towering summits of the Rocky mountains, which form at once the eastern boundary of Oregon, and are every way worthy to separate the waters of the Atlantic ocean from those of the Pacific. In fine, so far as the external appearance of this country is concerned, in contemplating its distinguished features, one is brought to the conclusion that there is nothing in all the descriptions of European or Oriental scenery, that surpasses that of this interesting country.

The rivers of Oregon form the next distinguishing trait of the country to be described. These are principally embraced in the Columbia and its tributaries.

This majestic river, which drains nearly the whole of Oregon, like most of the large rivers of North America, is supplied from the inexhaustible reservoirs of the Rocky mountains. Some of the more important confluents of this river require to be particularly noticed.

The most northerly branch of the Columbia is Canoe river, which rises near the fifty-fourth degree of latitude, and after running about one hundred miles in a southerly direction, unites with two others, one of which rises in a tremendous gorge of the Rocky mountains, under the fifty-third parallel, and the other flows from the soutb about two hundred miles along the base of the mountains. A traveler, in describing this gorge, says: " The country around our encampment presented the wildest and most terrific appearance of desolation. The sun, shining on a range of stupendous glaciers, threw a chilling brightness over the chaotic mass of rocks, ice and snow, by which we were environed. Close to our encampment one gigantjc mountain of conical form towered majestically into the clouds far above the others, while at intervals the interest of the scene was heightened by the rumbling noise of a descending avalanche."

The mountain here referred to, is supposed to be the highest point of land in North America. The south river, being the largest of the three, is entitled to be called the Columbia, to its rise, which takes place in a small lake situated in the mountains, nearly under the fiftieth parallel of north latitude. After the junction of the three, the Columbia pursues a course nearly due south, for two hundred miles, receiving a number of small rivers in its passage, and then unites its waters with those of the Mc Gillivry and the Clark rivers, both of which come rushing down from the Rocky mountains, to swell its increasing tide. The Clark takes its rise near the sources of the Missouri, and, in its passage to the Columbia, receives a number of smaller streams. This river rushes into the Columbia down a ledge of rocks, and the latter, in its passage through the Blue mountains, immediately after the junction, forms the Kittle Falls. From this point the river takes nearly a western course, one hundred miles, where it takes in the Okanagan from the north, having previously received the Spokan from the south and east. At this point the river makes another bend, and taking a due south course about one hundred and fifty miles, to the forty-sixth degree of north latitude, unites with its great southern branch, called the "Snake, or Lewis River."

This stream takes its rise in the Rocky and Snowy mountains, near the sources of the Colorado, the Platt, the Yellow Stone, and the Missouri rivers. It first takes a western course about two hundred miles, thence northwest about two hundred and fifty, to its junction with its kindred branch from the north. It passes through the Blue mountains, forming the Salmon Falls, and receives, in its course, the Henry, Melade, Wapicacoos, the Kooskooske, or Salmon river, and a number of other streams.

Below the junction of these two great branches, the Columbia receives, on the south, the Walla Walla, Unatilla, John Day's river, and the De Shoots, or Falls river; and, after shooting itself through the Dalls, or Narrows, where it becomes compressed to about one hundred and fifty feet wide, and in passing through the narrow chasm, forms, at some stages, the most frightful whirlpools, it glides gently and smoothly onward about forty miles, and then throws itself through a terrific chasm, which its accumulated waters have torn in the mountains, and rushing down a ledge of rocks, forms the beautiful cascades.

Above the Dalls, the river, in many places, is very

rapid, and in one place, a short distance from the De Shoots, in low water, there is a perpendicular fall of several feet. But, when the river is high, the water sets back from the narrows below, so as to admit of the passage of boats up and down. The Cascades cannot, however, be run with boats either in high water or low.

Many a poor voyager in the service of the Hudson's Bay Company, both at the Cascades and the Dalls, has lost his life in attempting to navigate these treacherous waters. A boat filled with American emigrants, in attempting to run the Dalls last fall, was drawn down in one of the tremendous whirlpools, and, though the shore was lined with people, two or three persons sunk and perished before their eyes.

Below the Cascades the river continues rapid a few miles, but soon becomes effected by the tide. The distance from the Cascades to the Pacific, is about one hundred and forty miles, and the river is navigable for vessels drawing fourteen feet, nearly the whole distance. The rivers which fall into the Columbia below the Cascades are, the Quicksand and the Wallamette, on the south, and the Cowilitz on the north. The Wallamette takes its rise in the Cascade mountains, and in that range of high lands which border the Pacific ocean. In passing up the Wallamette from its mouth, the first branch of importance you discover, is the Clakamas, on the east or left-hand side, as you go up the stream, and twenty-four miles from the upper mouth of the Wallamette. This river rises in Mount Hood, and passes through a rough country; though there is occasionally a fine plain on its banks. One mile above the mouth of Clakamas is the Wallamette falls.

Here the river rushes over a precipice of rocks thirty feet perpendicular in low water.

But the river below the falls often rises so high that there are but from six to ten feet perpendicular falls. This is a most beautiful cataract, and the hydraulic privileges which it affords, and which are beginning to be extensively used, are almost boundless.

Two miles above the falls you come to the mouth of

the Tuality, which comes into the Wallamette from the west, or on the right-hand as you ascend the river. This river rises in the high lands towards the coast, in a number of little streams which water the beautiful and somewhat extensive plains, which are called "The Tuality Plains."

This river, though small, will ultimately be of considerable importance to the country, as it can easily be made navigable for boats far into the plains, and some of the smaller branches, thirty and forty miles from the Wallamette, may be advantageously used for the purpose of driving different kinds of machinery. Ten miles above the Tuality you arrive at the mouth of the Molala and Hanchauke rivers. These two unite but a short distance before they empty into the Wallamette. The Molala rises in the Cascade mountains, but the source of the Hanchauke is in a lake situated midway between the Wallamette river and the base of that range. They both water extensive and beautiful plains, in their serpentine course to the Wallamette.

Fifteen miles above these rivers, you come to the mouth of the Yamhill, which rises in the Kilemook hills towards the ocean and, after meandering for thirty or forty miles through one of the most beautiful portions of the Wallamette valley, and, with its tributaries watering the extended plains through which it flows, it rushes down a ledge of rocks a few feet, forming a beautiful cascade, and hastens to mingle its waters with those of the Wallamette. Proceeding up the stream, and passing a number of small ones on each side, after going twenty-two miles, you arrive at what is called Mill Creek, which comes into the Wallamette from the south-east. It is a small stream, but from its flowing through a beautiful, excellent and central portion of the valley, and affording some very fine water-privileges, it is regarded as being a very important branch of the Wallamette.

Six miles above this comes in the Rickreal, from the west, which can also boast of its priviliges for milling operations, and of watering a splendid portion of the country.

Eight or ten miles above the Rickreal, comes dancing down into the Wallamette, from the east, the "Santa Am's Fork," being fed by the numerous rivulets which rise in the Cascade range. This is a very considerable stream, and from the facilities which it offers for water power, and from the nature of the country through which it flows, may be regarded as second in importance to none of the tributaries of the Wallamette.

Above this, as far as you are disposed to advance, the tributaries of the Wallamette are numerous on each side, but resembling those already described in their sources, dimensions and importance, as well as in the nature of the country through which they flow, do not require to be separately considered.

The principal branch of the Wallamette rises in a snow-clad mountain, called, by British fur traders, "Mount McLaughlin," but by Mr. Kelly, an American citizen, "Mount Madison." Its general course is north, and after running about two hundred and fifty miles, it divides, and forming a long narrow Island, called Wappato Island, the upper channel empties into the Columbia six miles below Fort Vancouver, and ninety miles from the Pacific ocean, and the lower channel, eighteen miles below the upper mouth. It has been generally supposed that the Wallamette river runs through a flat, sunken country, and is therefore a sluggish and muddy stream, than which nothing can be more erroneous. True, from its union with the Columbia, for fifteen miles up, it bears that character, but above this, the general velocity of the current is from three to six miles an hour, and its bed is either gravel, rock, or sand; while nothing can exceed the cleanliness and beauty of its shores. It is navigable for vessels drawing twelve feet, fifteen miles above its upper mouth, and for steamboats, quite up to the Falls. A great portion of the year it is navigable for light steamboats, for fifty or sixty miles above the Falls. In fine, the Wallamette, with its numerous tributaries, arising from its susceptibilities of navigation, its boundless water privileges, the extent, beauty, and amazing resources of the country which it waters, may be considered as the most interesting and important tributary of the Columbia.

This great artery of Oregon, twelve miles below the lower mouth of the Wallamette, receives the Cowilitz from the north, the last river of any magnitude, which contributes to swell its mighty flood, till it reaches the Pacific ocean. The Cowilitz rises in Mount St. Helen's, and in its passage to the Columbia, flows, in a rapid current, through a valley of considerable farming importance.

The Columbia below the Cascades, and after having swallowed up all its important tributaries, is from one mile to a mile and a half in width, until you reach to within twenty-five miles of the ocean. Here it opens to the width of four or five miles, forming, on the south shore, Swan Bay. In this bay, or rather broad space of the river, are a number of low sandy islands already formed, while others appear to be forming in various places. At the foot of this bay, is Tongue Point, which is a high rocky promontory extending into the river from the south shore. From this point to the high bluff on the north shore, the river is ix miles wide. Here the ship channel runs nearly straight across the river, and it generally requires, from the shallowness and intricacy of the channel, two or three days to pass through it. Below Tongue point, the river again widens to eight or ten miles, and a deep indentation on the north shore, and above Chenook point, is called "Gray's Bay," and nearly opposite and between Tongue point and George's point, and ten miles from the mouth, is the harbor of Astoria.

Between the latter point and Point Adams, is Young's Bay, which extends some ways back inland, and receives a river called Lewis' and Clark's river. This is a beautiful bay, about five miles broad, and the ship channel passes directly across its mouth. After swelling out and forming the two bays above described, the river becomes again contracted, so that from Point Adams to Chenook point, it is only five miles wide. On the north side, between Chenook point and Cape Disappointment, is Baker's Bay, which, being sheltered from the winds by the high lands and timber which surround it, is a safe and comfortable harbor. The distance from Point Adams to Cape Disappointment is six miles.

From the former is a channel which runs straight into the ocean in nearly a south-west direction, and no where less than thirty feet deep and one third of a mile wide. But the channel generally used, both for ingress and egress, turns north-west from Young's Bay, and passing round on the north-east side of Sand Island, which lies in the mouth of the river between the two Capes, takes a sweep around, close under Cape Disappointment, and thence in a southerly direction about three miles, where it unites with the south channel, and thus becoming one, their course across the last and most formidable bar of the Columbia, is south-west by west. Between the two channels there is an extensive bar, or island of sand, which is bare at low water, but the two channels together encompass this on all sides.

From Point Adams and from the shore around, and a little to the west of Cape Disappointment, and converging towards each other, proceed those two large sand-bars, which, meeting at the distance of four miles from each point, form that fearful obstacle to the navigation of these waters—the Bar of the Columbia. The channel across this bar is five fathoms deep and a half of a mile wide. When the wind is high from the south and west, the waves of the Pacific and the torrents of the Columbia meet upon this bar with the most terrific violence, producing a line of breakers, often extending from one point to the other, and calculated from their frightful appearance to appal even the heart of a storm-beaten sailor. Vessels bound to the Columbia have often been obliged to lie off and on at this point, for weeks in succession, before an opportunity offered for them to cross the bar. And on desiring to leave, they have sometimes been under the necessity of lying snug under the lee of Cape Disappointment for fifty or sixty days, the passage out meanwhile being continually blocked up by these formidable breakers. This, however, is not the case, except in the winter or spring.

Doubtless there are rivers in the world which afford a greater variety of fish, than this, but perhaps there are none that supply greater quantities. Sturgeon are caught in abundance, but salmon is the principal fish. Of these there are various kinds, but in this country they are generally distinguished by the names spring-salmon and fall-salmon. They literally fill the rivers of Oregon, in their season. And at all the falls and cascades in the various rivers of the country, the quantities taken and that might be taken, are beyond all calculation. As they penetrate far into the interior, they afford almost inexhaustible supplies to the Indian tribes of the country, as well as the whites, many of whom depend almost entirely upon such supplies, for the first year, after settling in the country. The Umpqua and Clameth rivers both rise in the Cascade range, and both empty into the Pacific ocean. They both pass through beautiful and extensive valleys, but toward the coast, are hemmed in by mountains of rock.

They afford also abundant supplies of salmon, which are caught at the Falls and Cascades. At the mouth of the Umpqua is a harbor into which small vessels may enter in safety, wind and tide favoring. This river is navigable for small steamboats twenty-five miles from its mouth.

The timber of Oregon is not of a great variety. The only forests are those composed of fir. This kind of timber abounds on the Columbia, for one hundred and fifty miles from its mouth, among the mountains that border the Pacific, or the lower parts of the Umpqua and Clameth rivers, in various parts of the Wallamette valley, and along the base, on both sides of the Cascade mountains. This timber, in various parts of the country, grows to an almost incredible size. It is no uncommon thing to find trees from twenty-four to thirty-six feet in circumference, and three hundred feet high. One was measured near Astoria or Fort George, and was forty-six feet in circumference, ten feet from the ground. This tree has been cut down, but the writer has examined the stump and is certain that the tree has not been misrepresented. If possible, on the Umpqua river, the fir grows longer than on the Columbia. Here, as also in some parts of the Wallamette valley, the forests are truly magnificent.

This is the principal timber used in the country, both for framing, joinery and fencing purposes. Cargoes of it are shipped annually to the Sandwich Islands, where it finds a ready market at a high price. Besides this, there is a species of the yellow pine, which, however, is not of a very excellent quality, nor does it grow in great abundance. The oak is quite plenty in the Wallamette and the Umpqua valleys, and is considered, next to the fir, the most valuable timber in the country.

In the upper parts of the Wallamette and Umpqua valleys, timber is very scarce, and if these portions are ever settled, as doubtless will be the case, building and fencing materials will be brought from the surrounding mountains, a few miles distant. Along the rivers of this lower country may also be found, in considerable quantities, the cotton-wood, alder, ash, willow, dog-wood, and white maple. The laurel is also indigenous to the country, and cedar of an inferior quality, abounds in some places.

Beside these, there is a variety of shrubbery, among which are the service-berry, crab-apple, hazle-nut, and swamp maple. In the middle region, or between the Cascade and Blue mountains, timber is very scarce; the trees are generally small, and of soft, useless woods, such as cotton-wood, sumach and willow, and found only in the neighborhood of the streams. In the Blue mountains are found quantities of pine, which, in the event of the settlement of the beautiful valleys of the middle country, may be rafted down the rivers, which pass through the mountains, to almost any point below, which, indeed is already done on the Clear Water and Walla Walla rivers. But many parts of the country, and particularly of the middle region, must forever remain destitute of timber, and if ever occupied by any people except savages, substitutes for building and fencing purposes must take the place of the fine fir, oak, pine and ash of the lower country. This scarcity of timber is quite a drawback on many portions of the country.

The climate of Oregon varies materially as you proceed from the coast into the interior. To a proper understanding of the nature of the climate of this country, it is necessary to consider the winter and the summer separately and somewhat particularly. The winds which prevail here, as in every other part of Oregon in the winter, are from the south and east, sometimes veering to the south-west. There is no definite period in the fall when these winds commence blowing, but the different seasons vary much in this respect. Sometimes we have a touch of them, about the twentieth of September, but this is regarded only as a timely monition of what we are subsequently to realize. Some seasons these winds set in for good about the tenth or fifteenth of October, but others, they do not come till late in November. It is impossible to calculate precisely when they will begin to blow, or, in other words, when an Oregon winter will decidedly set in. The commencement may be considered as ranging from the first of October to the first of January; and the medium is about the middle of November. Sometimes they come on gradually, but some seasons they burst upon the country at once, and with the violence of a thunder storm. These winds always bring with them continued falls of rain; and therefore the period of their continuance is properly called the rainy season.

Along the Pacific coast these storms are more violent and the rains more abundant than they are in the Wallamette valley. When fully set in, these rains generally continue, with occasionally a very short interval, for two or three months, and sometimes four, after which there is usually a month of warm, pleasant weather. This comes sometimes in February, sometimes in March, but is generally followed by three or four weeks of cold, chilly rains, from the south and west. During the latter part of winter, there are generally light falls of snow throughout the country, though in the valleys and particularly in the Wallamette valley it seldom falls to more than two or three inches deep.

Though the winters are disagreeable on account of the chilliness of the south-east winds, and the extreme humidity of the atmosphere, yet the cold is very moderate, the mercury seldom falling as low as freezing point. As a matter of course, the ground is seldom frozen, and therefore ploughing may be done a great portion of the winter. Occasionally, however, there is an exception to this. At one time the mercury fell in this valley to five degrees below zero, and at the Dalls, on the west side of the Cascade mountains, fifteen degrees. As this weather lasted for several days, the lakes were all frozen, so that cattle and horses could pass over them on the ice, and the Columbia river was bridged with it as far down as the mouth of the Wallamette, for twelve or fifteen days. But this was principally in consequence of the extreme cold above the Cascades, and the accumulation of ice in that region. A similar circumstance occurred in 1834.

Considerable snow falls every year in the region of the Cascade mountains and around the Dalls on the Columbia. In the middle region, or from the Cascade to the Blue mountains, the rains begin later in the year, are less constant and heavy, and do not continue so late in the spring as in the lower country. In the latter they begin to taper off, generally, in the month of March, but continue more or less through the month of April.

It will be inferred from what has been said, that there is quite a difference in the winters of Oregon. Some are vastly more rainy than others. The winters of 1844 and 1845 commenced with a storm on the twelfth day of October, and continued with a storm of great and uniform violence through the months of November, December, January and February ; then taking a respite for three weeks in the month of March, it closed with a storm, which continued through the month of April. But one-half of the winters in Oregon are not characterized by as much falling weather as is frequently experienced in the State of New York, and are, in consequence of their warmness, decidedly pleasant. It will be understood that none of the winters of this country are so stormy or so cold, but that cattle and horses, with all other animals in the country, subsist on no other feed than is found on the open prairies. In the upper country, or in that portion which lies immediately west of the Rocky mountains, it seldom rains, except in the spring, and then it is not protracted. But vast quantities of snow fall in the winter, particularly on the mountains. This part of Oregon is extremely dry, which, with the vast difference in temperature between the day and the night, forms its most remarkable trait, at least so far as climate is concerned. Between sunrise and noon there is a difference of from forty to sixty degrees of Fahrenheit.

If the winters of Oregon are rather stormy and unpleasant, the summers are sufficiently delightful to counterbalance all this. In the months of March and April, the weather usually becomes sufficiently warm to start vegetation, so that thus early the prairies become beautifully green, and many of Flora's choicest gifts appear to herald the approach of summer. But the summer winds do not generally prevail until the first of May. These are from the west and north, and there is seldom any pleasant weather except when they prevail. And after a long and rainy winter, the people of this country look for the cool and healthy breeze from the bosom of the Pacific ocean with great solicitude. At length the wished for change takes place ; the howl of the storm and the roar of the southern winds, are hushed to silence; the hills and valleys are gently fanned by the western zephyr ; and the sun, pouring his floods of light from a cloudless sky, causes nature, as by enchantment, to enrobe herself in all the glories of summer. The delightful weather thus ushered in, continues with but little variation, through the entire summer.

There are, however, some showers, but they are much "like angels' visit's, few and far between." Generally in the months of July, August and September, the ground becomes exceedingly dry. But the few rains that fall in May and June, with the moisture which is deposited in the heavy dews of the valleys, serve to bring the grains and vegetables to maturity. The temperature of the summer ranges from sixty-five to eighty degrees at noon, in the shade, but the evenings are much cooler. There are few nights through the summer, in which a person would be too warm, covered with two quilts and a flannel blanket. The cool evenings, however, are very pleasant, and doubtless go far to neutralize the effects of the malaria that is exhaled through the influence of the sun, from the swamp and marshy places, which are found in various parts of the country.

From a personal experience of more than five years, and from an extensive observation in reference to this particular, the writer is prepared to express the opinion that the climate of Oregon, not excepting the Wallamette valley, is decidedly favorable to health. And why should it not be? The temperature, particularly in this lower country, is remarkably uniform. This country is not subject to the evils resulting from sudden changes from extreme heat to extreme cold, as in some parts of the States. The exhilarating ocean breeze, which sets in almost every day during the summer, contributes greatly to purify the atmosphere. These circumstances, connected with the fact that there is but little decaying vegetable matter in the country, and but few dead swamps and marshes to send forth their poisonous miasma to infect the surrounding regions, are sufficient to show that this country must be the abode of health, and that human life is as likely to be protracted, and men as likely to die with old age in this country as in almost any other in the world. True, the Indians are generally diseased, and are fast dying off, but their diseases have not been generated in this country; they are the result of their connection with diseased and dissipated foreigners. Formerly it was not so. Besides this, the ague and fever, which attacks many of the whites who come to settle in the Wallamette valley, is easily controlled, and finally leaves the person with a vigorous, unimpaired constitution, and seldom recurs to them the second season. The persons in this country who appear to be the most healthy, are those who have been here the greatest length of time.

The members of the Hudson's Bay Company generally present, in the fullness and flushness of their features, the corpulency of their persons, and their sinewy and robust limbs, the most satisfactory evidence that the climate of Oregon must be friendly to the promotion of health. Indeed, but very few white persons have sickened and died in this country since its first occupancy by such, more than thirty years ago. Though these are the facts in reference to the health of the lower country, even yet there are persons in the States who are ready to publish far and near, that the climate of Oregon, and particularly of the Wallamette valley, is "decidedly unhealthy," that "the most malignant and fatal fevers rage in the country;" than which, no representation could be more erroneous.

It will be readily perceived from these remarks, that this climate is well calculated for wheat, barley, oats, peas, apples, potatoes, turnips, and all other vegetables which are cultivated in the Middle States. Indian corn, however, does not succeed very well, though some years considerable is raised. The country is exceedingly favorable for the raising of horses, cattle and hogs, all of which thrive and multiply beyond all conception.

If there is any difference in regard to health between the different portions of Oregon, probably the middle region, and immediately along the coast, are the most healthy parts.

The climate of the Wallamette valley is more favorable to agriculture than any other portion of the country; but that of the middle region is every way adapted to purposes of grazing and to all the pursuits of a pastoral life.

But with a uniform healthy and delightful climate, that is as well adapted to agricultural purposes as any within the same degrees of latitude in any part of the earth, Oregon loses much of its interest, if the fertility of the *soil* is not in keeping with the nature of the climate.

The soil of Oregon has been variously represented by persons who have traveled through the country. Some have spoken of it in altogether too favorable a light, while others have greatly underrated it. Some have placed it among the first in the world in point of fertility, and others have considered Oregon as a boundless desert, fit only to be the habitation of wild beasts and savage tribes. Some have viewed it as a second Eden, and others, one writer in particular, denounces it as a "God-forsaken country that never was designed to be the habitation of a Christian or civilized man." These conflicting representations arise doubtless from a superficial acquaintance with the country. They have either not continued in the country a sufficient length of time to become acquainted with its real productiveness, or they have depended upon that information which has been artfully designed to prevent the true nature of the country from being known.

To a proper understanding of the nature and productiveness of the soil, it will be necessary to consider it as it appears in different portions of the country. As the Clatsop Plains are exciting considerable interest at the present time in the country, a description of them, with a view to the examination of the soil, is desirable. These plains lie on the south side of the mouth of the Columbia river, back of that point of land which is known by the name of Point Adams. They are a portion of that low tract of country which lies in the form of a triangle, one of whose sides is washed by the waves of the Pacific, and the other by those of Young's Bay; while its base rests against the range of mountains extending back from Kellimook Head, and its point or apex is washed by the south channel of the Columbia. The height of this triangle, or the distance from Point Adams back to the mountains, is about twenty-five miles, while the mean width is probably not more than four miles. The plains themselves are about twenty miles long and from one to two and a half broad. They contain about forty square miles. They lie directly on the shore of the Pacific, and command a fine view of all the ships that pass over the bar of the Columbia. There is a beautiful sand-beach extending their entire length, which, at low water, forms a firm and commodious road. Between the plains and Young's Bay, there is a tract of timber land, comprising about twice as much as the plains, but similar in every other respect, except the dense forest of fir, spruce, pine, cedar, hemlock and alder, by which it is shaded. It is quite probable that the entire tract of land above described, has been formed by the vast quantities of sands and vegetable substances which have been conveyed from time immemorial, by the Columbia river to the ocean, and deposited by the ceaseless action of tide. The evidences of this are, first, the fact that the soil is of the same alluvial character that appears on the banks of the river above; secondly, from the several ridges, or undulations, which curve precisely with the shore of the ocean, and all of which appear to have successively formed the boundary of the deep; and, thirdly, from the fact, that shells and other marine substances are found deeply embedded in the sands thus deposited, in a perfect state of petrifaction. But it is only necessary for a man to walk up from tide-water to the ridge nearest the ocean, and cast his eye over the gentle undulations of this tract, for him to become convinced that it has been redeemed from the waters of the Pacific. These remarks have been deemed important, in order to show the true nature of the soil of this important point of Oregon.

It will be perceived that the foundation of the soil is sand. In some places this sand is bare, but even here, where the winds admit of vegetation taking root, its growth shows clearly that this sand is far from being destitute of vegetative properties. On the plains, however, this sand is covered with a black mould, which is from six to ten inches deep, and which doubtless has been formed by the constant decay of the various kinds of vegetation, which here grow in abundance. This black mould, with a portion of the sand beneath, forms a rich and productive soil, which, from its proximity to the ocean, and perhaps from the nature of the soil itself, is not so well adapted to wheat, but produces potatoes, turnips, and indeed all kinds of vegetables in abundance. It is also tolerably well adapted to the raising of peas and oats. Cattle, horses and hogs thrive on this soil as well as in any part of Oregon.

The bottom-lands of the Columbia, from the Cascades to the ocean, are subject to an annual inundation from the great rise of the river, occasioned by the melting of the vast quantities of snow, which fall on its upper branches among the mountains. This flood continues through the month of June and into July, so that whatever may be the fertility of the land thus overflown, but small portions of it, without immense labor and expense, will ever be brought to contribute greatly to the support of man. However, those portions of it which lie above high water, are remarkably fertile, and produce in abundance, all the grains and vegetables common to the best portions of the country. Fort Vancouver is situated on the most choice portion of this tract, and here a farm of two or three thousand acres is cultivated, and produces annually several thousand bushels of grain. Here also apples, pears and peaches are cultivated successfully; with care the grape also is brought to a degree of perfection.

The uplands, or timbered lands, differ in some respects from the prairies. Though but few attempts have been made to cultivate them, yet sufficient has been done to prove that the soil is rather of a superior quality. And, indeed, this is attested by the immense growth of timber itself. No inferior soil could send forth those enormous trunks, which, in their upward progress, spread their magnificent branches to the skies, and often place their heads three hundred feet from the ground. Though the cost of clearing these lands is great, yet time will doubtless cause the richness and fertility of this soil to contribute to the support of its future cultivators.

The soil of the country around Puget's Sound is of a very different character. The country to appearance is beautiful. The prairies are extensive; the harbor is fine, and the scenery delightful; but, strictly speaking there is no soil to the country. The prairies are all composed of shingle land, or small stone, or gravel, without scarcely any mixture of soil. Indeed, there are but few places, and these are very small spots, where any thing can be raised. Attempts have been made to redeem it from its native barrenness, but as yet all have failed.

The Hudson's Bay Company transported some of their surplus population at Red river, on the east side of the Rocky mountains, to this region; but, in consequence of the amazing sterility of the country, they soon became discouraged, and, contrary to the wishes of the Company, they have abandoned the place and have settled elsewhere. This is sufficient to show the nature of the soil in this portion of the country. And in view of these facts, how has it come to pass that some persons after having visited this region, publish it as being distinguished alike for the salubrity of its climate and the fertility of its soil? The climate indeed is delightful, but the soil is exceedingly forbidding, and cannot, perhaps, be recovered from its extreme barrenness.

Of all the different parts of Oregon, it is unquestionable that the Wallamette valley is entitled to be called the garden of the country, so far as the fertility of its soil is concerned. The close observer, in traveling through this valley, will discover several kinds of soil. On the lower, or first bottoms, in some places, a sandy soil appears, in others, a kind of black marl or loam. There is but little difference in the productiveness of the two kinds. They both appear to be the alluvial deposits of the Wallamette river. On the second bottoms, or high prairies, as they are called in the country, the soil is a dark loamy clay, and is equally as strong and fertile as that on the lower grounds. Higher up the river, in the region of the Santa Am's fork, and embracing tracts of considerable extent, you come to a gravelly soil, which is less productive than any other in the valley. However, this last embraces but a small proportion of the valley. As the most of the country is embraced in the high prairies, there is much more of the clayey land than of any other kind. But the goodness of the soil is better ascertained by examining the crops which are annually taken from the land.

The writer of this has formerly resided, for years together, in the great wheat growing country of the State of New York, and has been an attentive observer of the amount of labor necessary to be performed to put into the granary the wheat raised from an acre of ground. He has also, for several succeeding years, observed the same in the Wallamette valley; and the result of these observations has brought him to the conclusion, that it requires less labor in this country to raise one bushel or a thousand bushels of wheat, than it does on any part of the Genesee flats. The prairies of this country, in many important respects, are unlike those of any other country. They are naturally very mellow, and appear, as one is passing over them, as though it had been but a year or two since they were cultivated. They are not swarded over with a thick strong turf, as in the Western States. They can be easily ploughed with one good span of horses the first time, and when thus ploughed, they are ready to receive the seed, and seldom fail, even the first crop, of yielding from fifteen to twenty-five bushels per English acre. The first crops are never so good as the succeeding ones. Farmers have, in a number of instances, without using any extraordinary means, taken from fifty to sixty-five bushels of wheat from an acre, and this has been an average of fields containing from ten to fifteen acres. But this is, by no means, the common yield after the first crop, though, doubtless, if farmers in this country would cultivate less ground and bestow on it the same quantity of labor, they would realize much more from the acre than they now do. Under the present system of cultivation in this country, the average amount taken from the acre is in the vicinity of twenty-five bushels.

Unlike any other portions of the world, a good crop of wheat, provided the seed is put into the ground in its season and in a proper manner, is as sure to reward the labor of the husbandman, as that day and night will continue until harvest time. This, perhaps, is not owing so much to the quality of the soil, as to the nature of the climate. And it is difficult to conceive of any circumstance that can prevent this result, so long as the present laws of nature, which regulate the seasons of Oregon, are allowed to operate. But this is not the case with regard to all other crops.

Potatoes frequently fail from a want of rain the latter part of the season; or, if they do not entirely fail, the crops are often very light.

This is the case with all spring crops, particularly if the seed is put in late. They are liable to suffer from drought before they ripen in the fall. However, during the last five years, there has not been a failure in any of the crops. Some years have not been as productive as others, in the spring crops, but a majority of the years, these have all succeeded to admiration, with the exception of Indian corn. This valuable species of produce will never be raised, to any considerable extent, in this country, though some seasons it succeeds tolerably well. The cool nights and dry summers are obstacles that it cannot overcome. The soil of this valley as well as the climate, is well adapted to the raising of melons, squashes, cucumbers, beets, cabbages, and all kinds of garden vegetables. Apples, peaches, and other kinds of fruit, flourish, so far as they have been cultivated; and from present appearances, it is quite likely that the time is not far distant, when the country will be well supplied with the various kinds of fruit which grow in the Middle States.

The soil of the middle region of Oregon differs materially from that of the low country. It bears one general character, and consists of a yellow sandy clay. It produces naturally a kind of bunch grass, which is very nutritious, and grows in abundance on the vast plains of the country; and here are also a variety of small shrubs, and the prickly pear. Persons in passing through the country along the banks of the Columbia river, are liable to entertain erroneous views, in reference to the fertility of this region. The land along the river, is a collection of sand and rocks, than which nothing can present a more sterile appearance. But back a few miles, the country wears a different aspect. And judging from the grass and herbage, which cover the ground, as well as from the appearance of the soil, the land may be pronounced at least as tolerably good. It is on the extended plains of this region that the Kayuses and Nez Perces raise their immense droves of horses. It is no uncommon thing for one Indian to own fifteen hundred of these animals. The writer once had the privilege of seeing at least two thousand from one eminence. And yet this portion of Oregon has been called "a barren waste;" an error which a correct knowledge of the country will certainly rectify.

It may be therefore concluded, as it has been already expressed, that, from the fertility of the soil of this region, as well as the salubrity of the climate, as a whole, it is most admirably adapted to purposes of grazing, while on many of the streams agricultural pursuits might successfully be prosecuted.

On the Walla Walla and Clear Water rivers, attempts at farming have been made, and have been crowned with success.

The upper region of Oregon, or that part which lies east of the Blue mountains, is less fertile than the middle. Though the soil of some portions of it is tolerably good, yet much the greater proportion of the plains are either covered with a course sand or gravel, or are so strongly impregnated with salts of various kinds, that it would be perfectly useless to make any attempts at cultivation, though the climate might be ever so favorable.

What has often been said of Oregon as a whole, may be said in truth, of this portion of the country, namely, that it is an extensive barren waste, not capable of supporting more than a very small number of inhabitants; but this remark only applies to the *third*, or *upper region*, of this vast territory. To apply it to that half of Oregon which extends from the Blue mountains to the Pacific ocean, would be doing the country great injustice. For, instead of this being the fact, it is the opinion of those who have been longest in the country, and consequently know best what its resources are, that this portion is capable of sustaining as large a population, as *all* of the New England States. In fact, the resources of this country are great; and it is only necessary for them to be known, to be duly appreciated by the people of the United States. A single consideration only is necessary to be presented to show what the country would be capable of doing, provided it was filled with an industrious population. It will be borne in mind that in the fall of 1843, an emigration arrived in this country numbering from eight to ten hundred persons, most of whom came so late that it was impossible for them to get locations where they could raise wheat the first year, and were consequently thrown upon the resources of the country. In the fall of 1844, another emigration arrived, numbering from seven to eight hundred persons. These all, with the entire population, depended upon the products of 1844, for a subsistence until the harvest of 1845. Probably not more than one quarter of the whole population had cultivated the land in 1844, yet they were all supported from the granaries of the country; fifteen thousand bushels of wheat were shipped to the Russian settlements; one thousand barrels of flour were exported to the Sandwich Islands, and thousands of bushels yet remained in the country unconsumed. With these facts before us, it does not require half an eye to see that Oregon *can* and *will* compete with any other portion of the world, in supplying the islands of the Pacific, the Russian settlements, and every other flour market contiguous, with their bread stuffs, which usually bear, in these portions of the world, a handsome price.

In connection with this it may be remarked that beef and pork can be raised in this country with greater ease and facility than wheat. And the climate of the country being favorable for salting and barreling, the time is not far distant when these articles also will be exported in abundance. The United States Navy and shipping in general in the Pacific, can be supplied with these articles of consumption from this country more reasonably, perhaps, than from any other. Already there are many settlers in this valley who have from two to five hundred head of cattle, and it is nothing strange for a man to be the owner of a hundred hogs. At present, however, from the great influx of population, these kinds of property bear a high price in the country, but the time may be anticipated, when the home market will not be so extensive, and then the vast supplies from this quarter must find an outlet.

The facilities for lumbering in the country have already been presented; and, in addition, it should be observed that, with the vast amount of salmon which may be barreled annually, and the products of dairies, for conducting which the country offers the greatest facilities, the exports of Oregon, in proportion to the number of its inhabitants, *may* equal those of any portions of the United States.

In this exhibition of the wealth and resources of Oregon, there is one more subject that ought not to be overlooked, viz: the facility with which a man comparatively poor, can place himself entirely above want. Individuals have, in some instances, arrived in this country in the month of September; have settled immediately on some of the fine prairies, and with but little, except good health and sound limbs, have harvested, the following season, of their own sowing, from fifty to one hundred and fifty acres of wheat.

And, indeed, there are few countries, perhaps none, in which a poor man, when once he has surmounted the difficulties of getting here, in which he can get a better living, and get it easier, than in this. Such is the testimony of every person who tries it for one or two years. But every country has its defects, and this is not entirely free from them. It is neither the garden of Eden, nor is it a barren desert. It does not "flow with honey," like the land of Canaan; but in some places it literally flows with milk. And, though it is not a "land of wine," yet, in the more necessary articles of "corn and oil," it greatly abounds.

That it is a land of mountains and valleys, of rivers and streams, of mighty forests and extended prairies, of a salubrious and healthy climate, and a rich and productive soil, the foregoing remarks will clearly show. In fine, it is every way entitled to be called a good country.

CHAPTER XVII.

Oregon territory — Its history — Spanish discoveries — Measures of the English — Sir Francis Drake — Heceta — Isle of Grief — Bodega discovers Killemook Head — Discoveries of Captain James Cook — Captain John Mearls — Cape Disappointment — Robert Gray, of Boston — First visit to the coast — Second visit, discovers the Columbia river — Captain Vancouver — Braughton.

When America was first discovered, it was supposed to constitute the eastern limits of the continent of Asia; but, as discovery succeeded discovery in quick succession during the first twenty years after the arrival of Columbus in 1492, the astounding fact that the Genoese navigator had given to the nations of Europe a vast continent, was speedily and satisfactorily established. If there remained any doubts as to the separation of America from the eastern continent on the minds of any, they were all removed after Fernando Magellan had passed from the Atlantic to the Pacific ocean through the strait which separates Patagonia from Terra Del Fuego, and Vacco Nunez de Balboa had discovered the placid waters of the great ocean from the top of the Andes, at the Isthmus of Darien. Within a few years after Magellan sailed into the Pacific ocean, the Spaniards, under Hernan Cortez, discovered and made a conquest of the rich and populous empire of Mexico, and soon after followed the subjugation of Chili and Peru to the authority of Spain. The immense amount of silver which the Spaniards obtained by these conquests, excited the avarice of others, and crowds of adventurers of different nations and under daring leaders, came over and traversed the new world in every direction, eager to acquire distinction by plundering the rich countries which they might discover. Defeated in their objects, they, however, collected much information respecting those regions which otherwise might not have been explored, perhaps, for centuries.

In 1532, forty years after the discovery of Columbus, the coast of the American continent had been explored from the Gulf of Mexico on the Atlantic side, to the Strait of Magellan, and on the Pacific side from the same Strait to a place called Culiacan, situate near the eastern side of the entrance to the Gulf of California. Northward of these points, both of which are near the twenty-third degree of north latitude, nothing as yet was known of that vast region which was destined to teem with so many millions of human beings. Up to 1578, the Spaniards were the principal actors in prosecuting discoveries along the Pacific coast. Expeditions were fitted out by Cortez and by his successor in the viceroyalty of Mexico, Don Antonio de Mendoza, which sailed northward from time to time, touching at various points along the coast, but making no important discoveries until 1539, when Francisco de Ulloa, under the direction of Mendoza, sailed from Acapulco, north, for the purpose of ascertaining the situation and extent of that country which by this time began to be called California.

Ulloa discovered that California was a continuity of the American continent; for up to this time it was not known whether it was connected with Asia or America, or whether it was not a country by itself. There is satisfactory evidence that some of these early explorers saw the coast up as high as the thirty-fourth degree of north latitude, and in 1543, a navigator by the name of Ferrelo, is said to have extended his discoveries as far up as the forty-third parallel, and about the same time a land expedition was fitted out under Hernando de Soto, and performed a memorable march through the then unknown regions north of the Gulf of Mexico, till they reached the fortieth parallel of latitude, and then turning east, they fell in with the Mississippi river near the mouth of the Ohio, and descended it in boats back to the Gulf of Mexico, which they succeeded in crossing in open boats; and the few that survived the fatigues and perils of the enterprise, finally reached Pameco in safety. This expedition had a two-fold object in view, which was, first, to discover wealthy nations to subjugate like those of Mexico and Peru, and, second, to ascertain whether there were no navigable passages between the Atlantic and Pacific oceans, somewhere north of the Mexican Gulf. Being defeated in both these objects, the Spaniards desisted from any farther efforts to explore the north-west coast of the American continent, and did not renew their efforts for nearly half a century afterwards.

Though for the present they ceased to explore the north-west division of the New World, yet the commerce of the Spaniards in the Pacific ocean was continually increasing, and their "Government was adopting those measures of restriction and exclusion which were maintained with so little relaxation during the whole period of its supremacy in the American continent." * * * "The great object of its policy was to secure to the people of Spain the perpetual enjoyment of all the advantages which could be derived from the territories claimed by them, and, with that view, it was considered absolutely necessary, not only to prevent the establishment of foreigners in any part of those territories, but also to discourage the rapid advancement of the Spanish provinces themselves, in population, wealth or other resources. Agreeably to these ideas, the settlement and even the exploring of new countries in America, were restrained; colonies were rarely allowed to be planted near the coast, unless they might serve for purposes of defence, and when voyages or journeys of discovery were made, the results were generally concealed by the government. The subjects of all foreign nations were prohibited, under pain of death, from touching the section of the New World supposed to belong to Spain, or from navigating the seas in its vicinity."

About this time, 1570, the principles of civil and religious liberty were beginning to operate in England. They no longer acknowledged the Pope of Rome as their spiritual head, nor did they stand in fear of his fulminations. And, though the successor of St. Peter had granted to Spain a great part of the American continent, and, as far as possible, had confirmed her in her possessions, yet the English murmured bitterly against these excluding regulations of the Spanish government, and required "an acknowledgment of their right to occupy vacant portions of America, and to trade with such as were already settled."

These reasonable demands were refused by the Spanish government, and the Queen of England encouraged her subjects, openly and secretly, to violate laws which she declared to be unjustifiable and inhuman. Accordingly, on the Atlantic side of the continent, we see these restrictive laws immediately violated by bands of daring English, and, in the name of *free-traders* and *free-booters*, who set the Spaniards at defiance, plundering their ships and some of their towns along the coast. From the reports concerning the importance of the commerce of the Pacific, the English had long desired to share in its advantages, and at length all their dread of the difficulties and dangers of the passage through the strait of Magellan were overcome, and there appeared on the waters of the Pacific the most renowned naval captain of the age. This captain was Francis Drake; and, as an opinion has prevailed that he effected important discoveries on the coast of Oregon, it will be proper to notice his movements while he remained on this coast.

Mr. Greenhow in his able memoirs, has collected all the evidences of Drake's discoveries on this coast, and from an account of his voyage by his chaplain, and from nearly all the biographical sketches of the hero for a century after his voyage had been accomplished, and from the contradictions of those writers who attempt to establish the opposite, he arrives at the conclusion that "the English under Drake, in all probability saw no part of the west coast of America north of the forty-third degree of north latitude."

Drake's visit to this coast took place in 1579, and proceeding as high up as the forty-third degree, and finding the weather cold and boisterous, and knowing that his ship needed repairing before he could return to England, he turned about, and retracing his steps as far back as the thirty-eighth degree, entered the bay now called "San Francisco," where he spent the remainder of the winter. The following spring he put again to sea, and, by the way of China and the Cape of Good Hope, returned to England, where, immediately after his arrival, for his wonderful voyage and marvelous exploits, he was knighted by Queen Elizabeth, on the deck of his own ship. Doubtless the character of Drake as a hero and a great navigator, is well founded; but the assertion that he explored the whole extent of this coast, and discovered the Columbia river, is a fabrication, and is entitled to no more credit than the fabled voyage of Maldorado from the north-west coast, across the continent, into the Atlantic ocean.

That Francis Drake is not entitled to the credit of being the first discoverer of the coast as far up as the forty-third degree, appears from an account of a voyage performed by Cabrillo and Ferrelo, two Spaniards, in 1543, thirty-six years before the voyage of Drake. In the month of March they sailed to the forty-fourth degree, and in consequence of the suffering of their crews from cold, fatigue, and want of proper nourishment, they resolved to proceed no farther northward, and accordingly directed their course towards the south.* These were probably the first white men that ever saw any of the land embraced in the territory of Oregon, and they saw only about two degrees of the coast, at the south-west corner.

The next discoveries of importance made on the coast of Oregon, were by a Spanish navigator, by the name of Heceta, in 1774. He was sent by the viceroy of Mexico from San Blas, to explore the coast north of the forty-third parallel, and succeeded in reaching as high up as the fifty-fourth degree, where he made land, probably the north-west part of Queen Charlotte's Island. From this point he turned southward, entered a fine bay

---

* See Greenhow's Memoirs.

in latitude forty-nine and one-half, and proceeding down along the coast, saw land occasionally, but does not appear to have minutely examined the shore, and arrived at Monterey on the 27th of August.

The following year another expedition was fitted out, and Heceta was intrusted with the command. He proceeded northward, touched at port Trinidad in latitude forty-one, where he communicated with the natives, and, on leaving, erected a cross with an inscription setting forth the rights of the Spanish government to the country discovered. From this point he continued north as high as the forty-eighth or forty-ninth degree, then turned east, and soon saw land, which was probably the south-west side of Vancouver's Island, at the entrance of the Strait of Fuca.

Not being able to examine this part of the coast, they were driven southward to within eighty miles of the Columbia river, where they came to anchor inside of a small island, near the main land. Here they met with a cruel misfortune. They sent some of their men on shore to search for water, and while in the discharge of their duty, they were surrounded by savages and immediately murdered. As they were numerous, the Indians immediately put off in their canoes to the ships, evidently with the intention of taking them and destroying the crews. But the Spaniards finally succeeded in preventing them from boarding; and on their departure, in commemoration of the event, the island was called the Isle of Grief. At the same place, and in the same manner, twelve years afterwards, some of the crew of an English ship were destroyed, and by them the island was called Destruction Island. After this disaster, Heceta continued southward along the coast, and discovered the promontory which now bears the name of Cape Disappointment, but which the Spaniards called Cape San Roque. Directly south of this, and under the parallel of forty-six degrees sixteen minutes, he saw an opening in the land, which appeared to be a harbor, or the mouth of some river. As Heceta did not enter this harbor, the existence of the river subsequently was more a matter of conjecture than of certainty, though it was put down on the Spanish maps by the name of Rio de San Roque. From these circumstances, it is at least inferable that Heceta and his companions were the first civilized men that ever saw the Columbia river.

During the same year, 1775, another Spanish navigator, by the name of Bodega, made the Oregon coast about thirty miles south of the mouth of the Columbia. The land first seen by them was the high promontory now known by the name of Kilemook Head; but which the Spaniards called Cape Mizari. Bodega examined the coast, from this point to Cape Mendocino, in search of a large river, said to have been seen by Aguilar, in 1603. But not succeeding in his attempts, he took his departure from this part of the coast and returned to Monterey.

The next discoveries on the Oregon coast were made by the celebrated Captain James Cook, an English navigator, in 1778. This enterprising man left England early in the summer of 1777, and arrived on the American coast in March, 1778. The primary object of his voyage was the discovery of a north-west passage from the Pacific ocean to the Atlantic, an object which long engaged the attention of England and Spain. To accomplish this object, he was to explore the whole extent of coast, from the forty-fifth degree as far north as the weather and ice would allow him to proceed. He first made land near the forty-second degree of latitude; but by the violence of storms, was driven still farther to the south. However, the wind becoming more favorable, he proceeded on his course to the northward, and on the 22d of March, he found himself in sight of the coast a little beyond the forty-eighth degree. The land here discovered by Cook was the projecting point of the continent at the entrance of the strait of Juan De Fuca, to which he gave the name of Cape Flattery, and which is the north-west corner of Oregon territory. Cook examined the coast a few miles south of this point; but not succeeding in his object here. he soon continued north, and in latitude forty-nine and a half, cast anchor in a spacious and secure harbor, to which he subsequently gave the name of Nootka Sound. Here he continued several weeks, during which he held constant intercourse with the Indians, who appeared to be no strangers to white men ; and after making the necessary repairs, and taking in wood, water and refreshments, he again steered to the northward to buffet the ice and storms of the Arctic Ocean, in a vain attempt to discover a north-west passage. Thus terminated his discoveries on the Oregon coast. He was subsequently basely murdered by the natives of Hawaii.

It is worthy of remark, that this usually fortunate navigator and discoverer was driven past the mouth of the Columbia river, by a storm, during the night.

There seems to have been but little notice taken of the Oregon coast during the ten years which followed the discoveries of Cook, though at this time the coast farther north was very well known. As Nootka Sound was known to be a good harbor, after Cook's account of his voyage was made public, vessels, in visiting this region, generally steered their course for that place. But in 1788, Captain John Meares, an Englishman, fitted out an expedition at Macao for the purpose of discovering the harbor, or river, or rather opening, which was first seen by Heceta, in 1775, and subsequently noticed on the Spanish maps, by the name of the Rio De San Roque. The principal object that Meares had in view, on this part of the coast, was to ascertain whether there was such a river in existence ; and the account which he has given of his discoveries, at this point, will show the unreasonableness of the claims of the English, to be the first to ascertain the fact of the existence of the Columbia river. In latitude forty-six degrees and forty-seven minutes, he discovered a head-land which he called Cape Shoal Water, and proceeding south along the coast, he says — "An high bluff promontory bore us off south-east, at the distance of only four leagues, for which we steered to double, with the hope that between it and Cape Shoal Water, we should find some sort of harbor. We now discovered distant land beyond this promontory, and we pleased ourselves with the expectation of its being Cape Saint Roc of the Spaniards, near which they are said to have found a good port. By half-past eleven we doubled this Cape at the distance of three miles, having a clear and perfect view of the shore in every part, on which we did not discern a living creature, or the least trace of habitable life. A prodigious easterly swell rolled on the shore, and the soundings gradually decreased from forty to sixteen fathoms, over a hard sandy bottom. After we had rounded the promontory, a large bay, as we had imagined, opened to our view, that bore a very promising appearance, and into which we steered with every encouraging expectation.

"The high land that formed the boundaries of the bay was at a great distance, and a flat level country occupied the intervening space; the bay itself took rather a westerly direction. As we steered in, the water shoaled to nine, eight, and seven fathoms, when breakers were seen from the deck right ahead, and from the mast-head they were observed to extend across the bay; we, therefore, hauled out and directed our course to the opposite shore, to see if there was any channel, or if we could discover any port.

"The name of Cape Disappointment was given to the promontory, and the bay obtained the title of Deception Bay. By an indifferent meridian observation, it lies in the latitude of forty-six degrees and ten minutes north, and in the computed longitude of 235 degrees and 34 minutes east. We can now with safety assert, that there is no such river as that of Saint Roc exists, as laid down in the Spanish charts."

It follows, from this account of Captain Meares, first, that he became fully convinced, from personal observation, that no great river entered the Pacific ocean from the American continent at this point. And, second, that no such river had previously been discovered by English navigators, and that the assertion, that "the Columbia was discovered by Captain, afterwards Sir Francis Drake," must be totally unfounded. For, if the latter captain had made this discovery, the fact must have been known by Captain Meares, and he would not have been so ready to decide that "no such river exists." The truth appears to be this—up to the year 1788, it was not known by any civilized nation, that the great Columbia had an existence on the face of the globe.

The citizens of the United States appear to have taken no part in the discoveries on the north-west coast, and in the trade opened by such discoveries previously to the year, 1788. At that time a company of merchants from Boston, sent two ships around Cape Horn, commanded respectively by Captain Robert Gray and Captain John Kendrick.

The names of these vessels were, the Columbia and Washington. These were the first American ships that visited the north-west coast. After weathering a violent storm in which the Columbia, which Kendrick commanded, received some injury, they proceeded to Nootka Sound, where both vessels spent the winter. The object of this expedition was to collect the fine and valuable furs with which the country abounds, and ship them to Canton.

While these two American ships were in this part of the ocean, there was considerable difficulty between the Spaniards and the English, in reference to which had the best right to the country in the vicinity of Nootka Sound. In the settlement of this difficulty, the American captains took an active and efficient part, and from an understanding of the whole affair, were of the opinion that, from a previous discovery and occupancy, the Spanish claims were well founded, and that the possession of the country was an unjustifiable arrogancy upon the part of the British. But it is no part of the object of this sketch to investigate the subject of these conflicting claims. The Columbia and Washington continued on the coast until the month of August, 1789, when it was determined between them, that Captain Gray should take the command of the Columbia and proceed to China and the United States, with all the furs which had been collected, and Kendrick should remain on the coast in the Washington.

Gray accomplished this voyage in safety, and on the 27th day of September, 1790, again left Boston in the same ship for the north-west coast, and sometime in May of 1791, made land a little to the north of Cape Mendocino, or near the forty-first degree of north latitude. While proceeding northward towards Nootka, Captain Gray discovered an opening in the shore of considerable width in latitude forty-six degrees sixteen minutes, from which issued a strong current which prevented his entrance. He continued off against this opening for nine days, with an intention, if possible, to enter it, but the strength of the current and probably from the appearance of the breakers which previously had frightened Meares, he was unable at this time to accomplish his object. Though convinced that he had discovered the mouth of a great river, without waiting longer for an opportunity to enter it, he proceeded to the north, and in June arrived at Nootka Sound. From this point Gray continued his course north, and after making some important discoveries in the vicinity of Queen Charlotte's Island, returned to Clyoquot, near Nootka, where he continued during the winter. Captain Kendrick in the meantime had stayed on the coast, and about the time that Gray went into winter quarters, he set sail for the Sandwich Islands, where he first opened a traffic with the natives, in the article of sandal-wood. Though Kendrick first opened this trade, he did not long live to enjoy the benefit of his discovery, but in 1793, was murdered by the Islanders.

In the spring of 1792, the discoveries on the coast of Oregon were prosecuted both by the English and Americans. In the middle of April, Captain Vancouver arrived on the coast with two ships under his command, and commencing at Cape Mendocino, explored the whole extent of coast, as he proceeded to the north, and passed the opening which Gray attempted to enter in latitude forty-six degrees sixteen minutes, without considering it as being worthy of his particular attention, on account of the forbidding appearance which it presented. In his progress northward he says, that, "the coast was so minutely examined that the surf was constantly seen to break on its shores from the mast-head. And yet, that he saw no appearance of an opening in its shores, which presented any certain prospect of affording shelter." On his way up the coast he fell in with the ship Columbia, Captain Gray, who had just left his wintering place at Clyoquot. In their interview, Gray informed Vancouver that the previous summer he had been off the mouth of a river in latitude forty-six degrees ten minutes, where the outset was so strong as to prevent his entering for nine days. In referring to this, Vancouver says, that "this was probably the opening passed by us on the forenoon of the 27th, and was apparently inaccessible, *not from the current,* but from the breakers that extend across it." He also observes that he was thoroughly convinced, as were most persons on board, that he could not have passed any harbor or place of security for shipping, from Cape Mendocino to Cape Flattery.

From this it appears that Captain Vancouver did not yet believe that such a river as was represented by Gray, had any existence. And under this impression he proceeded on to the north, while Gray, to assure himself of the reality of his discovery of a great river, resolved, if possible, to enter it with his ship. While proceeding southward he entered a harbor, which he called Bulfinch's Harbor; but passing on, arrived, on the 11th of May, 1792, opposite the bay which Meares called the Bay of Deception, immediately south of Cape Disappointment, and in latitude forty-six degrees ten minutes north. Though the breakers presented a formidable obstacle before them, and they did not know but that they were rushing to inevitable destruction, yet Captain Gray and his gallant comrades dashed bravely on, and discovering a narrow passage through the breakers, passed them in safety, and as Gray had anticipated, found themselves in a large river of fresh water, up which they proceeded the distance of twenty miles. The point at which they arrived, was probably the narrow and shallow channel known by the name of Tongue Point Channel, and which is difficult to pass, though the river is well known. The natives flocked around the strangers and manifested the utmost surprise, at what they saw and heard. A traffic was opened with them in which furs were received from the Indians, in exchange for coarse goods; and after having continued in the river eight days, making repairs, trading with the natives, exploring the river, and taking observations of the surrounding country, Captain Gray again passed the breakers at the entrance, through the intricate channel, prepared to announce to the world the most important discovery that was ever made on the north-west coast.

Before taking his departure, Captain Gray bestowed the name of his vessel upon the majestic river which he had discovered, calling it the Columbia, a name which, in honor of the generous captain who bestowed it, and of the gallant ship that first anchored in its waters, it should forever retain. The high promontory on the north side of the entrance, which was called Cape Disappointment, by Meares, in token of his unsuccessful search, by Captain Gray was called Cape Hancock, and the low point on the south side Cape Adams.

It has been asserted by one writer, that the existence of this river was long known before Gray or Vancouver visited it.* Doubtless, it was known by the Indian tribes that lived upon its banks, but if any white man ever saw it he was not permitted to survive to tell of his discovery. From a survey of the whole ground, it appears clearly that Captain Robert Gray is entitled to the credit of being the original discoverer of this great river of Oregon; a river which, when viewed as the only convenient or practicable channel to and from one of the most extensive and fertile valleys in North America, will bear comparison with almost any river in the world.

From the mouth of this river, Gray returned to the north, and in the vicinity of Queen Charlotte's Island, while his vessel was under full sail, she struck a rock and received so great an injury that she was near

---

* Astoria.

foundering, but he finally succeeded in getting her into Nootka Sound, when his damage was soon repaired. Gray found at this place a Spaniard who had the command of the establishment, and to him he immediately communicated the results of his examinations, and particularly his discovery of the Columbia river, which proved a very fortunate circumstance, for he thereby obtained an unimpeachable witness in his favor. He continued in this region a few months actively employed in his trade with the natives, and other business, and in the ensuing fall took his final departure from the northwest coast.

In a discussion of the conflicting claims of the two governments, it had been arranged between the Spanish and English, that the former should surrender to the latter the country lying around the Nootka Sound, and Captain Vancouver was the commissioner from England to receive the surrender. The negotiations between Vancouver and the Spanish commissioner took place while Gray and other American captains were on the coast. The contest which was carried on between the two parties, however interesting, would be too tedious to introduce here. Suffice it to say, the place was not surrendered nor does it appear that the Spanish flag was ever struck to the British at Nootka Sound. Be this as it may, in the month of October, Vancouver left Nootka with his three vessels, the Discovery, Chatham, and Doedalus, having procured from Quadra, the Spanish commissioner, copies of the charts and descriptions of Gray, and proceeded southward to satisfy himself of the correctness of Gray's representations. Whidby in the Doedalus was sent to explore Bulfinch's Harbor, while Vancouver proceeded with the other vessels to the mouth of the Columbia. Vancouver's own ship, the Discovery, was not able to enter the river, and he therefore proceeded on to the Bay of San Francisco. But the Chatham, under Lieutenant Braughton, succceded, with great difficulty, in crossing the bar. He found lying at anchor in the bay the brig Jenny, from Bristol, which had left Nootka a few days previous. The Chatham ran aground soon after entering, and Braughton, from the intricacy of the channel, resolved to leave her about four miles within the bar and proceed up the river in a boat. Accordingly he set out, and thoroughly examining every part of the river, he penetrated to the distance of about ninety-six miles from the mouth, where the river takes a bend and where the strength of the current was such as to induce them to return. This bend or point in the river, they called Point Vancouver. Returning to their ship they gave a bay on the north side of the river, the name of Gray's Bay, but the bay back of Cape Disappointment, they called Baker's Bay, after the captain of the brig Jenny.

Having remained in the river twenty days, on the 10th of November they again crossed the bar, and proceeded south to join Vancouver in the bay of San Francisco. With the usual avariciousness of English aristocrats, Braughton, before his departure, formally took possession of the river and of the country in the vicinity, in the name of his Britanic Majesty, "*Having every reason to believe that the subjects of no other civilized nation or state had ever entered this river before;*" an act of justice the like of which the subjects of Great Britain are ever ready to perform towards American citizens.

At the bay of San Francisco, Braughton and Whidby reported the result of their observations to Vancouver, and the former was dispatched to England, while the latter proceeded to the Sandwich Islands.

Vancouver never again returned to the coast of Oregon, though he subsequently explored minutely the region round about Cook's Inlet. However, he sailed south as far as Nootka, from which place he took his departure for England, where he arrived in August, 1795, having been absent more than four years.

Braughton having been elevated to the rank of Captain, was again sent by the British government to the Pacific, and arrived on the coast of Nootka in the spring of 1796, empowered to receive the surrender of the place from the Spanish, but found it entirely abandoned by the whites, and in the possession of savages, under the treacherous, cruel and notorious Maquinna. It should be observed that Nootka Sound is on the west side of Vancouver's Island, consequently it does not properly belong to the coast of Oregon.

CHAPTER XVIII.

Oregon territory—History continued—European nations involved in war—Pacific trade carried by the Great Republic—Ship Boston siezed by the Indians—Land Expeditions—Captain Jonathan Carver—Sir Alexander McKinzie—Lewis and Clark—Project of John Jacob Astor—Captain Thorn and the Tonquin——McDougal and Concomley—Fate of the Tonquin—Wilson Price Hunt—Depression at the fort—Encouragement—Ship Beaver arrives—Declaration of war—Thompson and the north-west company—Ross Cox—Astoria in danger—Visit of McTavish and Stuart Alarming news—Effect on the American company—Sloop of war—Racoon and Captain Black—Astoria falls into the hands of the British—Astor's magnificent enterprise terminated.

For twenty years following 1796, the nations of Europe were involved in the most bloody and destructive wars, and consequently but little if any interest was taken by either Spain or England, in the north-west coast of America, either as it regards its occupancy or its trade; and seldom during that entire period, did the vessels of any other nations than those of the United States, appear in the North Pacific. The trade, therefore, between this coast and other parts of the world, was exclusively carried on under the flag of the great Republic.

Though they made no establishment on the coast for the first sixteen years, the Americans sent their vessels annually to this region, laden with such articles as the natives of the country desired, which they exchanged for furs. These were carried to Canton and exchanged for silks, porcelain, teas, and other articles suited to the various markets then open to American vessels. This trade engaged the attention of many persons from various parts of the Union, and in its earlier stages, fortunes were amassed, but it will be understood that, from the length of the voyages performed, the nature of the coast, the difficulty of the trade, and, above all, the treachery of the savages with whom the traffic was carried on, the persons employed therein were constantly exposed to the greatest perils. But the dangers to which they voluntarily subjected themselves, are no reason why they might pursue a fraudulent or abusive course with the Indians. Yet, doubtless, many of them did not render an equivalent for the furs received, and the natives were sometimes deceived by trinkets that were of no value. Spirits were also introduced among them, which had a direct tendency to inflame their savage passions. Difficulties and quarrels arose frequently between the Americans and Indians, and it required the most extraordinary skill and courage on the part of the former, to accomplish their business, with the ignorant and treacherous savages with whom they were surrounded. But very few vessels visited these shores during this period that did not suffer the loss of one or more of its crew, by the ruthless hand of the blood-thirsty Indian.

Those who have read the narrative of John R. Jewitt, will recollect the circumstances of the bloody massacre of the crew of the ship Boston, in 1803, by Maquinna and his followers, while she was lying at Nootka. Under the appearance of friendship and without exciting suspicion, this treacherous chief laid his plans to destroy the crew, and seize the vessel as his own, which he cruelly put into execution, murdering all the crew but two, who, after continuing in slavery three years, finally effected their escape.

Previous to this period (1803) the subject of land expeditions across the continent to the Pacific ocean, was agitated among the people of the United States, principally through the representations of Captain Jonathan Carver, who, in 1766, explored the sources of the Mississippi, and said he had discovered a river which flowed west, which he called the Oregon river, and which he had no doubt emptied into the Western Ocean.

It is in Carver's account that we first detect the name Oregon, a name which, it is conjectured, first originated with Carver himself. However it might have come into existence, it will probably be continued in connection with the country to the end of time.

In 1774, Captain Carver and Richard Whitworth projected what, in those days, was considered a bold and daring enterprise, which was to cross the continent from Missouri to the Pacific ocean, for the purpose of exploring the country and tracing out the sources of the Oregon river, which Carver said he had previously seen; of passing down that river to its supposed exit, there building a vessel and carrying on their discoveries by sea. But this project, which, if it had been carried out, might have been attended with important results, was defeated by the breaking out of the American Revolution.

A more successful attempt of this kind was made in 1793, by Sir Alexander McKenzie. This gentleman was employed by the "North West Company" to explore those regions of the west and north, which even to fur-hunters yet remained unknown. In 1789, he explored the Hyperborean regions to the Arctic ocean; but, in 1793, he took a more westerly route, and ascending Peace river to its sources, he passed the dividing ridge, and entering upon a river that flowed towards the Pacific, he pursued it, and finally arrived on the coast of the Pacific ocean, in latitude fifty-two degrees and twenty minutes north. He supposed the river he had discovered was the Oregon river of Carver, but subsequent discoveries have proved it to be the stream which now bears the name of Frazier's river. It empties into the ocean three degrees north of the Columbia river.

This was the first journey performed by a white man across the Rocky Mountains to the Pacific Ocean. This, however, took place north of the limits of the territory of Oregon.

In 1804, '5 and '6, the memorable expedition under Captains Merriweather Lewis and William Clark, was accomplished. This exploring journey was projected by the United States Government, through the recommendation of Thomas Jefferson, who was then President. Captain Lewis was made the commander of the expedition, and after much difficulty in preparing, on the 14th day of May, 1804, they began the ascent of the Missouri in boats.

After toiling the entire season, sometime near the last of October, they found themselves sixteen hundred miles from the mouth of the Missouri, and among savage tribes, prepared to spend the first winter of their campaign. In the spring of 1805, these indefatigable men continued their course up the Missouri to its sources in the Rocky Mountains; passed the stupendous gates of that mighty chain, and on the other side came to a river which flowed to the westward. They followed it down until it became a broad and noble river, and on the 7th of October, embarked in canoes, and in a few days found themselves at the confluence of two splendid rivers, which proved to be the two great branches of the Columbia. The branch they descended, which was the south branch, they called the Lewis, and the north they distinguished by the name of Clark.

Continuing their downward course they successively passed the Falls of the Columbia, the Dalls, the Cascades, below which they began to be affected by the rise and fall of the tide, and knowing by this that they must be drawing near the ocean they passed on, and on the 15th day of November, 1805, landed at Cape Disappointment, on the north side of the mouth of the Columbia.

As the rainy season was setting in they examined the country on both sides of the river, with a view to find a suitable place to make their encampment for the winter. They accordingly built a fort on the south side, not far from an Indian village, and called it Fort Clatsop, after the name of the Indian tribe.

Here they spent an agreeable winter, and as the weather would admit, explored the surrounding country. The savages were peaceable, and assisted in procuring them food, such as the river and sea afforded, of which there was no lack. Here they continued until the 13th day of March, at which time, having made the necessary preparations, they commenced their long and toilsome journey back to the United States. They ascended the river in canoes as far as they could, on account of the rapids, and then resolved to proceed by land. They divided themselves into two parties, with the design of re-crossing the Rocky Mountains by two different routes. That under Lewis took nearly a due east course to the Falls of the Missouri, while that under Clark took a more southern route to the head waters of the Yellow Stone, and the two parties were to unite at the junction of these rivers. In the month of August, the parties again united, according to agreement, and passing down the Missouri, arrived at St. Louis on the 23d of September, 1806, after an absence of two years and six months.

The journey of Lewis and Clark was one of discovery, and the first performed by white men across the territory of Oregon. The information which the account of these gentlemen gave to the people of the States, was received with great interest, and contributed to hasten the settlement of the north-west boundary question between the territories of Great Britain and those of the United States, as far west as the Rocky Mountains; and also to induce private individuals to extend their trade with the Indians beyond that chain.

In 1806, the British fur-traders of the north made their first establishment on the west side of the mountains. Mr. Simon Frazer, of the North-West Company, established himself on Frazer's Lake, near the fifty-fourth degree of north latitude, in a country since called by the English, New Caledonia. But the first establishment of the kind which was made on the waters of the Columbia, and within the limits of Oregon, was that of Manuel Lisa, a Spaniard, who was a member of the Missouri Fur Company, which was formed at St. Louis, in 1808. This was made on the head waters of Lewis' river, and was placed under the immediate direction of Mr. Henry, but, in consequence of the difficulty of obtaining supplies, and the continued hostility of the savages around, it was given up in 1810.

At this time was formed the magnificent project of John Jacob Astor, of New York, in reference to a trading establishment at the mouth of the Columbia river. The Company of which this distinguished merchant was the chief support, as well as the principal director, was formed in 1810, and called the Pacific Fur Company. Among the individuals that Mr. Astor admitted to a partnership in the company, were a number who had formerly belonged to the British fur companies, and being acquainted with the trade, Mr. Astor considered them a valuable acquisition. A gentleman, however, from New Jersey, by the name of Wilson Price Hunt, was to be the principal agent in the establishment.

Other posts were to be established also, as circumstances would admit. It was designed to send ships around Cape Horn to the Columbia, laden with articles of Indian trade, which were to be exchanged for furs, and these were to be sent to China and exchanged for goods that would suit the markets of the United States. The plan was well laid, and but for opposing circumstances which no sagacity, however penetrating, could previously discover, and over which the originator could have no control, it doubtless would have succeeded to admiration. The first ship which was sent out was the Tonquin, which was commanded by Jonathan Thorn.

McDougal, McKay, and one or two others, who were partners and clerks, went in her.

They left New York in September, 1810, and on the 22d day of March arrived at the mouth of the Columbia river. As they approached the mouth, they discovered that the water broke in dreadful surges across the bar, and there appeared to be no possibility of effecting an entrance. And now began the heart-rending sufferings of that ill-fated crew.

Captain Thorn sent off a boat to explore the entrance under one of his officers by the name of Fox. Fox at first declined, but the Captain insisted, and finally Fox consented by saying, "Yes, I will go and lay my bones by the side of those of my father, who was lost at this place but a few years ago." The party started off, and the boat passing over the mountain waves, slowly separated from the ship. Night came on, but the boat did not return. Another, but no boat; the ship in the meantime standing off and on. The utmost anxiety prevailed

16

on board. What should be done? Another boat was sent off to look for the former, and also to find the entrance. Two persons belonging to the latter boat only, survived to tell the story that all their companions were lost. They perished amid the breakers at the entrance of the river; and thus was given the remainder of the crew, a most solemn warning of the more tragic fate which awaited them.

Soon after this disaster the weather became more favorable, and the Tonquin passed the bar and came to anchor in Baker's Bay. After McDougal and others had examined the country round about, the site they pitched upon for the establishment of their post was about ten miles up the river, and on the south side. They built a trading house, and inclosed it with pickets, and gave it the name of "Astoria," after the name of the projector of the enterprise. Soon after they arrived, the partners crossed the river to visit Comcomly, the chief of the Chenooks.

When they got ready to leave to return to the fort, the wind was high, and the water in the bay was rough. Comcomly endeavored to dissuade them from crossing, but they resolved to make the attempt. The wary chief, however, sprang into his canoe with several of his men, and kept close along by the boat as she came into the high swells, believing that she would not endure the sea. His fears were well grounded, for scarcely had they started when the boat capsized, and the partners and their men were struggling in the water for life. Comcomly, however, was immediately among them in his canoe, and rescued them from a watery grave.

They were now willing to stay with the chief till the storm abated, which took place soon afterward, and they returned to the fort.

McDougal was to be the head of the concern until the arrival of Mr. Hunt. After considerable difficulty between Captain Thorn and the gentlemen of the establishment, the goods designed for Astoria were landed, and the ship proceeded northward for the purpose of trafficking with the Indians along the coast. McKay went in her as supercargo, and Mr. Lewis as clerk. The whole number of persons on board was twenty-three, besides an Indian, who accompanied them as interpreter. The ship proceeded to Vancouver's Island, and came to anchor in the harbor of Nittinat. Some of the natives came on board, but as it was too late in the day to traffick, McKay went on shore to see the chief, whose name was Wicananish, and six of the Indians remained on board as hostages. McKay was received with great professions of friendship by the chief, and a number of sea otter-skins were spread for his bed. In the morning great numbers of the Indians came off to the ship, apparently to trade, headed by two sons of the chief, and bringing with them great quantities of fur. The fur was spread upon the deck, and the goods were also displayed before the Indians by the unsuspecting crew. The bantering, which is peculiar to Indian traffick, commenced, and all for a few moments seemed to go on well; but at a concerted signal given by the chiefs, the knives, war-clubs, and tomahawks, which the savages had contrived to secrete about their persons, were at once displayed, the crew were immediately overpowered, and nearly all of them butchered upon the deck. Mr. Lewis, the clerk, and some others had succeeded in getting into the hold of the vessel, near the powder magazine, and Lewis had told the interpreter that he intended to blow up the ship, and in this way to avenge his own death, and that of his companions.

The ship was now in the full possession of the savages, who thronged her deck and were clambering up her sides, all intent upon securing their prize, and unconscious of the terrible fate which awaited them and which they so well deserved. At length the magazine was fired, and a scene which beggars description was then presented. The ship was torn to atoms, and the decks in broken fragments, mingled with shivered boxes, barrels, guns, and the dissevered limbs, heads, and trunks of savages, were blown high into the air, and falling upon the dark and agitated waters, presented the most gloomy picture of desolation. At the time of the explosion, the interpreter was in the main chains, and was thrown unhurt into the waters, where he succeeded in getting into one of the canoes which were floating tenantless in the bay, and in this he went ashore and finally got back to Astoria in safety, and from him the story of the fate of the Tonquin is known.

In January, 1811, Mr. Wilson Price Hunt, who had been appointed general agent of the concern on the Columbia, set out from St. Louis to cross the Rocky Mountains, and after he and his companions endured the most incredible sufferings from cold, fatigue, and want of food, they arrived at Astoria in the spring of 1812. Soon after they arrived, the shocking intelligence of the destruction of the Tonquin and her unfortunate crew, reached Astoria, and threw the whole establishment into the most gloomy forebodings. The disaster was calculated to depress the spirits and destroy the hopes of the persons engaged in the enterprise. But the arrival of the ship Beaver, from New York, which brought out supplies and reinforcements, encouraged the Astorians, and they resolved to prosecute vigorously their enterprise. It was determined that Mr. Hunt should leave the river in the Beaver, and go to the northward, for the purpose of advancing the interests of the company in that region. Astoria was left under the direction of Mr. Duncan McDougal, who had long been in the service of the North West Company.

In January, 1813, the news of the declaration of war by the United States against Great Britain, reached Astoria by persons who had been sent by Mr. Astor from New York for that purpose, and served to darken the prospects of the company.

On the 15th of July, Mr. David Thompson arrived at Astoria. This gentleman was a partner in the North West Company, and it appears that he designed to anticipate Mr. Astor in the occupancy of the mouth of the Columbia, but, to his disappointment, found the American Company already in full possession. Whatever was his object, he was doubtless the first person that descended from near its source, the north branch of the Columbia,

About this time the Astorians received information that a British naval force was on its way to take possession of the mouth of the river, which appeared to be a source of satisfaction to McDougal and other British subjects who were connected with him, some of whom immediately left the service of the Pacific Company and went over to the rival association. One of the persons that quitted the service of Mr. Astor was Ross Cox, who subsequently published a narrative of six years' residence on the Columbia.

At this time, which was in the month of January, 1813, nearly all the persons in the establishment at Astoria agreed to abandon the enterprise, unless they should speedily receive more supplies and assistance from New York. Months passed away, but no assistance from New York arrived. Mr. Astor had dispatched the ship Lark, for Astoria, with abundant supplies of men and property; but she was unfortunately wrecked on a coral reef, near the coast of one of the Sandwich Islands, and thus added another to the uncontrollable circumstances which served to hasten the dissolution of the company.

From the representations of Mr. Astor, the government of the United States had resolved to send a frigate to the North Pacific, to succor and protect the infant settlement at the mouth of the river; but as the naval operations on Lake Erie and Lake Ontario began to assume a decidedly important character, it was necessary to dispatch the men designed for the Pacific enterprise to that quarter; and the fact that the American ports were blockaded by British fleets, rendered it impossible to convey any farther succors to Astoria. Accordingly, the partners of the Pacific Company, at Astoria, resolved to abandon the enterprise and provide for their safety, as they began to fear that they might be attacked by the British, who were already establishing themselves on the upper waters of the Columbia.

A short time after the partners came to this conclusion, Mr. Hunt, the chief agent, returned to Astoria. During his absence he had visited the Russian settlements at Sitka, Unalashka and Kodiak, had collected a cargo of valuable furs and sent them to Canton; but, on arriving at the Sandwich Islands, he learned that England and the United States were at war, and that Commodore Hillyer was on his way to the Pacific ocean with a squadron, to take possession of the mouth of the Columbia. He, consequently, chartered a vessel immediately and sailed for Astoria to convey the news of war, and prepare to meet any hostilities that might threaten them at their headquarters. He arrived at Astoria in the brig Pedlar, on the 28th of February, 1814, and was astonished to learn that the concerns of the establishment had been wound up some time previous.

Some time before Hunt arrived, a company of British, belonging to the North West Company established far in the interior, and under the direction of McTavish and Stuart, came down the river to Astoria, and brought the alarming intelligence that a naval force was on its way to the Columbia, with the object of taking and destroying every thing American in that quarter. Notwithstanding the probability that the whole establishment would fall into the hands of the British, without their paying for it, yet McTavish and Stuart proposed to purchase the whole establishment, furs and other property, at a proper valuation; and also to receive into "The service of the North West Company any of the persons belonging to the Pacific Company, at the same wages they were then receiving, and to send back to the United States all that did not choose to be thus employed." The partners of the American Company resolved to comply with this proposition, and accordingly the entire establishment was sold to the North West Company for the sum of about 40,000 dollars.

While this negotiation was going on, the British sloop of war Racoon, Captain Black, arrived at Astoria with the expectation of sharing largely in the plunder of that place, and, though he found the stars and stripes still floating over the factory, yet all the valuable property, consisting of furs, peltries, &c., had passed into the hands of British subjects, and Capt. Black could do no more than to lower the stars and stripes, and hoist the colors of

Britain over the walls of the factory. This he did with the accompanying ceremony of breaking a bottle of port on the flag-staff, and changing the name from Astoria, to that of Fort George.

On arriving at Astoria, in the "Pedlar," Hunt found that he could do nothing farther in that part of the world, but to close up the concerns of the company to the best advantage, and return to the United States. Accordingly he re-embarked in the Pedlar, with three of his companions in trade, and returned home by the way of Canton. Of the other persons who had been his associates in this astonishing enterprise, some entered the service of the North West Company; some exposed themselves to the perils of re-crossing the Rocky Mountains, and others, of whom there are a few living to this day, took to themselves Indian wives, and fixed their habitations among the savages of Oregon.

Thus the magnificent enterprise, conceived and prosecuted by John Jacob Astor, against so many opposing circumstances, was brought to an unfortunate termination.

Doubtless, but for the unhappy war of that period, it would have succeeded to admiration. That it did not succeed, is to be sincerely regretted by every American; for, in that case, the country would never have been divided; long before this time, the whole of Oregon would have been in the peaceable possession of the citizens of the United States. But the circumstances which militated against the success of this mighty project, were purely providential, and such as no prudence or foresight in its originator could have possibly guarded against. Though defeated in its ulterior objects, it opened the way to Oregon to American citizens, and supplied the means, in the interesting journals of those who were connected with the enterprise, for Washington Irving to awaken an interest in the American public, in relation to Oregon, that has gone on increasing until the present time.

CHAPTER XIX.

Oregon territory — History continued — Astoria restored to the Americans — Description of the Fort — North West Company remain in the country — Rival companies — Hudson's Bay Company — How formed — Extent of its operations — War between the two companies — Both merged in one — The Honorable Hudson's Bay Company — Policy of the company — Number and situation of trading forts — Immense power of the company — Colonizing the country — Sir George Simpson's Colony — Settlements — Fort Vancouver — Gentlemen of the Fort — Perils of the fur-trade — A thrilling tragedy.

ACCORDING to the first article of the treaty of Ghent, which provided "that all territory, places and possessions whatsoever, taken by either party from the other, during, or after the war, should be restored without delay," measures were taken by the United States Government to re-occupy the post at the mouth of the Columbia river. In 1817, Captain J. Biddle and J. B. Prevost were commissioned to proceed to the Columbia, and there to assert the claim of the United States to the sovereignty of the country. These gentlemen sailed from New York in the sloop-of-war Ontario, on the 4th of October, 1817. The British Government, hearing of the departure of the Ontario for the Columbia, dispatched an order to the agents of the North West Company, directing them to give every facility in their power to the agents of the United States Government, for the re-occupation of Fort George, as a place that had been captured during the war, and to be restored according to the above article in the treaty of Ghent. Captain Biddle entered the mouth of the Columbia in August, 1818, and on the 19th of the same month, the flag of the United States was again floating over the stockades of old Astoria. But a more formal surrendering of the place by Great Britain and occupation of it by the United

States, took place the following October. On the first day of this month, the British frigate Blossom, Captain Hikey, arrived in the Columbia, bringing Mr. Prevost, who had left the Ontario in Chili, to attend to some business there, and who was empowered to receive the surrender of the place from the constituted British authorities. Captain Hikey and James Keith, the latter of whom was the superintendent of the North West Company at that time, were the persons appointed to deliver up the settlement in due form. The following is the instrument by which the country captured by the British, at the mouth of the Columbia, reverted to the United States:

"In obedience to the commands of his Royal Highness the Prince Regent, signified in a dispatch from the right honorable the Earl Bathurst, addressed to the partners or agents of the North West Company, bearing date the 27th of January, 1818, and in obedience to a subsequent order, dated the 26th of July, from W. H. Shireff, Esq., captain of his majesty's ship Andromache, we, the undersigned, do, in conformity to the first article of the treaty of Ghent, restore to the government of the United States, through its agent, J. B. Prevost, Esq., the settlement of Fort George, on the Columbia river. Given under our hands in triplicate, at Fort George, (Columbia River), this 6th day of October, 1818.

"F. Hikey, Capt. of his Majesty's ship Blossom.
"J. Keith, of the North West Company."

Mr. Prevost accepted this delivery in the following language:

"I do hereby acknowledge to have this day received, in behalf of the government of the United States, the possession of the settlement designated above, in conformity to the first article of the treaty of Ghent. Given under my hand in triplicate, at Fort George, (Columbia River), this 6th of October, 1818.

"J. B. Prevost, agent for the United States."

This transaction took place in 1818, and as Fort George had then been in the possession of the North West Company for more than four years, the trade of that company on the Columbia had become firmly established. The fort at that time consisted of a stockade, inclosing a parallelogram of one hundred and fifty feet by two hundred and fifty feet, extending in its greatest length from north-west to south-east. Within this inclosure were all the buildings attached to the establishment, such as dwelling-houses, stores, mechanic' shops, &c. On the fort were mounted two eighteen-pounders, four four-pounders, two six-pound cohorns, and seven swivels. The number of persons belonging to the factory, besides a few women and children, were sixty-five, of whom twenty-three were whites, twenty-six Sandwich Islanders, and the remainder persons of mixed blood from Canada. In the restitution of Fort George by Mr. Keith, to the Americans, it was understood that the North West Company would continue their occupancy of the country, and traffick therein according to the provisions of the article of agreement entered into between the United States and Great Britain, in October, 1818; which was, "That any country that may be claimed by either party on the north-west coast of America, westward of the Stony Mountains, shall, together with its harbors, bays, and creeks, and the navigation of all rivers within the same, be free and open for the term of ten years, to the vessels, citizens, and subjects of the two powers."

The history of Oregon from 1814 to 1834, is embraced in the history of those rival companies of fur-traders, which have extended their operations, from time to time, from the Gulf of St. Lawrence to Vancouver's Island, and from New Spain to the country of the Esquimaux. To give a particular account of these companies would require volumes; a brief survey, therefore, must suffice.

While the French merchants of Quebec and Montreal were, by their agents, exploring the immense forests on both sides of the great lakes, and ransacking the extended prairies of the West and the valley of the Mississippi, in quest of the rich and valuable furs with which the wilds of North America abounded, and were furnishing France and other European countries with the precious luxury, the avails of which constituted their immense wealth, a rival power ushered into being a corporation which is now grasping the supreme dominion of the forest north of the United States, from the coast of Labrador to the Pacific Ocean, and exercising an iron despotism, not only over the numerous persons who are in its employ, but also over many of the Indian tribes residing within the limits of its jurisdiction. For a number of centuries the government of Great Britain made the most extraordinary efforts to discover a north-west passage from the Atlantic to the Pacific, during which Baffin and Hudson explored the two bays, which now bear their names. From the accounts given, the opinion was entertained that the communication could be effected by Hudson's Bay, and, as an encouragement to private enterprise, and to increase the facilities to explore the regions of the north, for the purpose of accomplishing this long desired object, Charles II, in 1669, granted a charter to a society of London merchants, under the designation of " The Hudson's Bay Company." Then commenced the operations of a monopoly, second only in power to the far famed East India Company, which has opened the way for the extension of British rule over a vast portion of the continent of Asia. For many years the Hudson's Bay Company confined its operations within the Hyperborean regions, where it had enthroned itself in solitary despotism, and where it opposed itself in successful rivalry against a French company of a similar character; but, finally, has extended itself throughout the entire western territories claimed by Great Britain and the United States, and has even laid under contribution a portion of the Russian American possessions. During its onward career it has experienced few reverses, though it has frequently been called upon to contend with powerful opposition.

During the year 1787, an association was organized among the principal fur-merchants of Montreal, for the purpose of carrying the trade between the posts of that country and such of the British territories of the interior as were not supposed to be included in the grant to the

Hudson's Bay Company; and so rapidly did it extend its operations, that within two years its establishments were advanced as far as Athabaska Lake, near the fifty-ninth parallel of latitude, about eight hundred miles north-west from Lake Superior. This company, in its increasingly extended operations, proved the most powerful competitor with which the Hudson's Bay Company had to contend, but finally merged itself in the latter company.

The Hudson's Bay Company, exercising supreme control over its frozen domains, at length found a new company advancing upon them with a menacing aspect, and both companies became immediately actuated by the spirit and motives of rivals. They became the most bitter enemies to one another, and as the different parties of the two companies would come in contact while exploring the north-western wilds, the most serious quarrels would take place, and result in the commission of injuries by each party against the other. At length, in 1814, a regular war broke out, and for some time was openly carried on between them. The scene of this fraternal war was the territory on the Red river, contiguous to the frontiers of the United States. A company of Scotch Highlanders had been established here by Lord Selkirk, in 1812, in virtue of a grant of the country by the Hudson's Bay Company. The North West Company, to which the Scotch settlement had proved injurious by wresting from them those supplies of provisions for their trading posts, which had been obtained almost wholly from the Red river lands, denied the validity of this grant. and hence arose many disputes and various acts of violence, until finally, the Scotchmen were driven away, and their houses destroyed by their opponents. The Hudson's Bay Company re-established the colony the following year, and consequently hostilities were renewed.

Posts were taken and burnt by each party, and on the 19th of June, 1816, a general battle was fought, in which the North Westers were victorious. The Scotchmen were routed, and their governor, Mr. Semple, and seventeen of his followers, were killed.

These affairs were represented by each party before the British Government, and in 1821 a compromise was effected between the rival companies, and they were united by an act of Parliament, under the title of "The Honorable Hudson's Bay Company." At the same time an act was passed, granting to this company the exclusive right to trade in the Indian territories in Northern America, owned or claimed by Great Britain, for the period of twenty-one years. Under the protection of this act, after the coalition of the two companies took place, the arms of the giant monopoly were thrown around the entire territory west of the Rocky Mountains, extending from the Russian settlements to the Gulf of California. Oregon, from fifty-four degrees forty minutes, south as far as they pleased to go, and from the Rocky Mountains to the Pacific, was dotted with forts and trading posts, and every valley and mountain was made to contribute to swell the coffers of the co-partners of this extensive concern.

The grand operations of the Hudson's Bay Company are managed by a governor, deputy-governor, and a committee of directors, established in London, to whom all the reports of the company's affairs are annually transmitted. The trade of this company is under the immediate control of a governor, residing within the field of its operations, who is responsible only to the committee in London. Under him are inferior officers, consisting of superintendents, factors, traders and clerks. The higher officers have a direct interest or share in the profits of the business, but the lower are engaged at small salaries, with the promise of a pension for life, after a given period of faithful service. But the most numerous class of agents in the business of the company are the hunters, voyagers, and trappers, consisting of Hawaiians, French Canadians, half-breeds and Indians, who are paid a mere pittance for their services, and are kept in a state of entire subjection to the will of the company, by promises of future advancement, according as they shall render themselves of value to the trade. The strictest discipline and subordination are every where enforced by the officers, and generally observed by the servants, though occasionally there are violent outbreaks.

The furs and skins which constitute nearly the sole returns of the trade, are principally procured from the Indians in exchange for coarse manufactured goods, guns, and a variety of worthless trinkets, calculated to please the fancy of the savage, without proving of any benefit. Some, however, are procured by the company's trappers and hunters. The goods employed in this business are all brought from England, free of duty, and, for the department west of the Rocky Mountains, are deposited at Fort Vancouver. At this point, the goods that are wanted for the interior, are packed in bundles of such a size as to be easily carried by one man, as the transportation is performed alternately in boats and by portage, and sent to all the posts throughout the country. Recently, however, an additional depot has been established on Vancouver's Island, north of the forty-ninth parallel, called Victoria, which, probably, will become the principal one, as Vancouver is in the territory belonging to the United States. The furs collected are all sent to these two places, from which they are shipped directly to London, in vessels which arrive annually on the coast, with the goods and other supplies necessary to carry on the trade. Five or six ships of about three hundred tons burthen, are constantly employed for this purpose, in addition to several smaller craft which operate in the rivers and along the coast. Among the latter, is one steamboat, which is principally employed between Fort Nezqualy, on Puget's Sound, and Stikine, a post north of the fifty-sixth parallel.

The number of forts and trading-posts occupied by the company west of the Rocky Mountains, is twenty-two :—
Fort Vancouver, on the north side of the Columbia River, ninety-five miles from the ocean, in north latitude forty-five degrees and about forty minutes, and west longitude 122 degrees and 30 minutes; this fort was established in 1824, by Governor Simpson, and named after the distinguished navigator who was the second to enter the

mouth of the Columbia, but the first to explore the river as high up as the point of land on which Vancouver stands: Fort George, formerly Astoria, situated on the south side of the Columbia, ten miles from its mouth; Nezqualy, on Puget's Sound, latitude forty-seven degrees; Fort Langly, on Frazer's River, latitude forty-nine degrees and twenty-five minutes; Fort McLaughlin, on Mill Bank Sound, latitude fifty-two degrees; Fort Simpson, on Dundas Island, latitude fifty-four degrees and thirty minutes; Fort Stikine, on a river of the same name, latitude fifty-six degrees and thirty minutes: this fort is in the territory belonging to Russia, and, regardless of the rights of the Russians, the Hudson's Bay Company attempted, in 1834, to intrench themselves on the banks of the Stikine, which had been recently discovered, and abounded in the most valuable furs. Baron Wrangle, who was then the Governor of the Russian American possessions, having got wind of the project entertained by the English to wrest from them this important point, proceeded to the mouth of the river and fortified it by erecting a block-house and stationing there a sloop of war. The Russians had not been long in waiting before a vessel was discovered approaching the shore and bearing the men and materials for the contemplated establishment; but, to their surprise, the British found a sloop of war ready to dispute their passage into the river. They were informed that to save themselves, their property and their vessel, they must tack ship and return to their own possessions. All appeals to treaties, and all the fair promises of the English, were ineffectual; the Russians were inexorable, and the Hudson's Bay Company for once were foiled in their attempt, after having spent in preparations the sum of twenty thousand pounds. Subsequently they entered into a negotiation with the Russians and proposed to purchase the right of trading on the Stikine River, for a certain number of years. To this the Russians listened favorably, and at length a bargain was completed, in which the English bound themselves to pay to the Russians annually, for a term of years, a certain sum, to be paid in the produce of the extensive farm which the English cultivated on the Columbia River, connected with what they could procure from the settlers in the country. On the conclusion of this contract the post was immediately occupied, a strong fort erected, and munitions of war provided to defend the establishment against the hostile Indians by which it is surrounded.

With the exception of Victoria on Vancouver's Island, the forts and posts of the company are situated inland, as follows : Frazer's Lake, McLeod's Lake, Fort George, Alexandria, Chilcotins, Babine, and Bear's Lake, in that portion of the country called by the English, New Caledonia ; the posts of Walla-Walla, Okanagan, and Colville, high up on the Columbia River ; the Flathead and Kootania post, between the two main branches of the Columbia; Fort Hall, near the Rocky Mountains and on the south branch of the Columbia, and Umpqua post, situated in latitude forty-three degrees and thirty minutes, on a river of the same name, and about fifty miles from the ocean. The company also have two migratory trapping and trading expeditions of between fifty and seventy-five men each ; to the one is appropriated the country from the Columbia south to the Bay of San Francisco along the coast ; the other explores the interior between the Columbia and the head-waters of the Colorado and Sacramento.

The average annual value of the furs and peltries derived from these territories, has been in the vicinity of one hundred and forty thousand dollars, for which have been given about twenty thousand dollars worth of goods, prime cost, the services of about five hundred men, employed in various parts of the business, shipping to bring supplies and take back returns, with various other incidental expenses. The net profits, however, arising from the Columbia trade, according to the representations of Dr. John McLaughlin, who is the superintendent of the affairs of the Hudson's Bay Company, west of the Rocky Mountains, have not usually amounted to more than ten thousand dollars, the principal profits of the trade being derived from countries not embraced in the **western department.**

It has always been the policy of the Hudson's Bay Company to monopolize the trade of those immense regions in North America, occupied by civilized man, and it has appeared destined to swallow up all other commercial enterprises coming within its reach. With this view, its posts have been pushed onward from time to time, until every important point has been occupied from Hudson's Bay to Puget's Sound, and its brigades of boats have appeared on every navigable river of that vast region, bearing British manufactures into the deepest recesses of savage life, or, on their backward route, loaded with furs for the great depository on the seaboard. On every Indian trail have been seen the sure-footed mule and the Indian mustang, reeling under burdens of three hundred pounds, sometimes in troops of scores, driven by a squadron of weather-beaten mountaineers, with their rifles before them, and their long knives hanging at their belts; now ascending the mighty mountain chain; now plunging to the bottom of the deep, dark ravine; now diving into the solitudes of the primeval forest, untrodden but by the feet of wild beasts, and savages as wild as they, and now emerging upon the extended prairies, calling, wherever the rising smoke indicates, the presence of an Indian, and bartering the wampum, the gaudy ribbon, the scarlet cloth, and the Indian blankets, for the precious beaver, otter, and marten, until their supply of goods is exhausted, and their animals loaded with the fruits of their toils. They may be seen winding along the serpentine trail which leads back to the grand depot, happy if their numbers have not been diminished by the numerous casualties incident to the business in which they are engaged. The wonderful efforts of those who have controlled the destinies of this company, and the indefatigable exertions of the numerous agents employed to promote its interests, nave succeeded, equal to the most sanguine expectations. Possessed with inexhaustible resources, and sustained with the most vigorous policy, they have been advancing in a sure march of commercial conquest. They have left no posts behind them unsubdued, but wherever they have made an attack, they remain masters of the field. Their concentration of capital and interest gives them a decided advantage over the scattered capital of individual merchants, and to this we may attribute a great share of their success. A number of years ago they succeeded in ridding themselves of all American competition on the north-west coast, of which, until very recently, they have enjoyed the undivided monopoly. And whether on the coast or in the interior, wherever the Hudson's Bay Company has placed its giant foot, there American trade has been sure to decline.

Another feature of the policy of the company, is the course which they have pursued in relation to colonizing the country. They have always been opposed to its settlement by any people except such as, by a strict subjection to the company, would become subservient to their wishes. This has, doubtless, arisen from two circumstances : First, the fur-trade of Oregon has been rapidly declining for a number of years past, and the Hudson's Bay Company are fully aware that this trade alone will not be sufficient to sustain them in the country for many years to come, and to abandon the country would involve themselves in an immense loss. These liabilities they wish to guard against by opening sources of wealth in other branches of business, to be under their control. Secondly, they have had in their employment, every year, many hundreds of persons, consisting of Canadian French, Hawaiians, half-breed Iroquois, and others, who are under their absolute control, so long as they remain in the Indian country. Many of these, from year to year, either by having large families, by the decline of the fur-trade, or by superannuation, become unprofitable servants, and by the company are settled in various parts of the country, where they support themselves, and become, indirectly, a source of profit to the company. They wished to preserve Oregon as an asylum for their servants, on both sides of the Rocky Mountains, where they could use them to advantage, in agricultural, pastoral, and manufacturing pursuits, when they could be no longer serviceable to them in the business of the fur-trade. That the company have comtemplated a rapid decline, and probable termination of the fur-trade, west of the Rocky Mountains, appears from the fact of their having been formed into a new company, under the name of "Puget's Sound Agricultural Company," with a capital of two million pounds. This company has pretended to hold large tracts of land in the vicinity of Puget's Sound, under grants of letters patent from the English Government; and here they have attempted to establish a colony, but without success.

This attempt was made in 1842. The half-breed descendants of the gentlemen and servants of the Hudson's Bay Company, had been collecting together in a colony, on a small tract of fertile land lying on Red river, east of the Rocky Mountains, for more than thirty years, and so rapid was the increase of the colony, and so limited the arable country on the Red river, that the company resolved to send off a colony of the numerous Scotch and English half-breed ssettled on that river, to the shores of the Pacific ocean. Accordingly, in 1842, Sir George Simpson, who for many years has been the resident Governor of the Hudson's Bay Company, by holding out the most flattering inducements, succeeded in forming a colony of some thirty families, of which he took the charge in person. They left the Red river settlement late in the spring, with their scanty supplies packed upon the backs of mules and Indian ponies, and passing through the stupendous gates of the Rocky Mountains, they arrived on the borders of Puget's Sound some time in the month of October. If the fertility of the soil where they were planted by Sir George, had corresponded with the picturesque beauty of the face of the country, doubtless the colony would have succeeded; but in consequence of a total failure of the crops the first year, the colonists abandoned the place, contrary to the wishes of the company, and settled in a more fertile portion of the country.

Two other settlements intended for the reception and support of retiring servants of the company, have been established in Oregon; one in the valley of the Cowilitz, north of the lower Columbia, the other on the delightful plains watered by the Wallamette river, south of the Columbia. As interested motives first induced the company to establish these settlements, so it has always been their policy to keep them in a state of absolute dependence. The colonists have not only been responsible to the company for the course of conduct they have pursued, but from it alone, until very recently, they have been obliged to receive all their supplies of foreign necessaries, consisting of clothing, groceries, &c., for which they have been obliged to pay in the produce of the soil, at prices to suit the avaricious propensities which have developed themselves in the whole policy of the Hudson's Bay Company.

The oppressive measures adopted by the company, in reference to these settlements, were such as to cause them to languish for years, and to induce some of the most active and enterprising among the settlers, to take refuge in the United States.

Fort Vancouver, after it became the grand depot of the company west of the mountains, was the most important point occupied by them, and the settlement there established, differed from those already described, in the important particular, that every person connected with it, was in the *immediate* service of the company. The fort, in 1845, consisted in a stockade, inclosing a space of ground of about eight hundred feet long, and five hundred broad, with a bastion at one corner, with three gates in front, for ingress and egress, and one in the rear. In addition to the artillery mounted in the bastion, there were two eighteen-pounders and two swivels planted in front of the residence of the chief factors, and commanding the principal entrance to the fort.

Within this inclosure were situated some thirty buildings, serving as dwelling-houses, stores, magazines, and work-shops. Near the fort are the buildings occupied by the servants, as also a hospital, barns, and a large boat-house. In the rear of the fort the company have a splendid garden in the highest state of cultivation, which produces all kinds of fruit for which the climate is adapted, such as apples, peaches, pears and grapes. Here is also cultivated a large farm of some three thousand acres, producing wheat, barley, oats, peas, potatoes, &c., in great abundance; and herds of many thousands of cattle are supported on the adjacent plains.

Connected with the fort, and about four miles distant, up the Columbia, are a flouring-mill and saw-mill, which have been in operation for several years.

At the head of this establishment stands Dr. John McLaughlin, and second to him is James Douglass, Esq., the former being a native of Canada, and the latter of Scotland. These gentlemen, as far as social habits are concerned, have acquired for themselves, and for the company of which they are chief factors, an enviable reputation for hospitality and kindness. Few persons, whether coming by land or by sea, have ever visited Vancouver without being received with a hospitality which knew no bounds, until every want of the traveler was supplied. Innumerable have been the favors conferred by them upon the American missionaries, and their assistance has been rendered at times when great inconvenience, and even suffering, would have resulted from neglect. For all these acts of kindness these gentlemen, with many others at the various posts in the country, equally as well disposed, are deserving of much praise. But to particularize here would extend this account beyond the limits originally marked out; and I shall therefore close this sketch of the history of the Hudson's Bay Company, by presenting a few circumstances and incidents illustrative of the perils of the fur-trade, and of the character of those under-agents employed to prosecute it.

The trading-post situated at the confluence of the Thompson's and Frazer's river, had been long under the superintendence of an English gentleman by the name of Black, who, in view of many amiable qualities, was in good repute among the gentlemen of the company, and had already risen to the office of chief trader. By some means he had excited the jealousy of an Indian chief belonging to a tribe residing in the vicinity of the fort, upon whom he had lavished many favors, but who resolved to imbrue his hands in the blood of his benefactor.

One day, in 1842, the Indian came to the fort with his musket in his hand, which probably Black had sold him. The unsuspicious trader received him into the fort, and even into his dwelling, without disarming him. As the Indian appeared unusually friendly, Black became uncommonly confiding. At length, to fulfil some request which the Indian artfully made, he turned his back upon him, and while retiring, his secret foe deliberately brought his musket to his face, and taking a deadly aim, fired, the bullet passing directly through his heart. He fell; and as the Indian saw him stretched upon his own floor, weltering in his gore, he walked deliberately out of the house, passed through the gate of the stockade, and disappeared; and three years subsequently the Indian was still at large, and the crime unrevenged.

Different was the closing scene of another tragedy, acted the following year, on the Columbia river. A half-breed Iroquois, by the name of McKay, was employed for the company, on the lower waters of the Columbia, and resided in a small house on the north shore of the river, where he kept the Indian goods with which he carried on his trade. A few Indians of the Chenook tribe, knowing him to be alone, proceeded to his house, murdered him, and took possession of his goods. A friendly Indian carried the news immediately up to Vancouver, and an expedition was fitted out to pursue and take the murderers. Armed with muskets, they proceeded down the river, and at length came in sight of a canoe filled with Indians, and were informed that the murderers were in that canoe. They immediately gave chase, and the suspicions of the Indians being aroused, they also plied the paddle with all their might, to keep at a safe distance from their pursuers. Finding that the white men gained upon them, the Indians run their canoe ashore; but, as they were landing, they received a volley of musket balls, which unfortunately killed one Indian woman, and wounded some others, while the murderers, for the time being, made their escape. Dr. McLaughlin, of whom all the Indians in the country stand in the greatest fear, sent word to the Chenooks that they must deliver up the principal instigator of the crime, or he would adopt some other way to avenge the murder of McKay. Fearing that the wrath of the company might burst upon the whole tribe, every man became intent upon delivering up the murderer. At last he was found far north of the mouth of the Columbia, where he had secreted himself, and brought in triumph to Fort George, and delivered up to the authorities of the Hudson's Bay Company.

Dr. McLaughlin was present, and some thirty or forty others, besides the Indians who had collected to see what would be done. A trial was instituted, the Indian was pronounced guilty of wilful murder, and sentenced to be hung forthwith. A gallows was prepared, and one end of a long rope thrown over the top of the gallows, and tied around the Indian's neck. All the white men present, with the exception of Rev. J. H. Frost, who witnessed the scene, took hold of the other end of the rope, the Indian standing like a statue under the gallows, and, at a given signal, all pulled upon the rope, drawing the Indian up so that his feet were some distance from the ground. As his neck did not break, he merely strangled; but the mode of his death filled the tribes around with horror, and impressed every Indian with a sense of the fearful character of the white man's vengeance. This summary execution proved a salutary lesson, especially to the Indians in the vicinity where it took place.

In the prosecution of the fur-trade, it has frequently been necessary for the members of the company to adopt the most sanguinary measures against the Indians, in order to secure their own safety and ultimate success. Hundreds of their trappers and voyagers have fallen by the ruthless hand of the savage, while pursuing their game along the valleys, or scouring the mountain chains of the west, and none have ever prosecuted this perilous enterprise, who have not had repeated occasions to revenge the death of a comrade, perhaps a brother, or an intimate friend. Out of the pale of the law, the fur-traders became a law unto themselves, or rather adopted such laws, from time to time, as the exigences of the case required. At one of the forts, situated in the interior, a servant of the company was murdered by an Indian chief, who subsequently boasted that he had committed the deed. This chief belonged to a powerful migratory tribe that, at the time of the murder, was encamped in the vicinity of the fort, and, as he possessed considerable influence in the tribe, and could rally around him a large number of warriors, he concluded that the few white men at the fort would not dare to molest him.

The commandant of the fort knowing that if this daring crime remained unrevenged, there would be no safety for the remainder of the whites, offered a heavy reward to any Indian or white man that would take the life of the murderer. Some time elapsed, and, as no one dared to make the attempt, the murderer was still at large. One day it came to the ears of the commandant that the murderer was in camp, and might be found in a certain lodge at the farther extremity of the encampment. The commandant, who had long waited with the deepest anxiety for such an opportunity, seized his unerring rifle and, secreting it under the folds of his cloak which he had thrown around him, passed outside the stockade, and taking a narrow trail which wound along among the lodges, marched directly to the one where sat the doomed, but unsuspecting, chief, surrounded by his companions, and rehearsing his deeds of marvelous prowess in his numerous fights with the men of King George. Pulling aside the door of Buffalo skin, he stepped inside the lodge and presented himself in full view of the astonished Indians. He fixed his eye upon the well known form of the murderer, and, without uttering a word, let fall the folds of his cloak, and poising his rifle, aimed directly at the murderer's heart. The Indian perceiving that his hour had come, threw his arms above his head, gave a horrid yell, fell backward and expired; the ball had pierced his heart. The commandant retraced his steps unmolested back to the fort, leaving the Indians thunderstruck with his astonishing bravery. He has since been elevated to the important and honorable office of chief factor, to which, by long and faithful service, as well as by every qualification of the gentleman, he is justly entitled.

The incidents above related are not isolated, but have been selected from many of a similar character, which appear in the history of the Hudson's Bay Company. Indeed, it has been necessary, in order to succeed in their enterprise, for this corporation to carry forward their operations in the wilds of Oregon by the terror of arms. Their private trapping parties have frequently been waylaid by the Indians and destroyed; their trading expeditions have often been obliged to fight their way through hostile tribes, from one portion of the country to another, or perish with starvation. Sometimes they have left behind them a trail of butchered Indians, who fell before their unerring rifles, and then have halted to commit to a hasty grave the remains of a comrade, who had fallen by a poisoned arrow, from the quiver of a vengeful foe. Sometimes whole parties have been cut off, and not a solitary person left to bear to civilized man the story of their tragic fate.

On one occasion, a party in the northern wilds, at the head of which was the son of Sir George Simpson, was attacked by the Indians, and after killing a number of their assailants, every soul perished. Young Simpson owned a large grey-hound, which he had with him, and which defended his master to the last extremity. In the battle the hound received a musket ball in his leg, and finding he could render his master no farther assistance, effected his escape. Subsequently the remains of these unfortunate men were found through the sagacity of the faithful dog, which led persons to the spot where perished his master and his comrades. Frequently the forts of the company have been attacked by numerous bands of savages, and it has required all the skill of the commandant, and the hard fighting of the men, to prevent them from falling into the hands of their foes. These means have sometimes failed to repulse them, and forts have been taken, pillaged and burned. Commandants have been insulted, trampled upon, and murdered. And it is not surprising that the company, in view of the immense loss of life and property they have from time to time sustained by their warlike and perfidious enemy, should frequently take severe measures to awe them into submission. This they have done by sending out war parties to attack indiscriminately the offending tribe; and frequently in these excursions, women and children have been the greatest sufferers. Individual cases have doubtless transpired, where Indians have been wantonly butchered and their property seized by the servants of the company, but the company cannot be held responsible for the outrages committed by individuals, unless it can be shown that the individuals are authorized by the company to commit them. Whoever has been intimately acquainted with the Hudson's Bay Company, and has observed its operations for any length of time, must be aware that the policy pursued by them with reference to the Indians, is one of the greatest forbearance and conciliation, and that they never resort to severe measures except when robberies are committed, their servants murdered, or the safety of the company is at stake.

Perhaps no calling under the sun, whale-fishing not excepted, is more perilous than the fur-trade, or in which a greater proportion of those who engage in it lose their lives. The following incident is illustrative of the character of many of the under servants employed by the company, at the various forts in the country of the Columbia :—

In the summer of 1842, Sir George Simpson, who is at the head of the affairs of the Hudson's Bay Company, in America, and who resides at Red river, east of the Rocky Mountains, in one of his exploring tours, arrived at Vancouver, and thence in a ship, proceeded up the north-west coast to a fort of the company, situated at Stikien, for the purpose of investigating the case of the murder of John McLaughlin, Jr., which took place in the previous April. The murder of this gentleman had produced great excitement in the country, particularly among the servants of the company, on account of the deceased being the son of Dr. John McLaughlin, chief factor, and superintendent of the affairs of the company west of the Rocky Mountains, and of his having been killed by the servants of the company, and not by Indians, who are the usual actors in such bloody scenes. It had been reported, and after he had investigated the matter, it was believed by Sir George Simpson, that the murderers had been influenced to commit the deed by the cruel and overbearing conduct of the deceased towards them, he being at the head of the company's business in that place; that they had previously stolen from the fort several bottles of ardent spirits, of which they made a free use on the night of the murder, to render themselves as desperate as possible, and to nerve themselves for the accomplishment of their sanguinary purposes. It appears from the testimony given, that every individual belonging to the establishment under the direction of Mr. McLaughlin, had mutually bound themselves to accomplish his destruction. And, as no evidence could be procured, except from interested persons, whose object would be to secure themselves, it might be expected that, in the first investigation by Sir George Simpson, the interested party would attempt to make it appear that the killing of Mr. McLaughlin was no more than a justifiable homicide. Accordingly, when Sir George returned to Vancouver, he expressed this view of the subject, as Dr. McLaughlin informs the writer, and stated that the deceased was a quarrelsome, drunken fellow, and had unmercifully beaten his men from time to time, and by his cruelty and wickedness had procured his own death.

A subsequent investigation seems to throw more light upon this affair; and as second-hand report is not always to be credited, I solicited permission to examine the original depositions, which were readily put into my hands by the afflicted and venerable father of the unfortunate man, who is the subject of this short sketch.

Pierre Kanaquassee, one of the men employed in the establishment at the time of the murder, and in whose testimony the gentlemen of the company place the utmost reliance, gives the following narrative, in answer to questions proposed by James Douglass, Esq., the magistrate that examined him :—

Q. Where were you on the night of the murder of the late Mr. John McLaughlin?

A. I was in my room, in the lower part of the main house, where I lived with George Heron, in an apartment in the lower story, immediately under the kitchen. My door opened into the passage which led to the apartment of Mr. John McLaughlin in the second story.

Q. What occurred on the night of the murder?

A. I will tell you the whole story to the best of my recollection.

A few days preceding the murder, five Indians from Tako, with letters from Dr. Kennedy, arrived at the fort about midnight. The watchmen hearing the knocking, called Mr. John. When he got up, he mustered a few hands to defend the gates in case of any treacherous attack from the Indians, whom they did not, as yet, know. They were then admitted into the fort, delivered up their arms according to custom, and were lodged in a small room in the lower story of the main house A day or two after this, he beat, and put one of these Indians, a native of Nop, in irons, as Peter was told, for having committed some theft in Tako. About eight o'clock of the evening of the 20th of April, Mr. John gave liquor to the Indians, and made them drunk; after which he called the white men, viz: Laperti, Pripe, Lulaire, Heroux, Bellinger, Simon, Fleury, McPherson, Smith, and Antoine Kawanope. During this time, Peter was in his own, which was the adjoining room, lying awake in bed, and overheard all that passed. He heard Mr. John say to McPherson, " Peter is not among us—where is he?" McPherson replied, that he was in bed, and he was sent for him, by Mr. John. Peter in consequence went into the room and saw all the men seated in a ring, on the floor, around a number of bottles standing within the ring, and the Indians lying dead drunk on another part of the floor. Mr. John himself was standing outside of the ring, and McPherson placed himself on the opposite side of the ring; neither of them appeared to be partaking of the festivities of the evening, but were looking on, and forcing the people to drink. Antoine Kawanopee was seated on his bed, apart from the other men, perfectly sober, as he told Peter afterward. Mr. John had ordered him not to drink, observing, "You are not to drink at this time, as I am going to die to-night, and you will help me in what I am going to do." On entering the room, Mr. John told Peter to sit down with the other people, and ordered his servant Fleury to give him a good dram, which he did in a tin-pan. Peter could not drink the whole, and was threatened by Mr. John with violence if he did not finish it. He succeeded in emptying the pan, by allowing the liquor to run into the bosom of his shirt. Mr. John, in doing this, did not appear to be angry, but in a half playful mood. Peter remained there about a quarter of an hour, during which time he was careful not to drink too much, as a few hours previously Antoine had called at his room and said, "My Uncle, take care of yourself to-night; the master is going to die." Peter said, "Who is going to kill him?" and Antoine said, "The Bluemen," meaning the Kanakas, "are going to kill him." This, Peter thought, was likely to be the case, as the men, some time before Christmas preceding, had agreed among themselves to murder him, and had signed a paper, which McPherson drew up to that effect. Every one of the men of the place agreed to the commission of this deed, Smith and Heron, as well others. Peter's name was signed by McPherson and he attested it by his cross. This paper was signed in Urbaine's house, where the men severally repaired by stealth for the purpose, as Mr. John kept so vigilant a watch upon them, that they were afraid he might suspect their intentions, if they were there in a body. The same impression made him also remark, in a low tone of voice, to Laperti, on his first entering the room, when he observed Mr. John forcing the people to drink, "I really believe our master feels his end near, as he never used to act in this manner."

As above mentioned, after Peter had been about fifteen minutes in the room where the men were drinking, Mr. John retired, followed by Antoine. Mr. John had not on that occasion drank any thing with the men, neither did he (Peter) ever see him at any time preceding, drink in their company. He, however, supposed that he must have taken something in his own room, as he appeared flushed and excited, but not sufficiently so as to render his gait in the least unsteady. McPherson also did not taste any thing in the room. As soon as Mr. John was gone, Peter also left the room, and went to bed in his own room.

Peter was informed by Antoine that Mr. John, on leaving the room where the men were drinking, went up stairs to his own apartment, and he heard him say to his wife, "I am going to die to-night." And he and his wife both began to cry. Mr. John soon rallied, and observed, "Very well, if I die, I must fall like a man." He then told Antoine to load his rifles and pistols, and ordered him also to arm himself with his own gun. He and Antoine then went out, and Peter thinks he heard the report of more than fifteen shots. Antoine afterwards told Peter that Mr. John fired at Laperti, but missed him, and afterwards ordered Antoine to fire at Laperti. Antoine refused to do so, until his own life was threatened by Mr. John, when he fired in the direction, without aiming at Laperti. He also told the Kanakas to kill the Canadians, and it was in part them who fired the shots that he (Peter) had heard. Peter then got up and placed himself behind his door, and saw Mr. John come in and go up stairs with Antoine, when he took the opportunity of going out, armed with his gun and a stout bludgeon, and found the men standing here and there on the gallery watching an opportunity to shoot Mr. John. Laperti's position on the gallery was fronting the door of the main house, towards which he had his gun pointed; when Peter saw him, he was on his knees, the small end of the gun resting on the top rail of the gallery, in readiness to fire. Laperti exclaimed, on seeing Peter, "I must kill him now, as he has fired two shots at me." Peter objected to this, and proposed to take and tie him. Nobody answered him. At that moment, Smith came up to Laperti and told him to hide himself or he would certainly be killed. Laperti said, "Where can I hide myself?" And Smith said, "Come with me and I will show you a place in the bastion where you can hide yourself," and they went off together in the direction of the bastion at the corner of Urbaine's house. Peter, after a few minutes' stay on the gallery, returned to his house, as he had previously agreed upon with George Hebram, who was lying sick in bed, and who had entreated him not to leave him alone. At the door of the main house, he met Mr. John coming out, followed by Antoine, who was carrying a lamp. Mr. John said to Peter, "Have you seen Laperti?" Peter answered, "No, I have not seen him." And then Mr. John said, "Have you seen Urbaine?" And Peter again answered that he had not. The minute before this, as he (Peter) was returning from the gallery, he had seen Urbaine standing at the corner of the main house, next to Urbaine's own dwelling, in company with Simon. Urbaine said, "I don't know what to do; I have no gun, and do not know where to hide myself." Simon said, "I have a gun, if he comes I will shoot him, and will be safe." Mr. John, after Peter passed him, said to Antoine, "Make haste, and come with the lamp," and proceeded with a firm step to Urbaine's house, as Peter, who continued watching at the door, saw. After he saw them go to Urbaine's house, he proceeded towards his own room, and he and Antoine called out, "Fire! fire!" The report of several shots, probably five, immediately followed, and he heard Antoine exclaiming, "Stop! stop! stop! He is dead now." Antoine afterwards related to Peter, that on reaching Urbaine's house, Mr. John ordered him to go round by one corner, while he went round by the other, directing Antoine to shoot any of the Canadians he might meet. Mr. John then proceeded in a stooping position, looking very intently before him, when a shot was fired from the corner of the house towards which he was going, which caused his death, the ball having entered at the upper part of the breast-bone, a little below the gullet, and came out a little below the shoulder, having broken the spine in its passage. Peter was also told by one of the Kanakas, that as soon as Mr. John fell, Urbaine sprung forward from the corner of the house within a few paces of the body, and put his foot savagely on his neck, as if to complete the act, should the ball have failed in causing death. The Kanakas immediately asked Urbaine, who had killed the master? Urbaine replied, "It is none of your business who has killed him!" Peter, who during this time had removed to his house, seeing Herron go out without his gun, went out round the body and said, "My friend, we have now done what we long intended to do; let us now carry the body back to the house." Urbaine, Laperti, Bellinger, and other white men who were present, replied, "When we kill a dog, we let him lie where we kill him." And Antoine told him they had previously given him the same reply to a similar proposition from him. Peter then approached the body and, with one hand under the neck, raised the head and trunk, when a deep expiration followed, which was the last sign of animation. He had previously perceived no signs of life, nor did he hear any one say that any appeared after the deceased fell. The white men being unwilling to assist him, he carried the body, with the aid of the Kanakas, into the main house, where he had it stripped, washed clean, decently dressed, and laid out. In doing so he received no help from any but the Kanakas. The wounds made by the balls were very large, both openings being circular, and severally three inches in diameter. The body bled profusely, there being a deep pool of blood found around it, which was washed away afterwards by the Kanakas. Peter never heard that he spoke or moved after he fell. There was a perpendicular cut on the forehead, skin-deep, in a line with the nose, which Peter thinks was caused by his falling on the barrel of his rifle, though Urbaine said that he had received it from an Indian with his dog. It was as Peter supposes about eleven o'clock, P. M., when he had done washing and laying out the body; the watches had not then been changed, therefore he thinks it could not be midnight. The people continued coming and going during the night, to see the body, and Peter proposed praying over the body, as is customary in Canada; but they objected, saying, they did not wish to pray for him. He did sit up with the body all night, having soon after gone, first to Urbaine's and then to Lulaire's house, who each gave him a dram, which he took, saying, "There is no need of drinking now; they might drink their fill now." He soon afterwards went to bed.

He inquired of Martineau, who also lived in the same room, if he had fired at the deceased. He replied, that he had fired twice. He then asked him if it was he that had killed him, and he said, I do not know if it was me or not. He (Peter) put the same question to several of the other men whom he saw afterwards; they all said that they had not shot him, and Martineau afterwards said that he had not directed his gun at him, but had fired in the air.

The following morning he asked Antoine Kawanope if he knew who had killed the deceased. He replied, "I know who killed him, but I am not going to tell you, or any one else. When the governor comes, I will tell him. He asked Antoine why he would not tell; he said he was afraid it might cause more quarrels, and lead to other murders. He then advised Antoine not to conceal it from him, as he would tell no one. Antoine then said, he thought it was Urbaine who had done the deed. Peter observed that Urbaine had no gun. Antoine replied, "I think it was Urbaine, because as soon as the deceased fell, Urbaine rushed out from his lurking place at the corner of the house, where, I was informed by the people, he always kept his gun secreted, with the intention of shooting the deceased." Peter says Laperti, Urbaine and Simon were all concealed in the corner whence the shot came, and he thinks it to be one of the three who fired it. Urbaine always denied having committed the murder, and said, "I am going to the Russian Fort for trial, and will be either banished or hung. I will let the thing go to the end, and will then inform upon the murderers."

Simon always said that he was never in the corner from whence the shot was fired, and knew nothing about the matter; but Peter thinks that he must have been there, as he saw him, as before related, at the corner of the main house, when he promised to protect Urbaine, and from the situation of the fort, he must have passed that spot with Urbaine, as there was no other passage from the place where they had been standing. Laperti also said he never fired at all. When Peter, as before related, went upon the gallery after the first firing had ceased, while Mr. John and Antoine had gone into the house, he saw all the men on the gallery, except Pripe, Lulaire and McPherson, and he asked each of them, respectively, if they were going to shoot the master that night, and they all answered, (as well as himself,) they would do so at the first chance, except Pchou, a Kanaka, who would not consent to the murder. Smith was then without a gun.

Before the Christmas preceding Peter put the question to Smith, how he should like to see him kill Mr. John? He replied, "I should like it very well; I would have no objection, because his conduct is so very bad that he can never expect to be protected by the Company." Peter Manifree says, that Mr. John appeared to be aware of the plot formed by the men against his life, as he supposes, through the information of Fleury, his servant, who was aware of every thing that passed among them. Mr. John had often said to the men, "Kill me, if you can. If you kill me, you will not kill a woman—you will kill a man." And he kept Antoine as a sentinel to watch his room. One evening George Herron proposed taking his life, and said if he could find a man to go with him, he would be the first to shoot him. Peter refused to go, and Herron watched a great part of the night in the passage leading to Mr. John's room, holding his gun pointed towards its door, with the object of shooting Mr. John if he appeared, as he usually did at night when going to visit the watchmen; but he did not go out that night, or Peter thinks that he would have been shot by Herron. The following morning Peter asked Antoine if he would defend Mr. John, were he attacked by the people. Antoine said he would not, and would be the first man to seize or shoot him, should any attempt be made against his life or liberty. He put the same question to McPherson; but McPherson said, "No! Do not kill him till the Governor comes, by and by, and then we shall have redress."

Peter also says that all the unmarried men were in the habit of secretly going out of the fort at night, contrary to order, to visit the Indian camp, and that one evening when he wished to go out, he met George Herron on the gallery, who showed him where a rope was slung to the picket, by which he might let himself down to the ground outside of the fort, saying, "This is the way I and others get out, and you may do the same without fear of detection." On the morning after the murder he went into Urbaine's and Lulaire's house and got a dram in each of them, out of two bottles of rum which he saw there. He said, now Mr. John is dead, I shall go out of the fort and spend the day with my wife. Urbaine replied, "No! No one shall go out of the fort. We keep the keys, and we shall keep the gates shut." Peter was angry at this and said to Antoine, "When Mr. John was alive, he kept us prisoners, and would not allow us to run after women; and now that we have killed him. the Canadians wish to keep us as close as he did. I see we must raise the devil again with these Canadians, before we can get our liberty."

Peter also says that one principal cause of their dislike to John, and their plots against his life, was the strictness with which he prevented their sallying from the fort in quest of women; that he flogged Martineau for having given his blanket to a woman with whom he maintained illicit commerce, and he also flogged Lamb and Kakepe for giving away their clothes in the same manner. This, Peter says, exasperated the men.

The day after the murder many of the men went up to Mr. John's room to see the body, and McPherson remarked to them, that when the master was living they were not in the habit of coming up there; but they did so now that he was dead. On hearing this, Peter and Urbaine went away and never returned. On their way to their own house, they met Pripe and Bellinger.

Urbaine told them what McPherson had said, and in a threatening manner said, "McPherson is getting proud as the other, and will be telling tales about us. We will not murder him, but we will give him a sound thrashing." And Peter says that he soon after went to Smith and told him to put McPherson on his guard, as the Canadians intended to attack him. Smith asked Peter what he would do, now the master was dead, and Peter said he would obey McPherson's orders. Smith replied, "That is good, Peter. If we do not do so, we shall lose all our wages." All the Canadians, and, he thinks, Simon, continued drinking the whole of the day following the murder; the other men of the fort, did not drink. He thinks it was the remains of the liquor they had been drinking the preceding night. Peter also says that, for a month previous to the murder, Urbaine, Laperti and Simon were in the habit of getting drunk every night on rum purchased from the Indians. Peter told them to take care of themselves, because Mr. John would be angry if he knew it. Mr. John took no notice of their conduct, because, as Peter thinks, he knew of the plot against his life, and felt intimidated. He also says that Laperti was excited against Mr. John on account of a suspected intrigue which he carried on with his wife. The night following the murder, they all went to bed quietly. The next day all was also quiet, and all work suspended, except watching the Indians, which they did very closely, as they were afraid they might be induced to attack the fort, on learning that the master was no more. They continued watching turn-a-bout. The second day a coffin was made, and the corpse removed from the main house to the bath, when McPherson gave the men a dram. The third day the corpse was buried and the men had another dram. He does not know whether the men asked for the dram, or whether McPherson gave it of his own accord. The corpse was carried to the grave by Laperti, Pripe, Luclaire and some Kanakas, but Urbaine did not touch it; does not think it was through fear. Peter often heard Laperti say, I wish the Governor was here, to see what he would do. He also says there was no quarrel in the room where they were drinking, on the night of the murder; but he thinks there might have been a quarrel after they left, as Pripe was put in irons after that time. He also says that the Canadians must have fixed on that night to murder him, and that Fleury told him so, which accounts for his apparent dejection of mind, and of his having shed tears in presence of his wife and Antoine, when he said, " I know that I am going to die this night." He also thinks this might have led to the outbreak, but of this he is not sure. It is a mere matter of opinion. Mr. John was a little in liquor, but knew perfectly well what he was about. He never saw him so far gone with liquor as not to be able to walk actively about, except on one occasion, the preceding Christmas Eve, when he appeared to walk unsteady, but nevertheless could mount the gallery. They only knew he had tasted liquor from the excitement and changed appearance of his countenance. He does not know who first suggested the idea of murdering Mr. John.

Since the above disclosures were made, a few other facts have come to light, which, however, do not materially effect the character of these atrocities. Mr. John McLaughlin, Jr., was doubtless intemperate, reckless, and tyrannical, and often unnecessarily cruel in the punishments inflicted upon his men; but he was surrounded by a set of desperadoes, who, for months before the arrival of the night, during the darkness of which, the fatal shot ushered him into the presence of his Judge, had been seeking an opportunity to rob him of life. Some time before this event, he flogged Peter for the crime of stealing fish. Peter was exceedingly angry, and resolved upon the destruction of his master. At a time to suit his purpose, he went to the bastion, where were fire-arms, loaded to his hands, and rung the bell of alarm, with the intention of shooting Mr. McLaughlin when he should make his appearance. A man by the name of Perse, came out to see what was the matter, instead of the intended victim, when Peter fired, but missed him, the ball hitting a post near his head. For this offence, Peter was again seized, put in irons, and subsequently severely flogged and liberated. Nearly all the men had been flogged from time to time, for various offences, and all conspired against the life of their master. As might have been expected, when the case was examined by Sir George Simpson, the murderers attempted to cast all the odium upon Mr. McLaughlin, doubtless for the purpose of exculpating themselves, in which attempt they but too well succeeded, in the estimation of Sir George. Whether the persons who procured his death, would be pronounced, by an intelligent jury, guilty of wilful murder, or whether, from the mitigating circumstances connected with these transactions, the verdict should assume a more modified form, is not for me to determine. But it cannot be denied by any one, that the circumstances must be indeed extraordinary, that will justify any man, or set of men, to cut short the probation of an immortal being, and usher him, with all his unrepented sins, into the presence of his God.

CHAPTER XX.

Oregon territory — History continued — Mr. Ashley's expedition — Smith, Jackson, and Sublette — Rocky Mountain Fur Company — Interesting journey — Country explored — Independent parties — Boneville — Red Wolf — Captain Wyeth — Opposed by H. B. C. — Results — Immigration for settlement — Character of population — Sources whence it proceeds — Enterprise — Portions of country occupied.

FOR eight years after the surrender of Astoria to the British, and the destruction of the Pacific Fur Company, in 1814, a British corporation held undisputed sway over the wilds of Oregon. Hordes of English trappers scoured its mountain chains upon their fleet horses, and ransacked its deepest valleys, while the Americans, worsted in the affair of Astoria, confined their operations on the east side of the Rocky Mountains. The North American Company, of which Mr. Astor was also the head, explored the country of the great Lakes, the headwaters of the Mississippi, the Missouri, and had established posts high up on the Yellow Stone, when another company was organized, in 1822, under the name of the Columbia Fur Company, with the design of extending its operations into those western regions hitherto under the monopoly of the Hudson's Bay Company. Accordingly, in the spring of 1823, Mr. W. H. Ashley, of St. Louis, fitted out an expedition for the Oregon country, crossed the Rocky Mountain chain, between the sources of the Platte and Colorado, near the forty-second parallel, obtained a large amount of furs, and, in the fall, transported them in safety to St. Louis. In the following year he returned across the mountains with about one hundred men, whom he left in the country to hunt and trap; and, although they were opposed by the Hudson's Bay

Company in every way, yet the furs collected by them in three years, amounted to the sum of one hundred and eighty thousand dollars. In these first expeditions of Ashley from St. Louis, the goods were all transported on the backs of horses; but in 1827, he sent sixty men across the mountains with a piece of cannon drawn by mules, which was planted in the vicinity of the great Salt Lake, or Lake Yauta, which lies south of the forty-second parallel; and, after collecting the furs, and distributing supplies among the hunters, they returned to Missouri, having been absent just seven months.

In 1826, a company was formed in St. Louis by Messrs. Smith, Jackson and Sublette, and, having subsequently purchased Mr. Ashley's establishments and interests, they carried on a successful trade with the countries of the Columbia, under the name of the Rocky Mountain Fur Company. The first expedition with wagons to the Rocky Mountains was made by this company in 1829, and as an account of it will serve to show both the mode and the route usually pursued by the emigrants at the present day, I subjoin the following, which appeared in connection with President Jackson's Message in 1831;

"On the 10th of April last, (1829,) we set out from St. Louis with eighty-one men, all mounted on mules, ten wagons, each drawn by five mules, and two dearborns, (light carriages or carts,) each drawn by one mule. Our route was nearly due west to the western limits of the State of Missouri, and thence along the Santa Fe trail, about forty miles from which the course was some degrees north of west, across the waters of the Kansas, and up the great Platte River to the Rocky Mountains, and to the head of Wind River where it issues from the mountains. This took us until the 16th of July, and was as far as we wished to go with the wagons, as the furs to be brought in were to be collected at this place, which is, or was this year, the great rendezvous of the persons engaged in that business. Here the wagons could easily have crossed the mountains, it being what is called the Southern Pass had it been desirable for them to do so, which it was not for the reasons stated. For our support at leaving the Missouri settlements, until we should get into the buffalo country, we drove twelve head of cattle besides a milch cow. Eight of these only being required for use before we got to the buffaloes, the others went on to the head of Wind River. We began to fall in with buffaloes on the Platte, about three hundred and fifty miles from the white settlements, and from that time lived on buffaloes, the quantity being infinitely beyond what we needed. On the 4th of August, the wagons being in the mean time loaded with the furs which had been previously taken, we set out on our return to St. Louis. All the high points of the mountains then in view were white with snow; but the passes and valleys, and all the level country, were green with grass. Our route back was over the same ground nearly as in going out, and we arrived at St. Louis on the 10th of October, bringing back the ten wagons, four of the oxen, and the milch cow, as we did not need them for provisions. Our men were all healthy during the whole time; we suffered nothing from the Indians, and had no accident, but the death of one man, being buried under a bank of earth that fell in upon him, and another crippled at the same time. Of the mules we lost but one by fatigue, and two horses stolen by the Kansas Indians; the grass being along the whole route, going and coming, sufficient for the support of the horses and mules. The usual weight in the wagons was about one thousand eight hundred pounds. The usual progress of the wagons was from fifteen to twenty-five miles per day. The country being almost all open, level and prairie, the chief obstructions were ravines and creeks, the banks of which required cutting down, and for this purpose a few pioneers were generally kept in advance of the caravan. This is the first time that wagons ever went to the Rocky Mountains, and the ease and safety with which it was done, prove the facility of communicating overland with the Pacific Ocean. The route from the Southern Pass, where the wagons stopped, to the Great Falls of the

Columbia, being easier and better than on this side of the mountains, with grass enough for the horses and mules; but a scarcity of game for the support of men."

This company continued its operations for a number of years, and its agents explored the whole country from St. Louis, by the way of Taos and Santa Fe, to the Bay of San Francisco; thence along the coast of the Pacific north to the mouth of the Columbia; and all the vast interior from Fort Vancouver to the country of the Blackfeet and Sioux was faithfully examined; but, in consequence of the deadly hostility of the Indian tribes, and the direct and unbending opposition of the great English monopoly, the company withdrew from the territories west, and for years has confined its operations on the east side of the Rocky Mountains.

The above named are the principal American companies which have extended their operations west of the Rocky Mountains, since the famous expedition of Astoria, under the direction of Wilson Price Hunt. Several independent parties of adventurers, however, have, from time to time, turned their backs upon civilization, and, some actuated by curiosity, and others by the love of gain, have traced the waters of the rivers which flow westward, to the Pacific ocean; and after spending years among the Indians, have returned to the world information concerning the regions hitherto but little known, which they had explored.

In 1832, Captain Bonneville, of the United States Army, led a band across the Rocky Mountains, of more than one hundred men, and remained in the country drained by the Snake river and its branches for two years, employed in the collection of furs. The adventures of this intrepid officer have been made known by Washington Irving, and need not be repeated here. Suffice it to say that when the writer visited the country of the Snake river, in 1842, an incident of Bonneville's experience in that country, was related to him by Red Wolf, an Indian chief of the Nez Perce tribe. Bonneville had met with the most violent opposition from the Hudson's Bay Company, in his trade, and in attempting to leave a portion of the country where every thing, even to the game, appeared to be under their control, he and his party, which, by desertion and other causes, had been greatly reduced, lost their way, and wandered without food for three days and nights. At length, in a state of starvation, they fell in with Red Wolf and his party on the Snake or Lewis river, and the chief received them kindly, and treated them with the best which his means afforded, which was the flesh of a fat horse, which he killed for that purpose. After giving them this timely relief, he prevailed upon them to tarry with him a few days, and recruit their exhausted strength. They accepted of his kind offer, and were astonished at their departure, on being supplied by their Indian benefactor with provisions to take with them, and a guide to conduct them on to their proper route.

About the same time that Bonneville was making his transit across the Rocky Mountains, Mr. Nathaniel Wyeth, of Massachusetts, was endeavoring to establish a direct trade between the United States and the Columbia river. In addition to the fur-trade, Wyeth had in view the establishment of a salmon-fishery in Oregon, from which he hoped to receive considerable profits. With these views he dispatched a vessel around Cape Horn, to the Columbia, and led two expeditions across the continent, the first in 1832, and the second in 1834. To facilitate his operations, Captain Wyeth formed two trading stations, one in the south-east corner of Oregon, near the junction of the river *Portneuf* with the Snake or Lewis river, called Fort Hall, and the other on Wappato Island, near the entrance of the Wallamette into the Columbia, and about seventy miles from the Pacific ocean, called Fort William. These forts were advantageously situated for trade, but in consequence of the numerous disasters which happened to the company, but principally on account of the unrelenting hostility of the Hudson's Bay Company to all American enterprise in Oregon, Wyeth was obliged to relinquish his expedition, and Fort Hall and Fort William fell into the hands of that monopoly. Scores of lives were lost in Wyeth's expedition; several men were drowned, but more killed by the Indians. Wyeth continued his effort to establish the trade for three years, and it is said that, at the close of that time, of two hundred men whom he had led into Oregon, but forty were known to be alive, all the rest having fallen victims to the dangers incident to the fur-trade.

This enterprise, though failing in its primary objects, was of great service, not only to the United States in furnishing important information respecting the territories of the Columbia, but also to Oregon itself in introducing the first American settlers, in assisting the first American missionaries across the Rocky Mountains, and in opening the way for future emigrations to the fertile plains of that distant country.

Though a number of persons, Americans and Canadian French, who accompanied the first exploring and commercial expeditions across the mountains, had previously taken up their residence in Oregon, yet the first emigrations for the purpose of settlement, were made in 1832. To a proper understanding of the character of the present population of Oregon, it will be necessary to consider the sources whence it has sprung.

Probably a more heterogeneous mass of human kind cannot be found in any land, than have sought an asylum in the wilds of Oregon. Here are found the Indian, who is the legitimate proprietor of the soil, Englishmen, Scotchmen, Irishmen, Americans, Germans, Prussians, Italians, Spanish, Frenchmen, Danes, Canadians, Hawaiians, Otehietans, and Africans. From continual intermarriages with one another, and particularly with the natives of the country ever since white men first visited these shores, an amalgamated population has been produced, presenting every variety of color, disposition, and character of which the human species is capable. The English, Scotch, French, and some others, have principally been introduced into the country through the instrumentality of the Hudson's Bay Company. Many of these still belong to the company, and occupy various stations, from those of servants and clerks up through the various grades of office to the chief factors and superintendents. Others, who were formerly the servants of the company, becoming in some cases superannuated, in others unprofitable, have been dismissed; and the company chose rather to settle them in the country and continue to exercise a controling influence over them, than to return them to the lands whence they came. The numbers which have sprung from this source, and are now residents of the wilderness, amount to nearly two thousand souls.

Many persons have found their way to Oregon from the numerous vessels which have touched at various points along its extended coast. Scarcely a ship has visited the Columbia for years, from which two or more have not made their escape, and, secreting themselves until the vessel has left, they have come forth to mingle with the inhabitants as citizens of Oregon. Some have deserted their ships on the coast of California, and have fought their way to the valley of the Multnomah, through the hostile tribes that roam among the Clameth and Umpqua mountains. Some of these adventurous seamen are among the most industrious, temperate, and wholesome settlers of Oregon.

The Islands of the Pacific open another source for the supply of inhabitants to Oregon. Hundreds of Hawaiians have been taken from the Sandwich Islands by the Hudson's Bay Company, and by private individuals, to act as house servants and day-laborers, for which they have been found much better adapted than the natives of the country. Though the persons employing them are obliged to enter into stipulations with the Hawaiian government to return them at the expiration of their term of service; yet, from the numerous casualties incident to their new relations, and, those who survive, becoming warmly attached to the country of their adoption, in connection with the superior facilities which Oregon presents to the Hawaiian, when compared with those of his native land, but few of them ever return to their sea-girt home.

Another somewhat fruitful source for the supply of inhabitants to the fertile valleys of Oregon, has been found, singular as it may appear, in that vast range, called "The Rocky Mountains." I do not now refer to emigrants direct from the United States, who are obliged to pass through the gates of that stupendous range on their way to that "better country" which they seek, but to those white men, who, in connection with the American companies established for purposes of traffick with the Blackfeet, Sioux, and other Indians, have been collecting for the last forty years among the snow-clad mountains which send their waters both to the Atlantic and Pacific Oceans. There are men still living in the Wallamette valley, who accompanied Lewis and Clark in their exploring expedition in 1805 and 1806; and I have often seen persons who were the companions and fellow-travelers of Wilson Price Hunt, one of the partners of John Jacob Astor, in his trading establishment at the mouth of the Columbia, and who shared with that intrepid traveler in all the perils of one of the most remarkable expeditions of the kind ever carried to a successful issue, and has been inimitably described in Washington Irving's popular "Astoria." Madame Dorio, the heroine of that interesting narrative, and her son, who was born under peculiar circumstances during one of their encampments on their journey across the mountains, are both still alive, and inhabitants of the Wallamette valley.

There are many others, most of whom are Americans who, after having spent many years in ranging the Rocky Mountains, experiencing the most surprising adventures among the Indians, and enduring every variety of hardships which human nature is capable of suffering, have at last found a peaceful and quiet retreat, where they are secure from the savage violence of the Blackfoot, and from the treachery of the Sioux, and where most of them will close their earthly career. With the most thrilling interest I have heard them relate their mountain adventures and "hair breadth-escapes." The history of some of them will doubtless form the subject of many a future legend replete with interest. It is very remarkable with respect to this class of inhabitants, that, while they doomed themselves to a precarious subsistence among the hostile clans of the mountains, they contracted the most roving, barbarous and depraved habits; yet, on settling down amidst the increasingly interesting society of Oregon, most of them become steady, peaceful and industrious citizens. While ranging the mountains they usually connected with their's, the fortunes of an Indian woman, and many of them, in process of time, became surrounded with large families of half-caste children. They had a natural love for their offspring, and they could but form an attachment for the mothers of their sons and daughters; consequently, on leaving the scene of their savage life, they took with them their wives and children, anxious that both might be benefited by mingling with civilized society. At the present time some of these reclaimed mountaineers are among the principal persons to whom the public interests of the colony are intrusted. This shows with what facility they can throw off their mountaineer habits, and assume those of civilized life.

At present the most fruitful source of supply for settlers in Oregon, is the United States of America. Emigrations have arrived in the country, direct from Missouri, every fall, since 1839. In 1840 and 1841, the parties were comparatively small, but in 1842 the emigration numbered one hundred and eleven persons in all. In 1843, it increased to eight hundred persons, who emigrated principally in ox-wagons, and drove before them fifteen hundred head of neat cattle. In 1844, the number was about the same as the preceding year. In 1845, it increased to nearly three thousand souls, with some two or three thousand head of cattle.

These emigrations, for the most part, are composed of persons from the Western States, but in them might be found persons from almost every State in the Union, even the most Eastern. Maine herself has supplied several.

Many of these adventurers are of that class of persons

who have always hovered on the frontiers of civilization, and have been pushing on in search of a "better country, not an heavenly," until they have passed the utmost borders of civilized society. Penetrating entirely through the deep recesses of savage life, they have finally emerged from the deep defiles of the Cascade Mountains, into the lovely valleys of Oregon, where they have found, at least in embryo, the blessings of Christianity and civilization ; and here most of them, some from choice, and others from the impossibility of getting away, come to the conclusion to erect their tabernacles for life. The enterprise of these parties has far out-stripped the most sanguine expectations of the English writer in a London paper, who, a few years ago, remarked, that, "Even the persevering Yankees would not think of emigrating to Oregon in their ox-wagons." If this writer had possessed the eye of omniscience, he would have seen, at the very time he was penning it, a score of Yankee wagons, drawn by sixty yoke of oxen, winding their way through the deep passes of the Rocky Mountains, bound for the Oregon.

The population of Oregon in 1846, embracing the members of the Hudson's Bay Company, would not vary far from twelve thousand. These are settled principally in the Wallamette valley on the south, and the Cowilitz valley on the north side of the Columbia, on the Clatsop plains, and at the various posts of the Hudson's Bay Company.

CHAPTER XXI.

Oregon territory — Political history — Necessity of organizing a body politic — First meeting of the people — Second meeting — Exigencies met — Organization dies — Exploring squadron — Great excitement — Commander Wilkes — Opposed to organizing — Subject slumbers — Sub-agent — Mass meeting — Old subject revived — Indians troublesome — Talk of war — Dr. McLaughlin — Third meeting — Government organized — Fourth meeting — Officers qualified — Laws enacted — Effect produced — New legislative committee — Laws revised — Alterations — Election of a Governor and House of Representatives — Peaceable state of community — Joel Turnham — Thrilling incident.

THE subject of this Chapter is not the political relation of Oregon to any other country; whether from the Spanish purchase, the right of first discovery, or contiguity of situation, it properly belongs to the United States; or whether, from long and uninterrupted possession by British subjects, as the servants of a British monopoly, or from the conveniency of a continued possession of the majestic Columbia as a port of entry to North Western British America, it more properly belongs to England; but, simply, the internal politics of Oregon.

Strange as it may appear, the people of Oregon have their politics, altogether aside from their relation with other countries, and these have sprung up among them, more from the necessity of the case, than from any other cause. Up to 1840, the number of people in the colony was so small, the business transactions so limited, and the difficulties so few, that the necessity of organizing the community into a body politic, did not appear to be very great, though for two years persons had been chosen to officiate as judges and magistrates. But a circumstance transpired in the winter of 1841, different in its character and bearings upon community from any thing that had previously happened, namely, the death of one of the principal men in the colony, by the name of Ewing Young, who left a large and very unsettled estate, without having made the least provision for its administration. On the very day of the burial of this man, who had not a single relative to follow him to the tomb, measures were taken to call a public meeting for the purpose of appointing officers for the government of the community, and particularly to provide for the proper disposition of the estate of Ewing Young. A committee of arrangements, chosen at his funeral, called a mass meeting of the inhabitants of Oregon, south of the Columbia river, on the 17th and 18th of February, 1841, to be held at the Methodist Mission premises in the Wallamette valley. Pursuant to the call, the people collected and held, what was properly called, "The Primary Meeting of the people of Oregon."

The meeting on the 18th was full—nearly every male inhabitant south of the Columbia, of full age, being present.

Rev. Jason Lee was excused from officiating as Chairman, and Rev. David Leslie was elected to fill his place. G. Hines and Sidney Smith were chosen Secretaries.

The doings of the meeting the previous day were presented to the assembly, and adopted, in part, as follows :—

Resolved, That a committee be chosen to form a constitution, and draft a code of laws, and that the following persons compose that committee :

Rev. F. N. Blanchat, Rev. Jason Lee, David Don Pierre, Rev. Gustavus Hines, M. Chanlevo, Robert More, J. L. Parrish, Etienne Lucia, and Wm. Johnson.

As it was not deemed necessary to elect a Governor that office was set aside.

Dr. J. L. Babcock was elected to fill the office of Supreme Judge, with Probate powers.

George W. Le Breton was elected to fill the office of Clerk of the Courts and Public Recorder.

Wm. Johnson was elected High Sheriff. Zavier Ladaroot, Pierre Billique and Wm. McCarty were chosen Constables.

It was then resolved, that, until a code of laws be drafted by the Legislative Committee, and adopted by the people, Ira L. Babcock, the Supreme Judge, be instructed to act according to the laws of the State of New York.

It was then resolved to adjourn to meet the first Thursday in June, at the new building near the Roman Catholic church.

THURSDAY, June 11, 1841.

The inhabitants of the Wallamette valley met according to adjournment, and the meeting was called to order by the Chairman, Rev. D. Leslie.

On motion, the doings of the former meeting were read, on which the report of the committee for drafting a constitution and code of laws was called for, and information was communicated to the meeting by the chairman of the committee, that, in consequence of his not having called the committee together, no report had been prepared.

F. N. Blanchat was excused from serving on that committee at his own request.

On motion, it was then resolved, that a person be chosen to fill the place thus vacated in the committee for drafting a constitution and code of laws, and Wm. J. Baily was chosen that committee man.

On motion, it was resolved, that this committee be instructed to meet for the transaction of their business on the first Monday of August next.

On motion, resolved, that the committee be instructed to report to an adjourned meeting, to be held the first Thursday in October next.

On motion, resolved, that the committee be advised to confer with the commander of the American Exploring Squadron now in the Columbia river, concerning the propriety of forming a provisional government in Oregon.

Resolved, That the motion to adopt the report of the nominating committee presented at a previous meeting, be rescinded.

Resolved, That the committee to draft a constitution be instructed to take into consideration the number and kind of offices it will be necessary to create, in accordance with their constitution and code of laws, and to report the same at the next meeting.

It was also resolved, that the report of the nominating committee be referred to the legislative committee.

It was then moved and carried, that this meeting adjourn to meet at the Methodist Mission at eleven o'clock, A. M., of the first Thursday in October next.

    (Signed,)   DAVID LESLIE, *Chairman.*
GUSTAVUS HINES, } *Secretaries.*
SIDNEY SMITH,

I have previously stated that the origin of these attempts to form a kind of provisional government, was the removal by death of the late Ewing Young, leaving, as he did, a large and unsettled estate, with no one to administer it, and no laws to control its administration. The exigencies of this case having been met by the appointment of a Judge with probate powers, who entered immediately upon his duties, and disposed of the estate of Ewing Young, to the entire satisfaction of the community; and the fact that some of the most influential citizens of the country, and especially some of the members of the legislative committee, were adverse to the idea of establishing a permanent organization so long as the peace and harmony of the community could possibly be preserved without it, the subject was permitted to die away, and the committee for drafting a constitution and code of laws did not meet according to their instructions, nor did the meeting at which they were expected to report, ever take place.

What contributed more, however, to defeat this first effort to establish a regular government in Oregon than any thing else, was the arrival, during the summer in which the organization was pending, of the United States Exploring Squadron, under the command of Captain Wilkes. The results of the observations of the officers and scientific corps connected with the squadron, in the Oregon Territory, as well as a description of the different casualties which happened to them in the loss of the Peacock on the bar of the Columbia, and in their different conflicts with the natives of the interior, are already before the public in the voluminous works of Captain Wilkes, and therefore it is not necessary to introduce them here. The arrival on the coast of Oregon of so extensive an armament, consisting of four or five vessels of war, for the express purpose of exploring, not only the coast and rivers, but also the country itself, produced a very great excitement in the community, and but little was heard of but the Exploring Squadron during its somewhat protracted stay in the Columbia river. In addition to this, the officers of the squadron were consulted on the subject of organizing the country into a civil compact, and were found to be decidedly opposed to the scheme, and recommended that the subject be allowed to rest. They encouraged the people in the belief that the United States Government would probably soon extend jurisdiction over the country.

This put a quietus on the subject for the time being, and, as the number of settlers in the country was yet small, and the difficulties to be settled of such a nature as easily to be adjusted by arbitration, nothing took place to call up the subject of organizing until several months after the departure of the squadron from the Columbia river.

The subject of organizing a government was again revived in September, 1842; but Dr. White, who was now in the country as Sub-agent of Indian Affairs, contended that his office was equivalent to that of Governor of the Colony. Some of the citizens contended that the Doctor's business was to regulate the intercourse between the Indians and the whites, and not to control the whites in their intercourse among themselves. Without arriving at any thing definite on this point, after hearing the documents brought to the country from Washington by Dr. White, the people scattered away to their homes upon the plains, pleased with what they considered to be a preliminary step of the United States towards extending jurisdiction over the Territory of Oregon.

About this time the Indians became quite troublesome, in various parts of the country. At Waialetpee, on the

Walla-Walla river, where a mission station had been established by Dr. Marcus Whitman, they took advantage of the Doctor's absence and broke into the house, in the dead of the night, and even into the bed-chamber of Mrs. Whitman, who, with much difficulty, escaped out of their hands. At Laperai, on Clear Water river, where the Rev. Mr. Spaulding was conducting a mission station, they committed some outrages; also, at the Falls of the Wallamette river. A number of individuals of Dr. White's party, who had separated themselves from the main company, were robbed of their effects while passing down the Columbia river.

The Nez-Perces and Kayuses, two of the most powerful tribes in the country, had talked much of making war upon the American settlement on the Wallamette river. These things, with many others of more or less importance, produced a high degree of excitement, and served to arouse the people again to the subject of entering into some measures by which their mutual protection might be secured. The Canadian French, who had settled in the country, and who, up to the beginning of 1843, were more numerous than the Americans, were at first, agreed with them as to the necessity of organizing; but, at this time, as it was supposed through the influence of Dr. John McLaughlin, who, himself was opposed to such a measure, they broke off, almost to a man, on the pretence, that, as they were the subjects of Queen Victoria, and did not wish to forswear their country, they could not, consistently, enter into any measures that might prove prejudicial to her Majesty's government. This served to harmonize the views of the Americans, so far as to bring them unanimously to the determination immediately to organize; but they still differed as to the nature of the government that should be established. Some were favorable to an independent form, some to a form similar to a territorial government, while others were in favor of a few simple rules and regulations, which might operate satisfactorily for the time being, until the United States government should do something more effectual in their behalf. With these conflicting views a meeting of about fifty of the settlers, chiefly Americans, took place at the Wallamette Falls in the month of March, 1843, and the subject of organizing the community into a body politic, became the order of the evening. After a spirited and interesting discussion, the meeting resulted in the appointment of a committee to notify a public meeting to be held at Champoeg, the 2d day of May, 1843. In the mean time, there being no law in Oregon, every man was left to do what was pleasing in his own eyes. At length the 2d day of May arrived, and the people assembled according to notice, the French as well as the Americans, the former, doubtless, for the purpose of thwarting the designs of the latter, and these with the determination of carrying their purposes into execution. The following is an account of the meeting as taken from the public records.

A public meeting of the inhabitants of the Wallametie settlement was held at Champoeg, on the 2d day of May, 1843, in accordance with the call of a committee, chosen at a previous meeting, for the purpose of taking steps to organize themselves into a civic community, and provide themselves with the protection secured by the enforcement of law and order.

Dr. J. L. Babcock was chosen Chairman, and W. H. Gray, G. W. Le Breton and W. H. Wilson were chosen Secretaries.

The committee appointed for the purpose of bringing forward the business of the meeting, presented their report, and a motion was made to accept it, which was lost. Considerable confusion existed in consequence; but it was moved by G. W. Le Breton, and seconded by W. H. Gray, that the meeting divide themselves preparatory to being counted; those in favor of the objects of the meeting taking the right, and those of the contrary mind, the left. The motion prevailed, and a large majority being found in favor of organizing, the greater part of the dissenting withdrew.

The report of the committee was again presented and accepted. It was then taken up, item by item, and disposed of as follows:—

First item, that a Judge, with Probate powers, be chosen to officiate in this community. Adopted.

It was also resolved, that the second, third, fourth and fifth items, providing for the election of a Clerk, Sheriff, three Magistrates, and three Constables, be adopted.

The sixth item, recommending the election of a committee of nine persons for the purpose of drafting a code of laws for the government of the community, and to report to a public meeting to be hereafter called by said committee, and to be held at Champoeg, on the 5th day of July, 1843, was also adopted.

The seventh and eighth were adopted, which recommended the election of a Treasurer, a Major and three Captains.

It was then resolved, that the meeting proceed to choose persons to fill the various offices by ballot.

A. E. Wilson was chosen to act as Judge, with Probate powers.

G. W. Le Breton was chosen Clerk of the Court, and Recorder.

Joseph L. Meek was chosen to fill the office of Sheriff.

W. H. Wilson was chosen Treasurer.

Messrs. Hill, Shortess, Newel, Beers, Hubbard, Gray, O'Neal, More and Dougherty were chosen to act as the Legislative Committee.

Messrs. Burns, Judson and A. T. Smith were chosen to act as Magistrates.

Messrs. Ebberts, Bridges and Lewis were chosen to act as Constables.

John Howard was chosen Major.

Messrs. McCarty, McKay and S. Smith were constituted Captains.

It was then resolved, that the Legislative Committee be required to make their report on the 5th day of July, 1843, at Champoeg.

On motion, it was resolved, that the services of the Committee be paid for at the rate of one dollar and twenty-five cents per day, and that the money be raised by subscription.

A motion was made and carried, that the Major and Captains be instructed to enlist men, to form companies of mounted riflemen.

A fourth Magistrate and a fourth Constable were also elected, and it was then resolved, that the Legislative Committee should not be allowed to sit over six days.

In addition to the above business, this important primary meeting recognized the officers who had been elected immediately after the death of Ewing Young, and passed a vote that they should have power to exercise the functions of their office until the day of the public meeting should arrive, when the newly elected officers should be duly initiated.

During the interim between the above described meeting and the 5th of July, little transpired worthy of note, with the exception of the celebration of the Fourth. This day, glorious in the recollection of every American, wherever he may be found, as the birth-day of liberty, was appropriately celebrated at Champoeg, where nearly all the Americans in the country, and many of the French and English assembled to listen to an oration, and a temperance address, and to enjoy the socialities of a public dinner. The festivities of the day were enjoyed in the true spirit of liberty, there being no other *spirit* to exert an influence on the occasion. As there were no houses to entertain the people during the night, they nearly all camped upon the ground, and the morning of the 5th found them prepared to enter upon the important business that was to come before them, and which resulted in giving to the Oregonians a tangible form of government.

The minutes of the meeting are as follows:—

CHAMPOEG, July 5th, 1843.

The inhabitants of Oregon met at Champoeg, pursuant to adjournment, to hear the report of the Legislative Committee, and to perform such other business as might come before them.

Rev. Gustavus Hines was elected Chairman, and W. H. Gray, W. H. Wilson and H. Campbell were chosen Secretaries.

Robert More, Esq., Chairman of the Legislative Committee, then presented his report, which was read by the Clerk of the Court, and adopted, as follows :—

Section 1*st*.—We, the people of Oregon Territory, for purposes of mutual protection, and to secure peace and prosperity among ourselves, agree to adopt the following laws and regulations until such time as the United States of America extend their jurisdiction over us.

Be it therefore enacted by the citizens of Oregon Territory, that the said Territory, for the purposes of temporary government, be divided into not less than three, nor more than five Districts, subject to be extended to a greater number when the increase of population shall require.

For the purpose of fixing the principles of civil and religious liberty as the basis of all laws and constitutions of government that may hereafter be adopted, Be it enacted, that the following articles be considered articles of compact among the free citizens of this Territory :

Article 1*st*. No person demeaning himself in an orderly and peaceful manner, shall ever be molested on account of his mode of worship, or religious sentiments.

Article 2*d* The inhabitants of said Territory shall always be entitled to the benefit of the writ of habeas corpus, and trial by jury, of a proportionate representation of the people in the legislature and judicial proceedings, according to the course of common law ; all persons shall be bailable, unless for capital offences, where the proof shall be evident, or the presumption great. All fines shall be moderate, and no cruel or unusual punishments inflicted. No man shall be deprived of his liberty but by the judgment of his peers, or the laws of the land ; and should the public exigencies make it necessary for the common preservation to take any person's property, or to demand his particular services, full compensation shall be made for the same. And, in the just preservation of rights and property, it is understood and declared, that no law ought to be made or have force in said Territory that shall, in any manner whatever, interfere with, or effect, private contracts or engagements, *bona fide* and without fraud, privately framed.

Article 3*d.* Religion, morality, and knowledge, being necessary to good government and the happiness of mankind, schools and the means of education shall forever be encouraged.

The utmost good faith shall always be preserved towards the Indians; their land and property shall never be taken from them without their consent; and in their property, rights and liberty, they shall never be invaded or disturbed, unless in just and lawful wars authorized by the representatives of the people. But laws founded in justice and humanity, shall from time to time be made for preventing injustice being done to them, and for preserving peace and friendship with them.

Article 4*th.* There shall be neither slavery nor involuntary servitude in said Territory, otherwise than for the punishment of crime, whereof the party shall have been duly convicted.

Section 2*d.*—Organic Law.

Article 1*st.* Be it enacted by the authorities aforesaid, that the officers elected upon the 2d day of May, 1843, shall continue in office until the second Tuesday in May, 1844, and until others are elected and qualified.

Article 2*d.* Be it further enacted, that an election of civil and military officers shall be held annually upon the second Tuesday in May, in the several districts, in such places as shall be designated by law.

Article 3*d.* Each officer heretofore elected, or that shall hereafter be elected, shall, before entering upon the duties of his office, take an oath, or affirmation, to support the laws of the Territory, and faithfully to discharge the duties of his office.

Article 4*th.* Every free male descendant of a white man, inhabitant of this Territory, of the age of twenty-one years and upwards, who shall have been an inhabitant of this Territory at the time of its organization, shall be entitled to vote at the election of officers, civil and military, and be eligible to any office in the Territory.

Provided, that all persons of the description entitled to vote by the provisions of this section, who shall emigrate to this Territory after organization, shall be entitled to the rights of citizens, after having resided six months in the Territory.

Article 5*th.* The executive power shall be vested in a committee of three persons elected by the qualified voters at the annual election, who shall have power to grant pardons and reprieves for offences against the laws of the Territory; to call out the military force of the Territory, to repel invasions or suppress insurrection; to take care that the laws be faithfully executed, and to recommend such laws, as they may consider necessary, to the representatives of the people for their action. Two members of the committee shall constitute a quorum for the transaction of business.

Article 6*th.* The legislative power shall be vested in a committee of nine persons, to be chosen by the qualified voters at the annual elections, giving to each district a representation in the ratio of its population, excluding Indians, and the said members of the committee shall reside in the district for which they shall be chosen.

Article 7*th.* The judicial power shall be vested in a Supreme Court, consisting of the Supreme Judge and two Justices of the Peace, a Probate Court, and in Justices of the Peace. The jurisdiction of the Supreme Court shall be both appellate and original. That of the Probate Court and Justices of the Peace, as limited by law; provided, that individual Justices of the Peace shall not have jurisdiction of any matter of controversy when the title or boundaries of land may be in dispute, or when the sum claimed shall exceed fifty dollars.

Article 8*th.* There shall be a Recorder elected by the qualified electors at the annual election, who shall keep a faithful record of the proceedings in the Legislative Committee, Supreme and Probate Courts; also, record all boundaries of land presented for that purpose, and all marks and brands used for marking live stock; procure and keep the standard weights and measures required by law; seal weights and measures, and keep a record of the same; and also record wills, deeds and other instruments of writing, required by law to be recorded. The Recorder shall receive the following fees, viz: for recording wills, deeds, and other instruments of writing, twelve cents for every hundred words, and the same price for copies of the same; for every weight and measure sealed, twenty-five cents; for services as Clerk of the Legislature, and for all other services required of him by this act, the same fees as are allowed for similar services by the laws of Iowa.

Article 9*th*. There shall be a Treasurer elected by the qualified electors of the Territory, who shall, before entering upon the duties of his office, give bonds to the Executive Committee in the sum of fifteen hundred dollars, with two or more sufficient securities, to be approved by the Executive Committee of the Territory, conditioned for the faithful discharge of the duties of his office. The Treasurer shall receive all moneys belonging to the Territory that may be raised by contribution or otherwise, and shall procure suitable books in which he shall enter an account of his receipts and disbursements.

Article 10*th*. The Treasurer shall in no case pay money out of the Treasury, but according to law; and shall annually report to the Legislative Committee a true account of his receipts and disbursements, with necessary vouchers for the same, and shall deliver to his successor in office all books, moneys, accounts, or other property belonging to the Territory, as soon as his successor shall become qualified.

Article 11*th*. The Treasurer shall receive for his services the sum of five per cent. upon all moneys received and paid out, according to law, and three per cent. upon all money in the Treasury when he goes out of office, and two per cent. upon the disbursements of money in the Treasury when he comes into office.

Article 12*th*. The laws of Iowa shall be the laws of this country, in civil, military and criminal cases, *when not otherwise provided for;* and where no statute of Iowa Territory applies, the principles of common law and equity shall govern.

Article 13*th*. The law of Iowa, regulating weights and measures, shall be the law of this Territory; Provided, that the Supreme Court shall perform the duties required of the County Commissioners, and the Recorder shall perfom the duties of the Clerk of the County Commissioners, as provided in said laws of Iowa. And, provided, that sixty pounds avoirdupois weight, shall be the standard weight of a bushel of wheat, whether the same be more or less than two thousand one hundred and fifty and two-fifths cubic inches.

Article 14*th*. The laws of Iowa respecting wills and administrations, shall be the laws of this Territory, in all cases not otherwise provided for.

Article 15*th*. The laws of Iowa respecting vagrants, are hereby adopted as far as adapted to the circumstances of the citizens of Oregon.

Article 16*th*. The Supreme Court shall hold two sessions annually, upon the third Tuesday in April and September, the first session to be held at Champoeg, on the third Tuesday in September, 1843, and the second session at Tuality Plains, on the third Tuesday in April. At the sessions of the Supreme Court, the Supreme Judge shall preside, assisted by the Justices; Provided, that no Justice of the Peace shall assist in trying any case that has been brought before the Court by appeal from his judgment. The Supreme Court shall have original jurisdiction in cases of treason, felony, and breach of the peace, and in civil cases when the sum claimed exceeds fifty dollars.

Article 17*th*. All male persons of the age of sixteen years and upwards, and all females of the age of fourteen and upwards, shall have the right of engaging in marriage; Provided, that, when either of the parties shall be under twenty-one years of age, the consent of the parents or guardians of such minors shall be necessary to the validity of such matrimonial engagement. Every ordained minister of the gospel of any religious denomination, the Supreme Judge, and all the Justices of the Peace, are hereby authorized to solemnize marriage according to law, to have the same recorded, and pay the Recorder's fees. All marriages shall be recorded by the Territorial Recorder within one month from the time of such marriage taking place, and being made known to him officially. The legal fee for marriage shall be one dollar, and for recording fifty cents.

Article 18*th.* All offices subsequently made shall be filled by election and ballot in the several districts, in the most central and convenient place in such district, upon the day appointed by law, and under such regulations as the laws of Iowa provide.

Article 19*th.* Resolved, that a Committee of three be appointed to draw up a digest of the doings of the people of this Territory, with regard to an organization, and transmit it to the United States Government for their information.

In every other particular connected with the Judiciary and Military regulations of the country, the laws of Iowa were considered applicable, and were consequently formally adopted by the people assembled *en masse* at Champoeg, on the 5th of July, 1843.

As the country remained quiet as it regarded the Indians, and no particular danger menaced her from without, the military laws slumbered a dead letter, and the military officers remained without a militia. The organization, however, continued, and all the rest of the laws were uniformly put in force. The expenses of the government for two years after the organization, were met by voluntary contributions; some of the officers, however, serving without fee or reward.

In the spring of 1844, a new Legislative Committee was elected, which embraced two or three lawyers, who arrived in the country the previous fall. This Committee passed a vote, recommending several important alterations in the Organic Laws, which were found to be, in their practical operations, somewhat defective. As the people had not yet surrendered their law-making power into the hands of the Legislative Committee, it was necessary to call an election, to ascertain the will of the people in reference to the proposed alterations and amendments. This election took place, and resulted in the adoption of the Organic Laws, with the proposed alterations and admendments, by an overwhelming majority. The principal alterations thus effected relate to the three powers of Government, the Legislative, Executive, and Judicial. Instead of a Committee of nine, whose acts were to be confirmed or rejected by a subsequent vote of the people, the Legislative power was vested in a House of Representatives, to consist of not less than thirteen, nor more than sixty-one members, possessing all the powers usual to such bodies.

Instead of a Committee of three, the Executive power was vested in one person, to be elected by the qualified voters at the annual election, and possessing the powers common to the Governors of the different States.

The Judicial power was vested in a Supreme Court, and such Inferior Courts of law, equity and arbitration, as should, by law, from time to time, be established. It was also provided, that the Supreme Judge should be elected by the House of Representatives, and not by the people, according to the provisions of the former Code.

All the officers, civil and military, were required to take an oath as follows, to wit :—

I do solemnly swear, that I will support the Organic Laws of the Provisional Government of Oregon, so far as said Organic Laws are consistent with my duties as a citizen of the United States, or a subject of Great Britain, and faithfully demean myself in office ; so help me God.

Important changes were also effected in the Organic Laws, respecting land claims. By the previous arrangement, the different missions in the country were confirmed in their occupancy of the tracts of land of which they had taken possession, for the benefit of the Indian tribes, but in the amended Code, no such mission claims were allowed.

As the Land Law is quite important, particularly to persons interested to know how such matters are regulated in Oregon, perhaps it will not be improper to copy it *verbatim* :—

"Any person now holding, or hereafter wishing to establish a claim to land in this Territory, shall designate the extent of his claim by natural boundaries, or by marks at the corners and upon the lines of such claim, and have the extent and boundaries of said claim recorded in the office of the Territorial Recorder, in a book to be kept by him for that purpose, within twenty days from the time of making such claim; Provided, that those who shall be already in possession of land, shall be allowed twelve months, from the passage of this act, to file a description of his claim in the Recorder's office; and provided, further, that the said claimant shall state in his record, the size, shape and locality of such claim, and give the names of the adjoining claimants; and the Recorder may require the applicant for such record to be made, to answer on his oath touching the facts.

"All claimants shall, within six months from the time of recording their claim, make permanent improvements upon the same, by building or inclosing, and also become an occupant upon said claim, within one year from the date of such record, or, in case not occupied, the person holding said claim shall pay into the Treasury the sum of five dollars annually; and, in case of failure to occupy, or failure of payment of the sum above stated, the claim shall be considered as abandoned; Provided, that no non-resident of this Territory shall have the benefit of the Law; and provided, further, that any resident of this Territory, absent on his private business for two years, may hold his claim by paying five dollars, annually, to the Treasury.

"No individual shall be allowed to a claim of more than one square mile, or six hundred and forty acres, in a square or oblong form, according to the natural situation of the premises; nor shall any individual be allowed to hold more than one claim at the same time. Any person, complying with the provisions of these ordinances, shall be entitled to the same recourse against trespass, as in other cases by law provided.

"Partnerships of two or more persons, shall be allowed

to take up a tract of land, not exceeding six hundred and forty acres to each person in said partnership, subject to all the provisions of this law, and whenever such partnership is dissolved, the members shall record the particular parts of said tract which may be allotted to them respectively; provided, that no member of said partnership shall hold a separate claim at the time of the existence of said partnership."

It was also determined at the special election, by a vote of the people, that the amended Organic Law should become the law of the land, after the first Tuesday in June, 1845, when the election of a Governor and Members of the House of Representatives was to take place.

In the mean time the people of Oregon, though differing as much in their education, their degrees of civilization and refinement, and their constitutional habits, as they do in the color of their skin, continued in their intercourse with one another, to form a remarkably peaceable and quiet community. But, it will not be understood by this, that the Oregonians exhibited no irregularities, no wickedness in their conduct; but simply that in civil regulations, and daily intercourse in matters of business, and in efforts to promote the welfare of the country, the community was one of order, gentleness and unanimity. As a proof of this, when steps have been taken to adopt laws from time to time, as the exigencies of the case have seemed to require, though numbers have usually been opposed to the measures, yet, after having been adopted by the majority, they have been universally acknowledged. Those most opposed at first, like true-hearted republicans, would fall in with the majority, and sustain the laws with their entire influence.

Another thing that speaks well for the civil order that prevailed in the community before the present organization was established, is the fact, that crimes were very few. True, there were some petty quarrels between white men, but in a very few instances did they amount to blows.

So few were the cases of serious litigation, that when

the first Circuit Courts were held in the four different counties, there appeared but one case of assault in the whole country, and in that the circumstances were so extenuating that the defendant was fined only twenty-five dollars. The highest charge that came before either Justices or Judges, in Oregon, up to 1845, was against a man for challenging another to fight a duel, who, for a foolish violation of a law which had just been passed, was fined in the sum of five hundred dollars, and disfranchised for life. It being the first case of the kind in the country, the last part of the sentence was remitted by a special act of the Legislature.

There are vagabonds and scape-gallowses in almost every country, and it would be singular if none had found their way to Oregon. That this may have been the case, appears from a most desperate affray which greatly disturbed the quiet of the community, and which took place in the upper part of the settlement on the Wallamette river.

A man by the name of Joel Turnham, who possessed a most reckless and desperate disposition, committed several outrages upon a peaceful and inoffensive man by the name of Webley Hauxhurst. One day, Turnham took occasion to tie his horse in Hauxhurst's oat field, as he had frequently done before, without asking liberty, and then going to Hauxhurst's house, the latter expostulated with him for taking such undue liberties with his property. This so enraged Turnham that he seized Hauxhurst by the throat, with the intention of flogging him; but, while in the act of throwing him to the floor, the wife of Hauxhurst, who was an Indian woman of the Callapooah tribe, seized a board that lay near, and with one blow upon the head of Turnham, for an instant, paralized every muscle in his frame, and brought him staggering to the floor. Soon, however, Turnham gathered himself up and immediately left the house, swearing vengeance upon the woman, saying, "There is no law against killing Indians."

Hauxhurst, fearing as well for his own safety, as that Turnham would carry his threat into execution against the life of his wife, resolved upon taking immediate measures to secure the arrest of Turnham.

Turnham himself, at the previous election, had been chosen constable, and consequently, L. H. Judson, Esq., on application being made by Hauxhurst for a precept against Turnham, deputized a man by the name of John Edmonds to take him into custody. Edmonds immediately took the precept, and walking into a shop where Turnham was with a number of other persons, told him that he was his prisoner, and commenced reading the warrant. Not being able to read it readily, on account of an impediment in his speech, Turnham said, "Here, let me read it;" and snatching it out of the hands of Edmonds, tore it in pieces, and stamped it beneath his feet; and then, seizing a knife in one hand, and a hammer in the other, swore he would butcher the first man that attempted to take him. Edmonds called for help, but none dared to come near. Turnham, therefore, walked out of the shop, mounted his horse and rode off towards the house of Hauxhurst. Another warrant was issued, and Edmonds was advised to enter into all necessary precautions to take Turnham at any rate. Accordingly, he proceeded to the Oregon Institute and got Mr. Hamilton Campbell and some others, to go and assist him. Supposing that Turnham would fight, and from his desperate and sanguinary character would doubtless attempt to kill him, Edmonds armed himself with a revolving six-barreled pistol that was sure fire, and proceeded on to Hauxhurst's house. Turnham had been there and ground his large knife, which he usually carried in his belt under his coat, but had left a short time before Edmonds arrived.

Looking back from the prairie over which he was passing, he saw a company of men as they were dismounting from their horses, and immediately wheeled his horse around, and rode back upon the full gallop towards Hauxhurst's house. As Turnham approached, Edmonds placed himself inside of a small gate which led into the door-yard, with his right hand placed on the breech of his pistol, which he carried in his pantaloon's pocket. Turnham, paying no attention to him, came up immediately to the gate, and while passing through into the yard, Edmonds put his left hand upon Turnham's shoulder, and said, "You are my prisoner." Turnham immediately drew his long knife and brandished it in Edmonds' face, and Edmonds as quickly presented his six-shooter at Turnham's breast. They eyed each other for an instant, but Turnham, mad to desperation, exclaimed, "Shoot and be d——d;" and commenced throwing himself backwards and forwards, from one side of the yard to the other, for the twofold purpose of evading the bullets, and of placing himself in a position to enable him to make a successful drive upon his antagonist. Those who witnessed the affray, have no doubt but that he was bent upon the death of Edmonds. Some one within the house was heard to cry out to Edmonds, "Why don't you shoot?" At this Edmonds commenced his fire. The first two bullets missed Turnham altogether. The third wounded him in his knee, the fourth in his neck, the fifth in his face, and during all this time he was rushing forward upon Edmonds with the utmost vengeance.

When the fifth ball hit him, he clapped one hand to the wound, and cried out, "Oh!" and hesitated a moment as if he would yield; but gathering himself up for one more struggle, while making his last and most desperate effort to plunge his knife into the heart of Edmonds, the sixth ball pierced his temple, he fell and instantly expired.

This case was of such a nature, as in the estimation of the Supreme Judge, to demand an investigation by the Grand Jury. Accordingly, Edmonds gave bonds for his appearance at Court, and, though his enemies labored hard to convict him of murder, yet, when the matter was thoroughly investigated by the Jury, it was pronounced to be a clear case of justifiable homicide.

THE END.

The Far Western Frontier
An Arno Press Collection

[Angel, Myron, editor]. **History of Nevada.** 1881.

Barnes, Demas. **From the Atlantic to the Pacific, Overland.** 1866.

Beadle, J[ohn] H[anson]. **The Undeveloped West; Or, Five Years in the Territories.** [1873].

Bidwell, John. **Echoes of the Past:** An Account of the First Emigrant Train to California. [1914].

Bowles, Samuel. **Our New West.** 1869.

Browne, J[ohn] Ross. **Adventures in the Apache Country.** 1871.

Browne, J[ohn] Ross. **Report of the Debates in the Convention of California, on the Formation of the State Constitution.** 1850.

Byers, W[illiam] N. and J[ohn] H. Kellom. **Hand Book to the Gold Fields of Nebraska and Kansas.** 1859.

Carvalho, S[olomon] N. **Incidents of Travel and Adventure in the Far West; with Col. Fremont's Last Expedition Across the Rocky Mountains.** 1857.

Clayton, William. **William Clayton's Journal.** 1921.

Cooke, P[hilip] St. G[eorge]. **Scenes and Adventures in the Army.** 1857.

Cornwallis, Kinahan. **The New El Dorado; Or, British Columbia.** 1858.

Davis, W[illiam] W. H. **El Gringo; Or, New Mexico and Her People.** 1857.

De Quille, Dan. (William Wright). **A History of the Comstock Silver Lode & Mines.** 1889.

Delano, A[lonzo]. **Life on the Plains and Among the Diggings;** Being Scenes and Adventures of an Overland Journey to California. 1854.

Ferguson, Charles D. **The Experiences of a Forty-niner in California.** (Originally published as *The Experiences of a Forty-niner During Thirty-four Years' Residence in California and Australia*). 1888.

Forbes, Alexander. **California:** A History of Upper and Lower California. 1839.

Fossett, Frank. **Colorado:** Its Gold and Silver Mines, Farms and Stock Ranges, and Health and Pleasure Resorts. 1879.

The Gold Mines of California: Two Guidebooks. 1973.

Gray, W[illiam] H[enry]. **A History of Oregon, 1792–1849.** 1870.

Green, Thomas J. **Journal of the Texian Expedition Against Mier.** 1845.

Henry, W[illiam] S[eaton]. **Campaign Sketches of the War with Mexico.** 1847.

[Hildreth, James]. **Dragoon Campaigns to the Rocky Mountains.** 1836.

Hines, Gustavus. **Oregon:** Its History, Condition and Prospects. 1851.

Holley, Mary Austin. **Texas:** Observations, Historical, Geographical and Descriptive. 1833.

Hollister, Ovando J[ames]. **The Mines of Colorado.** 1867.

Hughes, John T. **Doniphan's Expedition.** 1847.

Johnston, W[illiam] G. **Experiences of a Forty-niner.** 1892.

Jones, Anson. **Memoranda and Official Correspondence Relating to the Republic of Texas, Its History and Annexation.** 1859.

Kelly, William. **An Excursion to California Over the Prairie, Rocky Mountains, and Great Sierra Nevada.** 1851. 2 Volumes in 1.

Lee, D[aniel] and J[oseph] H. Frost. **Ten Years in Oregon.** 1844.

Macfie, Matthew. **Vancouver Island and British Columbia.** 1865.

Marsh, James B. **Four Years in the Rockies; Or, the Adventures of Isaac P. Rose.** 1884.

Mowry, Sylvester. **Arizona and Sonora:** The Geography, History, and Resources of the Silver Region of North America. 1864.

Mullan, John. **Miners and Travelers' Guide to Oregon, Washington, Idaho, Montana, Wyoming, and Colorado.** 1865.

Newell, C[hester]. **History of the Revolution in Texas.** 1838.

Parker, A[mos] A[ndrew]. **Trip to the West and Texas.** 1835.

Pattie, James O[hio]. **The Personal Narrative of James O. Pattie, of Kentucky.** 1831.

Rae, W[illiam] F[raser]. **Westward by Rail:** The New Route to the East. 1871.

Ryan, William Redmond. **Personal Adventures in Upper and Lower California, in 1848-9.** 1850/1851. 2 Volumes in 1.

Shaw, William. **Golden Dreams and Waking Realities:** Being the Adventures of a Gold-Seeker in California and the Pacific Islands. 1851.

Stuart, Granville. **Montana As It Is:** Being a General Description of its Resources. 1865.

Texas in 1840, Or the Emigrant's Guide to the New Republic. 1840.

Thornton, J. Quinn. **Oregon and California in 1848.** 1849. 2 Volumes in 1.

Upham, Samuel C. **Notes of a Voyage to California via Cape Horn, Together with Scenes in El Dorado, in the Years 1849-'50.** 1878.

Woods, Daniel B. **Sixteen Months at the Gold Diggings.** 1851.

Young, F[rank] G., editor. **The Correspondence and Journals of Captain Nathaniel J. Wyeth, 1831-6.** 1899.